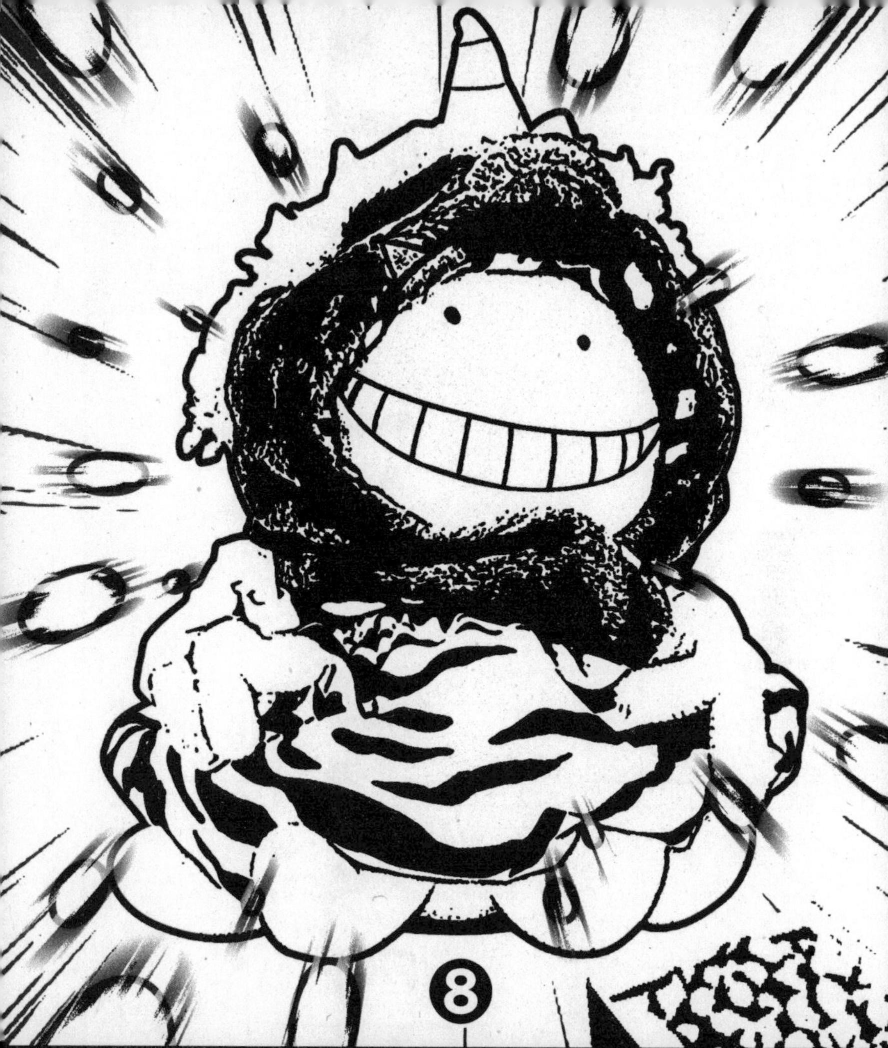

8

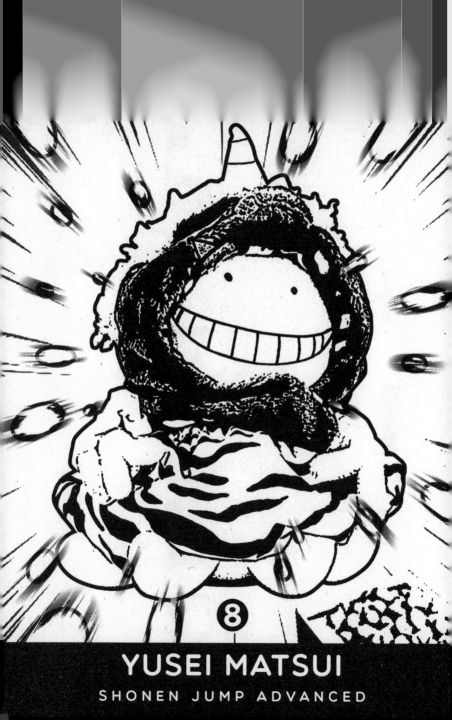

YUSEI MATSUI

SHONEN JUMP ADVANCED

Koro Tribune

August Issue

Published by: Class 3-E Newspaper Staff

Our new teacher is a creature who plans to destroy the world...?!

Story Thus Far

One day, something destroyed most of the moon.

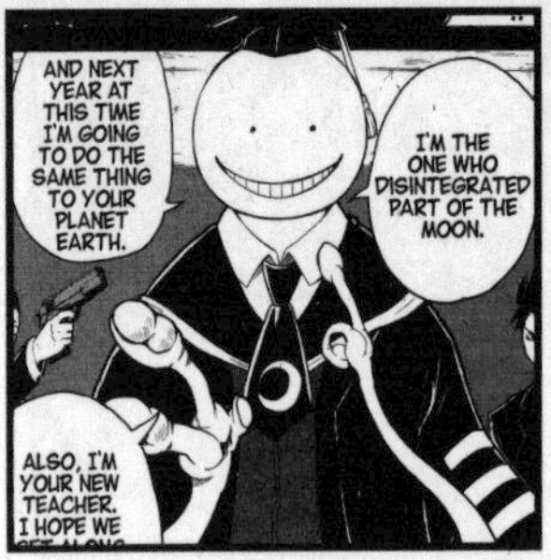

I'M THE ONE WHO DISINTEGRATED PART OF THE MOON.
AND NEXT YEAR AT THIS TIME I'M GOING TO DO THE SAME THING TO YOUR PLANET EARTH.
ALSO, I'M YOUR NEW TEACHER. I HOPE WE

A mysterious creature showed up in our junior high classroom claiming that he had attacked the moon and promising to destroy the Earth next March. And then...he took over as our teacher. What the—?! Faced with a creature beyond human understanding that no army could kill, the leaders of the world had no choice but to rely on the students of Kunugigaoka Junior High, Class 3-E, to do the job. For a reward of ten billion yen (100 million dollars)... SIGN ME UP!! Will the students of the so-called End Class, filled with losers and rejects, be able to kill their target Koro Sensei by graduation...?!

Koro Sensei

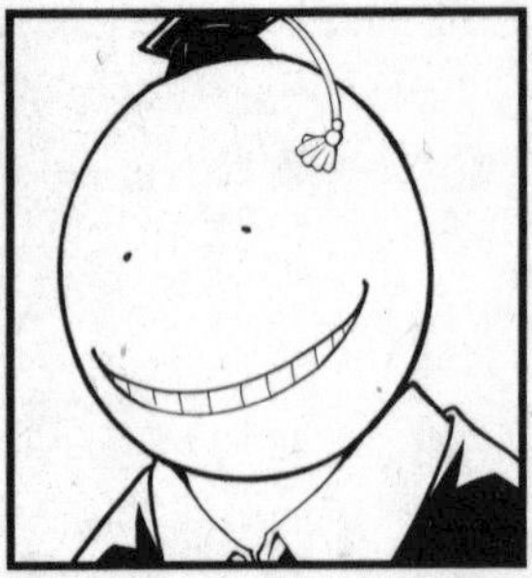

A mysterious octopus-like creature whose nickname is a play on the words "koro senai," which means "can't be killed." He is capable of flying at Mach 20 and his versatile tentacles protect him from attacks and aid him in everyday activities. Nobody knows why he wants to teach Class 3-E, but he has proven to be an extremely capable teacher.

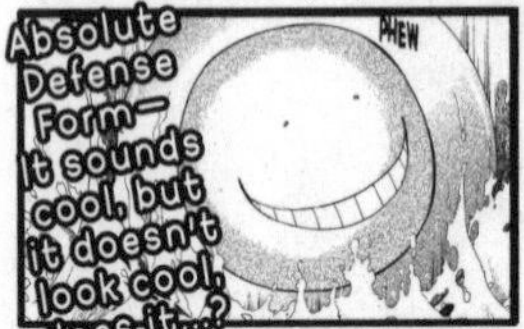

PHEW

Absolute Defense Form—It sounds cool, but it doesn't look cool, does it...?

Kaede Kayano

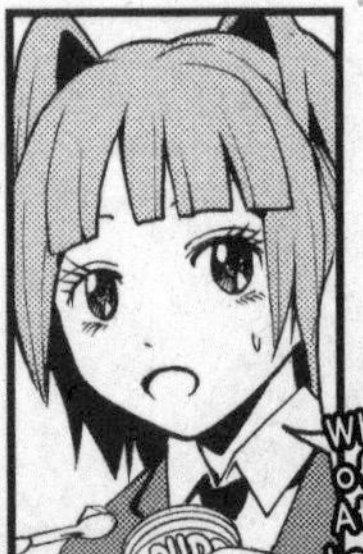

Class E student. She's the one who named Koro Sensei. She sits at the desk next to Nagisa, and they seem to get along well.

Nagisa Shiota

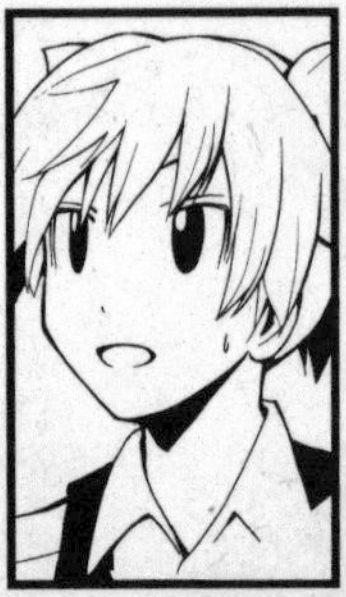

Class E student. Skilled at information gathering, he has been taking notes on Koro Sensei's weaknesses. Everyone is beginning to realize that he has a hidden talent for assassination.

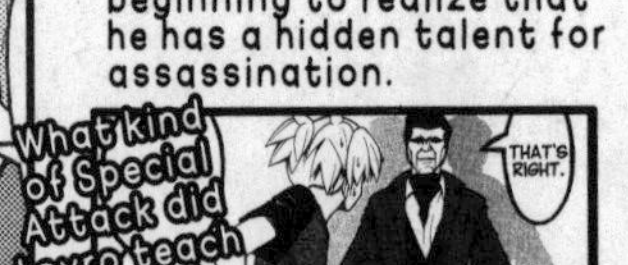

THAT'S RIGHT.

What kind of Special Attack did Lovro teach him?!

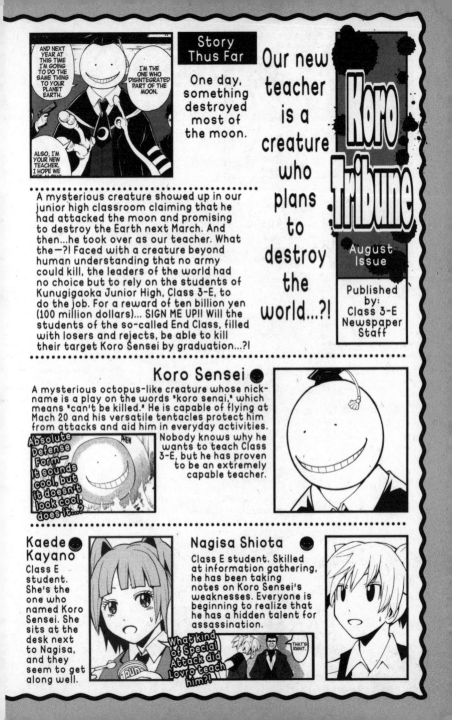

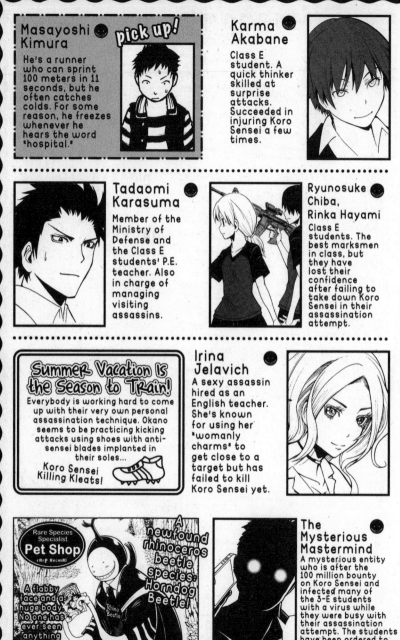

Masayoshi Kimura

pick up!

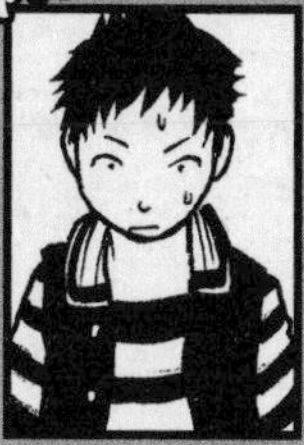

He's a runner who can sprint 100 meters in 11 seconds, but he often catches colds. For some reason, he freezes whenever he hears the word "hospital."

Karma Akabane

Class E student. A quick thinker skilled at surprise attacks. Succeeded in injuring Koro Sensei a few times.

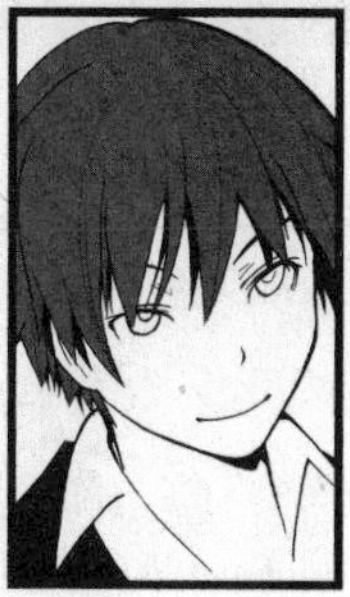

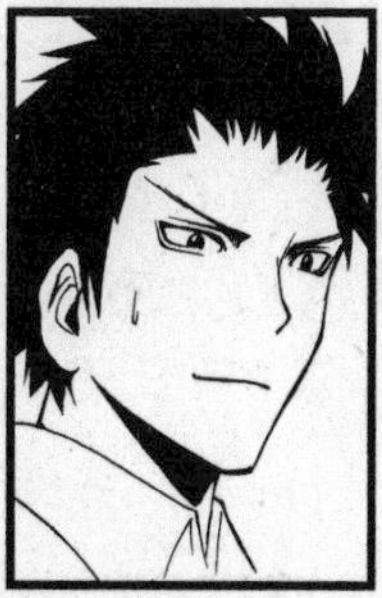

Tadaomi Karasuma

Member of the Ministry of Defense and the Class E students' P.E. teacher. Also in charge of managing visiting assassins.

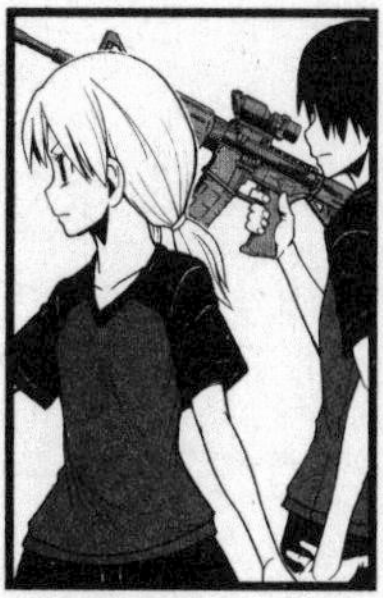

Ryunosuke Chiba, Rinka Hayami

Class E students. The best marksmen in class, but they have lost their confidence after failing to take down Koro Sensei in their assassination attempt.

Summer Vacation Is the Season to Train!

Everybody is working hard to come up with their very own personal assassination technique. Okano seems to be practicing kicking attacks using shoes with anti-sensei blades implanted in their soles...

Koro Sensei Killing Kleats!

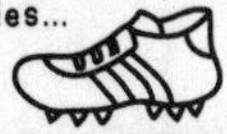

Irina Jelavich

A sexy assassin hired as an English teacher. She's known for using her "womanly charms" to get close to a target but has failed to kill Koro Sensei yet.

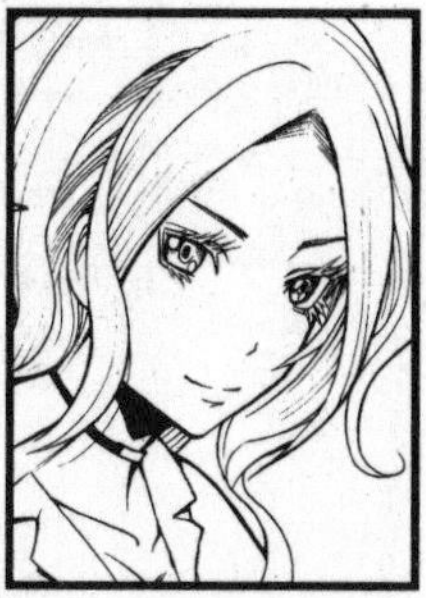

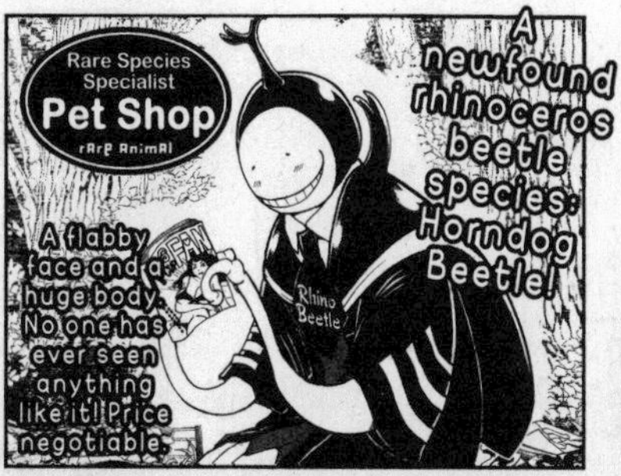
Rare Species Specialist
Pet Shop
rArE AnimAl
A newfound rhinoceros beetle species: Horndog Beetle!
A flabby face and a huge body. No one has ever seen anything like it! Price negotiable.
Rhino Beetle

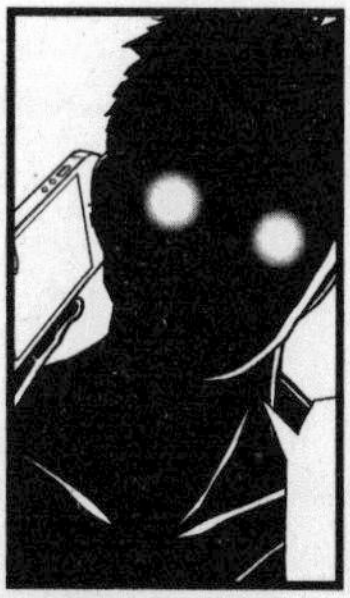

The Mysterious Mastermind

A mysterious entity who is after the 100 million bounty on Koro Sensei and infected many of the 3-E students with a virus while they were busy with their assassination attempt. The students have been ordered to hand over Koro Sensei in exchange for the antidote to the virus.

ASSASSINATION CLASSROOM 8 CONTENTS

(ANSWER SHEET)

Grade	3	Class	E	Name	CONTENTS	Score	

Fill in the blank with
t word choice. Use
h word only once!

slime
treat
infiltrate

a. [ ] the
emy territory.
Remove that
ty [ ].
] the
ed patients.

sed more
han once.

ancient Chinese classic.
wers, "Terasaka and Nagisa, which is superior?"
Karma asks, "In that case, can Terasaka be superior?"
Koro Tzu answers, "Terasaka is too extreme. Nagisa is [ ]."
Koro Tzu answers, "[ ]." Karma: Koro Tzu's disciple.
Terasaka: Koro Tzu's disciple: an extroverted student.
Nagisa: Koro Tzu's disciple: an introverted student.
Koro Tzu Sensei: a famed philosopher of China's
Spring, Autumn, and Warring States Period.

CLASS 62 TIME TO SEND IN THE PROS–2ND PERIOD

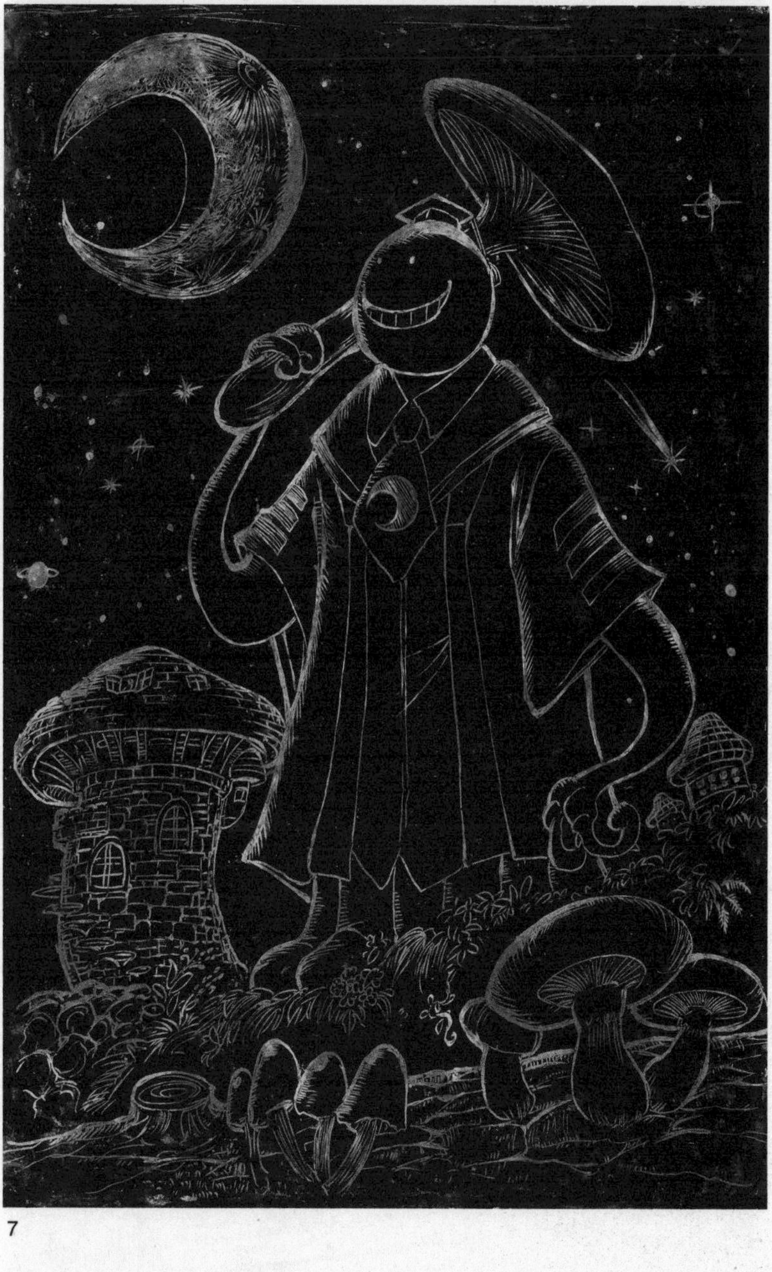

Update on the Tropical Island Assassination Trip

A new enemy appeared on the scene moments after the class's assassination attempt on Koro Sensei! Half of Class E's students have been infected by a deadly virus and the villain behind this biological warfare is demanding Koro Sensei's head (so to speak) in exchange for the antidote. It's hard to believe the evil mastermind behind such a dastardly plan would cut a fair deal, so the remaining healthy students have resolved to infiltrate the hotel within twenty-four hours to take their enemy down and save their classmates!

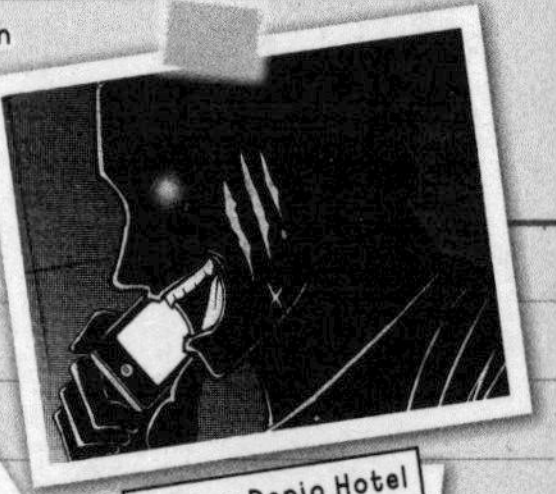

Raid Team Members

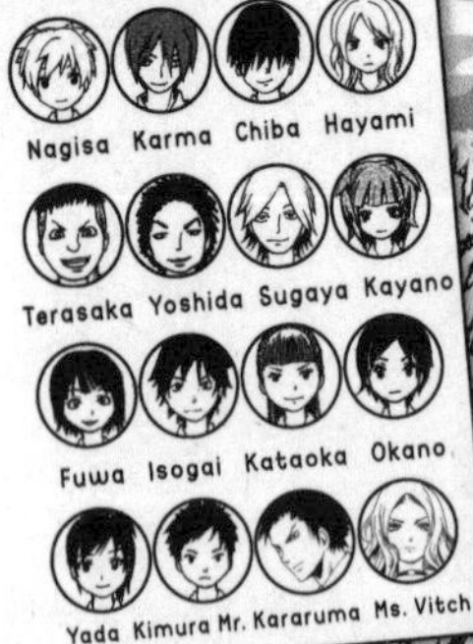

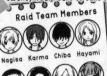

Nagisa, Karma, Chiba, Hayami
Terasaka, Yoshida, Sugaya, Kayano
Fuwa, Isogai, Kataoka, Okano
Yada, Kimura, Mr. Karasuma, Ms. Vitch

Infected Students

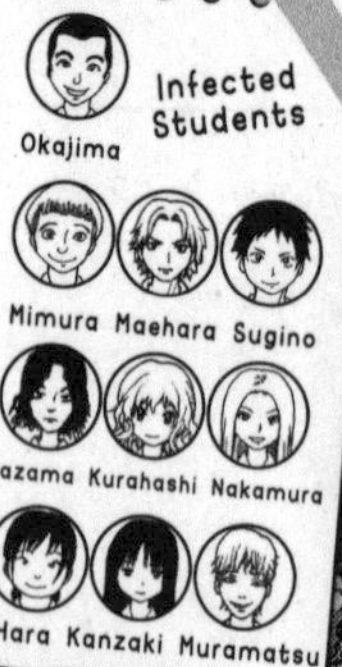

Okajima
Mimura, Maehara, Sugino
Hazama, Kurahashi, Nakamura
Hara, Kanzaki, Muramatsu

Nurses

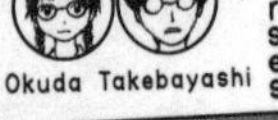

Okuda, Takebayashi

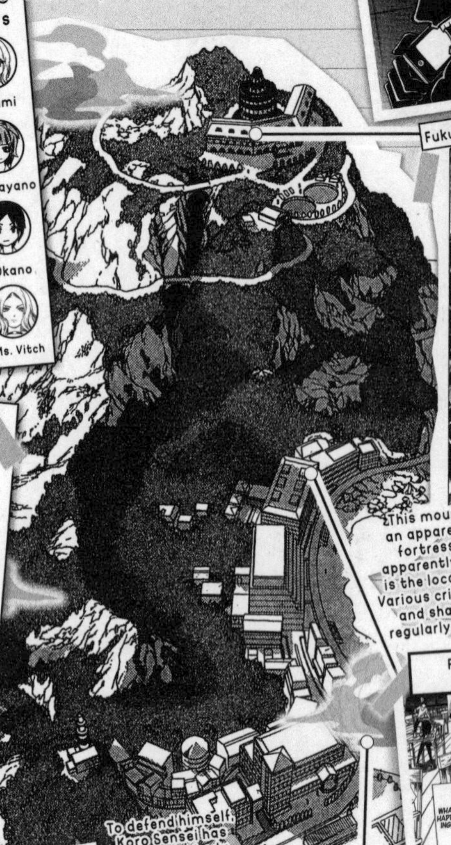

Fukuma Denjo Hotel

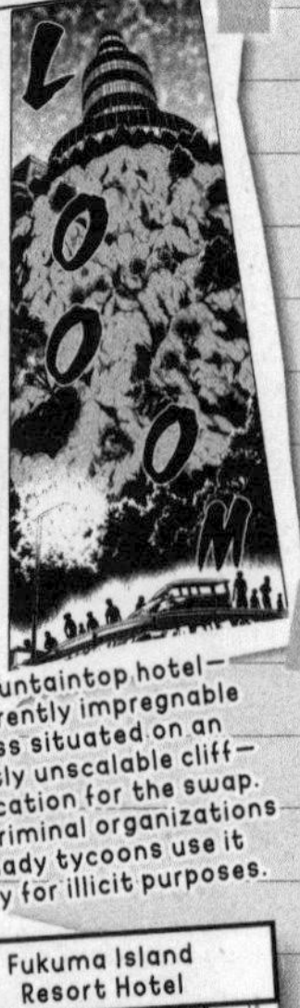
LOOOOM

This mountaintop hotel—an apparently impregnable fortress situated on an apparently unscalable cliff—is the location for the swap. Various criminal organizations and shady tycoons use it regularly for illicit purposes.

Fukuma Island Resort Hotel

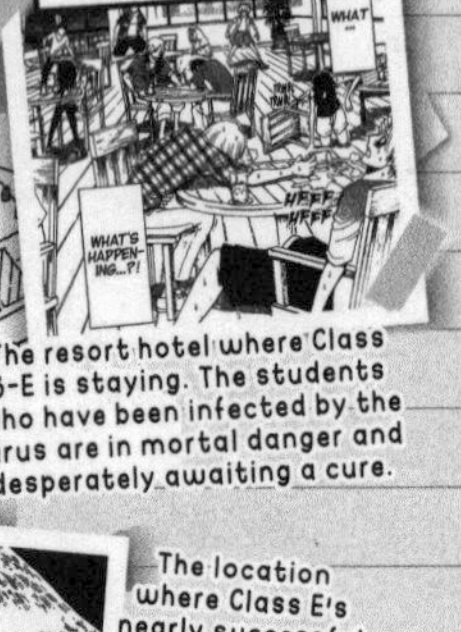
WHAT
HUFF HUFF
WHAT'S HAPPENING...?!

The resort hotel where Class 3-E is staying. The students who have been infected by the virus are in mortal danger and desperately awaiting a cure.

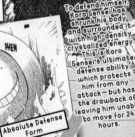

To defend himself, Koro Sensei has shrunk his body and surrounded it with high-density crystalized energy. This is Koro Sensei's ultimate defense ability, which protects him from any attack—but has the drawback of leaving him unable to move for 24 hours.

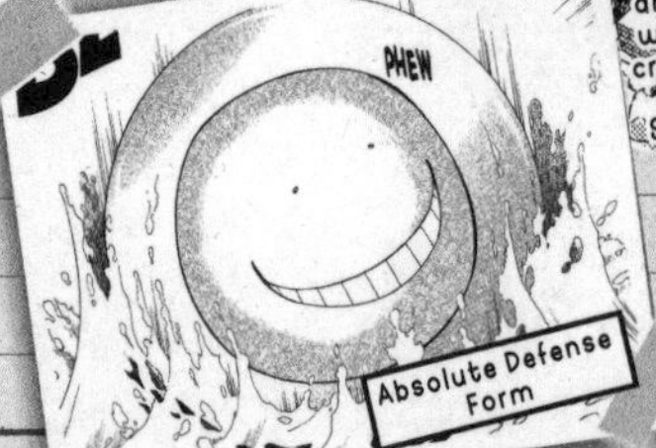
PHEW

Absolute Defense Form

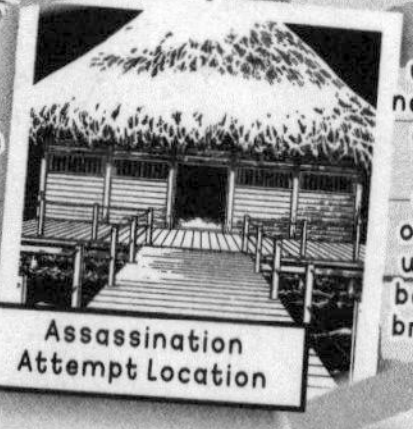

Assassination Attempt Location

The location where Class E's nearly successful assassination attempt was held—an overwater villa which can only be reached by a bridge from the island.

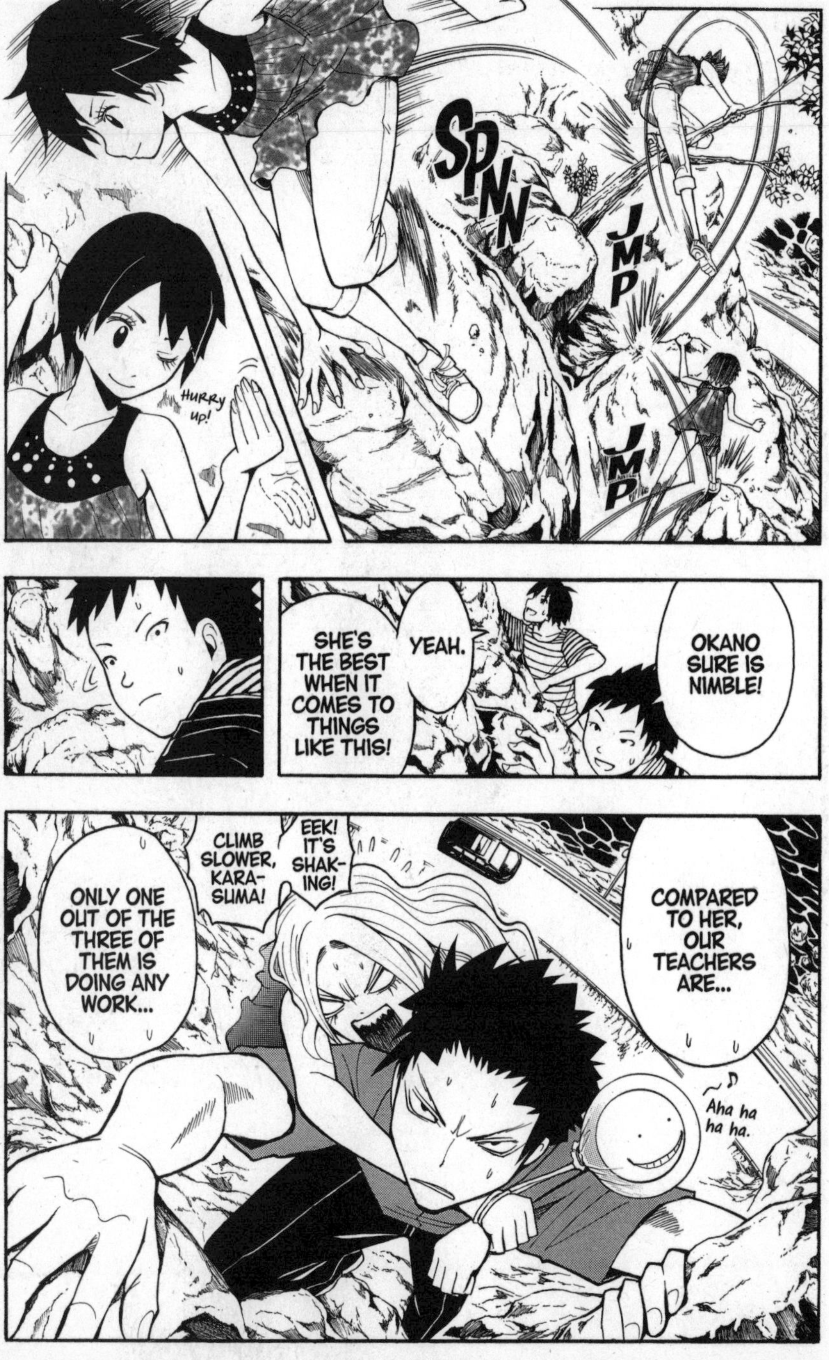
JMP
JMP
SPNN
Hurry up!
OKANO SURE IS NIMBLE!
YEAH.
SHE'S THE BEST WHEN IT COMES TO THINGS LIKE THIS!
COMPARED TO HER, OUR TEACHERS ARE...
~♪ Aha ha ha ha.
EEK! IT'S SHAK-ING!
CLIMB SLOWER, KARA-SUMA!
ONLY ONE OUT OF THE THREE OF THEM IS DOING ANY WORK...

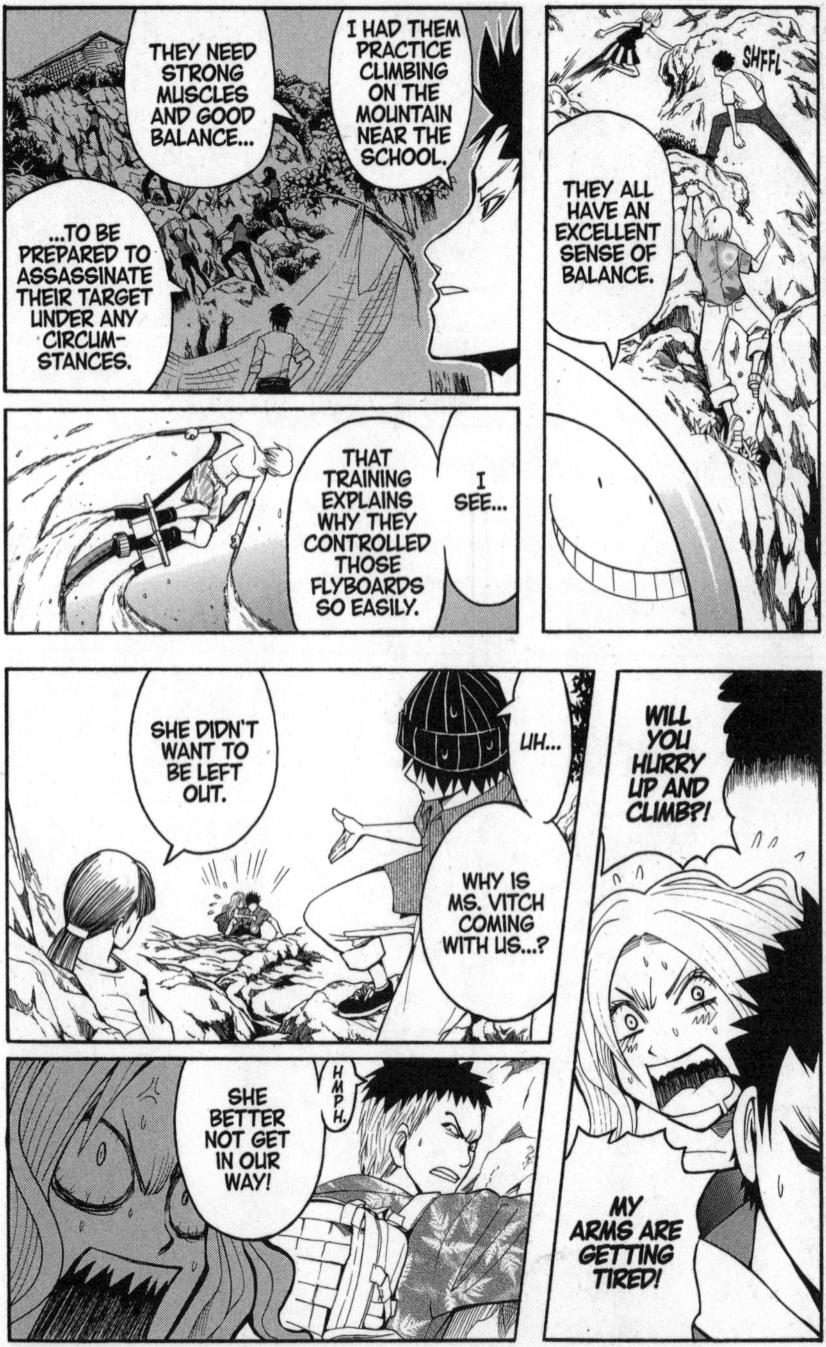
SHFFL
THEY ALL HAVE AN EXCELLENT SENSE OF BALANCE.
I HAD THEM PRACTICE CLIMBING ON THE MOUNTAIN NEAR THE SCHOOL.
THEY NEED STRONG MUSCLES AND GOOD BALANCE...
...TO BE PREPARED TO ASSASSINATE THEIR TARGET UNDER ANY CIRCUM-STANCES.
I SEE...
THAT TRAINING EXPLAINS WHY THEY CONTROLLED THOSE FLYBOARDS SO EASILY.
WILL YOU HURRY UP AND CLIMB?!
MY ARMS ARE GETTING TIRED!
UH...
WHY IS MS. VITCH COMING WITH US...?
SHE DIDN'T WANT TO BE LEFT OUT.
HMPH.
SHE BETTER NOT GET IN OUR WAY!

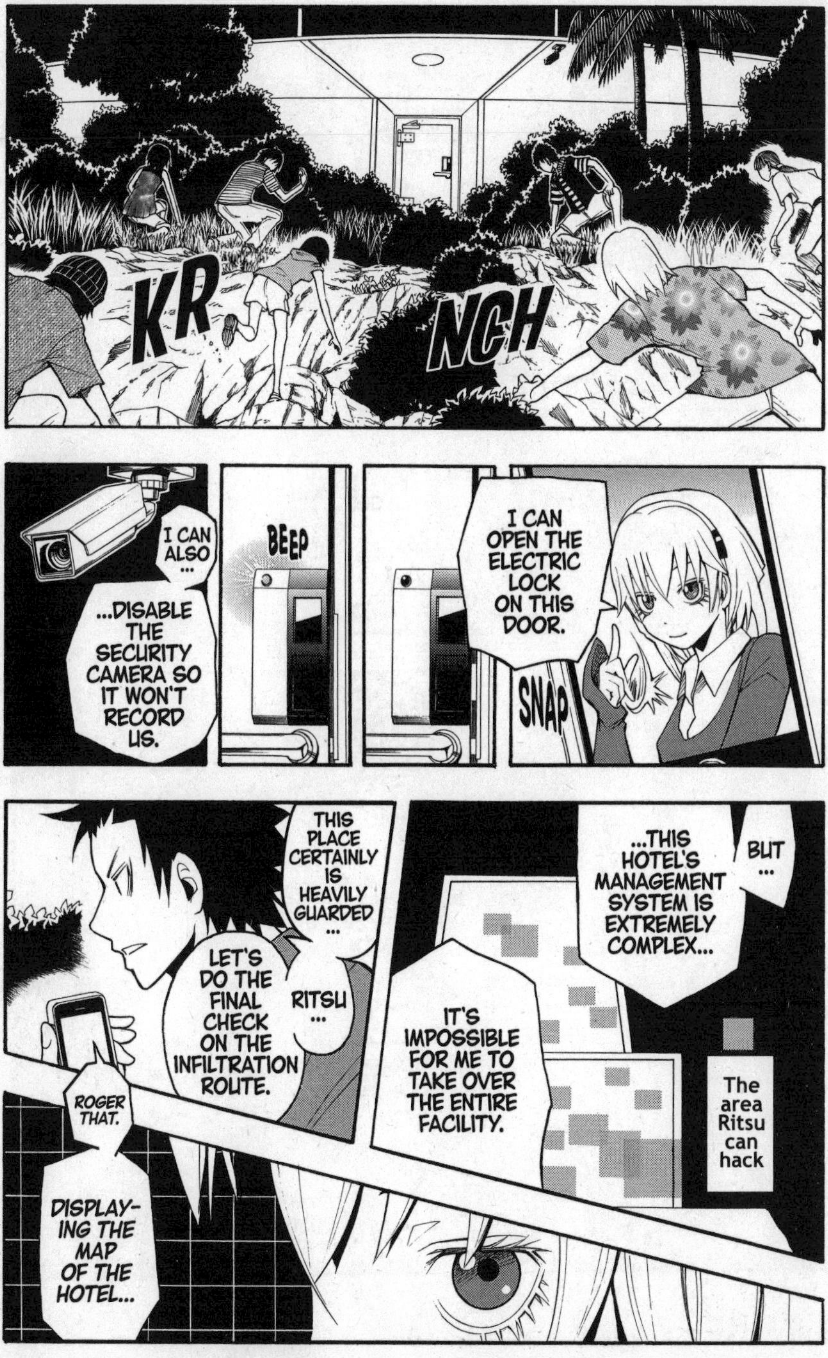
KRNCH
I CAN OPEN THE ELECTRIC LOCK ON THIS DOOR.
SNAP
BEEP
I CAN ALSO ...
...DISABLE THE SECURITY CAMERA SO IT WON'T RECORD US.
BUT ...
...THIS HOTEL'S MANAGEMENT SYSTEM IS EXTREMELY COMPLEX...
IT'S IMPOSSIBLE FOR ME TO TAKE OVER THE ENTIRE FACILITY.
The area Ritsu can hack
THIS PLACE CERTAINLY IS HEAVILY GUARDED ...
RITSU ...
LET'S DO THE FINAL CHECK ON THE INFILTRATION ROUTE.
ROGER THAT.
DISPLAYING THE MAP OF THE HOTEL...

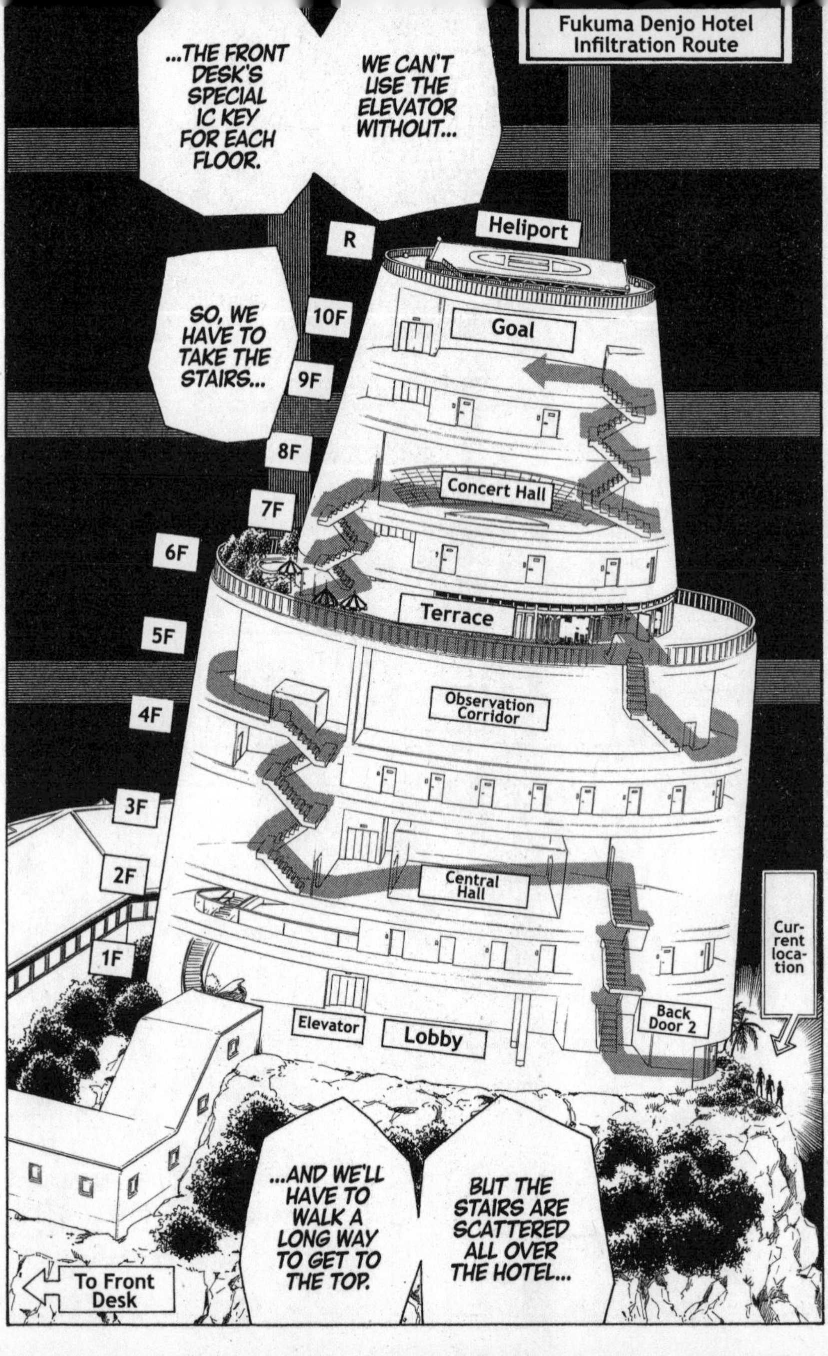
Fukuma Denjo Hotel Infiltration Route
WE CAN'T USE THE ELEVATOR WITHOUT...
...THE FRONT DESK'S SPECIAL IC KEY FOR EACH FLOOR.
SO, WE HAVE TO TAKE THE STAIRS...
Heliport
R
10F
Goal
9F
8F
Concert Hall
7F
6F
Terrace
5F
Observation Corridor
4F
3F
Central Hall
2F
1F
Cur-rent loca-tion
Back Door 2
Lobby
Elevator
BUT THE STAIRS ARE SCATTERED ALL OVER THE HOTEL...
...AND WE'LL HAVE TO WALK A LONG WAY TO GET TO THE TOP.
To Front Desk

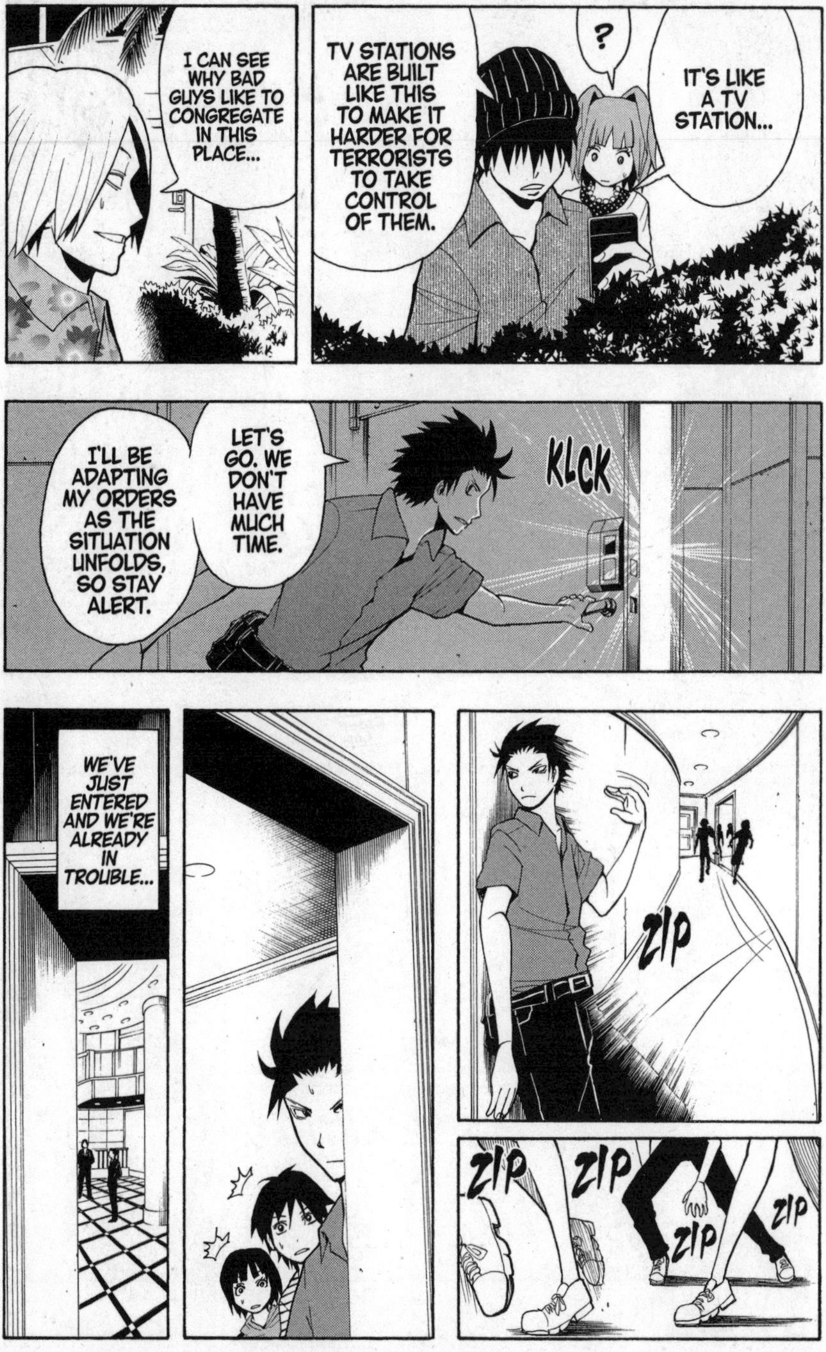
IT'S LIKE A TV STATION...
?
TV STATIONS ARE BUILT LIKE THIS TO MAKE IT HARDER FOR TERRORISTS TO TAKE CONTROL OF THEM.
I CAN SEE WHY BAD GUYS LIKE TO CONGREGATE IN THIS PLACE...
KLCK
LET'S GO. WE DON'T HAVE MUCH TIME.
I'LL BE ADAPTING MY ORDERS AS THE SITUATION UNFOLDS, SO STAY ALERT.
ZIP
ZIP
ZIP
ZIP
ZIP
WE'VE JUST ENTERED AND WE'RE ALREADY IN TROUBLE...

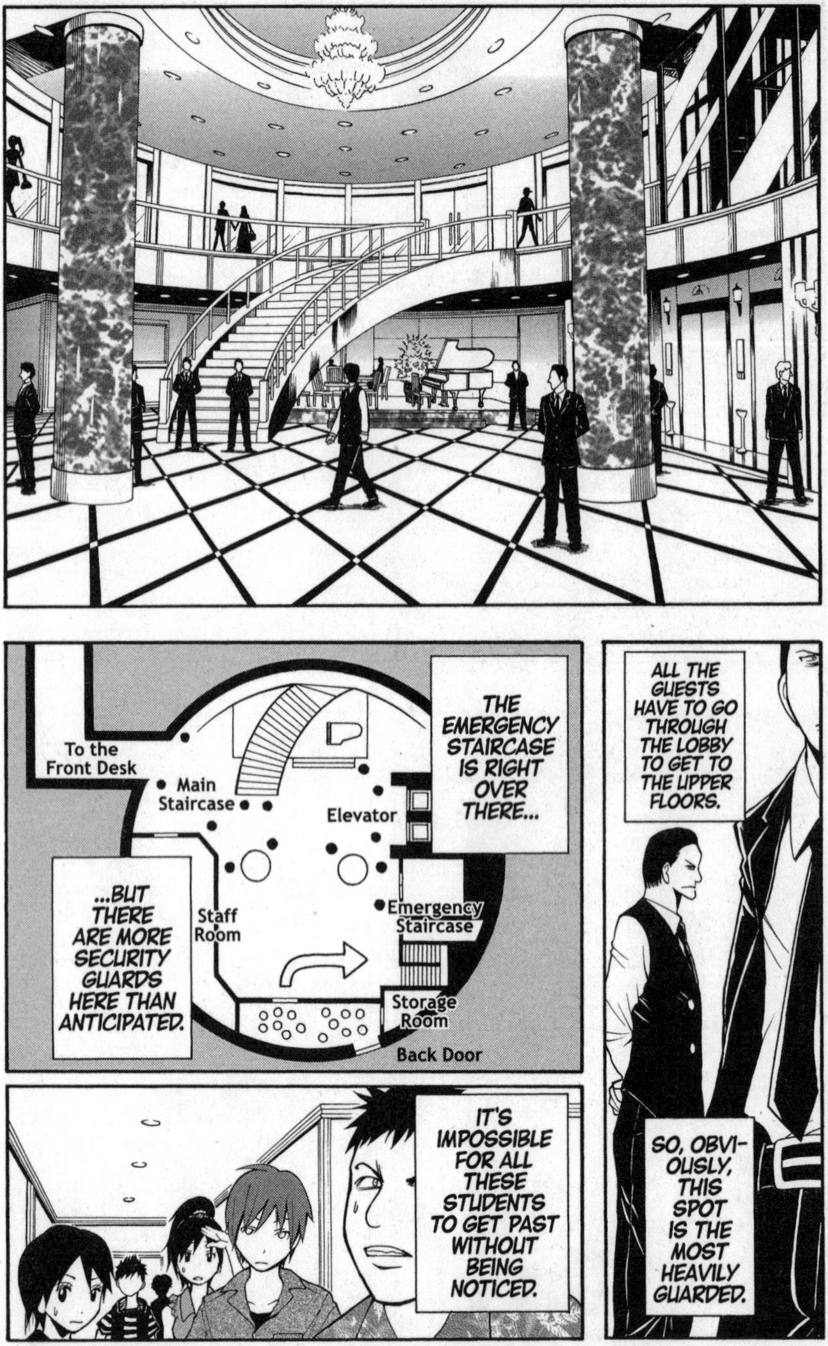
ALL THE GUESTS HAVE TO GO THROUGH THE LOBBY TO GET TO THE UPPER FLOORS.
SO, OBVIOUSLY, THIS SPOT IS THE MOST HEAVILY GUARDED.
THE EMERGENCY STAIRCASE IS RIGHT OVER THERE...
To the Front Desk
Main Staircase
Elevator
Staff Room
Emergency Staircase
Storage Room
Back Door
...BUT THERE ARE MORE SECURITY GUARDS HERE THAN ANTICIPATED.
IT'S IMPOSSIBLE FOR ALL THESE STUDENTS TO GET PAST WITHOUT BEING NOTICED.

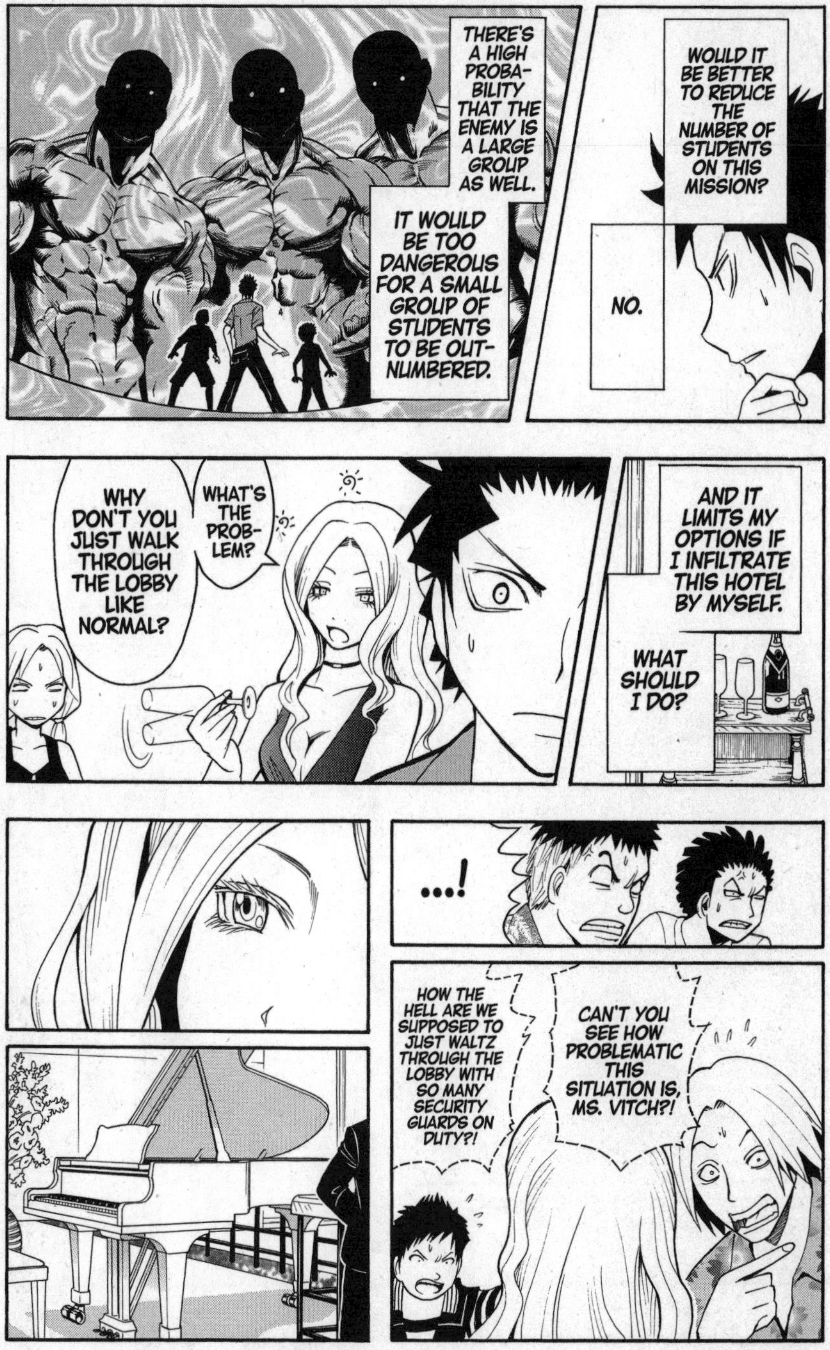
WOULD IT BE BETTER TO REDUCE THE NUMBER OF STUDENTS ON THIS MISSION?
NO.
THERE'S A HIGH PROBA-BILITY THAT THE ENEMY IS A LARGE GROUP AS WELL.
IT WOULD BE TOO DANGEROUS FOR A SMALL GROUP OF STUDENTS TO BE OUT-NUMBERED.
AND IT LIMITS MY OPTIONS IF I INFILTRATE THIS HOTEL BY MYSELF.
WHAT SHOULD I DO?
WHAT'S THE PROB-LEM?
WHY DON'T YOU JUST WALK THROUGH THE LOBBY LIKE NORMAL?
...!
CAN'T YOU SEE HOW PROBLEMATIC THIS SITUATION IS, MS. VITCH?!
HOW THE HELL ARE WE SUPPOSED TO JUST WALTZ THROUGH THE LOBBY WITH SO MANY SECURITY GUARDS ON DUTY?!

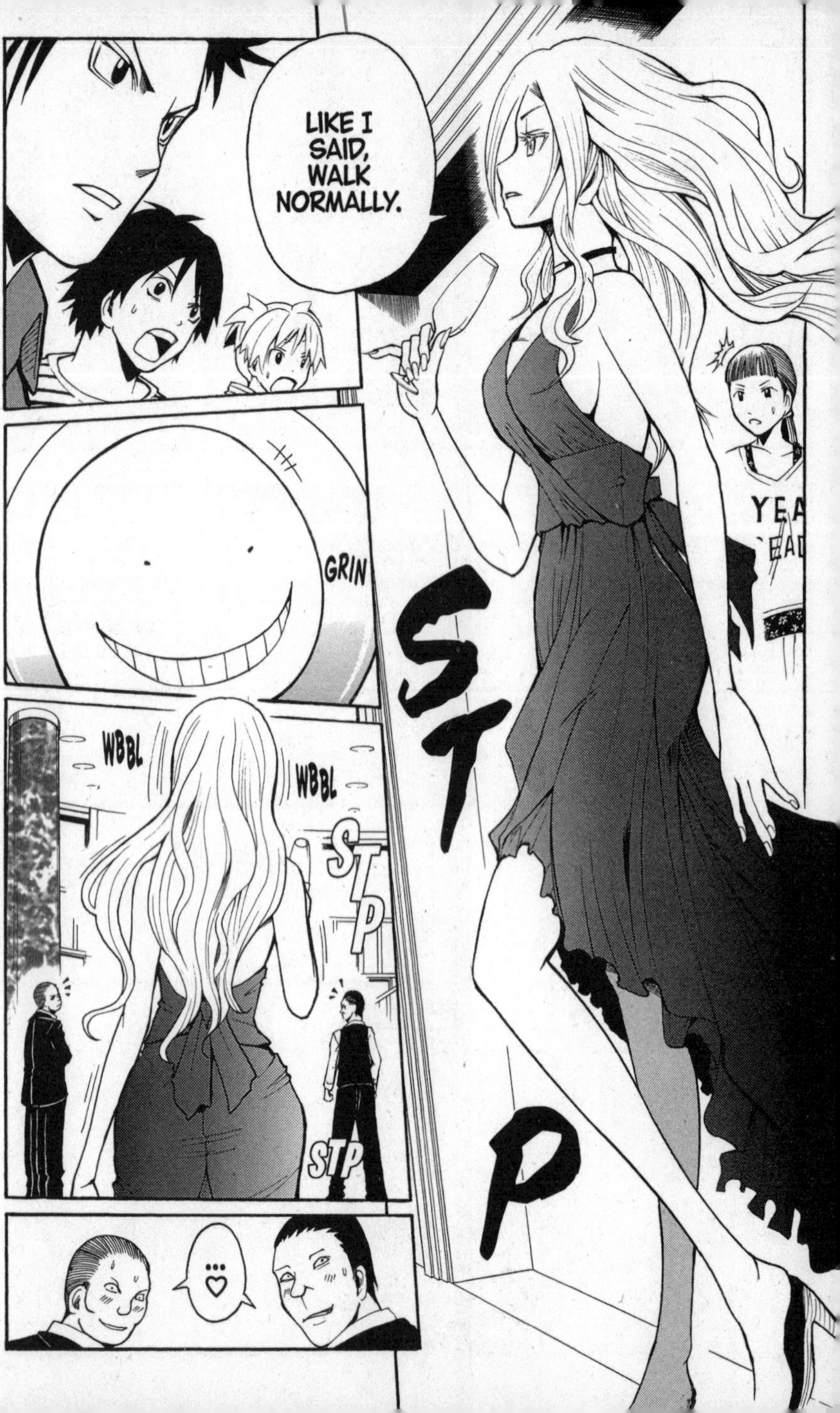
STP
LIKE I SAID, WALK NORMALLY.
GRIN
WBBL
WBBL
STP
STP
...♥

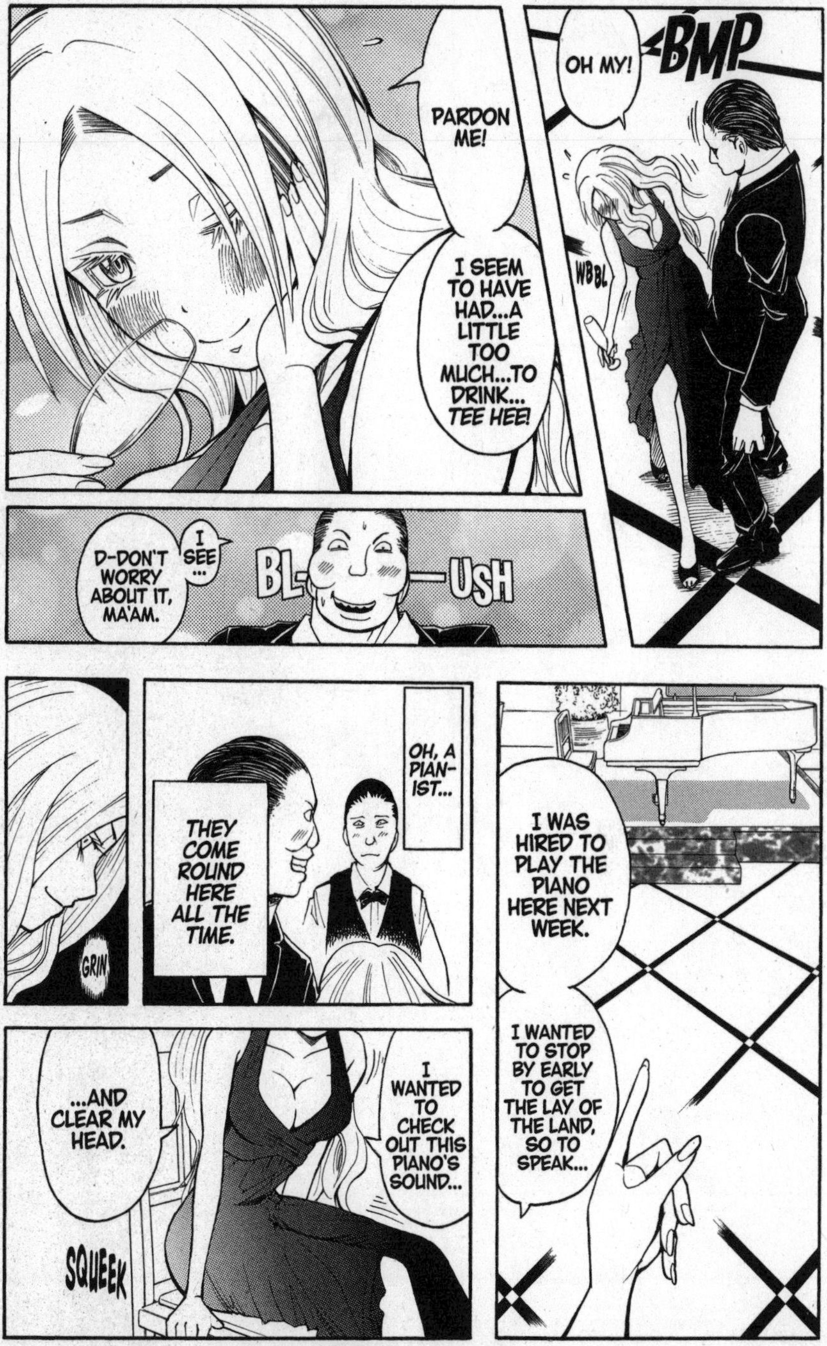
OH MY!
BMP
WBBL
PARDON ME!
I SEEM TO HAVE HAD...A LITTLE TOO MUCH...TO DRINK... *TEE HEE!*
I SEE...
D-DON'T WORRY ABOUT IT, MA'AM.
BL—USH
I WAS HIRED TO PLAY THE PIANO HERE NEXT WEEK.
I WANTED TO STOP BY EARLY TO GET THE LAY OF THE LAND, SO TO SPEAK...
OH, A PIANIST...
THEY COME ROUND HERE ALL THE TIME.
GRIN
I WANTED TO CHECK OUT THIS PIANO'S SOUND...
...AND CLEAR MY HEAD.
SQUEEEK

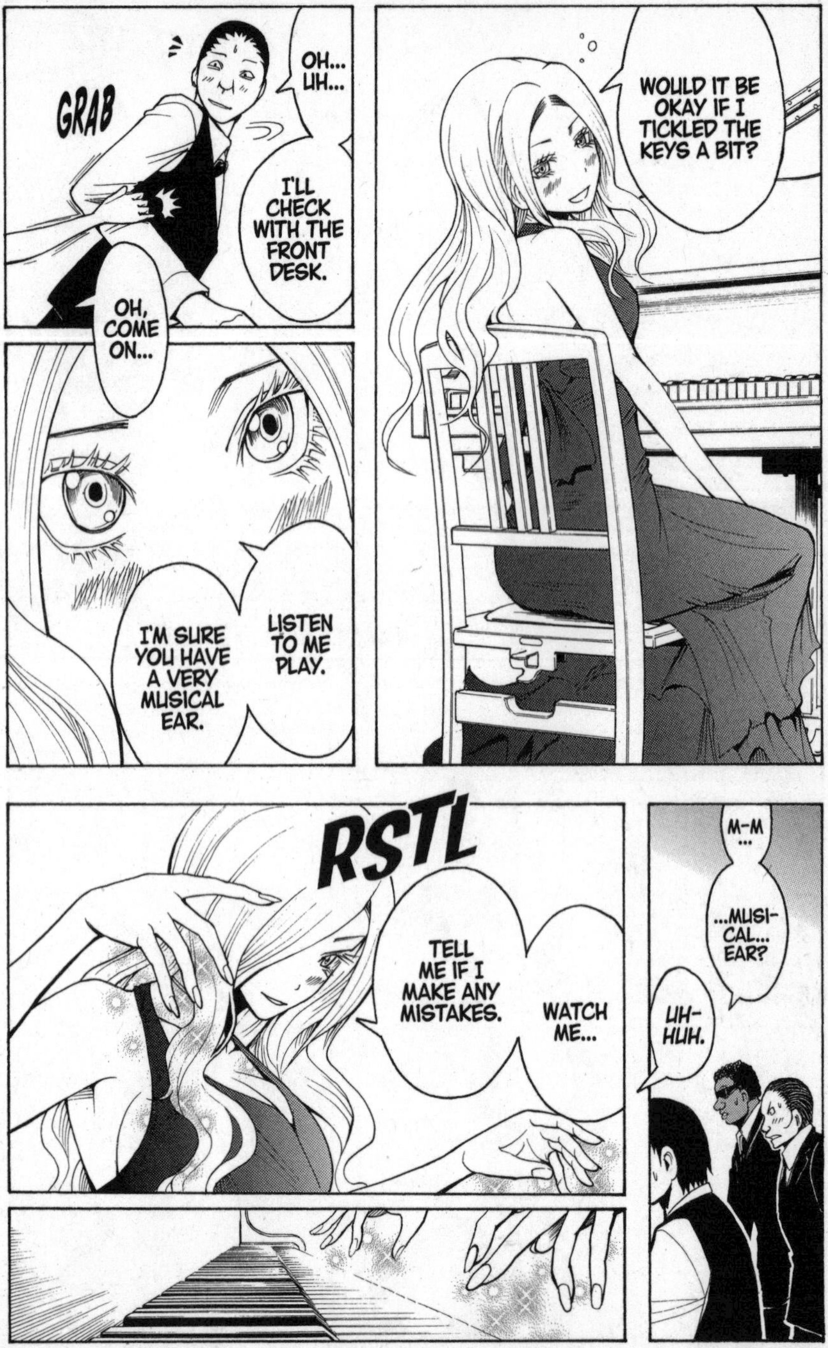
WOULD IT BE OKAY IF I TICKLED THE KEYS A BIT?
OH... UH...
GRAB
I'LL CHECK WITH THE FRONT DESK.
OH, COME ON...
LISTEN TO ME PLAY.
I'M SURE YOU HAVE A VERY MUSICAL EAR.
M-M...
...MUSI-CAL... EAR?
UH-HUH.
RSTL
WATCH ME...
TELL ME IF I MAKE ANY MISTAKES.

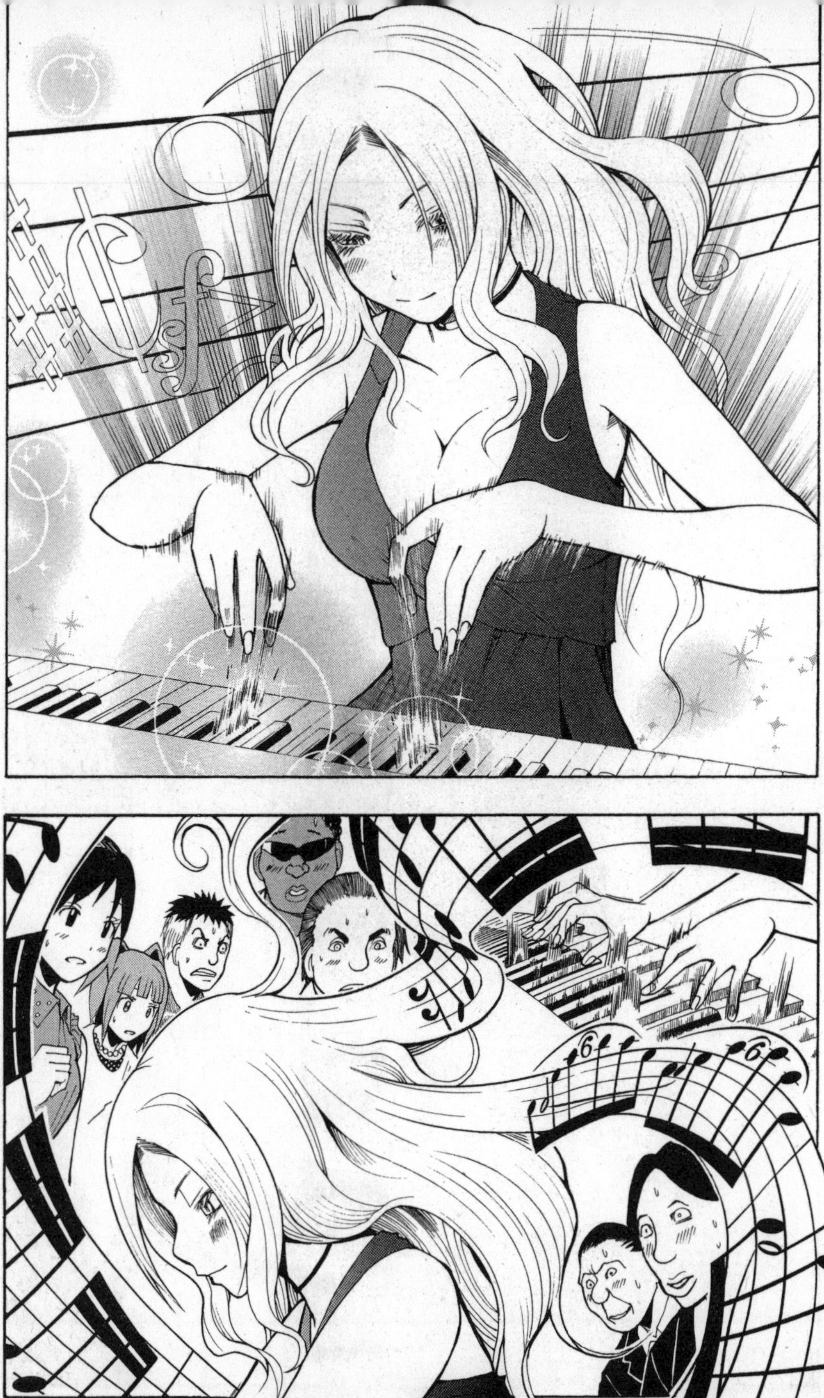

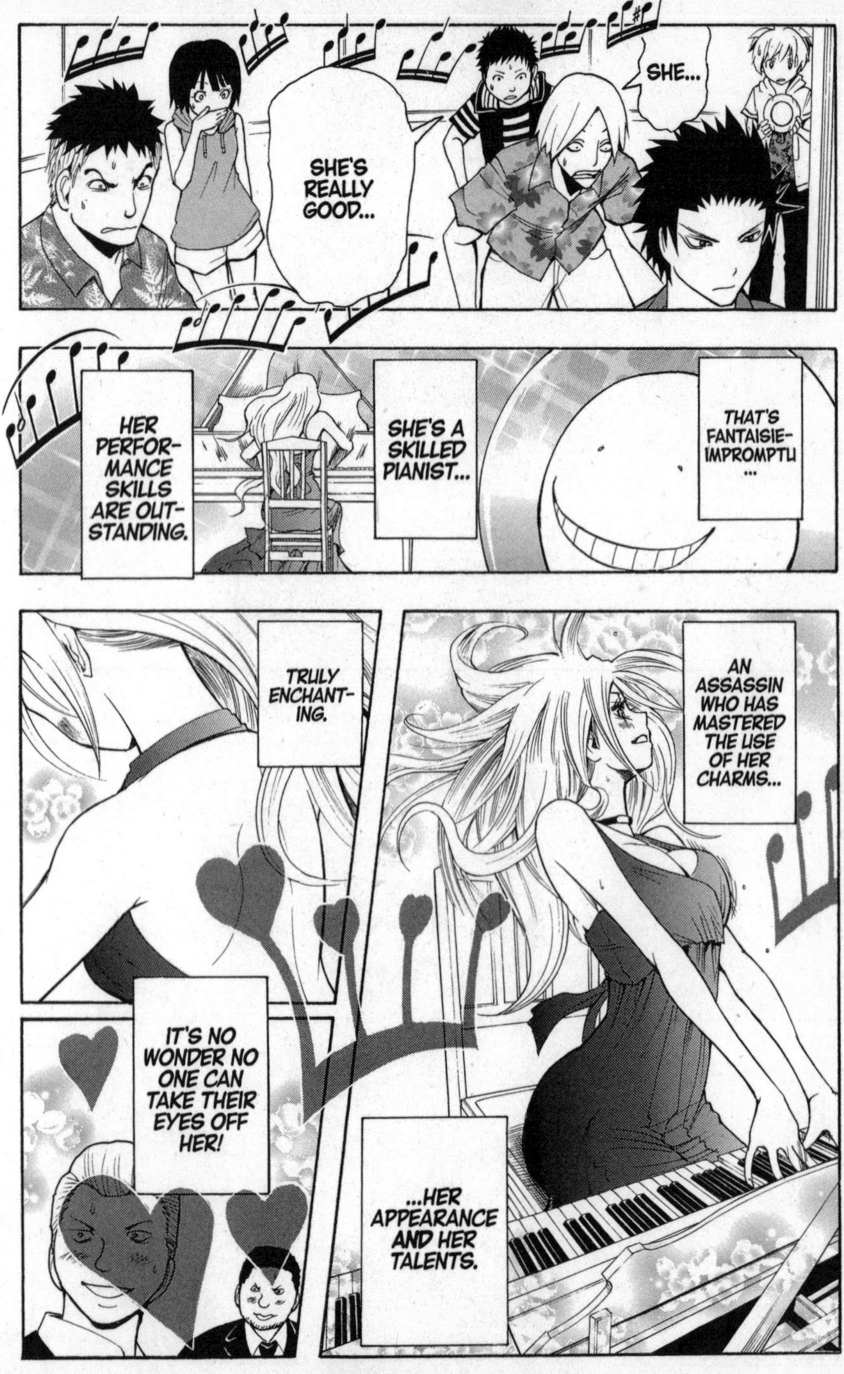
SHE...
SHE'S REALLY GOOD...
THAT'S FANTAISIE-IMPROMPTU ...
SHE'S A SKILLED PIANIST...
HER PERFORMANCE SKILLS ARE OUTSTANDING.
AN ASSASSIN WHO HAS MASTERED THE USE OF HER CHARMS...
...HER APPEARANCE AND HER TALENTS.
TRULY ENCHANTING.
IT'S NO WONDER NO ONE CAN TAKE THEIR EYES OFF HER!

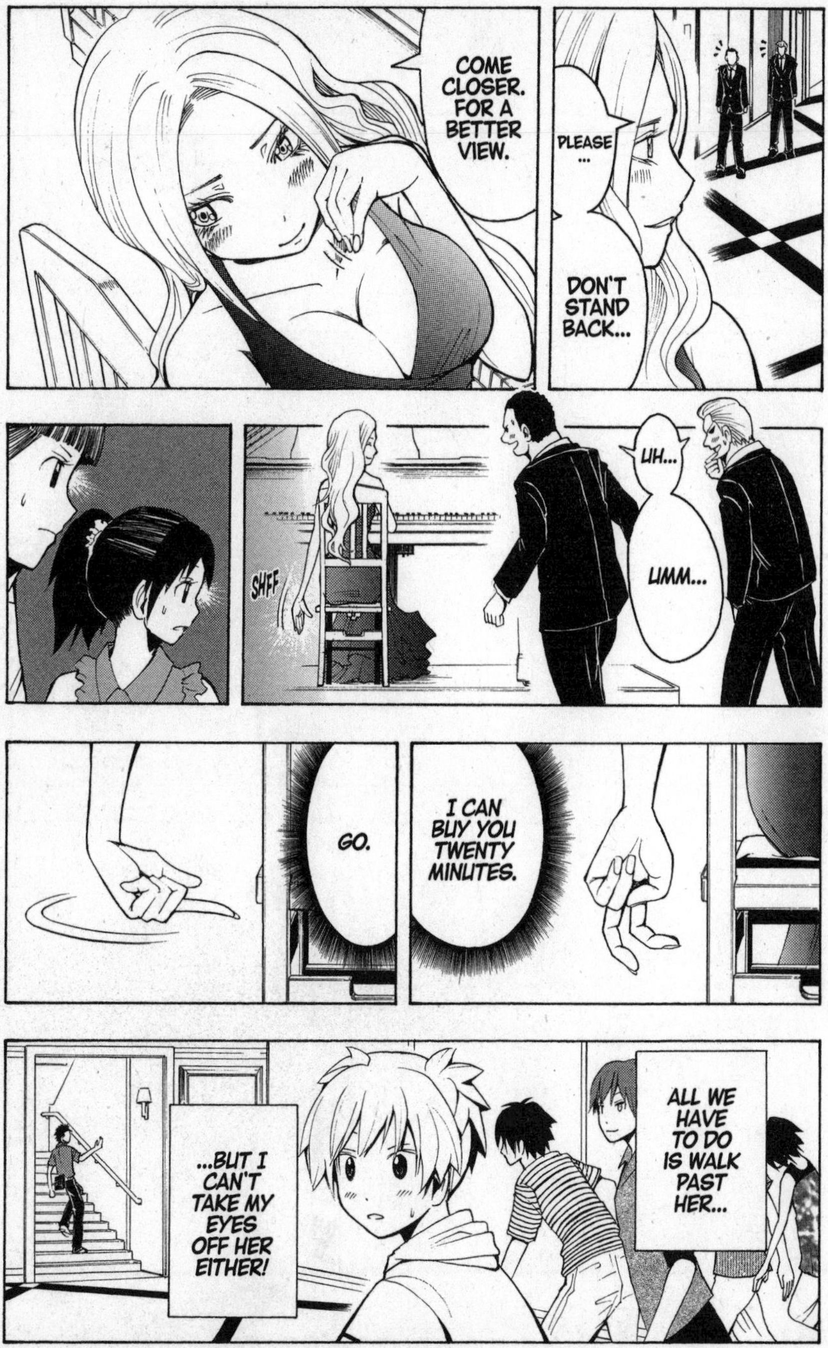
PLEASE ...
DON'T STAND BACK...
COME CLOSER. FOR A BETTER VIEW.
UH...
UMM...
SHFF
I CAN BUY YOU TWENTY MINUTES.
GO.
ALL WE HAVE TO DO IS WALK PAST HER...
...BUT I CAN'T TAKE MY EYES OFF HER EITHER!

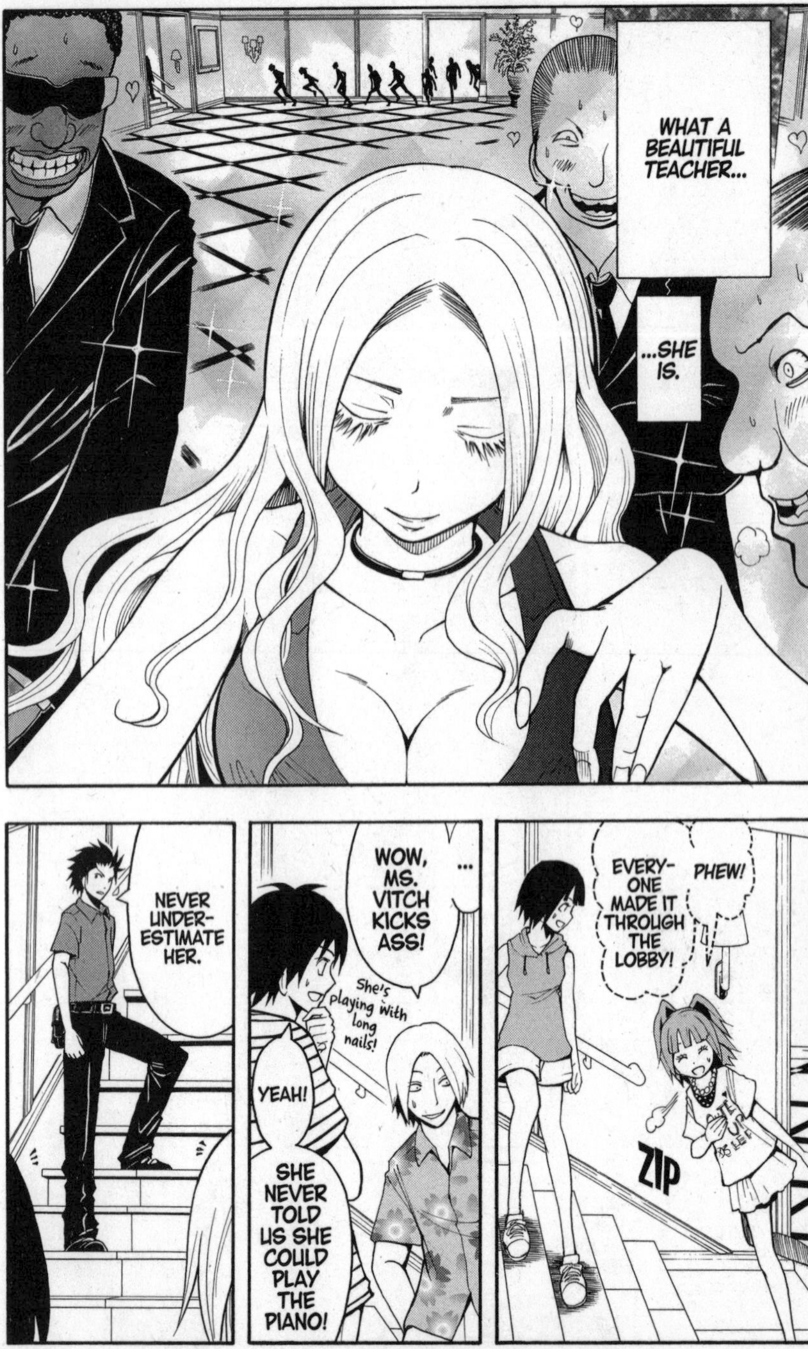
WHAT A BEAUTIFUL TEACHER...
...SHE IS.
PHEW!
EVERYONE MADE IT THROUGH THE LOBBY!
ZIP
...
WOW, MS. VITCH KICKS ASS!
She's playing with long nails!
YEAH!
SHE NEVER TOLD US SHE COULD PLAY THE PIANO!
NEVER UNDERESTIMATE HER.

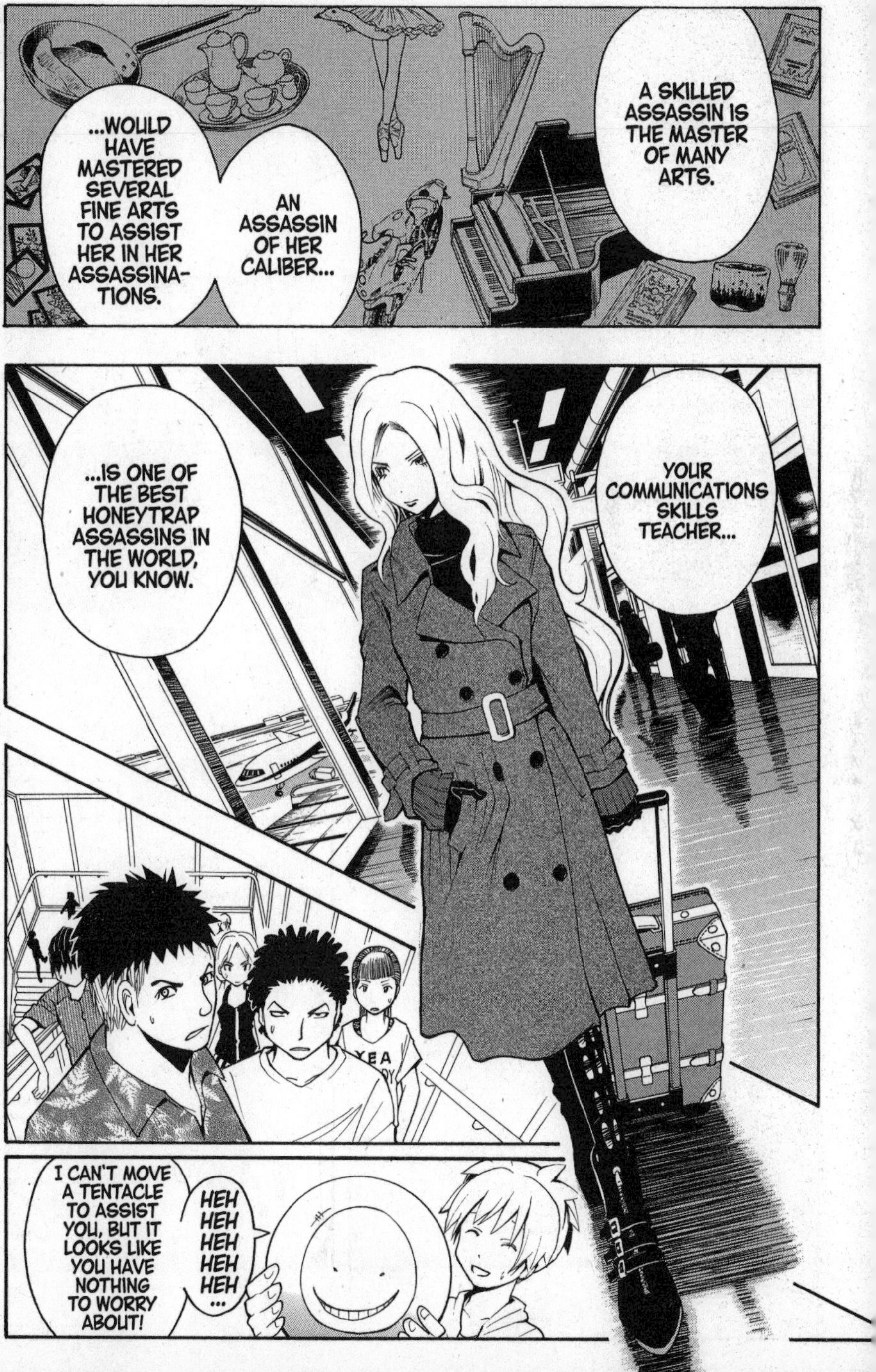
A SKILLED ASSASSIN IS THE MASTER OF MANY ARTS.
AN ASSASSIN OF HER CALIBER...
...WOULD HAVE MASTERED SEVERAL FINE ARTS TO ASSIST HER IN HER ASSASSINATIONS.
YOUR COMMUNICATIONS SKILLS TEACHER...
...IS ONE OF THE BEST HONEYTRAP ASSASSINS IN THE WORLD, YOU KNOW.
HEH HEH HEH HEH HEH...
I CAN'T MOVE A TENTACLE TO ASSIST YOU, BUT IT LOOKS LIKE YOU HAVE NOTHING TO WORRY ABOUT!

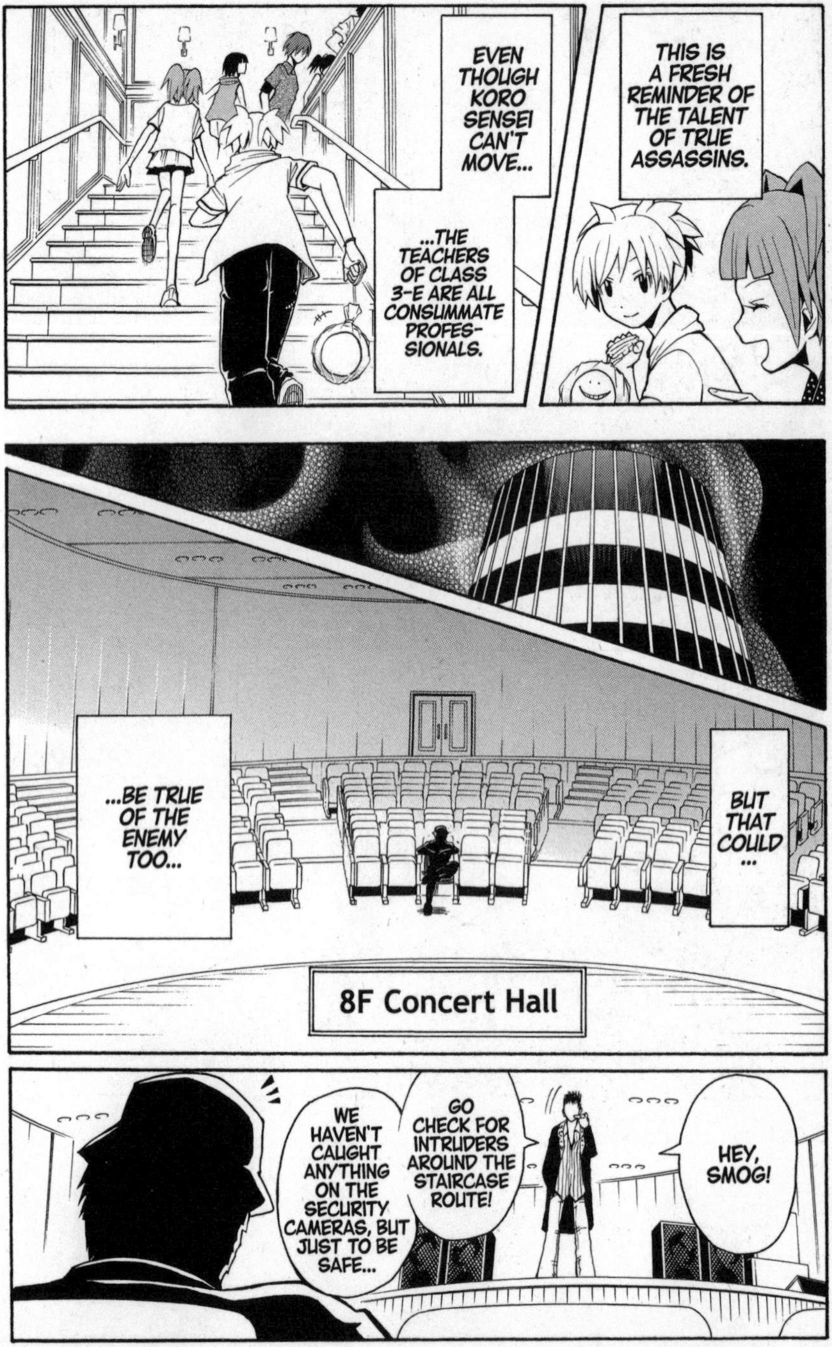
THIS IS A FRESH REMINDER OF THE TALENT OF TRUE ASSASSINS.
EVEN THOUGH KORO SENSEI CAN'T MOVE...
...THE TEACHERS OF CLASS 3-E ARE ALL CONSUMMATE PROFES-SIONALS.
BUT THAT COULD ...
...BE TRUE OF THE ENEMY TOO...
8F Concert Hall
HEY, SMOG!
GO CHECK FOR INTRUDERS AROUND THE STAIRCASE ROUTE!
WE HAVEN'T CAUGHT ANYTHING ON THE SECURITY CAMERAS, BUT JUST TO BE SAFE...

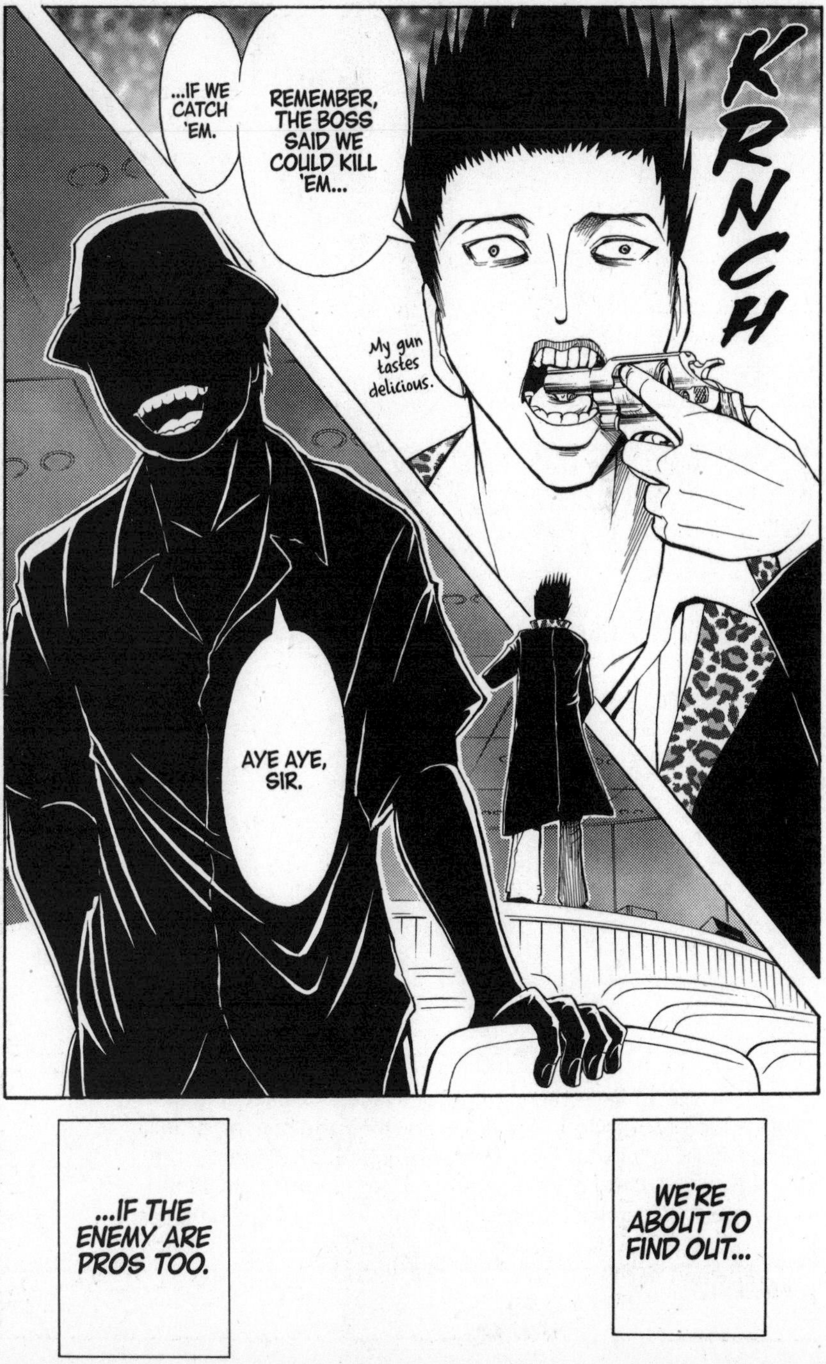
KRNCH
REMEMBER, THE BOSS SAID WE COULD KILL 'EM...
...IF WE CATCH 'EM.
My gun tastes delicious.
AYE AYE, SIR.

WE'RE ABOUT TO FIND OUT...

...IF THE ENEMY ARE PROS TOO.

Ms. Vitch's Super Amazing Techniques, Series 1: Facial Color Change

Normal   Red   Green

She can change the color of her face by controlling her blood circulation. Red is for blushing and playing drunk. Green is for looking vulnerable and ill. These looks can be incredibly useful for infiltration. But after showing them off to her students, she was told that her skills were nothing but "a cheap rip-off of Koro Sensei." This really turned her red with anger.

Class 63 Time for a Chaperone

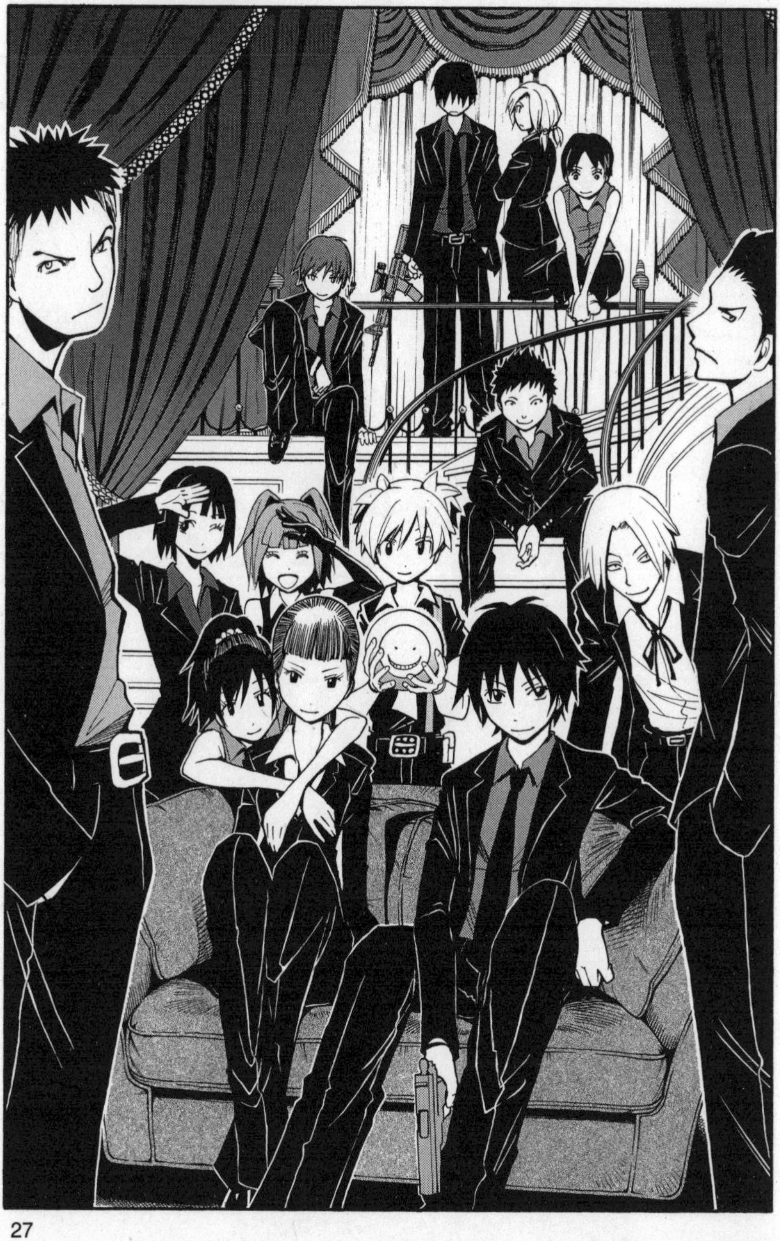

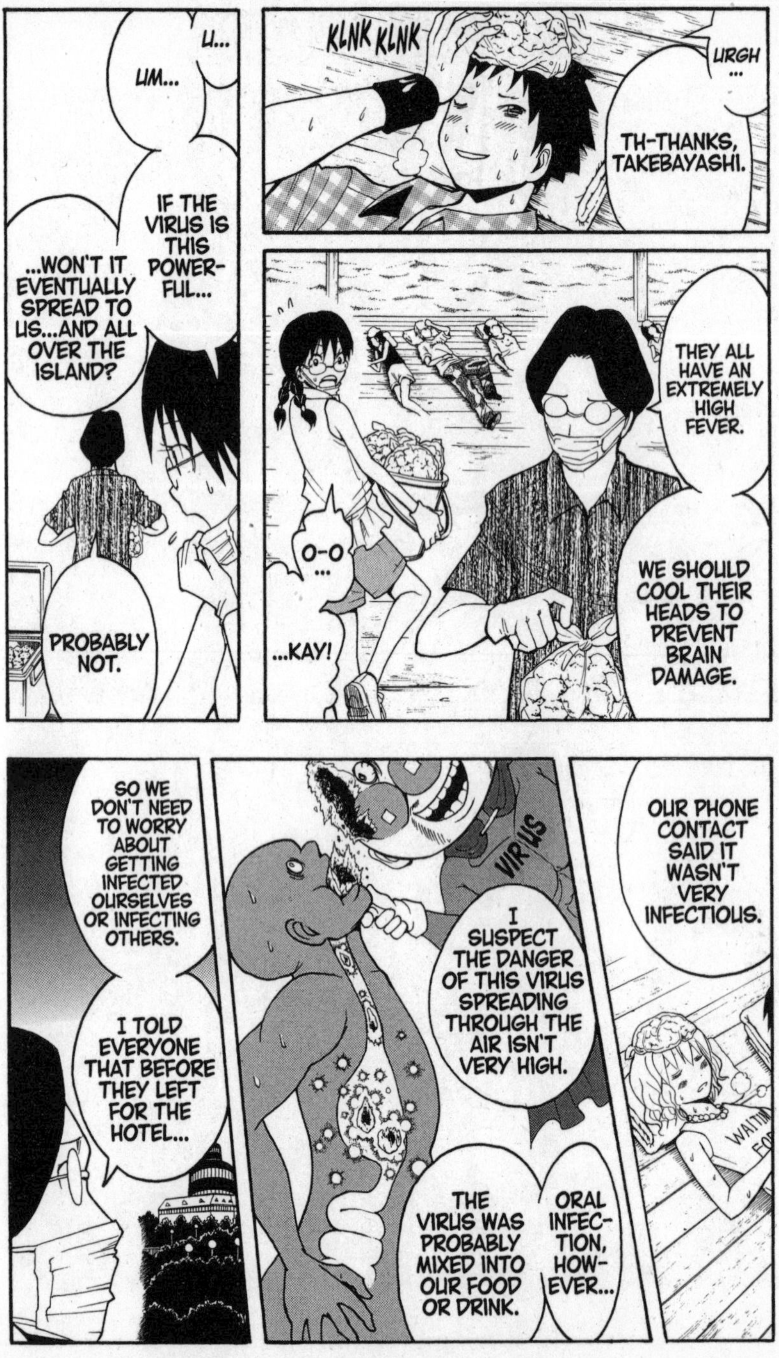
KLNK KLNK
URGH ...
TH-THANKS, TAKEBAYASHI.
THEY ALL HAVE AN EXTREMELY HIGH FEVER.
WE SHOULD COOL THEIR HEADS TO PREVENT BRAIN DAMAGE.
O-O ...
...KAY!
U...
UM...
IF THE VIRUS IS THIS POWERFUL...
...WON'T IT EVENTUALLY SPREAD TO US...AND ALL OVER THE ISLAND?
PROBABLY NOT.
OUR PHONE CONTACT SAID IT WASN'T VERY INFECTIOUS.
VIRUS
I SUSPECT THE DANGER OF THIS VIRUS SPREADING THROUGH THE AIR ISN'T VERY HIGH.
ORAL INFECTION, HOWEVER...
THE VIRUS WAS PROBABLY MIXED INTO OUR FOOD OR DRINK.
SO WE DON'T NEED TO WORRY ABOUT GETTING INFECTED OURSELVES OR INFECTING OTHERS.
I TOLD EVERYONE THAT BEFORE THEY LEFT FOR THE HOTEL...

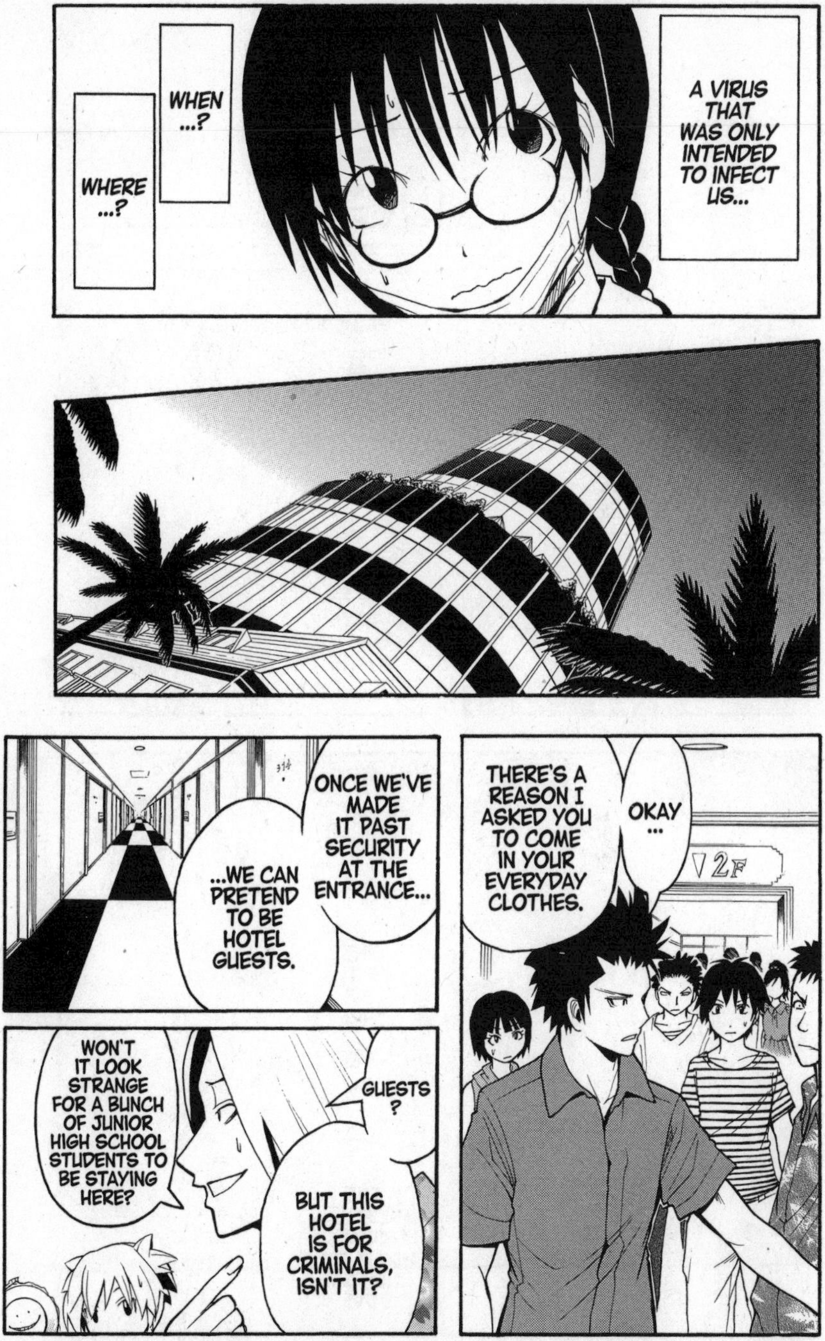
A VIRUS THAT WAS ONLY INTENDED TO INFECT US...
WHEN ...?
WHERE ...?
OKAY ...
THERE'S A REASON I ASKED YOU TO COME IN YOUR EVERYDAY CLOTHES.
2F
ONCE WE'VE MADE IT PAST SECURITY AT THE ENTRANCE...
...WE CAN PRETEND TO BE HOTEL GUESTS.
GUESTS ?
BUT THIS HOTEL IS FOR CRIMINALS, ISN'T IT?
WON'T IT LOOK STRANGE FOR A BUNCH OF JUNIOR HIGH SCHOOL STUDENTS TO BE STAYING HERE?

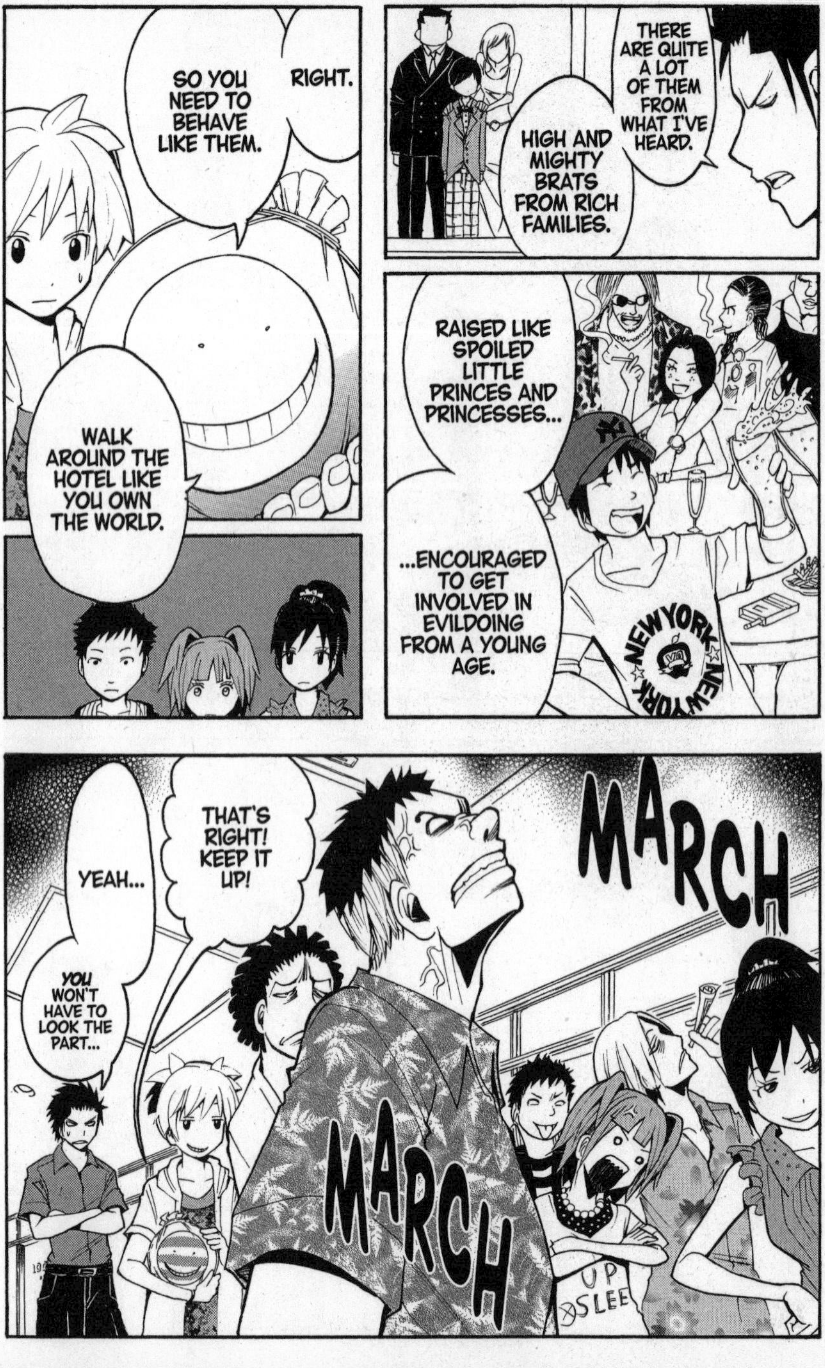
THERE ARE QUITE A LOT OF THEM FROM WHAT I'VE HEARD.
HIGH AND MIGHTY BRATS FROM RICH FAMILIES.
RAISED LIKE SPOILED LITTLE PRINCES AND PRINCESSES...
...ENCOURAGED TO GET INVOLVED IN EVILDOING FROM A YOUNG AGE.
NEW YORK NEW YORK
RIGHT.
SO YOU NEED TO BEHAVE LIKE THEM.
WALK AROUND THE HOTEL LIKE YOU OWN THE WORLD.
MARCH
THAT'S RIGHT! KEEP IT UP!
YEAH...
YOU WON'T HAVE TO LOOK THE PART...
MARCH

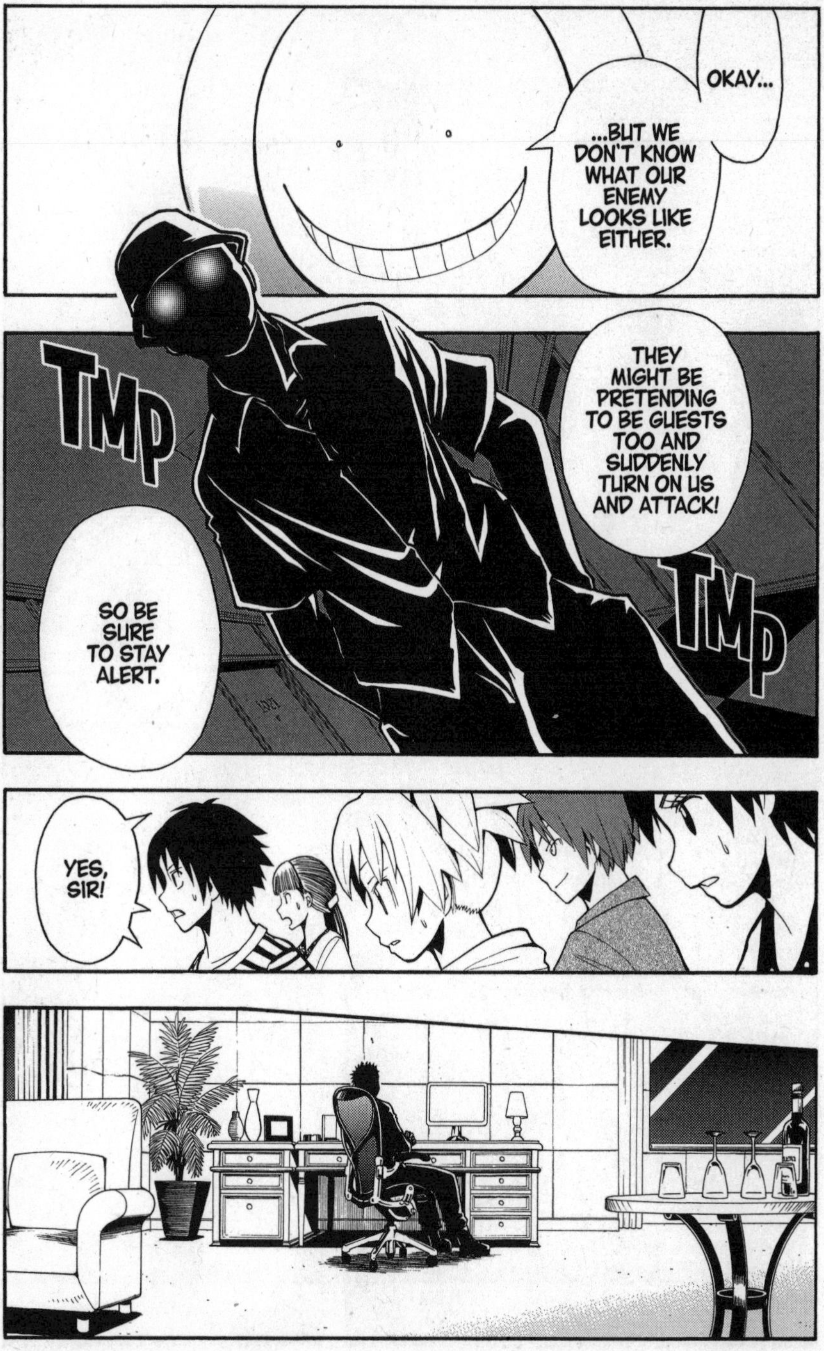
OKAY...
...BUT WE DON'T KNOW WHAT OUR ENEMY LOOKS LIKE EITHER.
THEY MIGHT BE PRETENDING TO BE GUESTS TOO AND SUDDENLY TURN ON US AND ATTACK!
TMP
TMP
SO BE SURE TO STAY ALERT.
YES, SIR!

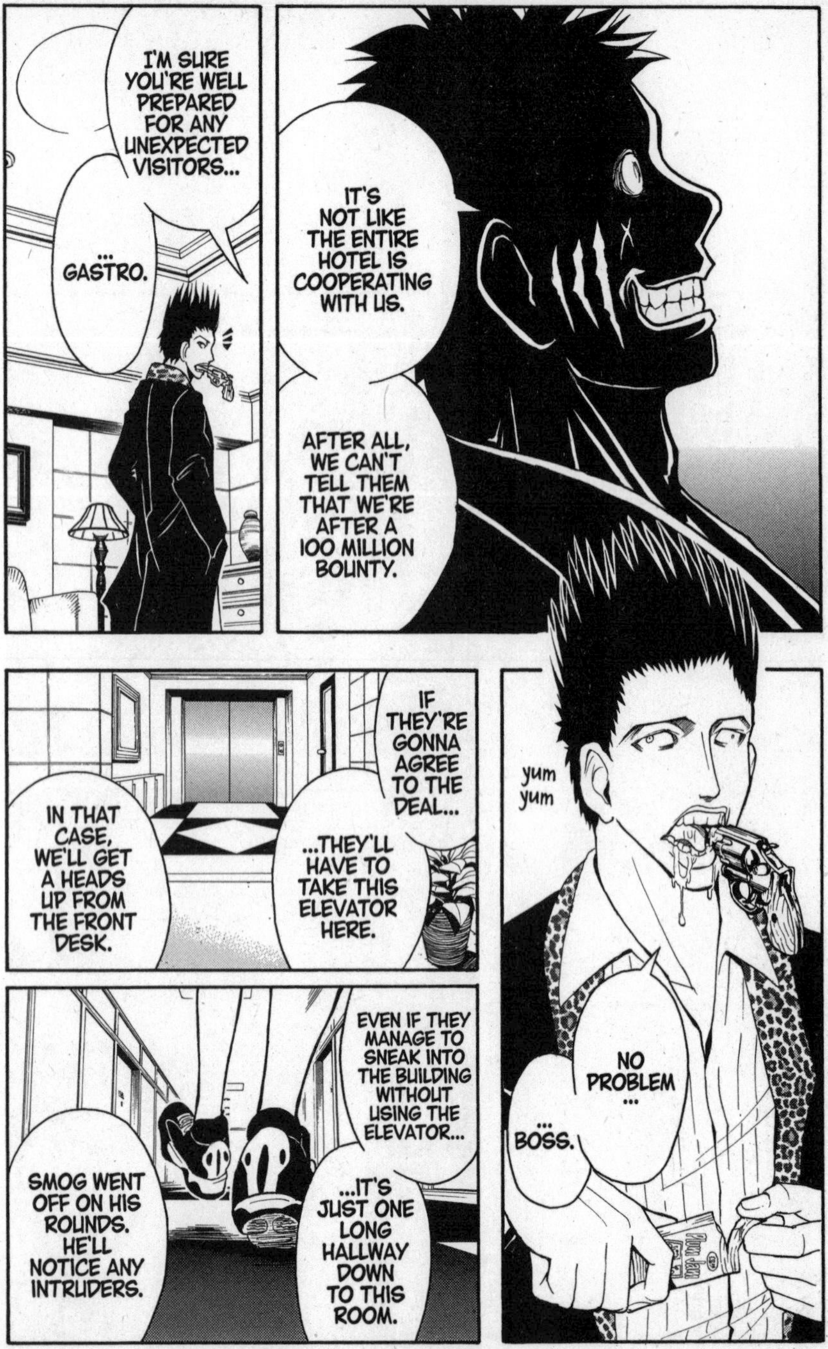
IT'S NOT LIKE THE ENTIRE HOTEL IS COOPERATING WITH US.
AFTER ALL, WE CAN'T TELL THEM THAT WE'RE AFTER A 100 MILLION BOUNTY.
I'M SURE YOU'RE WELL PREPARED FOR ANY UNEXPECTED VISITORS...
...GASTRO.
yum yum
NO PROBLEM...
...BOSS.
IF THEY'RE GONNA AGREE TO THE DEAL...
...THEY'LL HAVE TO TAKE THIS ELEVATOR HERE.
IN THAT CASE, WE'LL GET A HEADS UP FROM THE FRONT DESK.
EVEN IF THEY MANAGE TO SNEAK INTO THE BUILDING WITHOUT USING THE ELEVATOR...
...IT'S JUST ONE LONG HALLWAY DOWN TO THIS ROOM.
SMOG WENT OFF ON HIS ROUNDS. HE'LL NOTICE ANY INTRUDERS.

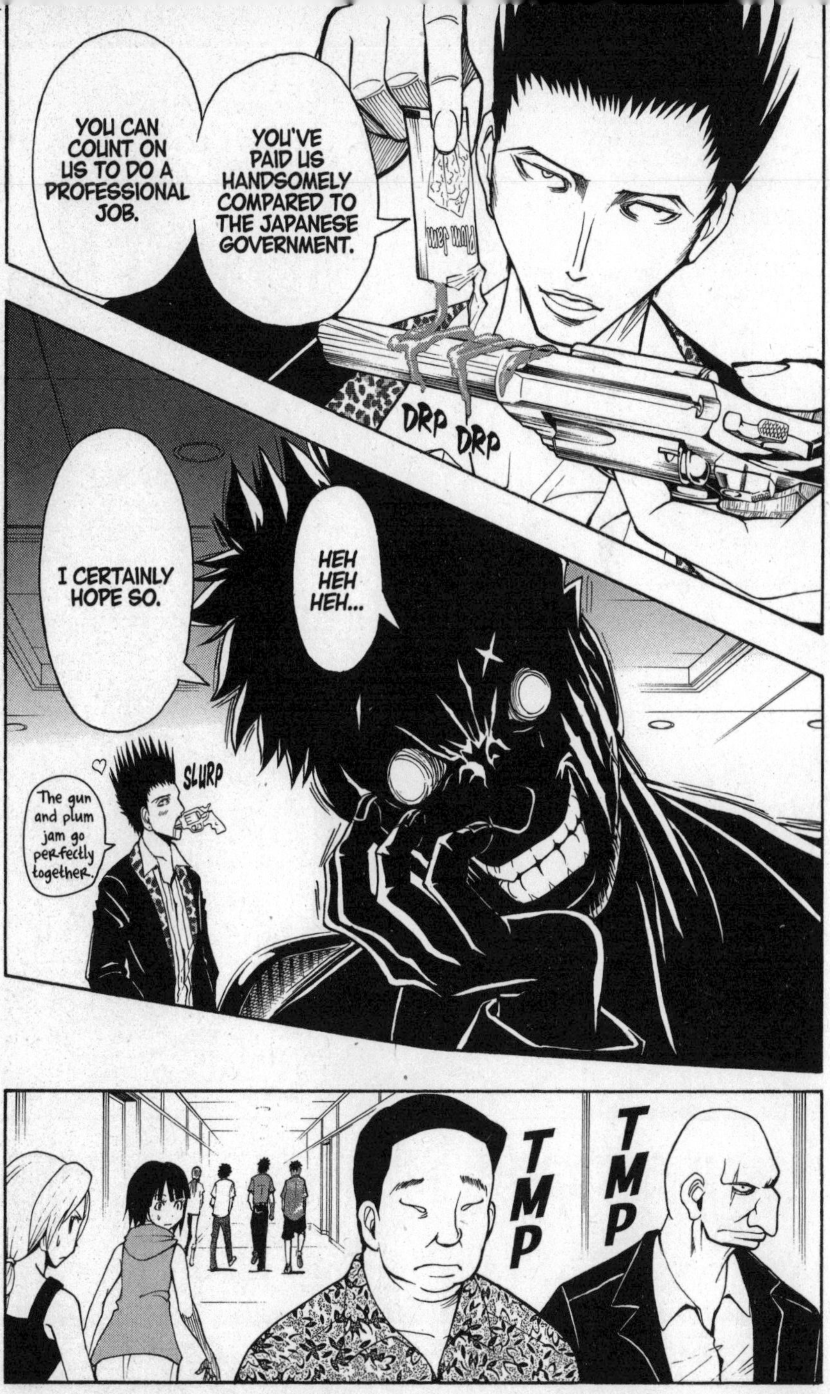
YOU'VE PAID US HANDSOMELY COMPARED TO THE JAPANESE GOVERNMENT.
YOU CAN COUNT ON US TO DO A PROFESSIONAL JOB.
Plum Jam
DRP DRP
HEH HEH HEH...
I CERTAINLY HOPE SO.
SLURP
The gun and plum jam go perfectly together.
TMP
TMP

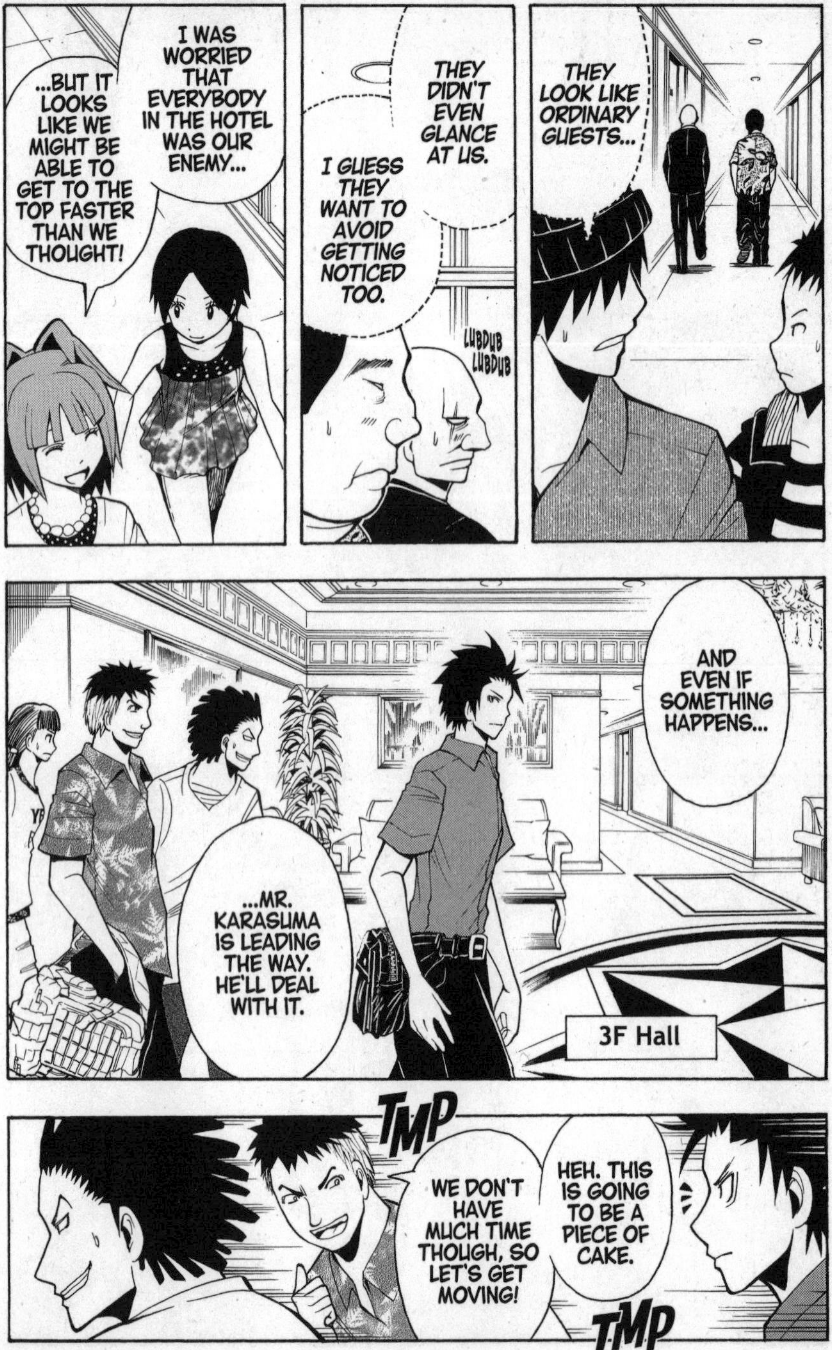
THEY LOOK LIKE ORDINARY GUESTS...
THEY DIDN'T EVEN GLANCE AT US.
I GUESS THEY WANT TO AVOID GETTING NOTICED TOO.
LUBDUB LUBDUB
I WAS WORRIED THAT EVERYBODY IN THE HOTEL WAS OUR ENEMY...
...BUT IT LOOKS LIKE WE MIGHT BE ABLE TO GET TO THE TOP FASTER THAN WE THOUGHT!
AND EVEN IF SOMETHING HAPPENS...
...MR. KARASUMA IS LEADING THE WAY. HE'LL DEAL WITH IT.
3F Hall
TMP
HEH. THIS IS GOING TO BE A PIECE OF CAKE.
WE DON'T HAVE MUCH TIME THOUGH, SO LET'S GET MOVING!
TMP

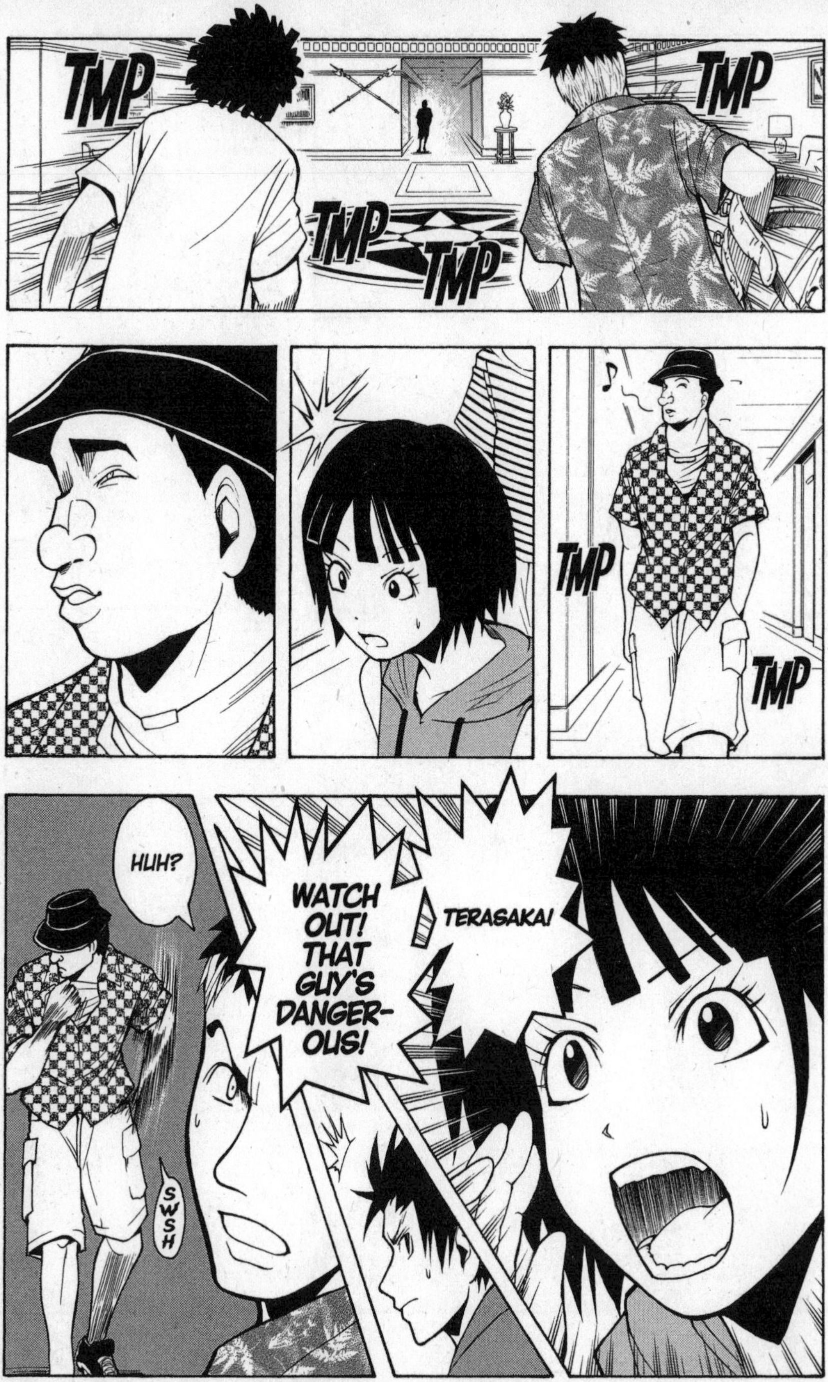
TMP
TMP
TMP
TMP
TMP
TMP
TERASAKA!
WATCH OUT! THAT GUY'S DANGER-OUS!
HUH?
SWSH

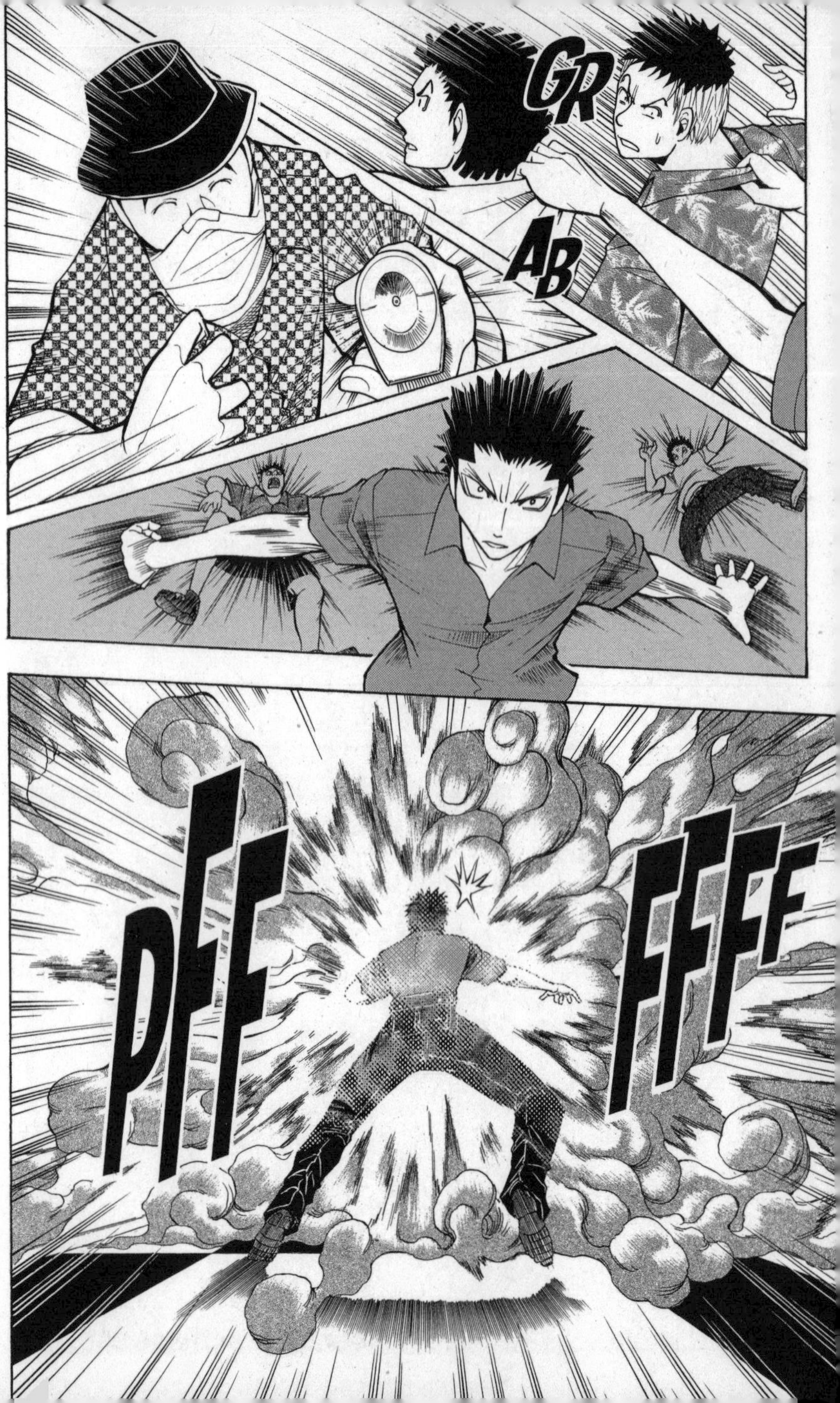
GR
AB
FFFF
PFF

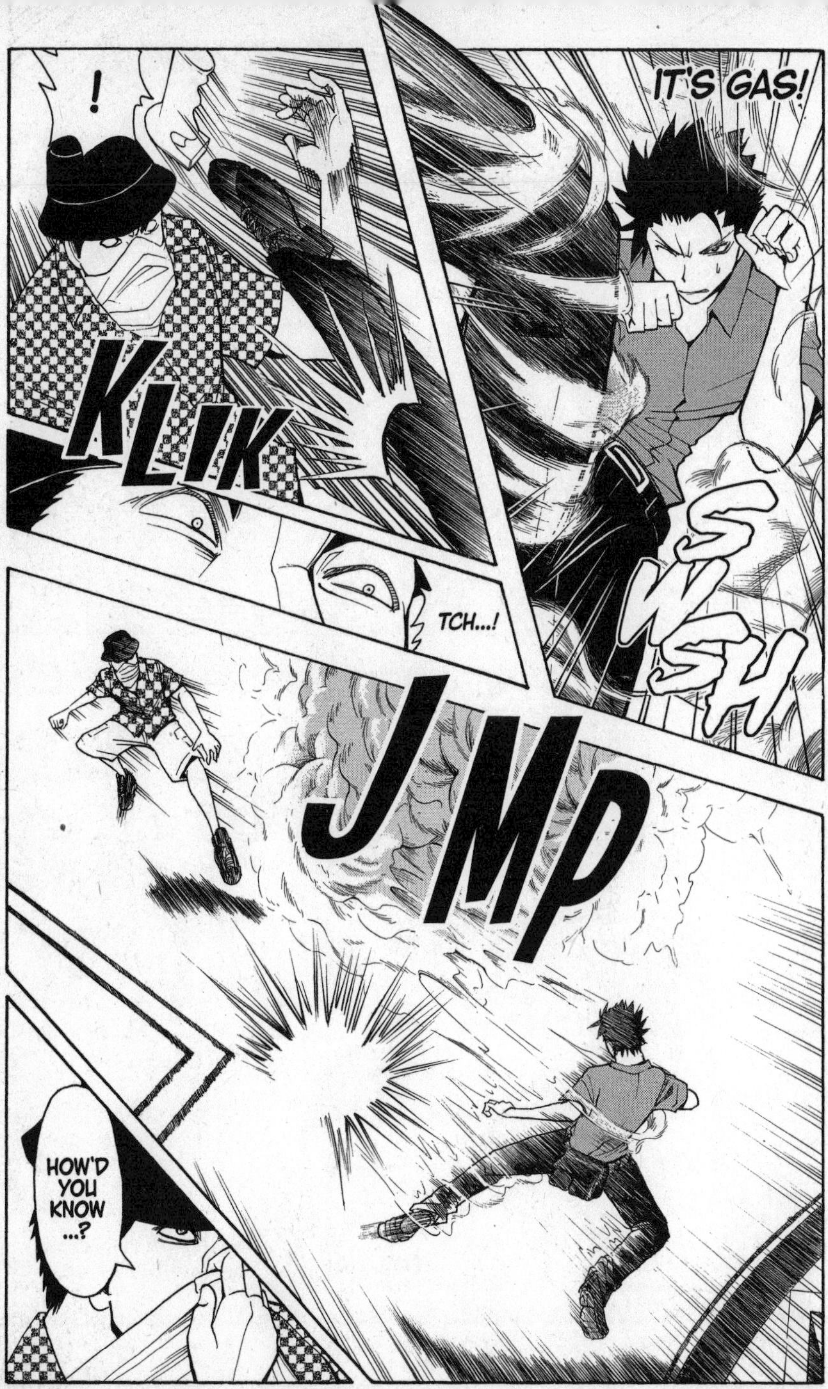
IT'S GAS!
SWSH
!
KLIK
TCH...!
JMP
HOW'D YOU KNOW ...?

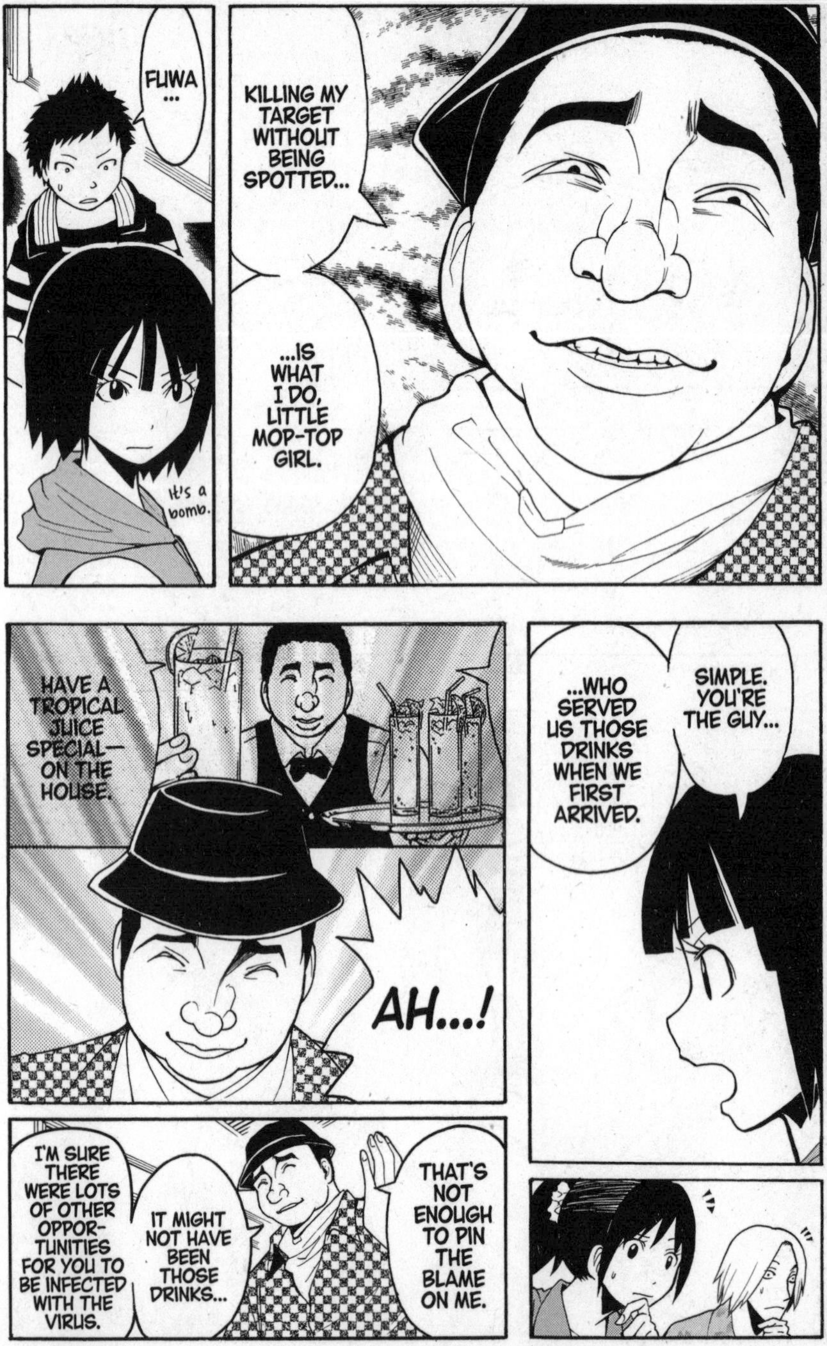

KILLING MY TARGET WITHOUT BEING SPOTTED...
...IS WHAT I DO, LITTLE MOP-TOP GIRL.
FUWA ...
It's a bomb.
SIMPLE. YOU'RE THE GUY...
...WHO SERVED US THOSE DRINKS WHEN WE FIRST ARRIVED.
HAVE A TROPICAL JUICE SPECIAL—ON THE HOUSE.
AH...!
THAT'S NOT ENOUGH TO PIN THE BLAME ON ME.
IT MIGHT NOT HAVE BEEN THOSE DRINKS...
I'M SURE THERE WERE LOTS OF OTHER OPPOR-TUNITIES FOR YOU TO BE INFECTED WITH THE VIRUS.

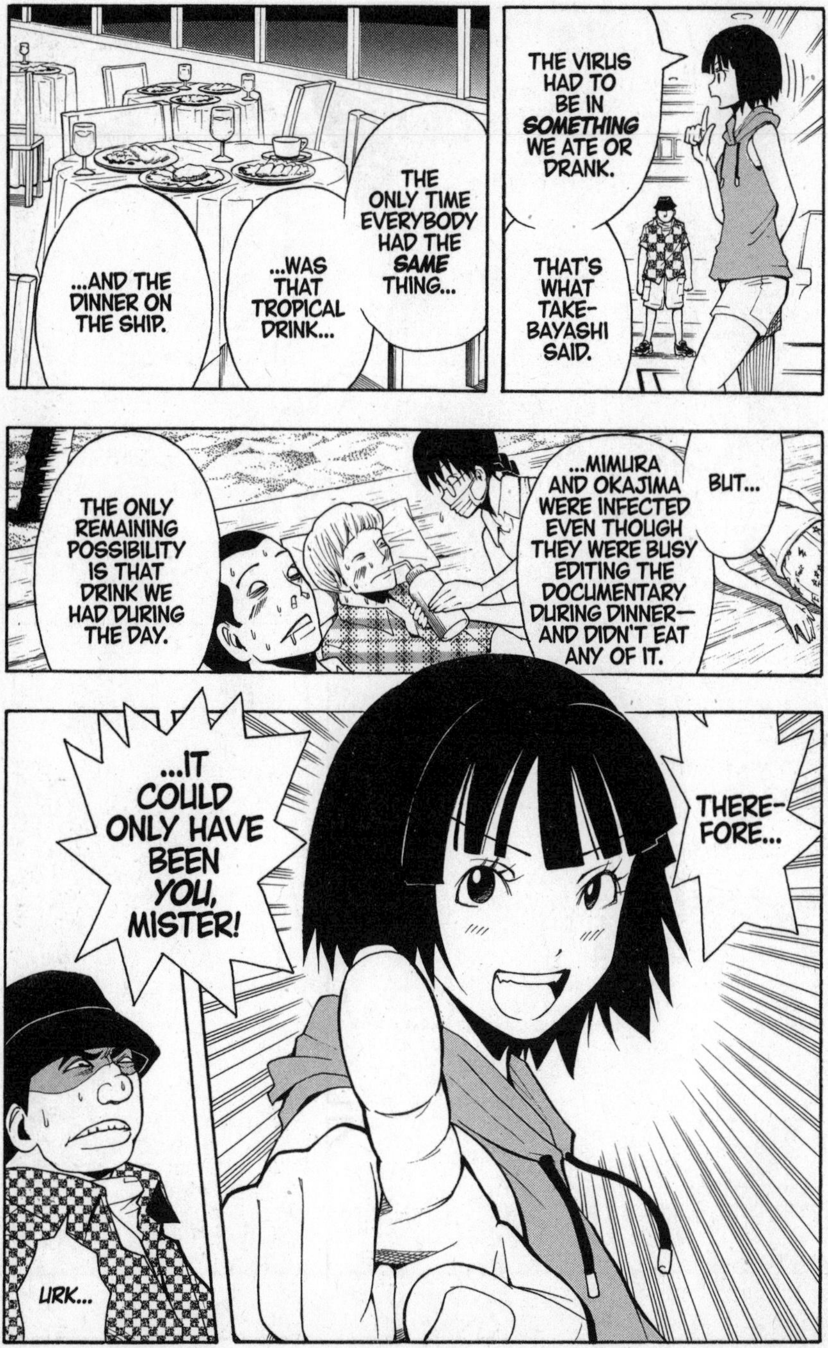
THE VIRUS HAD TO BE IN *SOMETHING* WE ATE OR DRANK.
THAT'S WHAT TAKE-BAYASHI SAID.
THE ONLY TIME EVERYBODY HAD THE *SAME* THING...
...WAS THAT TROPICAL DRINK...
...AND THE DINNER ON THE SHIP.
BUT...
...MIMURA AND OKAJIMA WERE INFECTED EVEN THOUGH THEY WERE BUSY EDITING THE DOCUMENTARY DURING DINNER—AND DIDN'T EAT ANY OF IT.
THE ONLY REMAINING POSSIBILITY IS THAT DRINK WE HAD DURING THE DAY.
THERE-FORE...
...IT COULD ONLY HAVE BEEN *YOU*, MISTER!
URK...

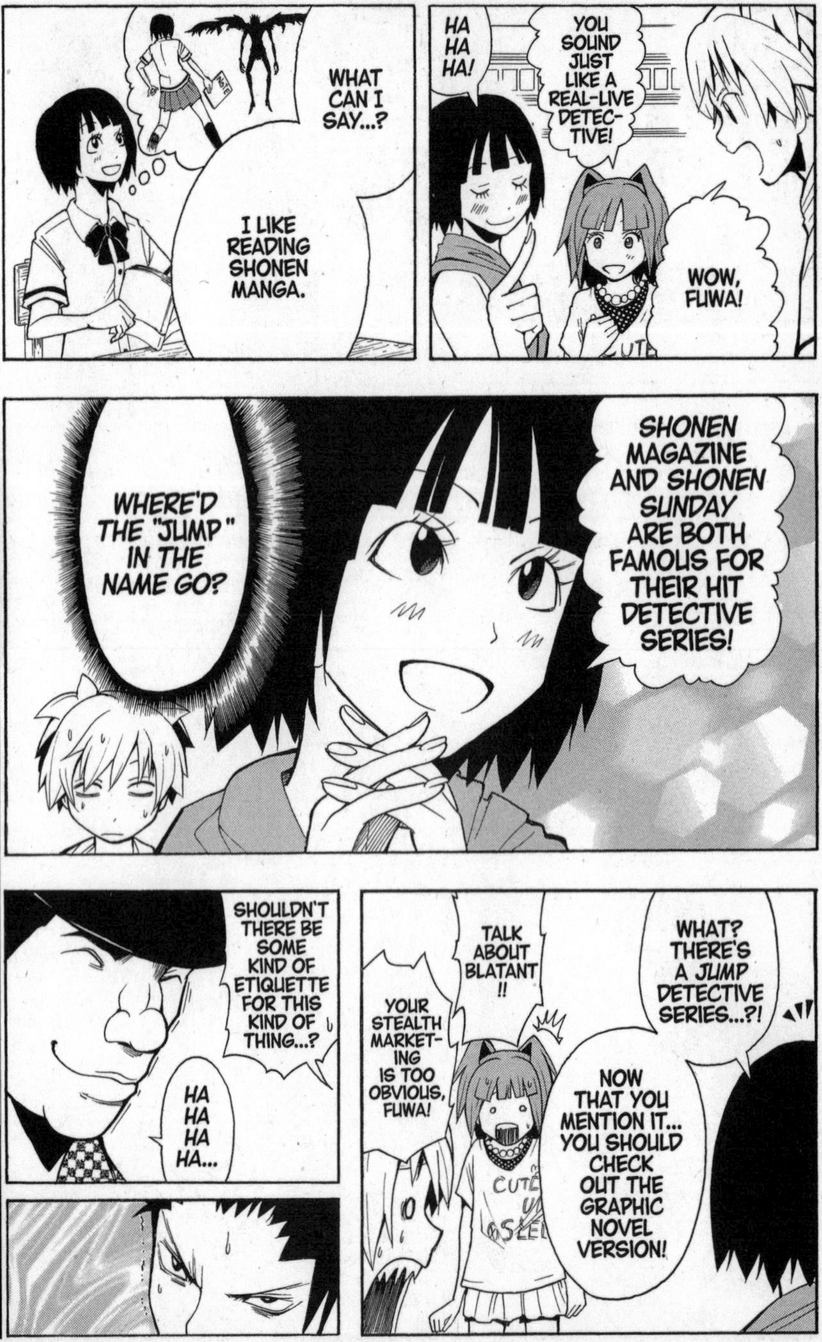
YOU SOUND JUST LIKE A REAL-LIVE DETECTIVE!
HA HA HA!
WOW, FUWA!
WHAT CAN I SAY...?
I LIKE READING SHONEN MANGA.
SHONEN MAGAZINE AND SHONEN SUNDAY ARE BOTH FAMOUS FOR THEIR HIT DETECTIVE SERIES!
WHERE'D THE "JUMP" IN THE NAME GO?
WHAT? THERE'S A JUMP DETECTIVE SERIES...?!
NOW THAT YOU MENTION IT... YOU SHOULD CHECK OUT THE GRAPHIC NOVEL VERSION!
TALK ABOUT BLATANT!!
YOUR STEALTH MARKETING IS TOO OBVIOUS, FUWA!
SHOULDN'T THERE BE SOME KIND OF ETIQUETTE FOR THIS KIND OF THING...?
HA HA HA HA...

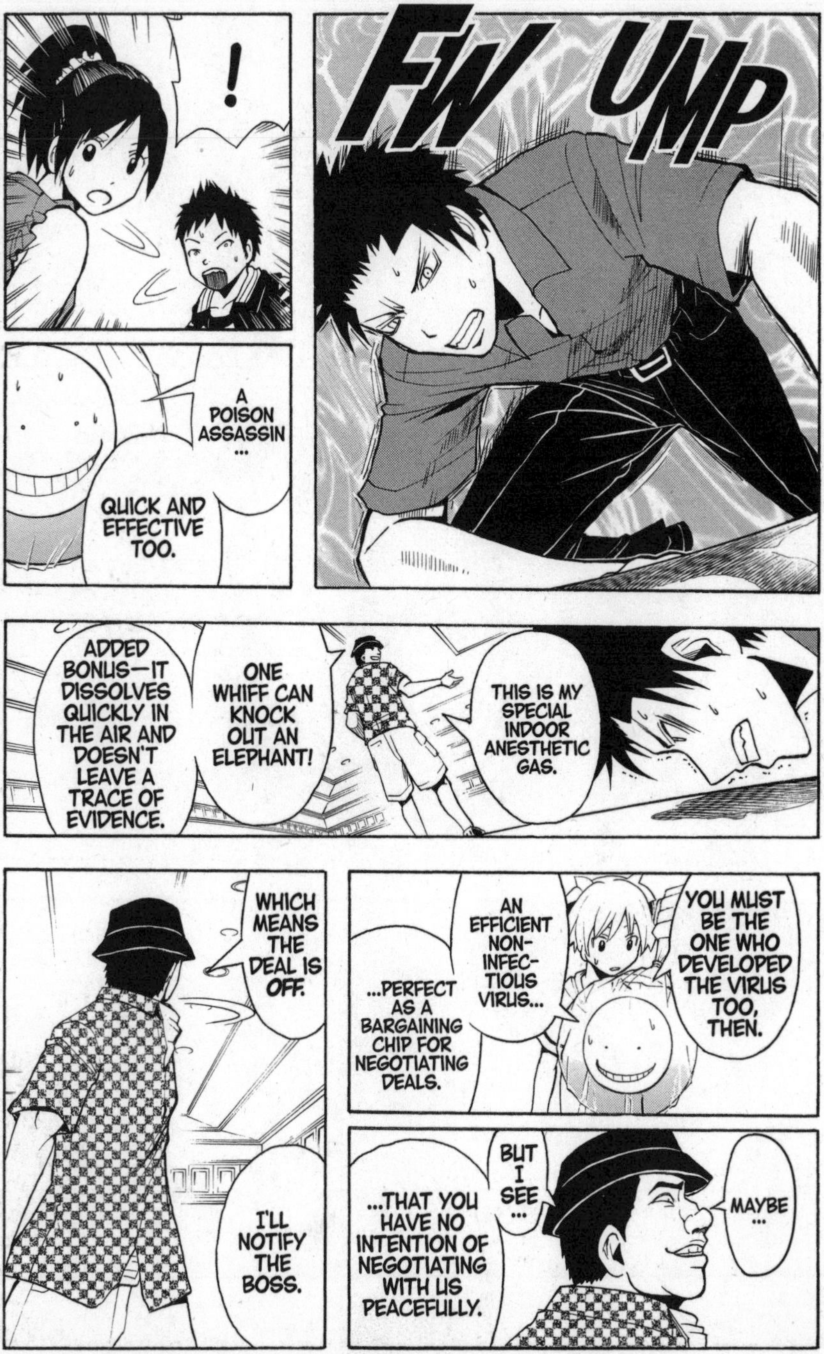
FWUMP
!
A POISON ASSASSIN...
QUICK AND EFFECTIVE TOO.
THIS IS MY SPECIAL INDOOR ANESTHETIC GAS.
ONE WHIFF CAN KNOCK OUT AN ELEPHANT!
ADDED BONUS—IT DISSOLVES QUICKLY IN THE AIR AND DOESN'T LEAVE A TRACE OF EVIDENCE.
YOU MUST BE THE ONE WHO DEVELOPED THE VIRUS TOO, THEN.
AN EFFICIENT NON-INFECTIOUS VIRUS...
...PERFECT AS A BARGAINING CHIP FOR NEGOTIATING DEALS.
MAYBE...
BUT I SEE...
...THAT YOU HAVE NO INTENTION OF NEGOTIATING WITH US PEACEFULLY.
WHICH MEANS THE DEAL IS OFF.
I'LL NOTIFY THE BOSS.

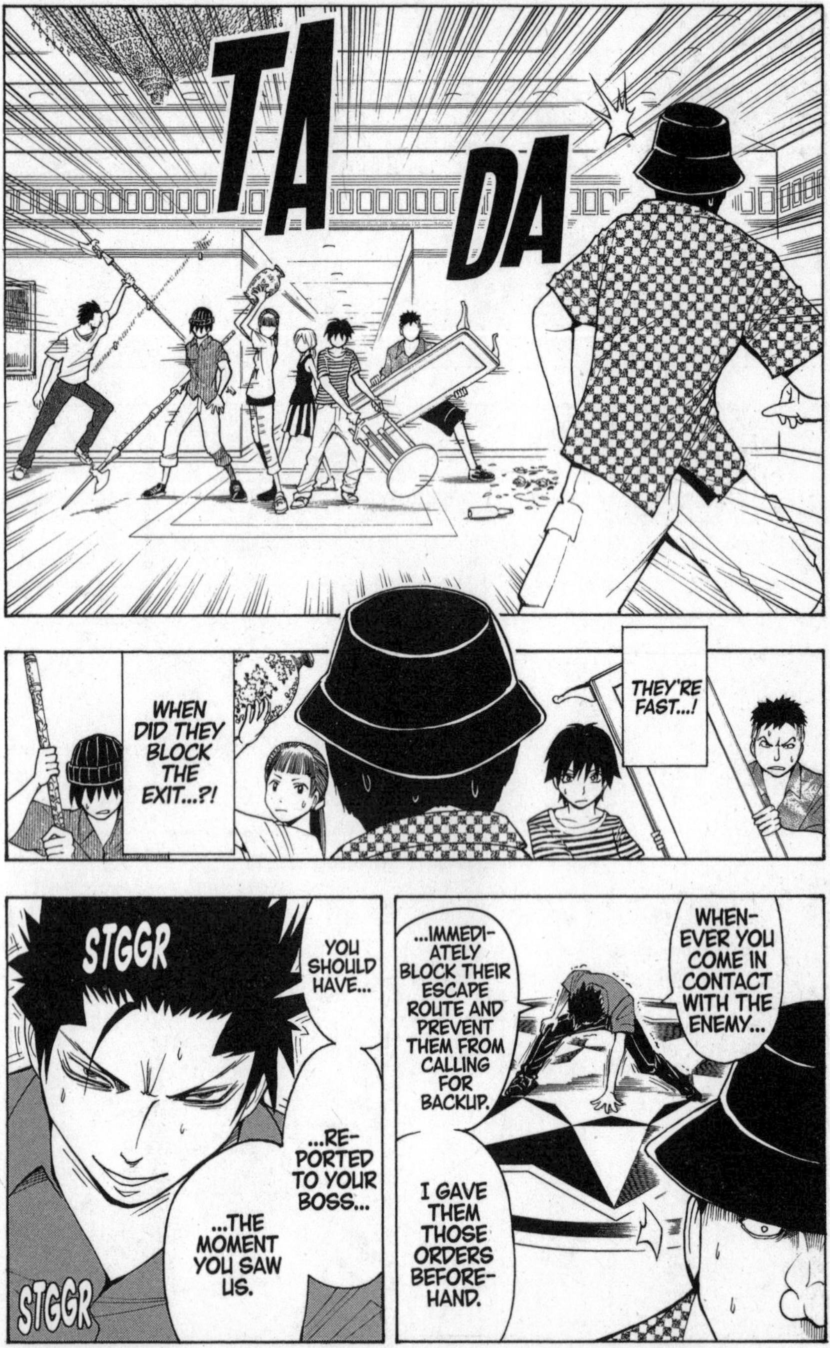
TA
DA
THEY'RE FAST...!
WHEN DID THEY BLOCK THE EXIT...?!
WHEN-EVER YOU COME IN CONTACT WITH THE ENEMY...
...IMMEDI-ATELY BLOCK THEIR ESCAPE ROUTE AND PREVENT THEM FROM CALLING FOR BACKUP.
I GAVE THEM THOSE ORDERS BEFORE-HAND.
STGGR
YOU SHOULD HAVE...
...RE-PORTED TO YOUR BOSS...
...THE MOMENT YOU SAW US.
STGGR

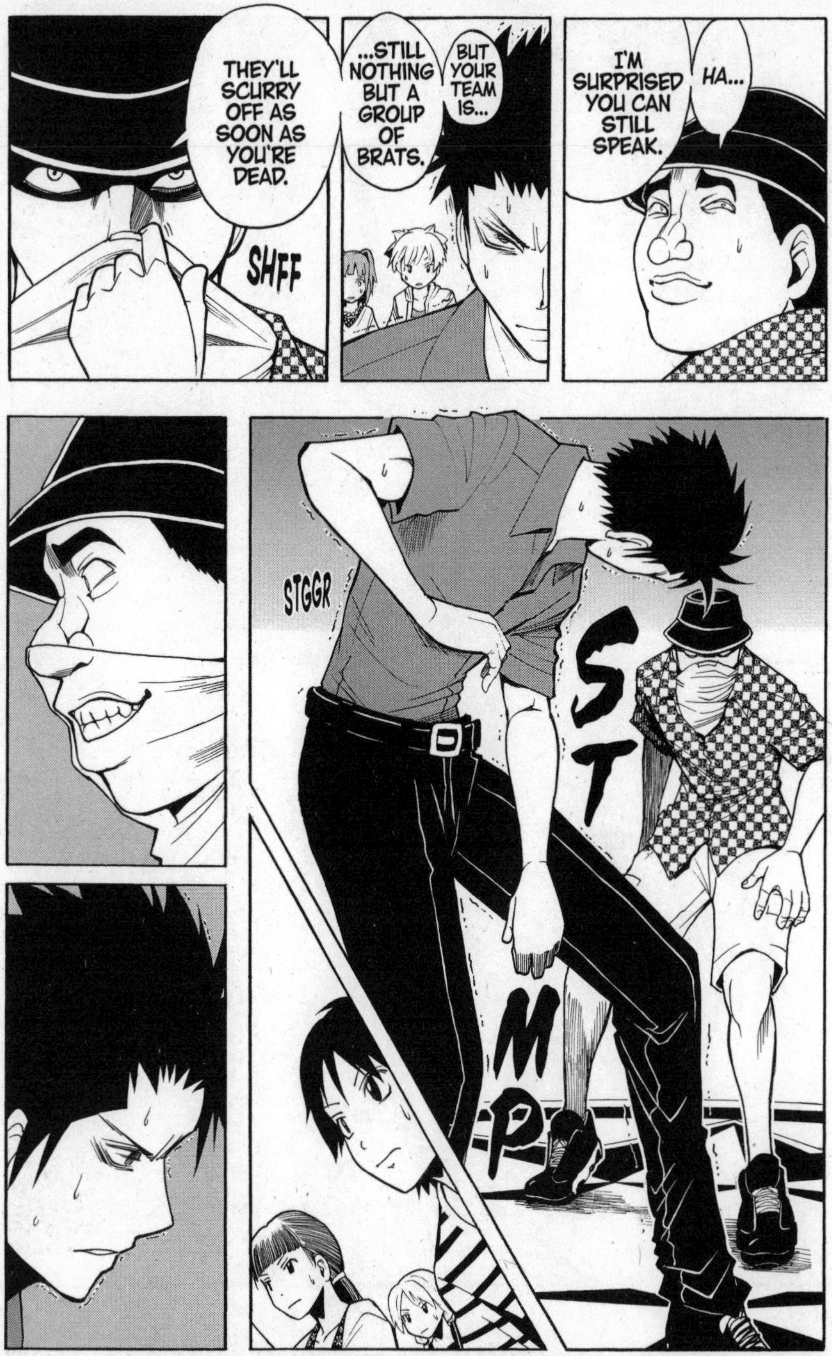
HA...
I'M SURPRISED YOU CAN STILL SPEAK.
BUT YOUR TEAM IS...
...STILL NOTHING BUT A GROUP OF BRATS.
THEY'LL SCURRY OFF AS SOON AS YOU'RE DEAD.
SHFF
STGGR
STMP

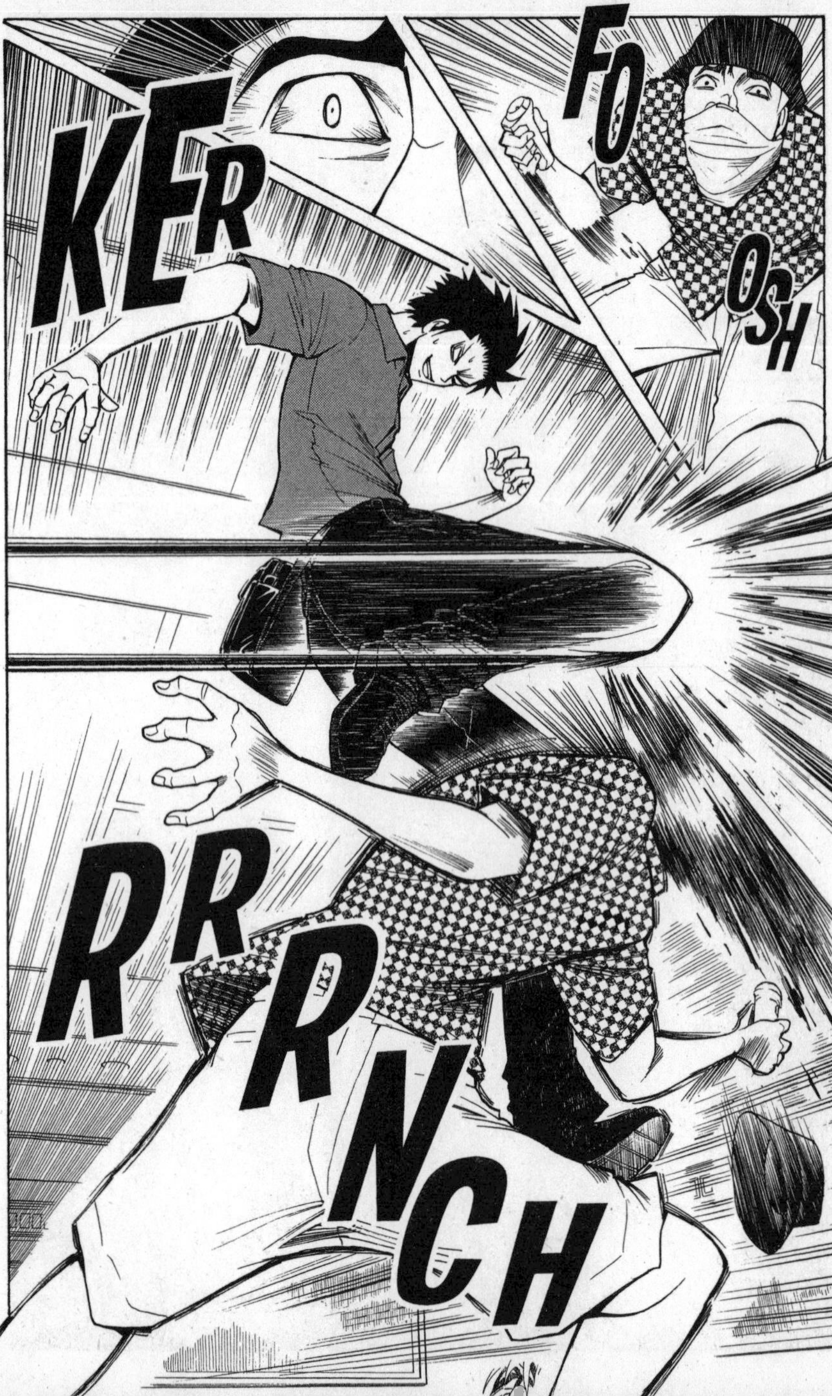
FOOSH
KER
RRRRNCH

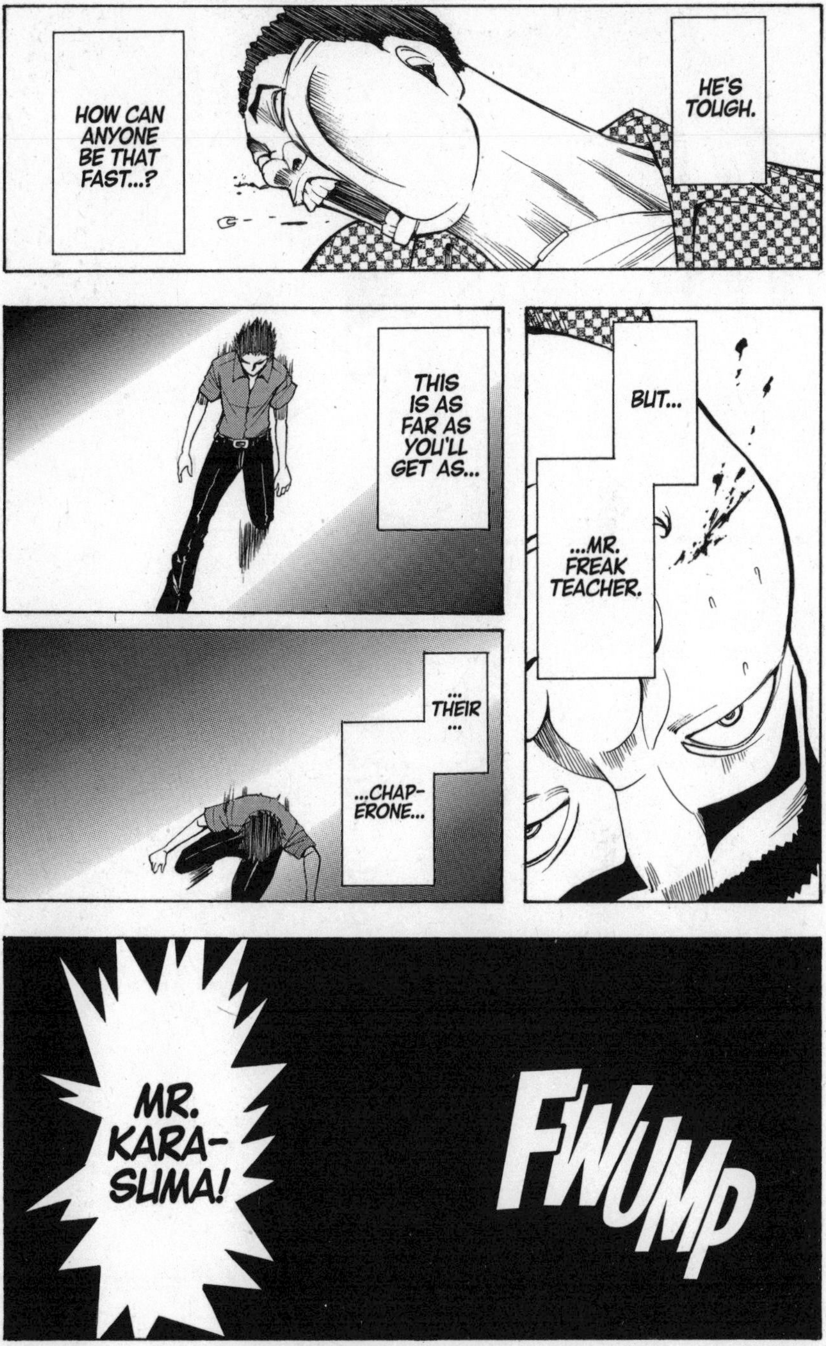
HE'S TOUGH.
HOW CAN ANYONE BE THAT FAST...?
BUT...
...MR. FREAK TEACHER.
THIS IS AS FAR AS YOU'LL GET AS...
...THEIR...
...CHAP-ERONE...
FWUMP
MR. KARA-SUMA!

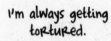

I'm always getting tortured.

It's that kind of manga...

Class 64 A Time for Peculiarities

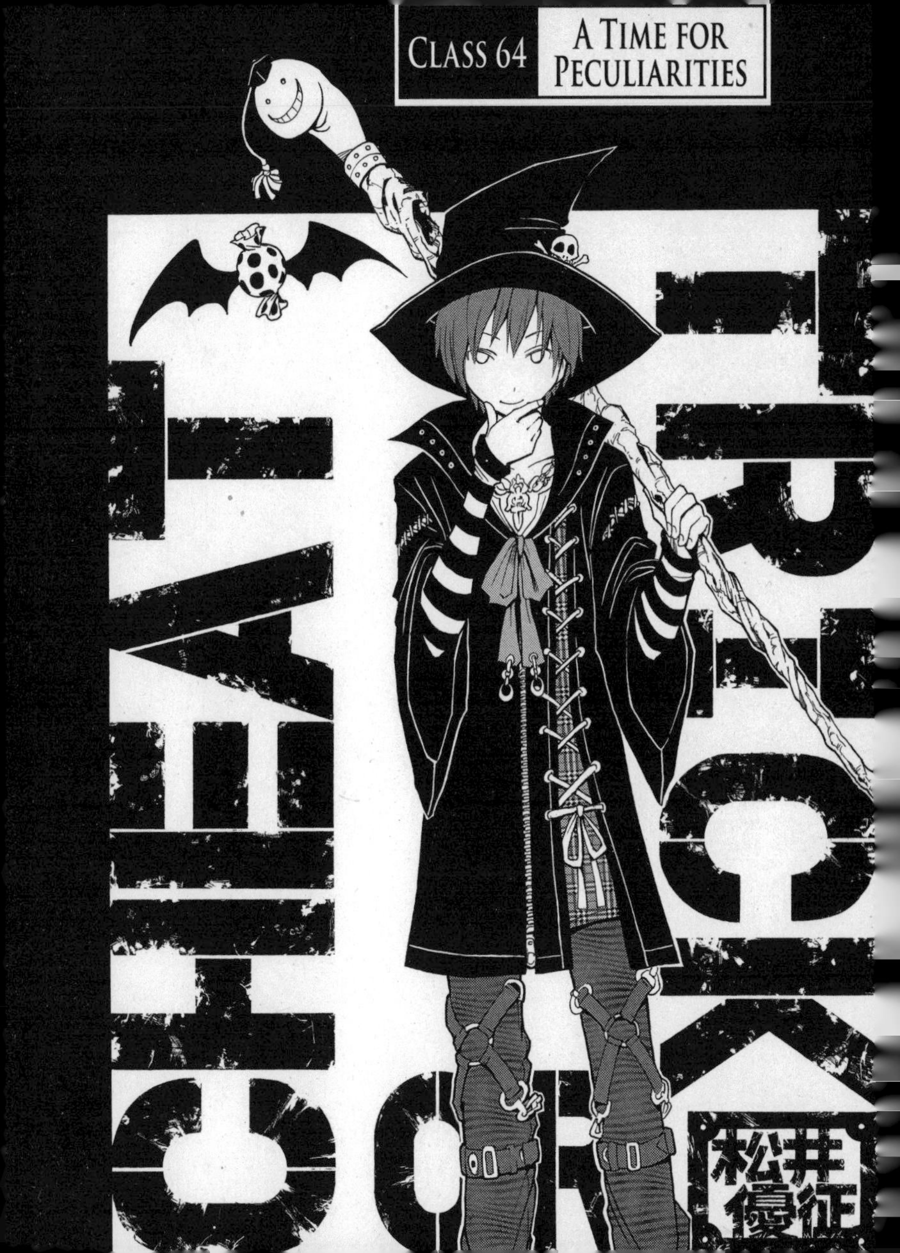
TRICK OR CHEAT
松井優征

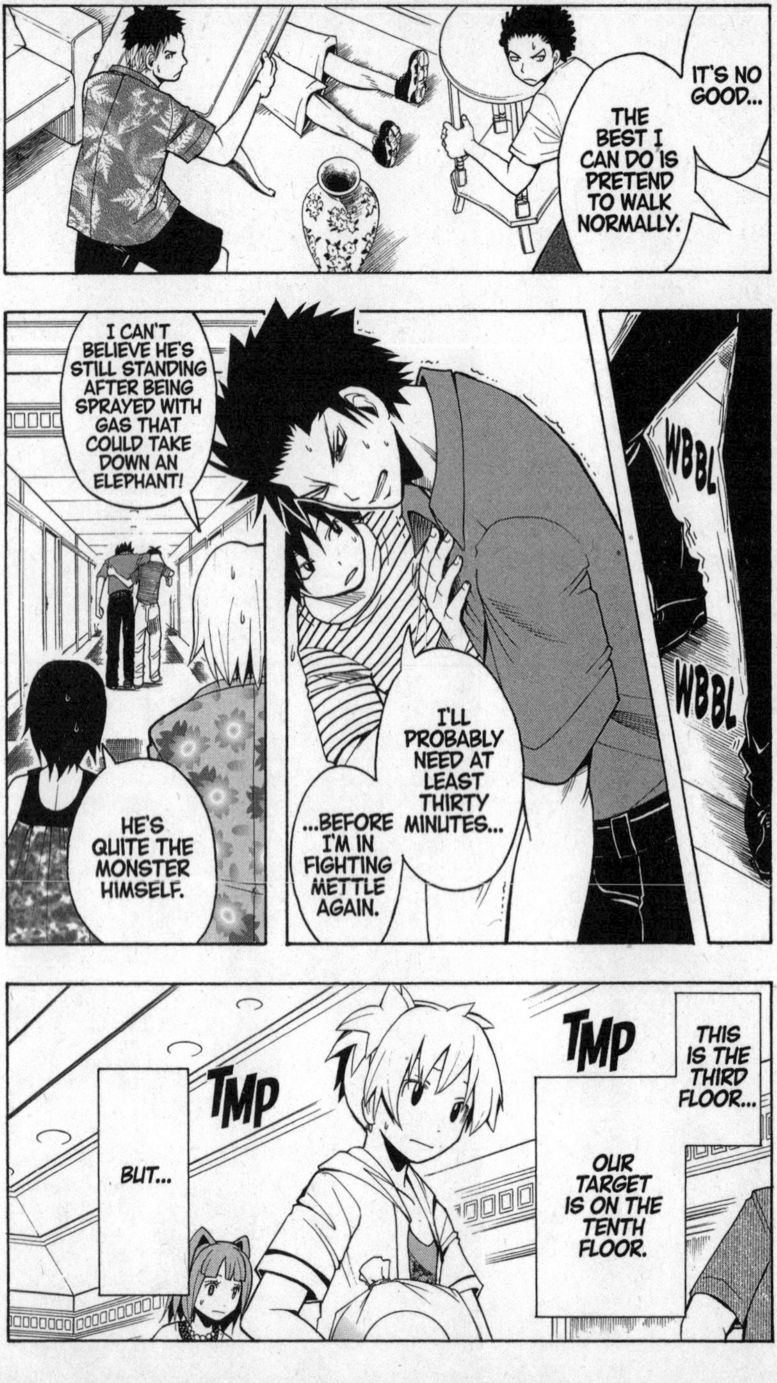
IT'S NO GOOD...
THE BEST I CAN DO IS PRETEND TO WALK NORMALLY.
WBBL
WBBL
I'LL PROBABLY NEED AT LEAST THIRTY MINUTES...
...BEFORE I'M IN FIGHTING METTLE AGAIN.
I CAN'T BELIEVE HE'S STILL STANDING AFTER BEING SPRAYED WITH GAS THAT COULD TAKE DOWN AN ELEPHANT!
HE'S QUITE THE MONSTER HIMSELF.
THIS IS THE THIRD FLOOR...
TMP
TMP
OUR TARGET IS ON THE TENTH FLOOR.
BUT...

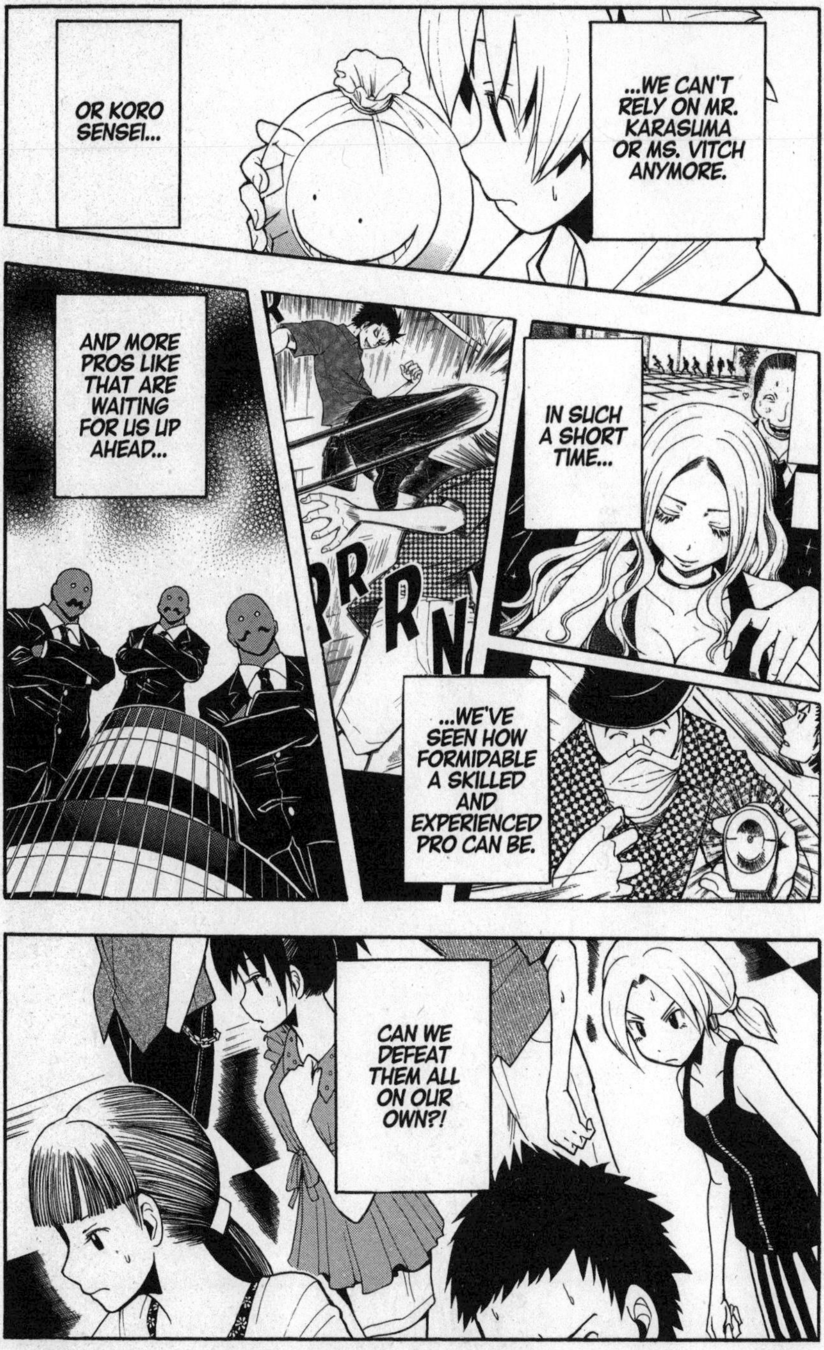

...WE CAN'T RELY ON MR. KARASUMA OR MS. VITCH ANYMORE.
OR KORO SENSEI...
IN SUCH A SHORT TIME...
...WE'VE SEEN HOW FORMIDABLE A SKILLED AND EXPERIENCED PRO CAN BE.
RRRRN
AND MORE PROS LIKE THAT ARE WAITING FOR US UP AHEAD...
CAN WE DEFEAT THEM ALL ON OUR OWN?!

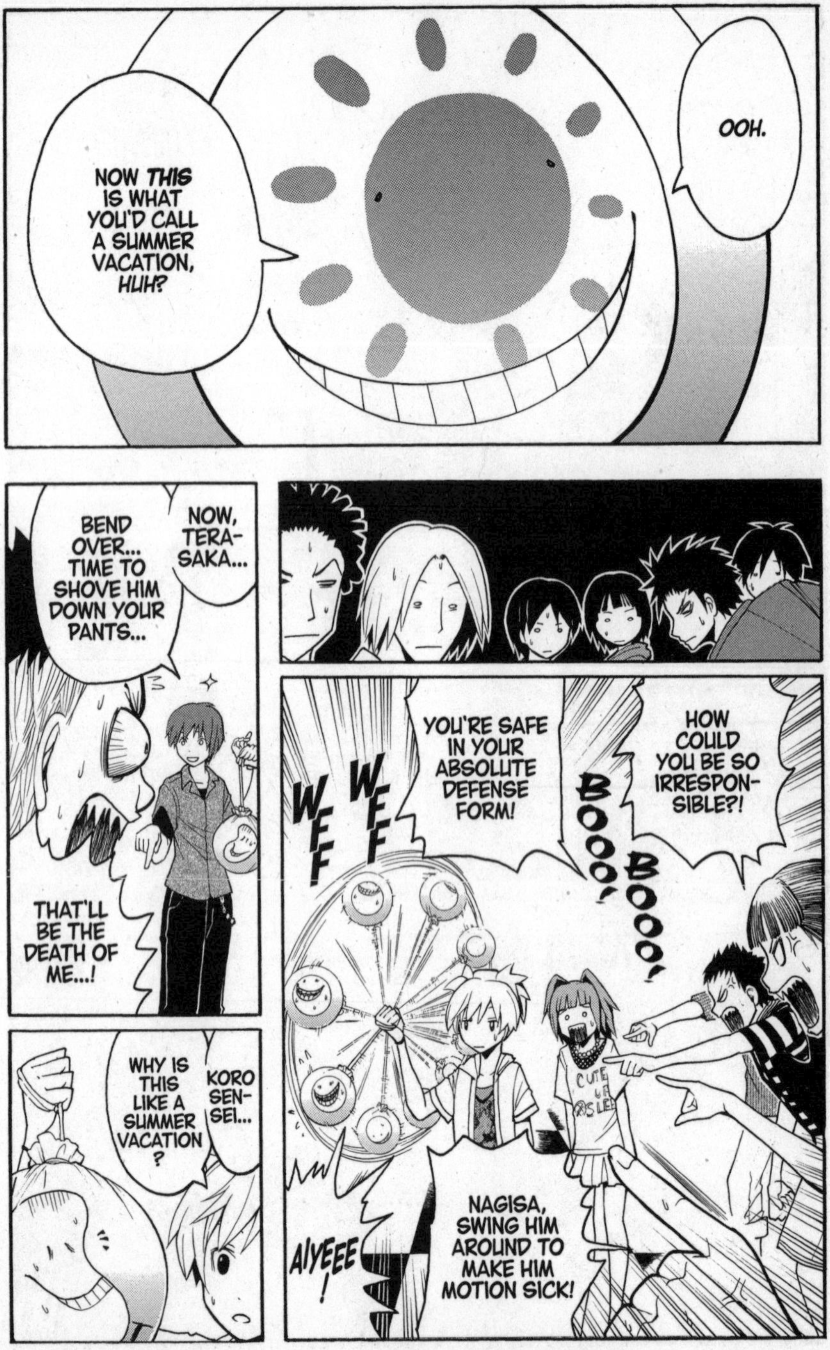
OOH.
NOW *THIS* IS WHAT YOU'D CALL A SUMMER VACATION, HUH?
HOW COULD YOU BE SO IRRESPONSIBLE?!
BOOOO BOOOO
YOU'RE SAFE IN YOUR ABSOLUTE DEFENSE FORM!
WFF WFF
NAGISA, SWING HIM AROUND TO MAKE HIM MOTION SICK!
AIYEEE!
NOW, TERASAKA...
BEND OVER... TIME TO SHOVE HIM DOWN YOUR PANTS...
THAT'LL BE THE DEATH OF ME...!
KORO SENSEI...
WHY IS THIS LIKE A SUMMER VACATION?

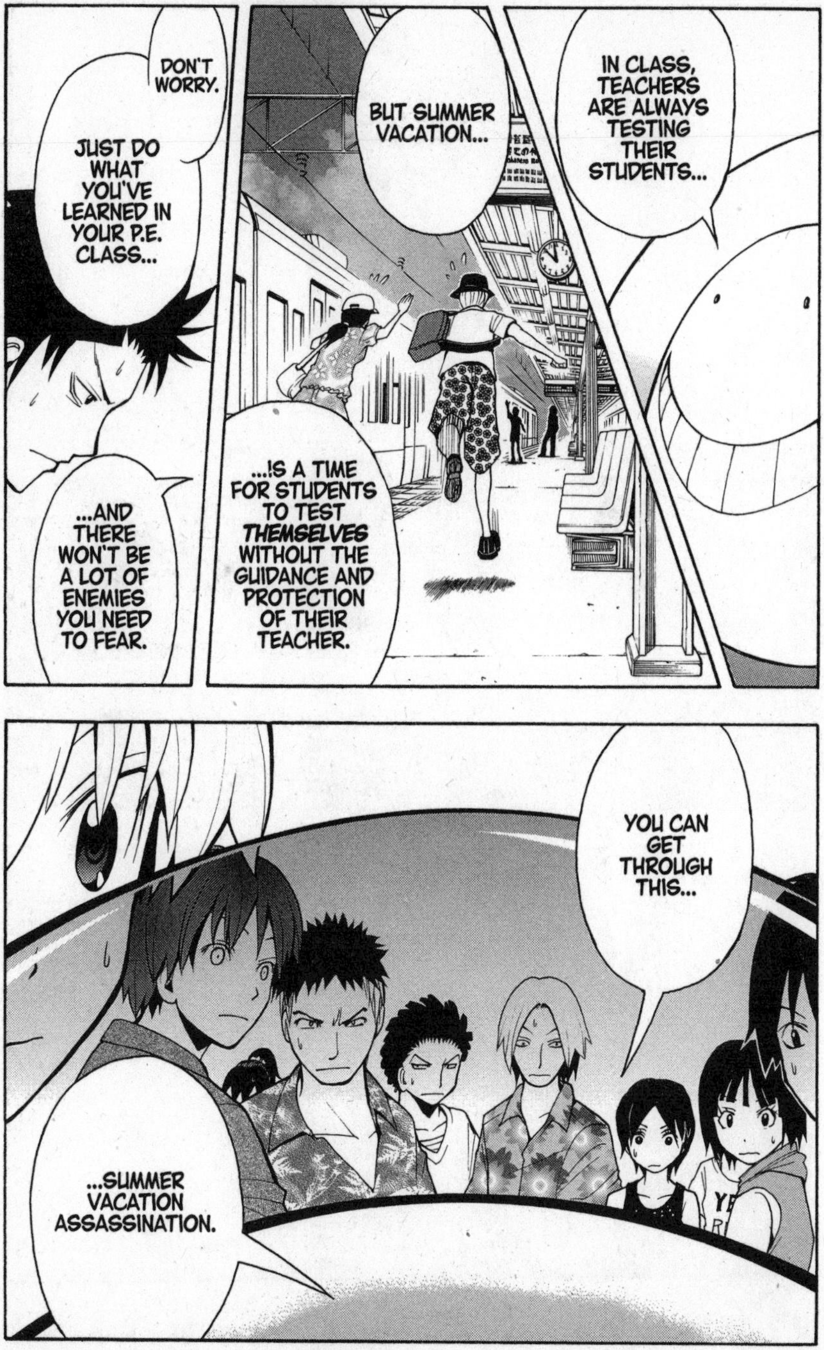
IN CLASS, TEACHERS ARE ALWAYS TESTING THEIR STUDENTS...
BUT SUMMER VACATION...
...IS A TIME FOR STUDENTS TO TEST *THEMSELVES* WITHOUT THE GUIDANCE AND PROTECTION OF THEIR TEACHER.
DON'T WORRY.
JUST DO WHAT YOU'VE LEARNED IN YOUR P.E. CLASS...
...AND THERE WON'T BE A LOT OF ENEMIES YOU NEED TO FEAR.
YOU CAN GET THROUGH THIS...
...SUMMER VACATION ASSASSINATION.

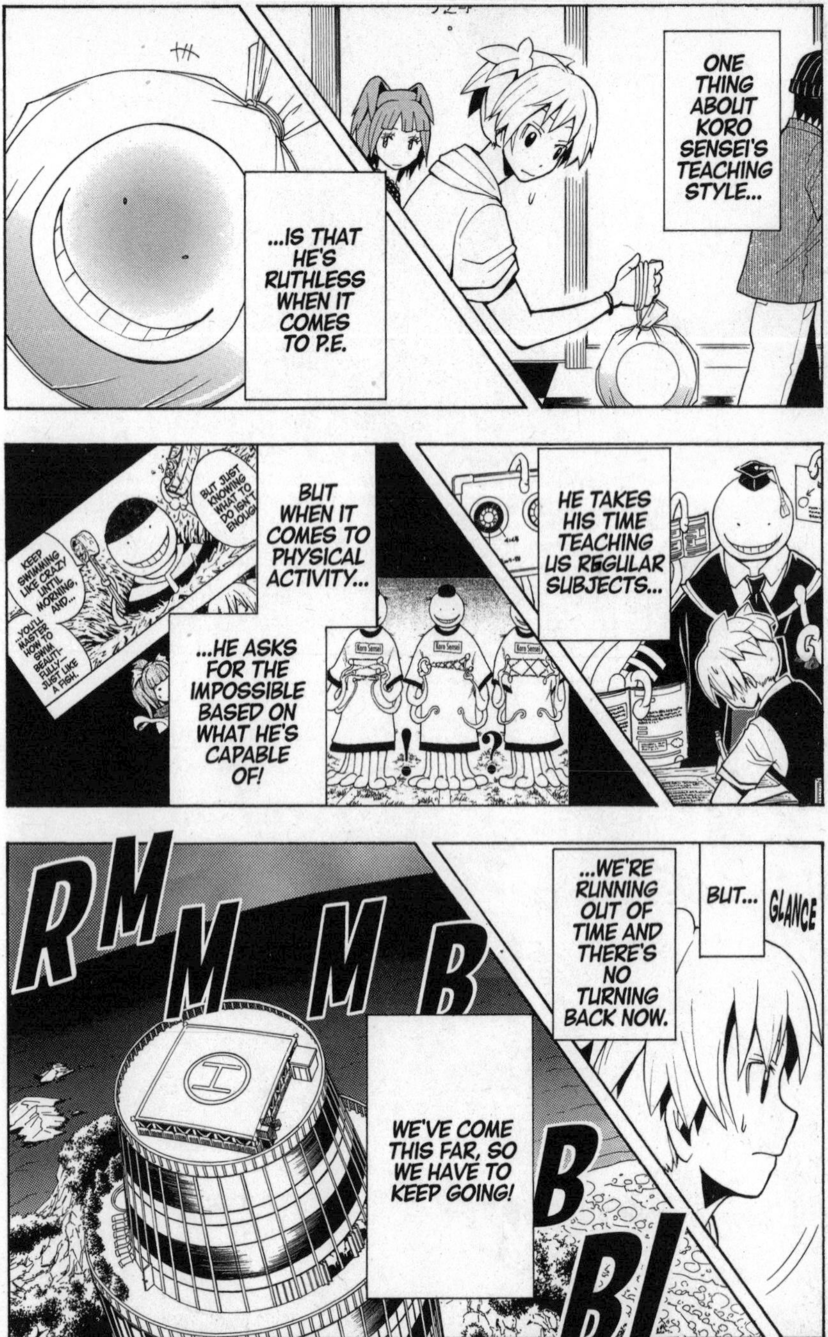
ONE THING ABOUT KORO SENSEI'S TEACHING STYLE...
...IS THAT HE'S RUTHLESS WHEN IT COMES TO P.E.
HE TAKES HIS TIME TEACHING US REGULAR SUBJECTS...
BUT WHEN IT COMES TO PHYSICAL ACTIVITY...
...HE ASKS FOR THE IMPOSSIBLE BASED ON WHAT HE'S CAPABLE OF!
BUT JUST KNOWING WHAT TO DO ISN'T ENOUGH
KEEP SWIMMING LIKE CRAZY UNTIL MORNING, AND...
...YOU'LL MASTER HOW TO SWIM BEAUTI-FULLY—JUST LIKE A FISH.
Koro Sensei
Koro Sensei
Koro Sensei
BUT...
GLANCE
...WE'RE RUNNING OUT OF TIME AND THERE'S NO TURNING BACK NOW.
RMMMMB
WE'VE COME THIS FAR, SO WE HAVE TO KEEP GOING!
BBL

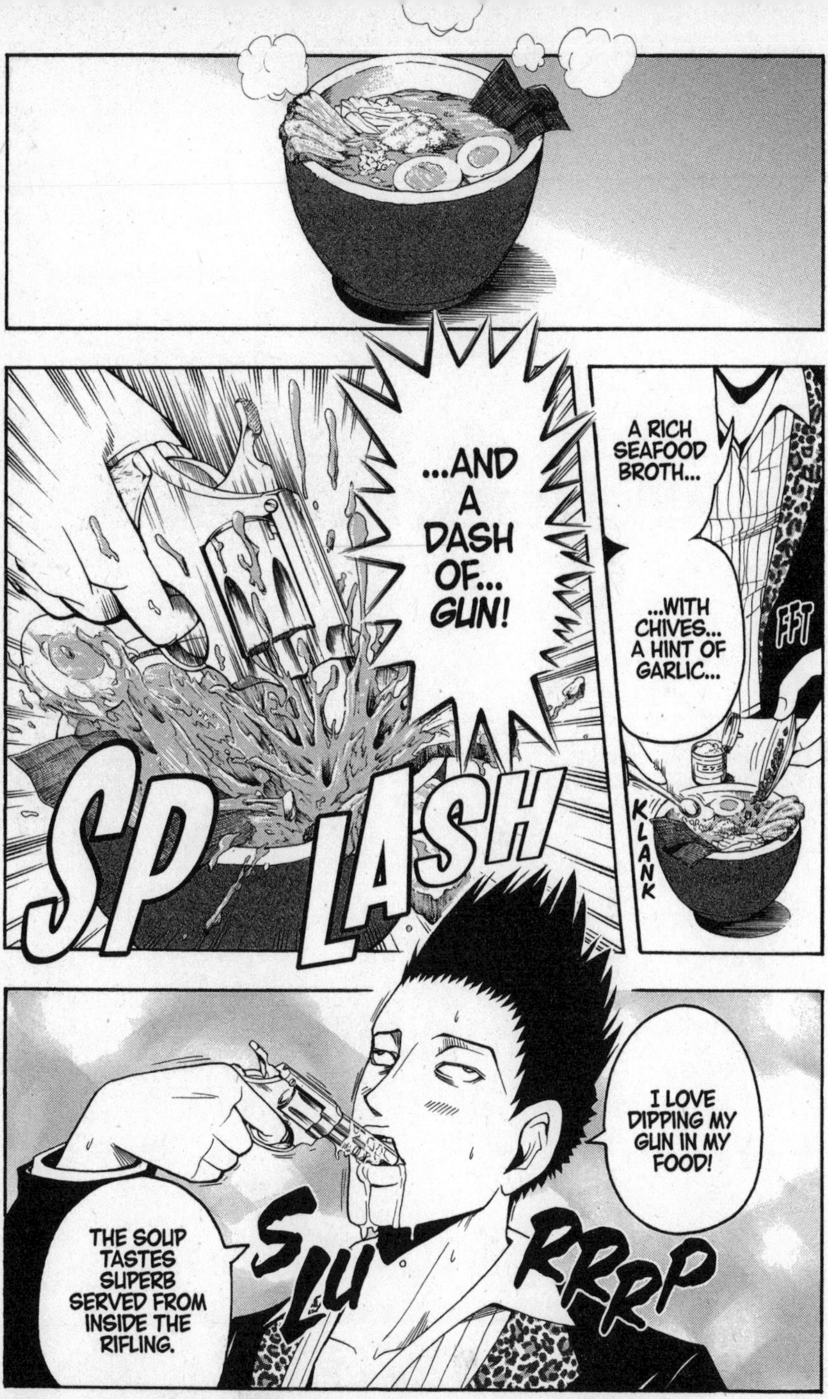
A RICH SEAFOOD BROTH...
...WITH CHIVES... A HINT OF GARLIC...
FFT
KLANK
...AND A DASH OF... GUN!
SPLASH
I LOVE DIPPING MY GUN IN MY FOOD!
SLURRRP
THE SOUP TASTES SUPERB SERVED FROM INSIDE THE RIFLING.

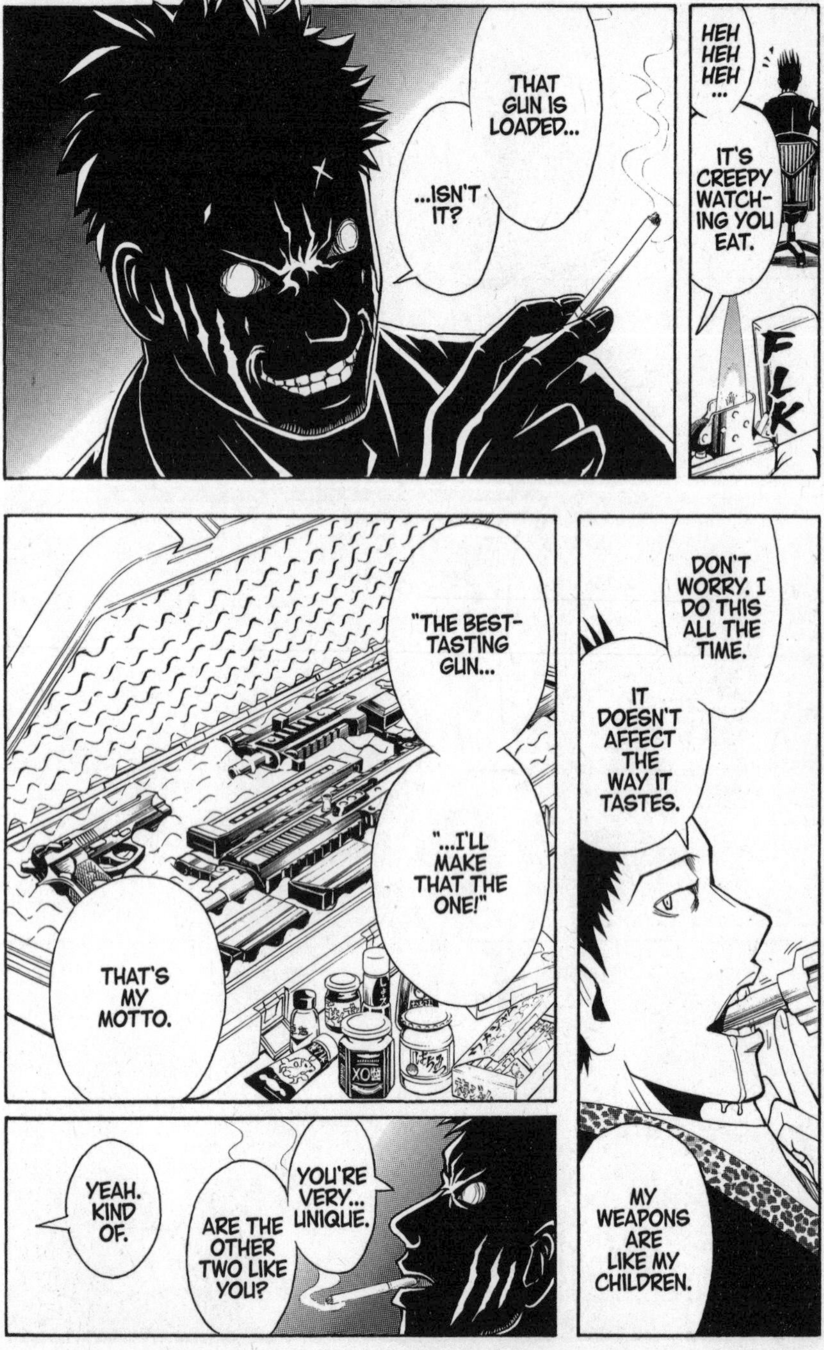
HEH HEH HEH ...
IT'S CREEPY WATCHING YOU EAT.
FLK
THAT GUN IS LOADED...
...ISN'T IT?
DON'T WORRY. I DO THIS ALL THE TIME.
IT DOESN'T AFFECT THE WAY IT TASTES.
MY WEAPONS ARE LIKE MY CHILDREN.
"THE BEST-TASTING GUN...
"...I'LL MAKE THAT THE ONE!"
THAT'S MY MOTTO.
YOU'RE VERY... UNIQUE.
ARE THE OTHER TWO LIKE YOU?
YEAH. KIND OF.

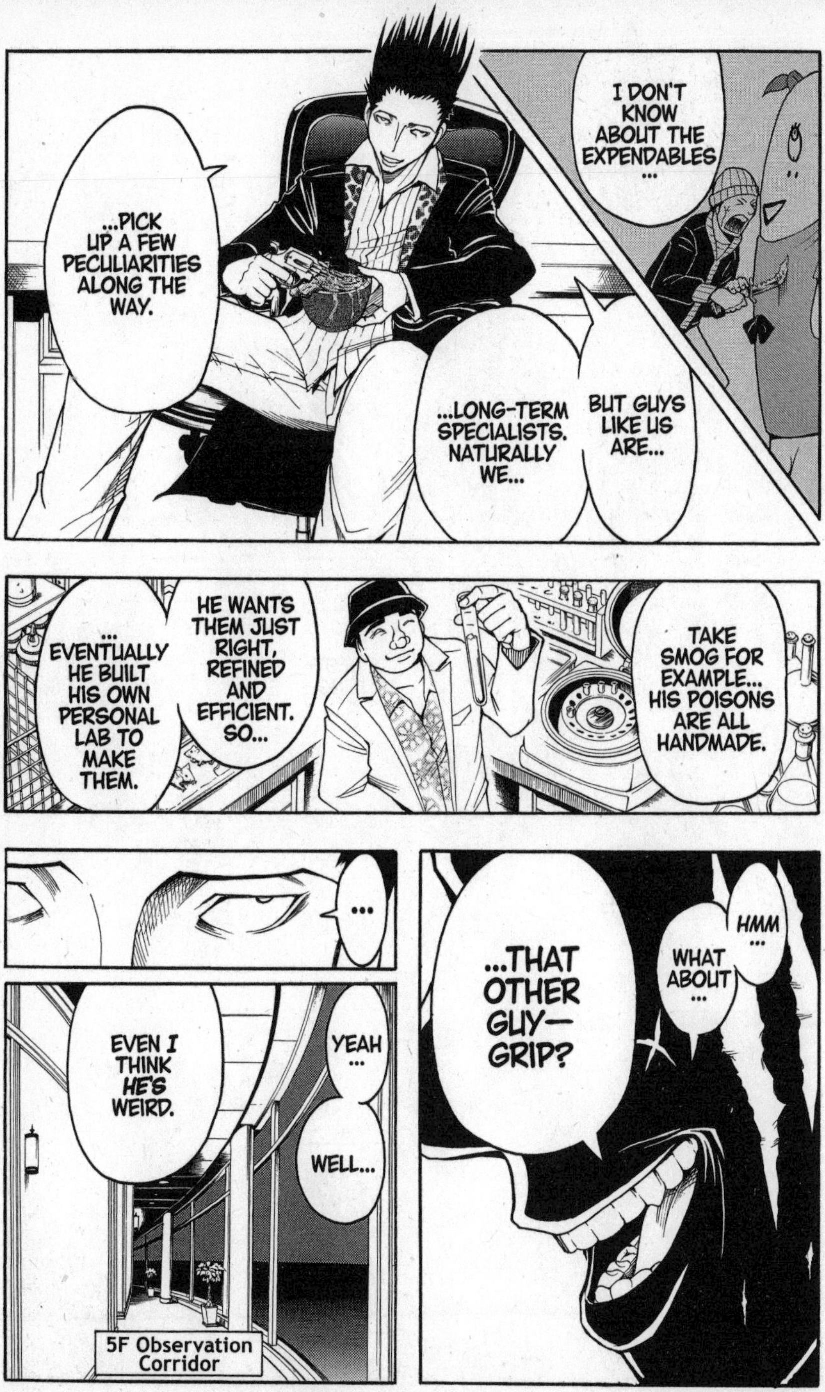
I DON'T KNOW ABOUT THE EXPENDABLES...
BUT GUYS LIKE US ARE...
...LONG-TERM SPECIALISTS. NATURALLY WE...
...PICK UP A FEW PECULIARITIES ALONG THE WAY.
TAKE SMOG FOR EXAMPLE... HIS POISONS ARE ALL HANDMADE.
HE WANTS THEM JUST RIGHT, REFINED AND EFFICIENT. SO...
...EVENTUALLY HE BUILT HIS OWN PERSONAL LAB TO MAKE THEM.
HMM...
WHAT ABOUT...
...THAT OTHER GUY—GRIP?
...
YEAH...
WELL...
EVEN I THINK *HE'S* WEIRD.
5F Observation Corridor

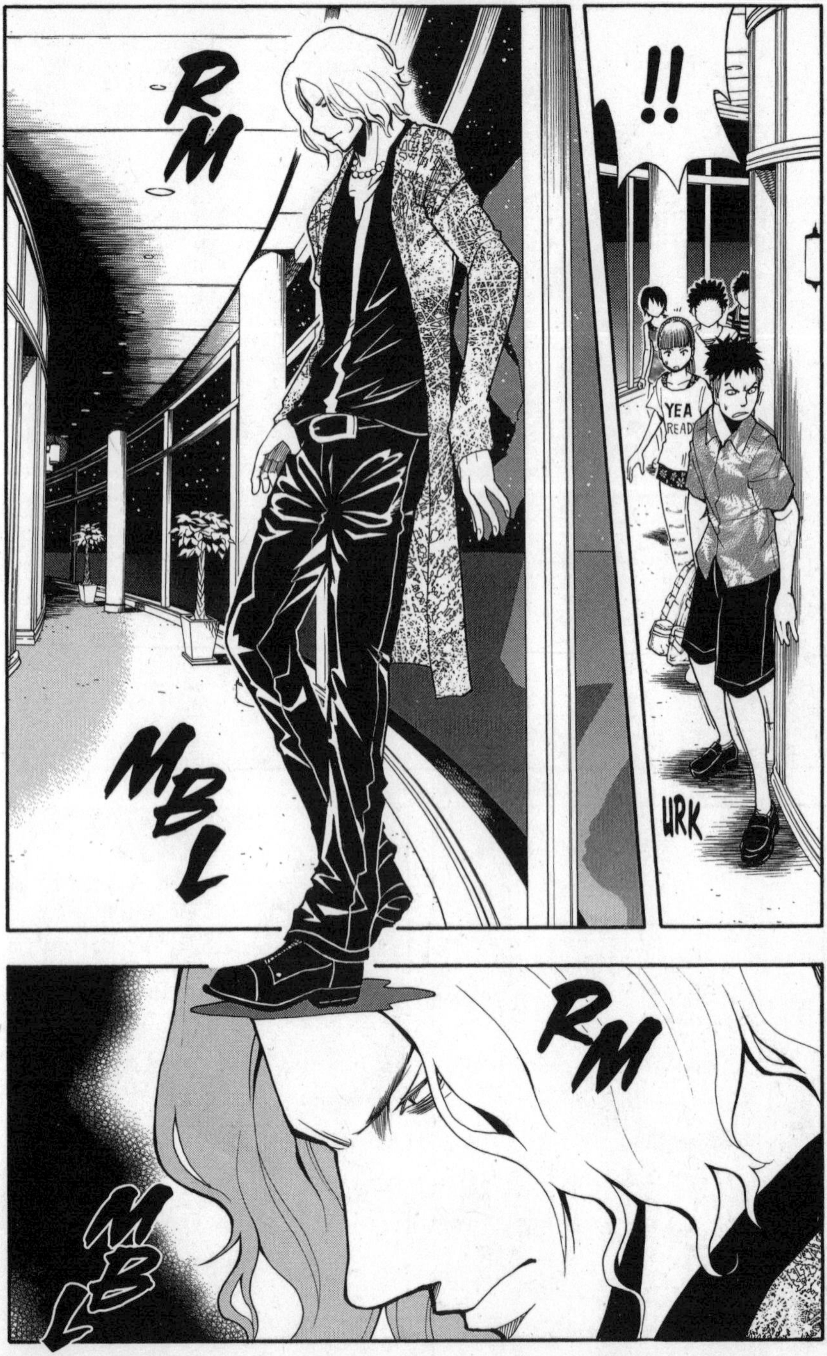
!!
YEA
READ
URK
RM
MBL
RM
MBL

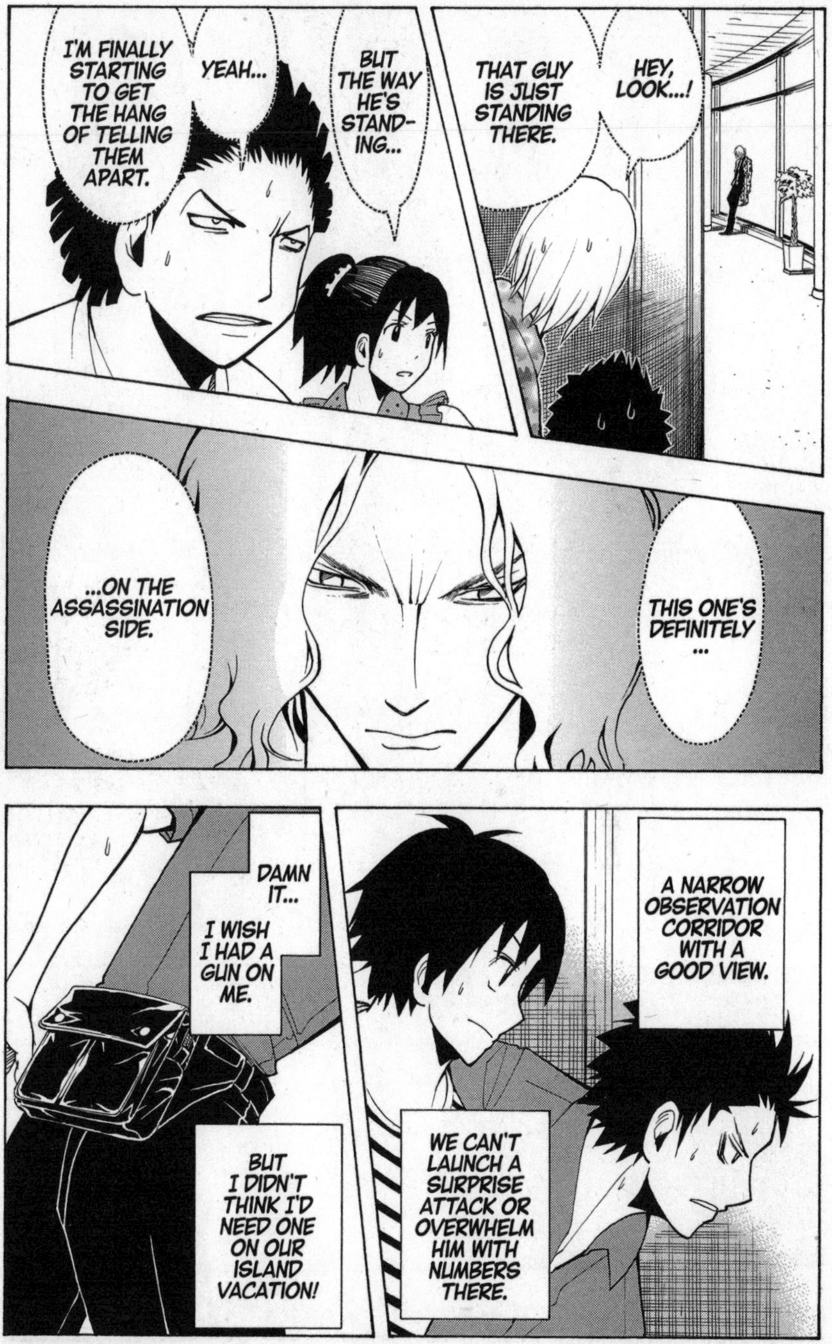
HEY, LOOK...!
THAT GUY IS JUST STANDING THERE.
BUT THE WAY HE'S STAND-ING...
YEAH...
I'M FINALLY STARTING TO GET THE HANG OF TELLING THEM APART.
THIS ONE'S DEFINITELY...
...ON THE ASSASSINATION SIDE.
A NARROW OBSERVATION CORRIDOR WITH A GOOD VIEW.
WE CAN'T LAUNCH A SURPRISE ATTACK OR OVERWHELM HIM WITH NUMBERS THERE.
DAMN IT...
I WISH I HAD A GUN ON ME.
BUT I DIDN'T THINK I'D NEED ONE ON OUR ISLAND VACATION!

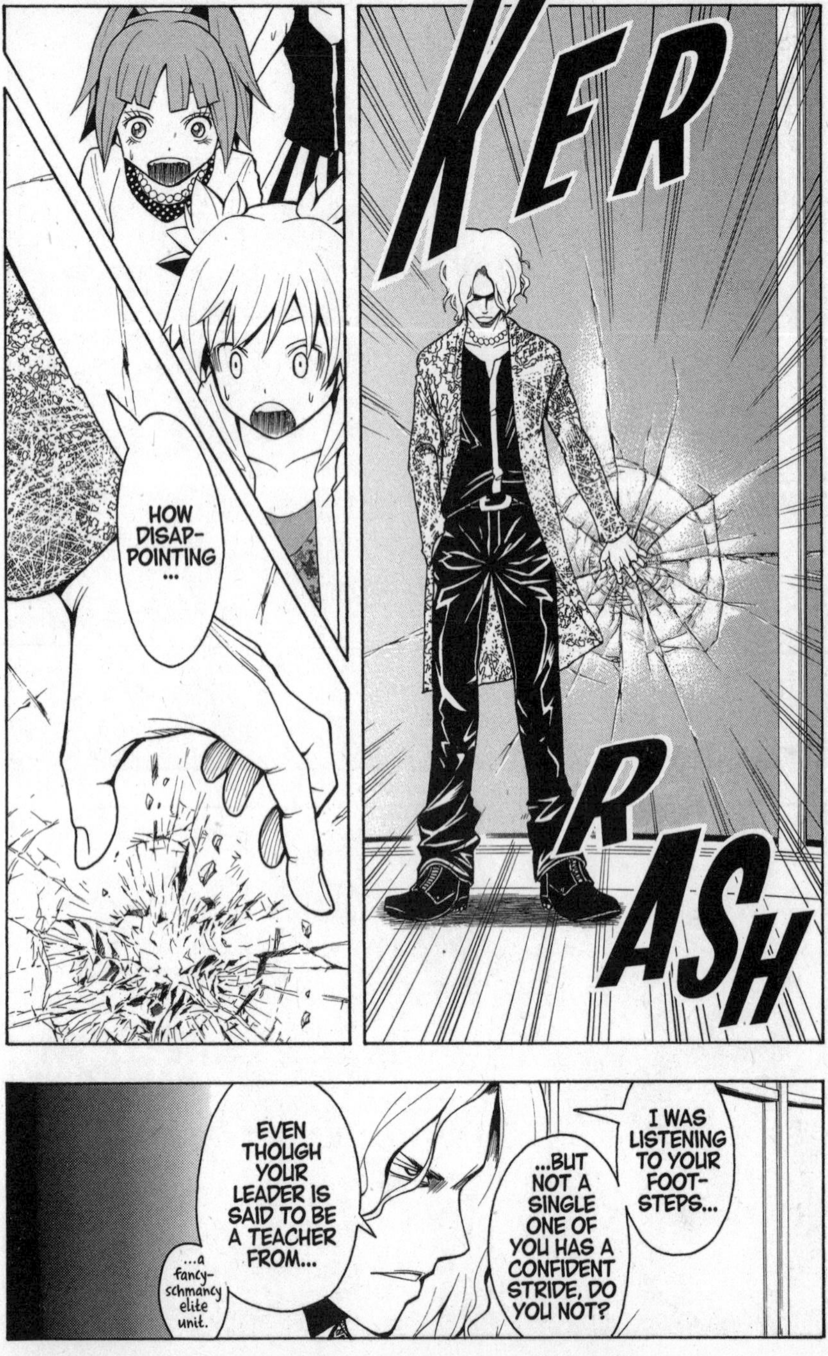
KERRASH
HOW DISAP-POINTING...
I WAS LISTENING TO YOUR FOOT-STEPS...
...BUT NOT A SINGLE ONE OF YOU HAS A CONFIDENT STRIDE, DO YOU NOT?
EVEN THOUGH YOUR LEADER IS SAID TO BE A TEACHER FROM...
...a fancy-schmancy elite unit.

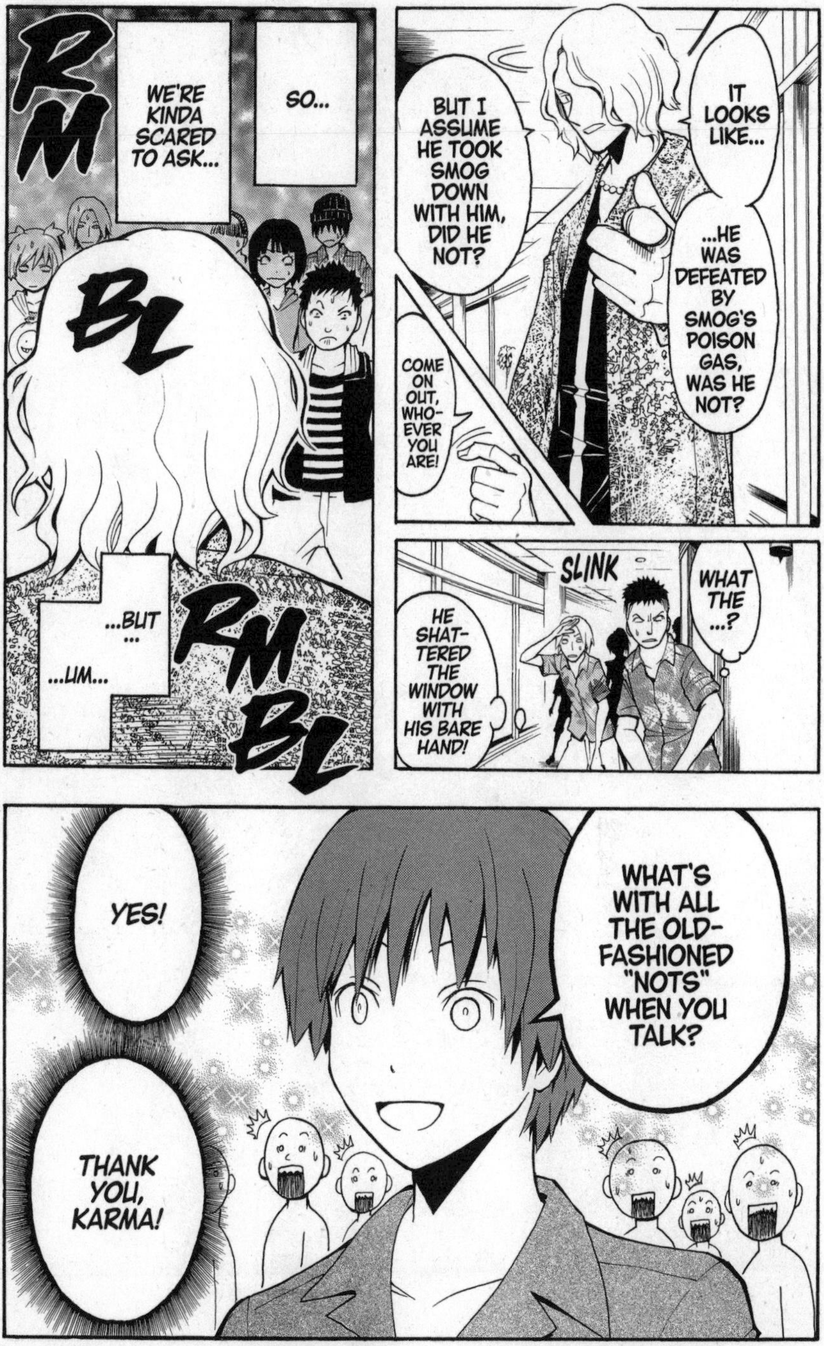
IT LOOKS LIKE...
...HE WAS DEFEATED BY SMOG'S POISON GAS, WAS HE NOT?
BUT I ASSUME HE TOOK SMOG DOWN WITH HIM, DID HE NOT?
COME ON OUT, WHO-EVER YOU ARE!
SLINK
WHAT THE ...?
HE SHAT-TERED THE WINDOW WITH HIS BARE HAND!
RM
SO...
WE'RE KINDA SCARED TO ASK...
BL
...BUT ...
...UM...
RMBL
WHAT'S WITH ALL THE OLD-FASHIONED "NOTS" WHEN YOU TALK?
YES!
THANK YOU, KARMA!

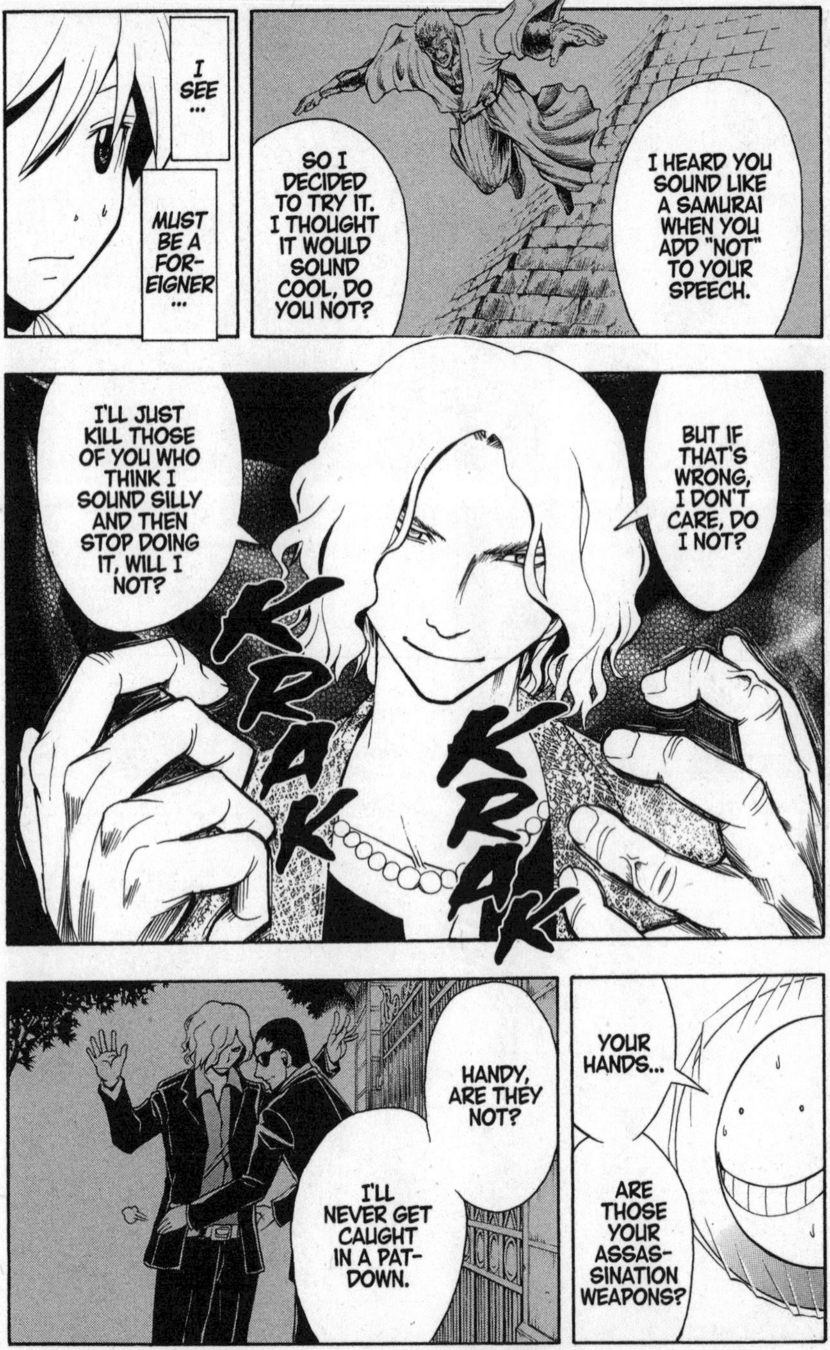
I HEARD YOU SOUND LIKE A SAMURAI WHEN YOU ADD "NOT" TO YOUR SPEECH.
SO I DECIDED TO TRY IT. I THOUGHT IT WOULD SOUND COOL, DO YOU NOT?
I SEE...
MUST BE A FOR-EIGNER...
BUT IF THAT'S WRONG, I DON'T CARE, DO I NOT?
I'LL JUST KILL THOSE OF YOU WHO THINK I SOUND SILLY AND THEN STOP DOING IT, WILL I NOT?
KRAK
KRAK
YOUR HANDS...
ARE THOSE YOUR ASSAS-SINATION WEAPONS?
HANDY, ARE THEY NOT?
I'LL NEVER GET CAUGHT IN A PAT-DOWN.

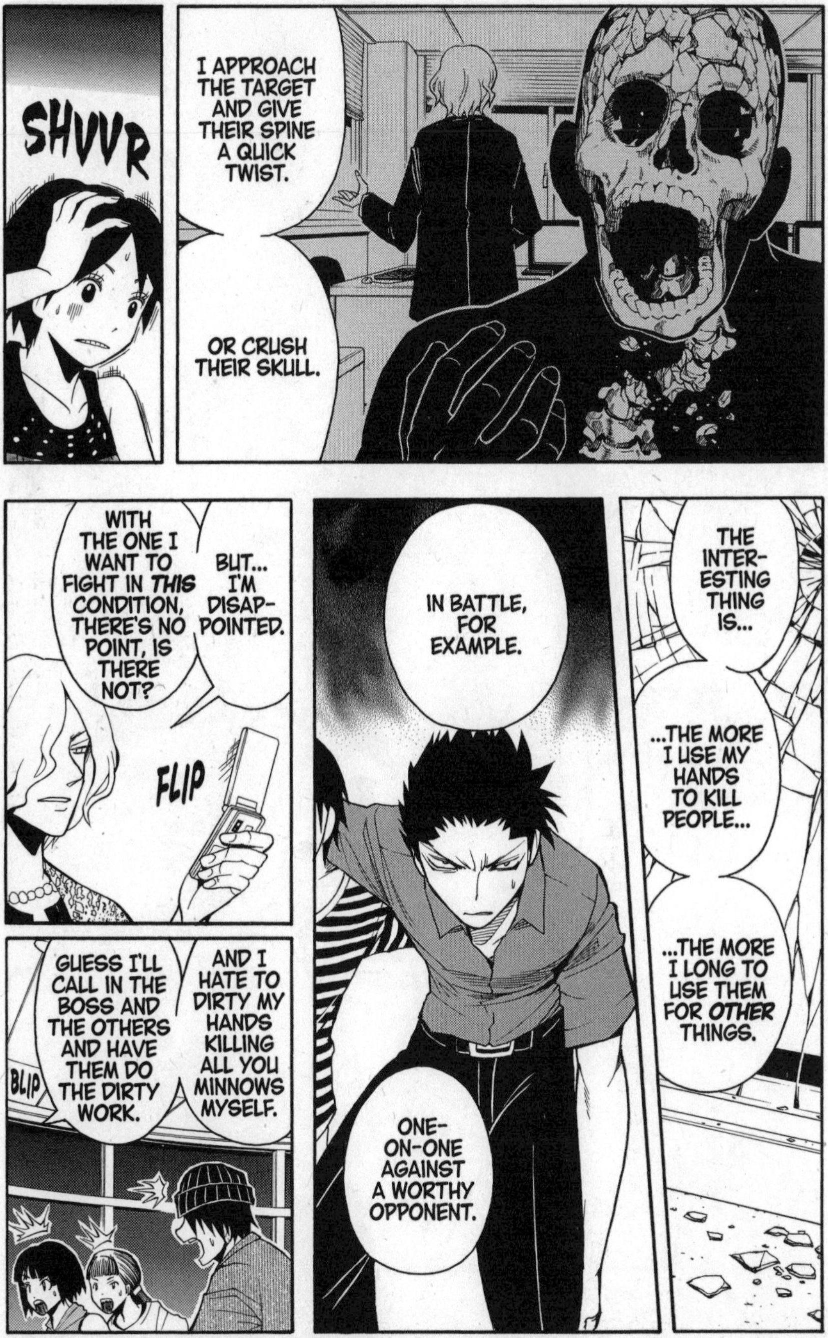
I APPROACH THE TARGET AND GIVE THEIR SPINE A QUICK TWIST.
OR CRUSH THEIR SKULL.
SHVVR
THE INTERESTING THING IS...
...THE MORE I USE MY HANDS TO KILL PEOPLE...
...THE MORE I LONG TO USE THEM FOR *OTHER* THINGS.
IN BATTLE, FOR EXAMPLE.
ONE-ON-ONE AGAINST A WORTHY OPPONENT.
BUT... I'M DISAPPOINTED.
WITH THE ONE I WANT TO FIGHT IN *THIS* CONDITION, THERE'S NO POINT, IS THERE NOT?
FLIP
AND I HATE TO DIRTY MY HANDS KILLING ALL YOU MINNOWS MYSELF.
GUESS I'LL CALL IN THE BOSS AND THE OTHERS AND HAVE THEM DO THE DIRTY WORK.
BLIP

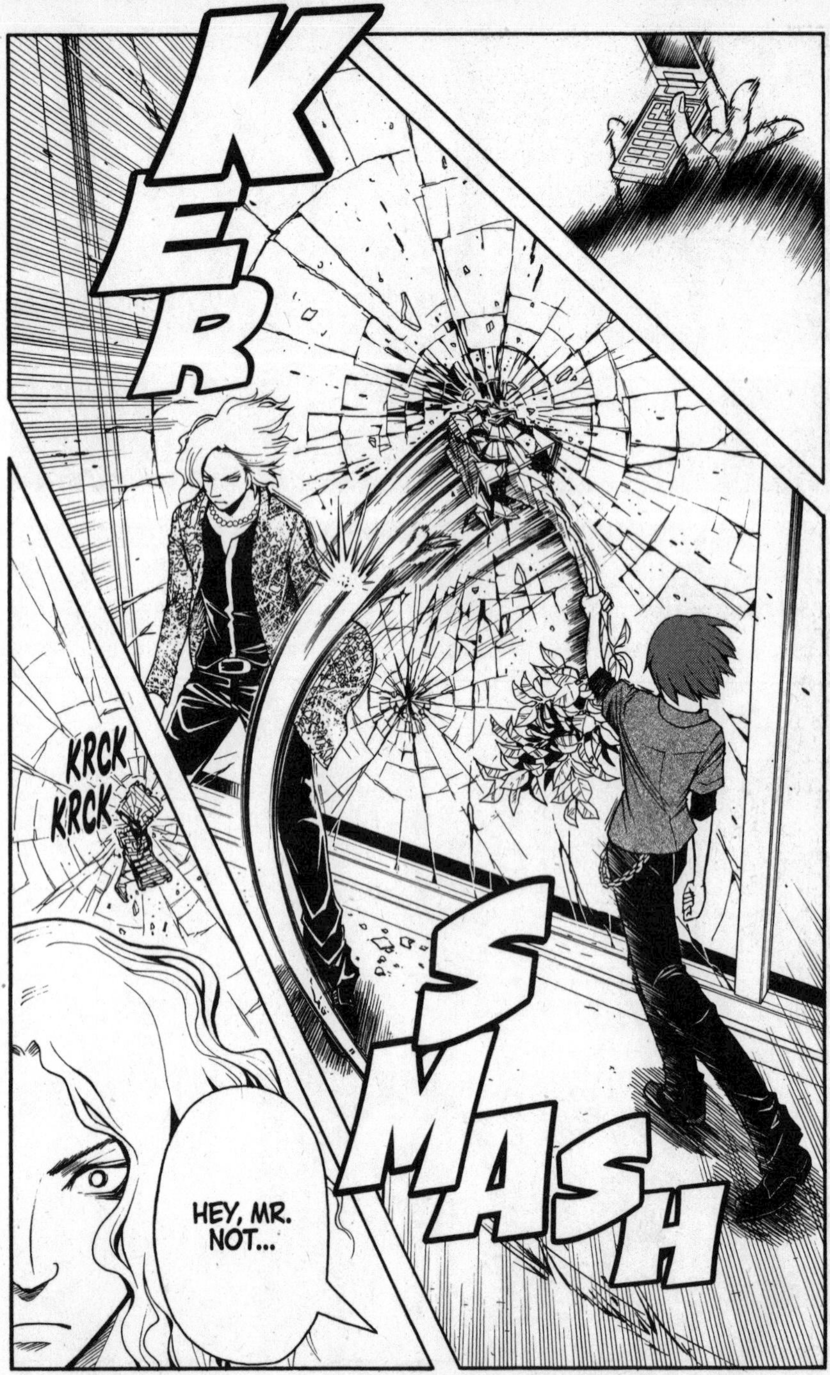
KER SMASH
KRCK KRCK
HEY, MR. NOT...

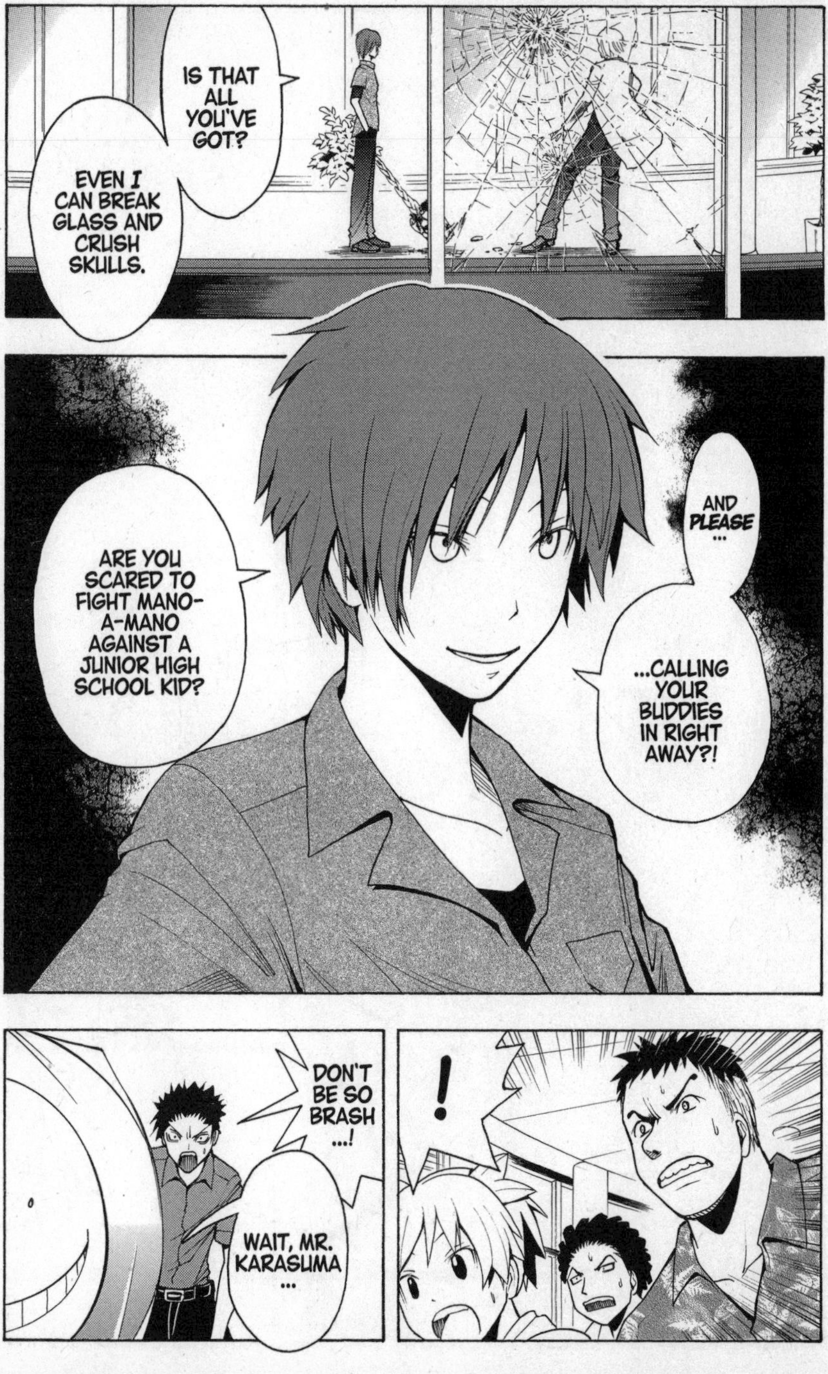
IS THAT ALL YOU'VE GOT?
EVEN I CAN BREAK GLASS AND CRUSH SKULLS.
ARE YOU SCARED TO FIGHT MANO-A-MANO AGAINST A JUNIOR HIGH SCHOOL KID?
AND PLEASE...
...CALLING YOUR BUDDIES IN RIGHT AWAY?!
!
DON'T BE SO BRASH...!
WAIT, MR. KARASUMA...

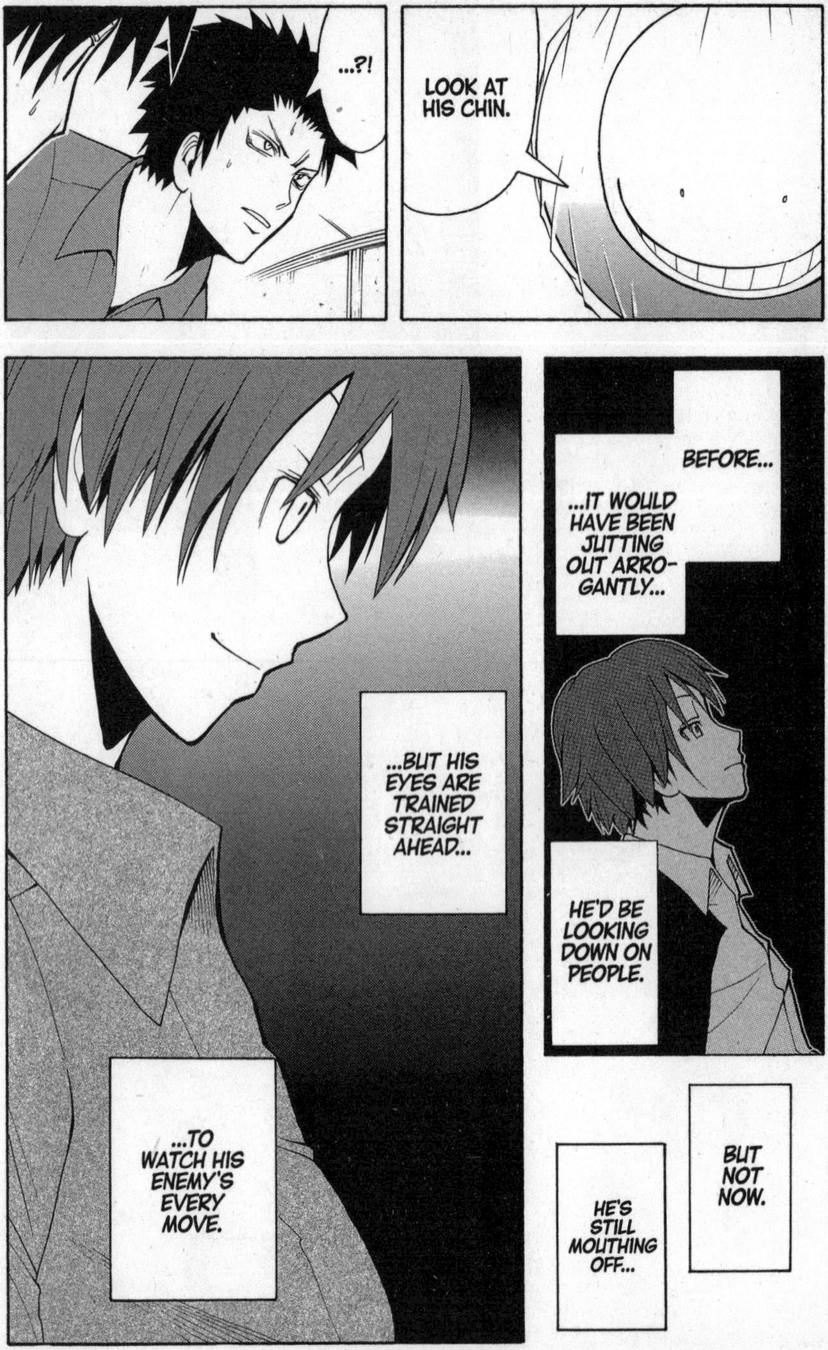
LOOK AT HIS CHIN.
...?!
BEFORE...
...IT WOULD HAVE BEEN JUTTING OUT ARROGANTLY...
HE'D BE LOOKING DOWN ON PEOPLE.
BUT NOT NOW.
HE'S STILL MOUTHING OFF...
...BUT HIS EYES ARE TRAINED STRAIGHT AHEAD...
...TO WATCH HIS ENEMY'S EVERY MOVE.

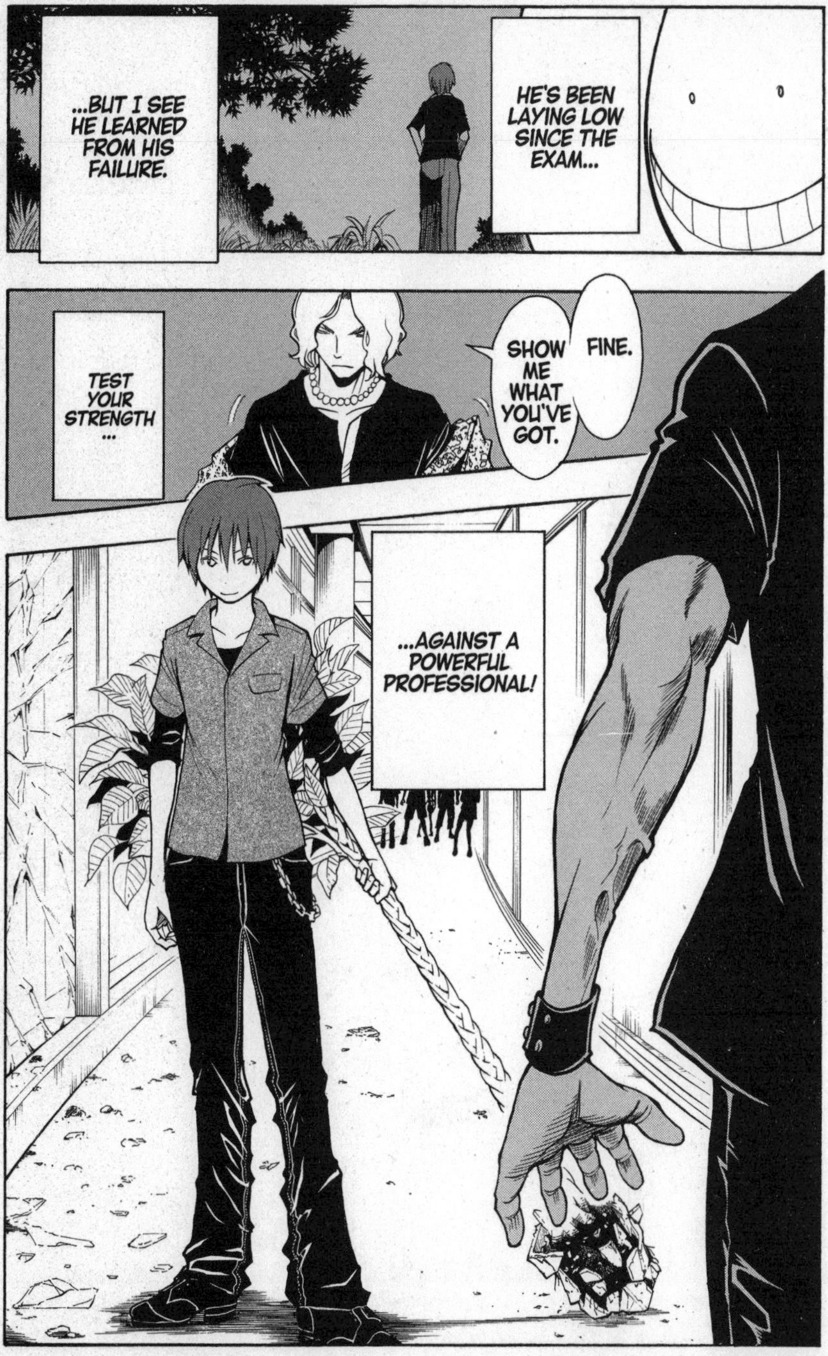
HE'S BEEN LAYING LOW SINCE THE EXAM...
...BUT I SEE HE LEARNED FROM HIS FAILURE.
FINE.
SHOW ME WHAT YOU'VE GOT.
TEST YOUR STRENGTH ...
...AGAINST A POWERFUL PROFESSIONAL!

There's more of this archaic samurai talk out there.

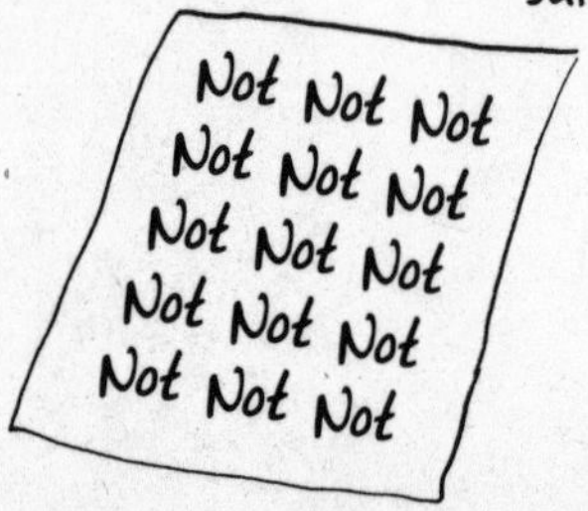
Not Not Not
Not Not Not
Not Not Not
Not Not Not
Not Not Not

It's in a legendary gag manga!*

*The use of the negative sound "nu" is associated with samurai's speech. It appears in the English version of Yoshio Sawai's Bobobo-bo Bo-bobo. For Assassination Classroom we decided to evoke this effect of archaic speech with phrasing like "Is it not?" How'd that work for you?

Class 65 Making Time for Karma–2nd Period

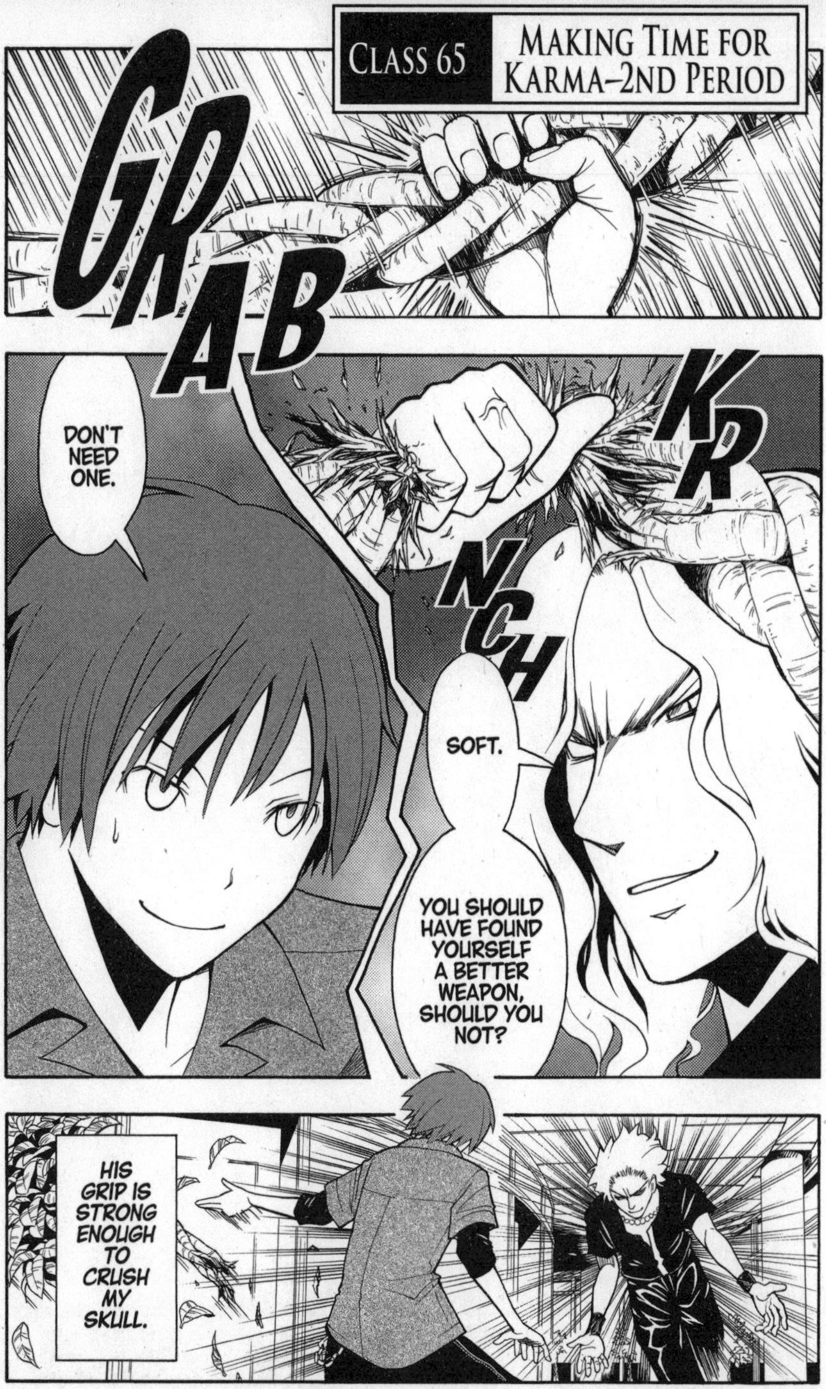
GRAB
KRNCH
SOFT.
YOU SHOULD HAVE FOUND YOURSELF A BETTER WEAPON, SHOULD YOU NOT?
DON'T NEED ONE.
HIS GRIP IS STRONG ENOUGH TO CRUSH MY SKULL.

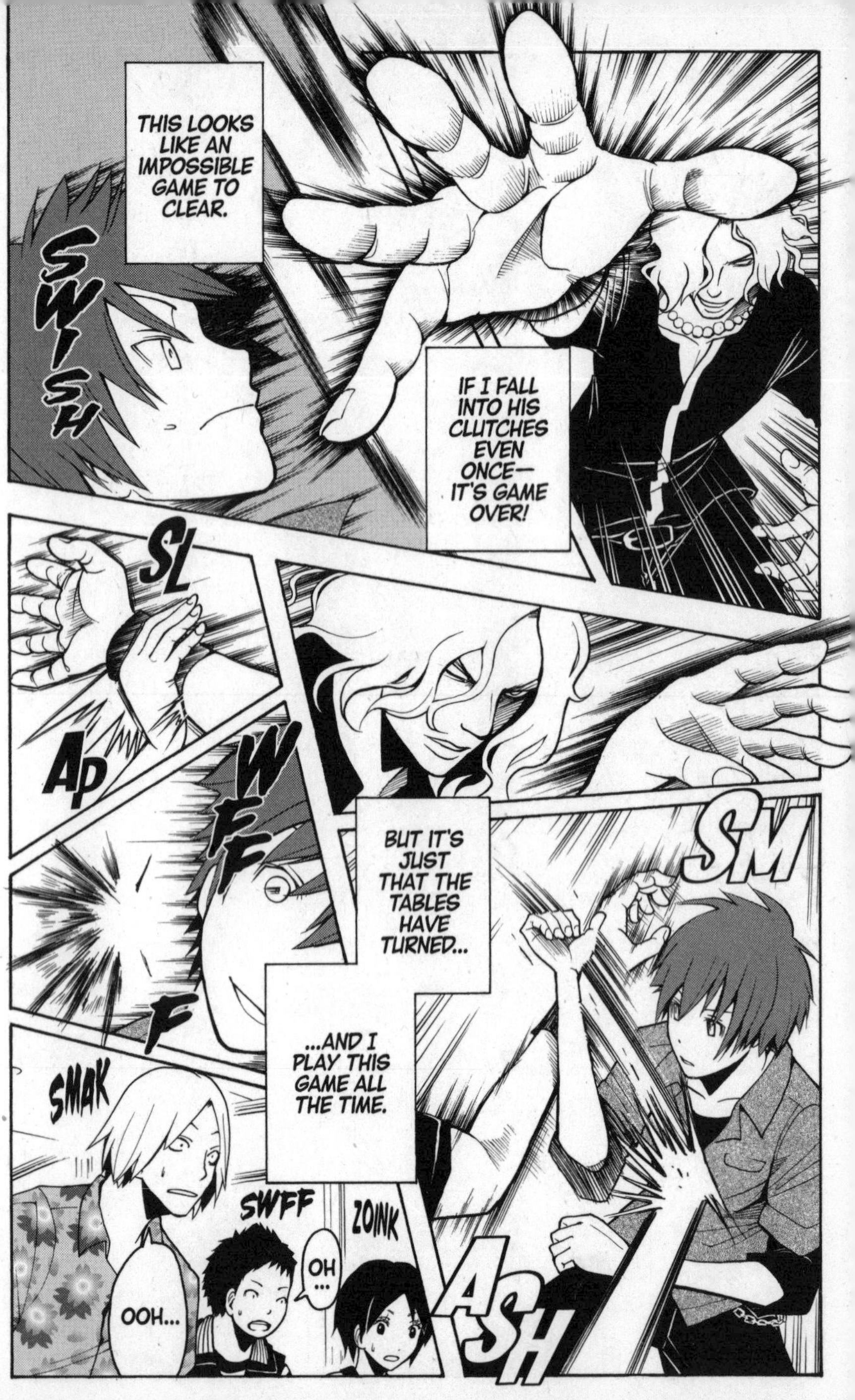
THIS LOOKS LIKE AN IMPOSSIBLE GAME TO CLEAR.
IF I FALL INTO HIS CLUTCHES EVEN ONCE— IT'S GAME OVER!
SWISH
SL
AP
WFF
F
BUT IT'S JUST THAT THE TABLES HAVE TURNED...
SM
ASH
...AND I PLAY THIS GAME ALL THE TIME.
ZOINK
OH...
SWFF
SMAK
OOH...

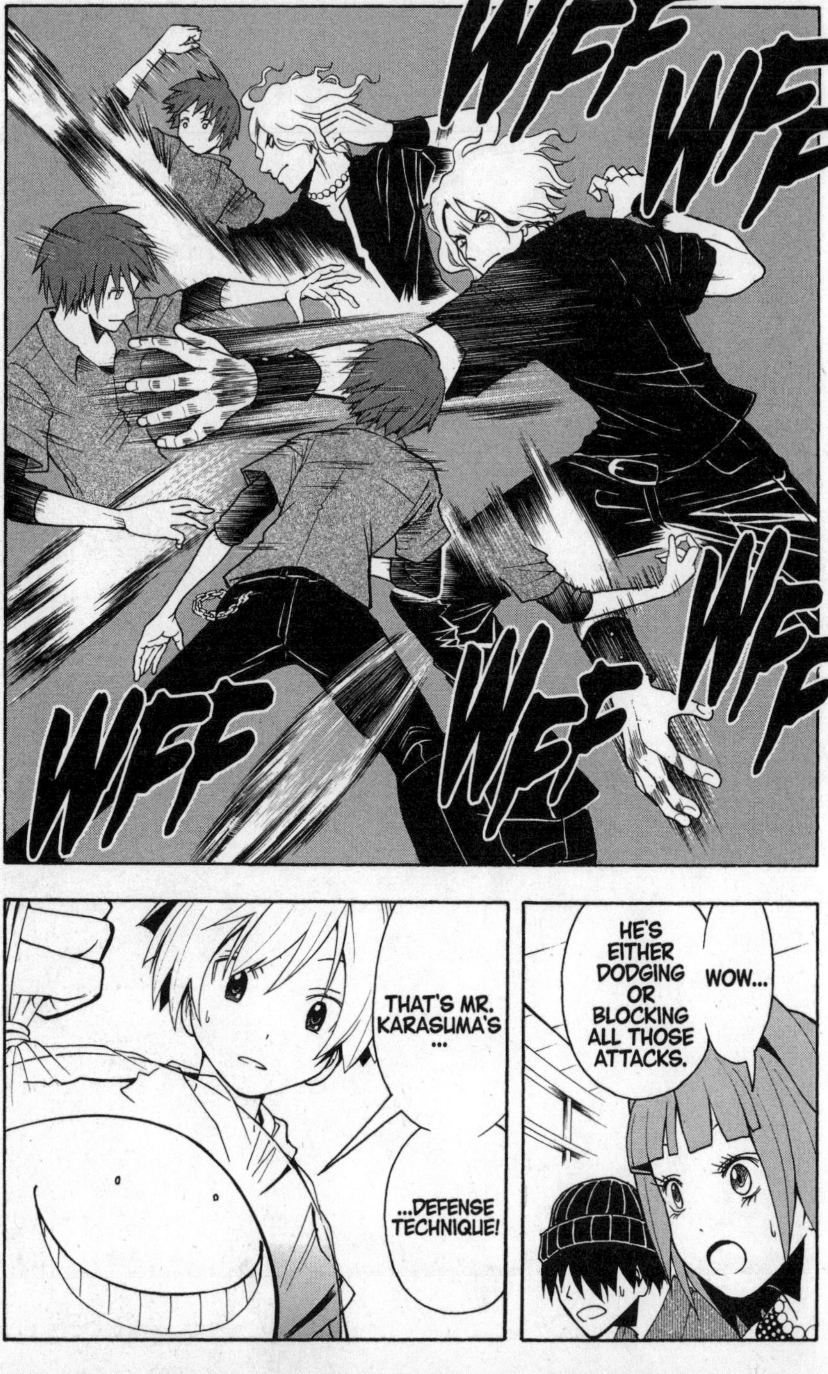
WFF
WIF
WIF
WFF
WFF
WOW...
HE'S EITHER DODGING OR BLOCKING ALL THOSE ATTACKS.
THAT'S MR. KARASUMA'S ...
...DEFENSE TECHNIQUE!

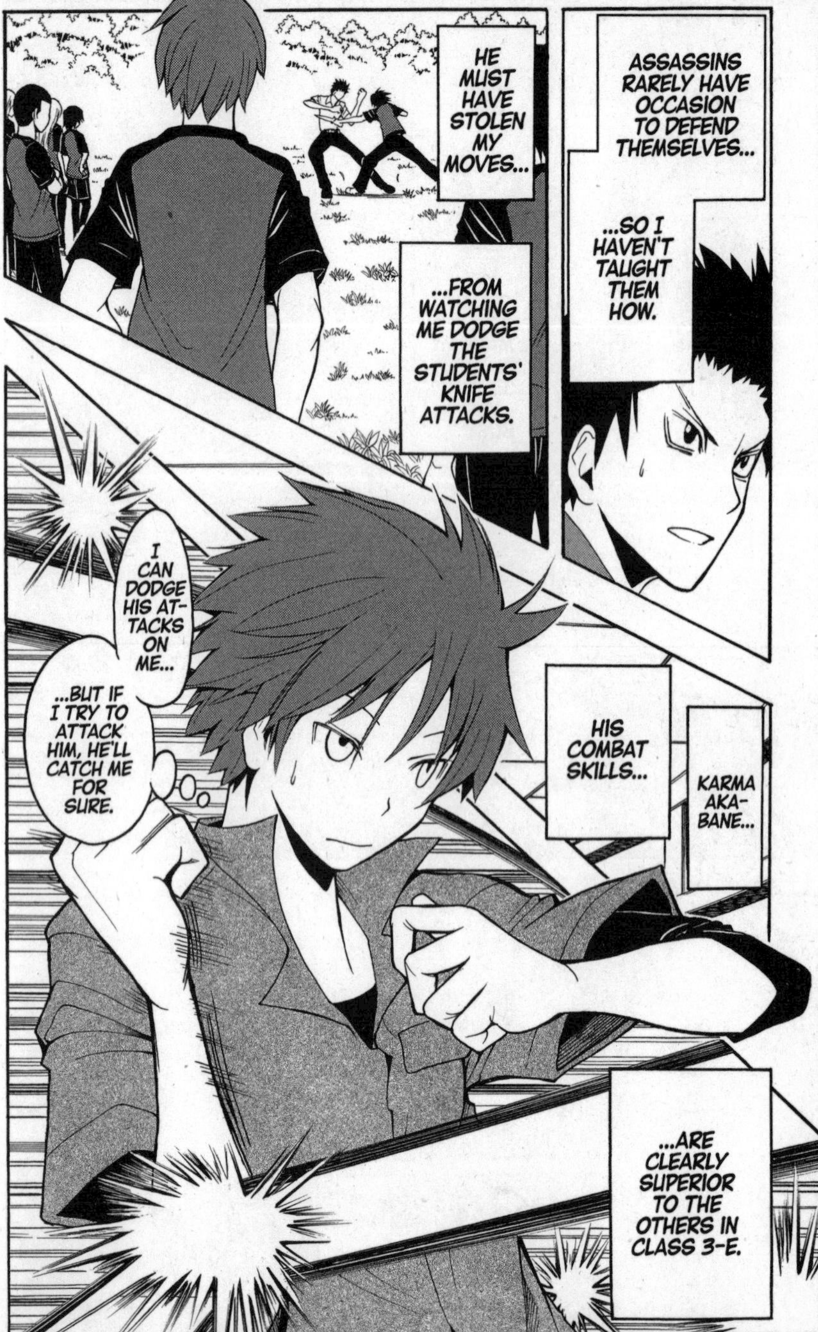
ASSASSINS RARELY HAVE OCCASION TO DEFEND THEMSELVES...
...SO I HAVEN'T TAUGHT THEM HOW.
HE MUST HAVE STOLEN MY MOVES...
...FROM WATCHING ME DODGE THE STUDENTS' KNIFE ATTACKS.
KARMA AKABANE...
HIS COMBAT SKILLS...
...ARE CLEARLY SUPERIOR TO THE OTHERS IN CLASS 3-E.
I CAN DODGE HIS ATTACKS ON ME...
...BUT IF I TRY TO ATTACK HIM, HE'LL CATCH ME FOR SURE.

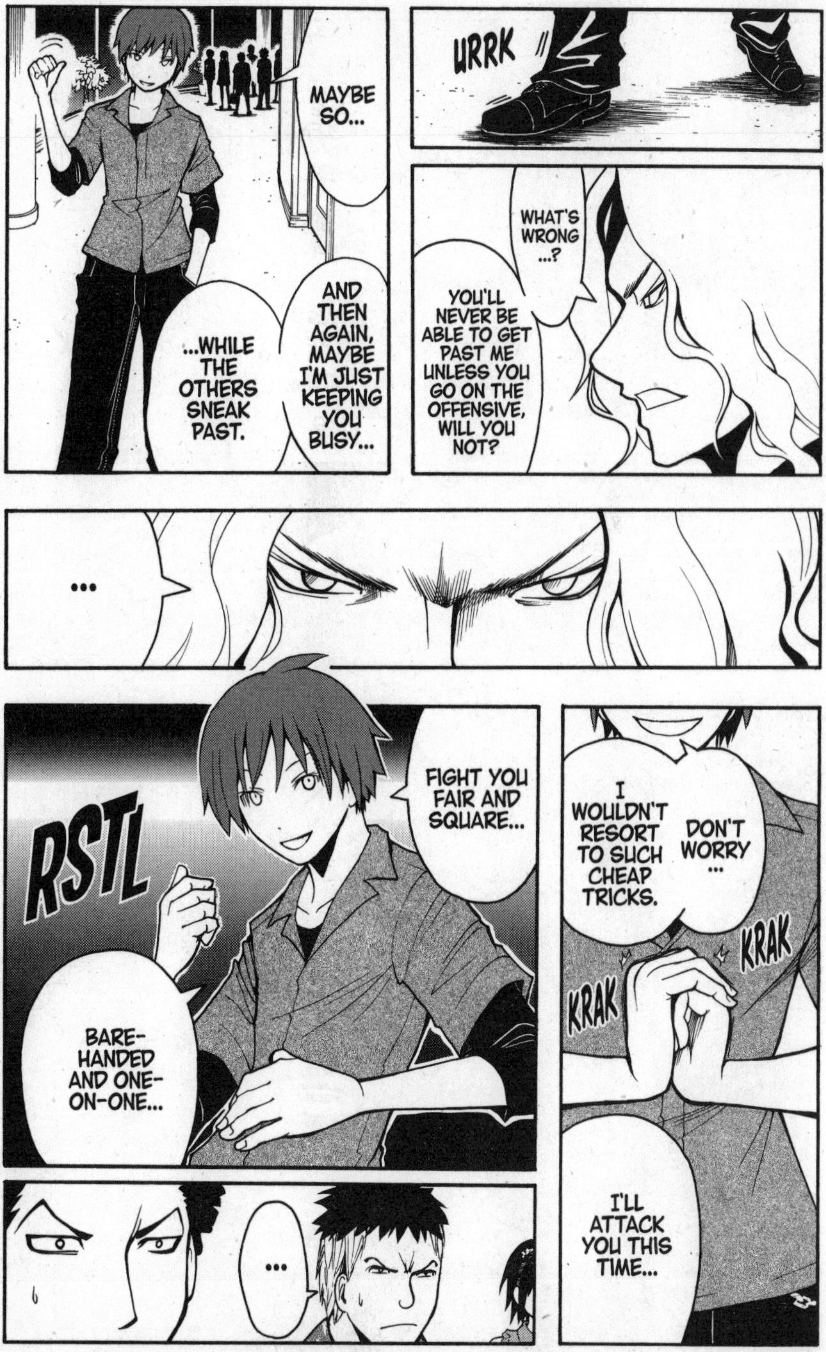
URRK
WHAT'S WRONG ...?
YOU'LL NEVER BE ABLE TO GET PAST ME UNLESS YOU GO ON THE OFFENSIVE, WILL YOU NOT?
MAYBE SO...
AND THEN AGAIN, MAYBE I'M JUST KEEPING YOU BUSY...
...WHILE THE OTHERS SNEAK PAST.
...
DON'T WORRY ...
I WOULDN'T RESORT TO SUCH CHEAP TRICKS.
KRAK
KRAK
I'LL ATTACK YOU THIS TIME...
FIGHT YOU FAIR AND SQUARE...
RSTL
BARE-HANDED AND ONE-ON-ONE...
...

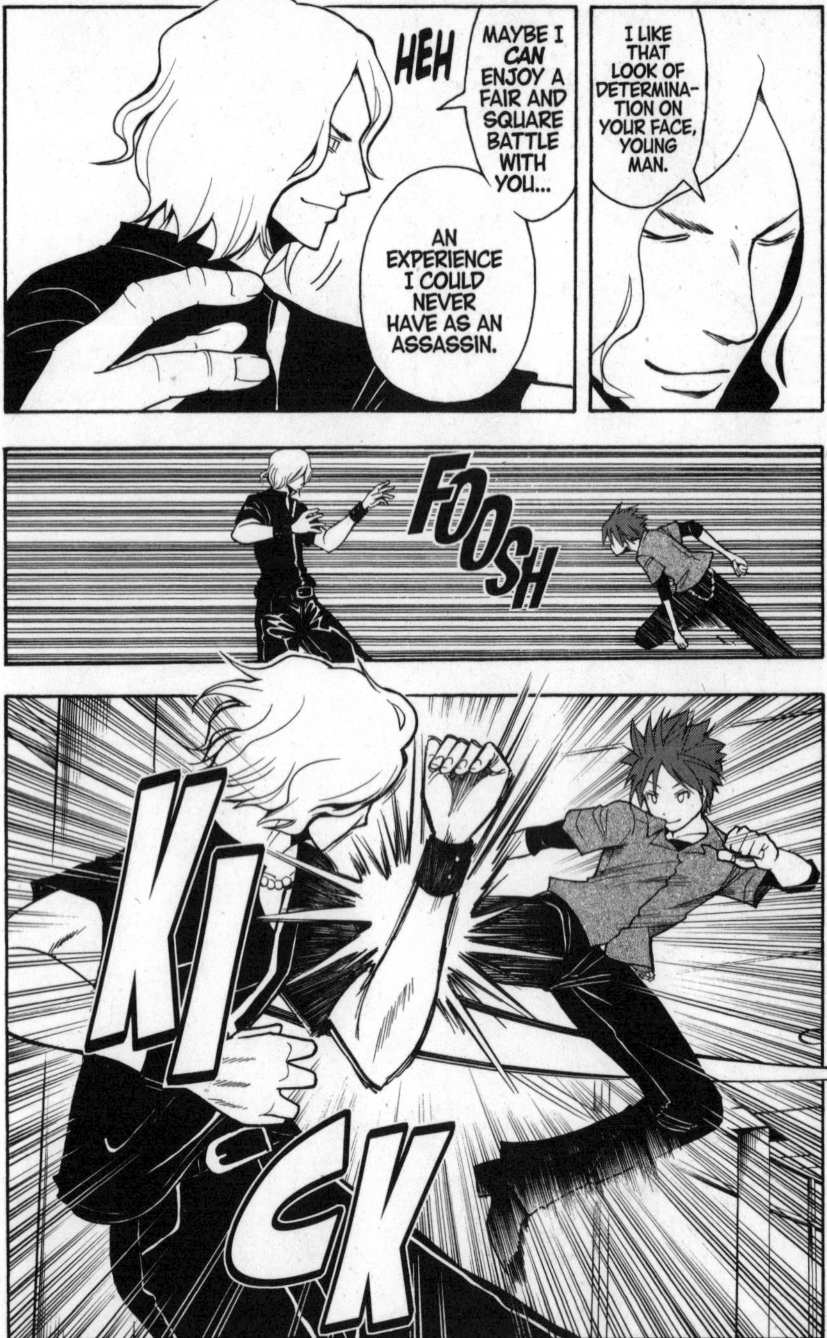
I LIKE THAT LOOK OF DETERMINATION ON YOUR FACE, YOUNG MAN.
HEH
MAYBE I CAN ENJOY A FAIR AND SQUARE BATTLE WITH YOU...
AN EXPERIENCE I COULD NEVER HAVE AS AN ASSASSIN.
FOOSH
KICK

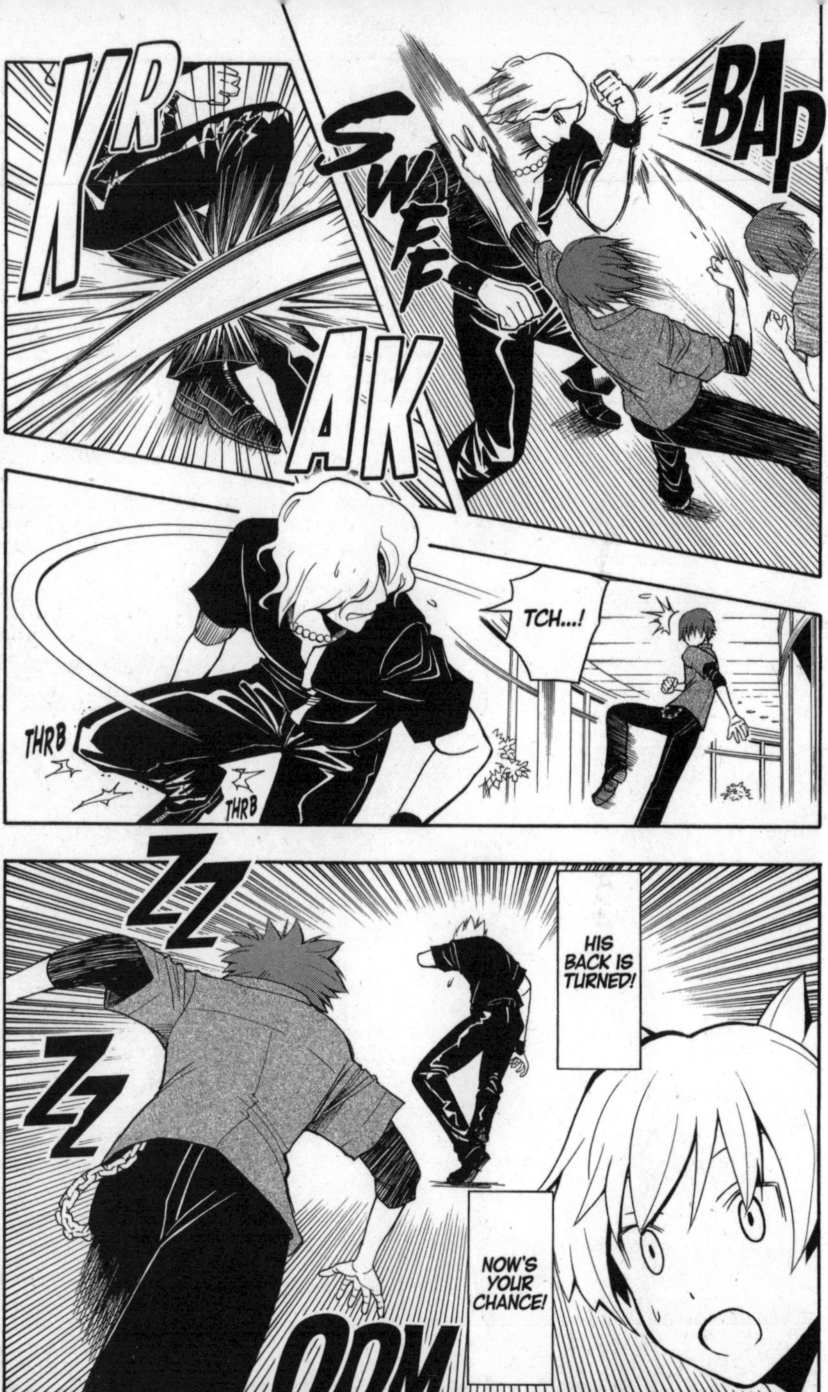
BAP
SWFF
KR
AK
TCH...!
THRB
THRB
HIS BACK IS TURNED!
NOW'S YOUR CHANCE!
ZZ
ZZ
OOM

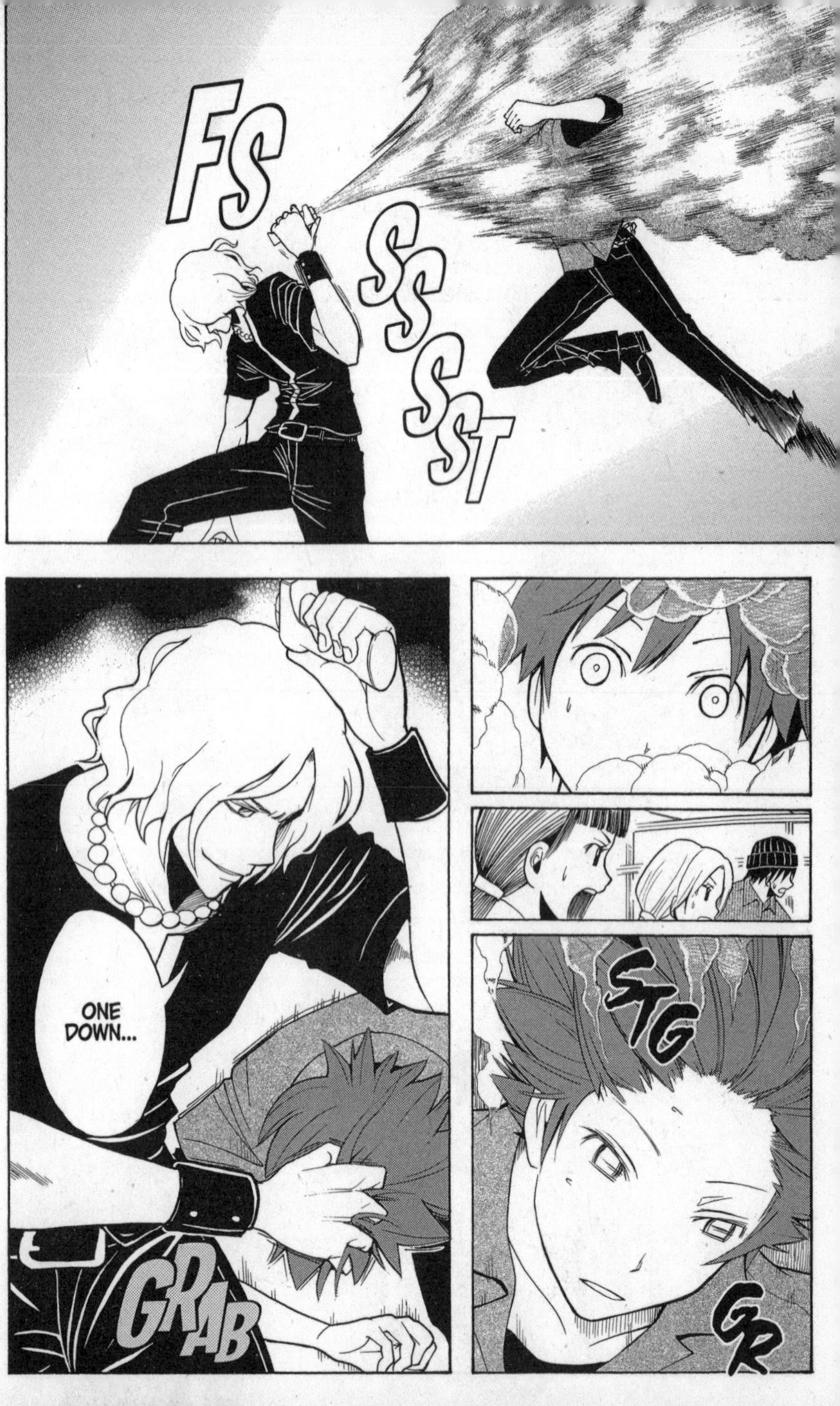
FS
SSSST
STG
GR
ONE DOWN...
GRAB

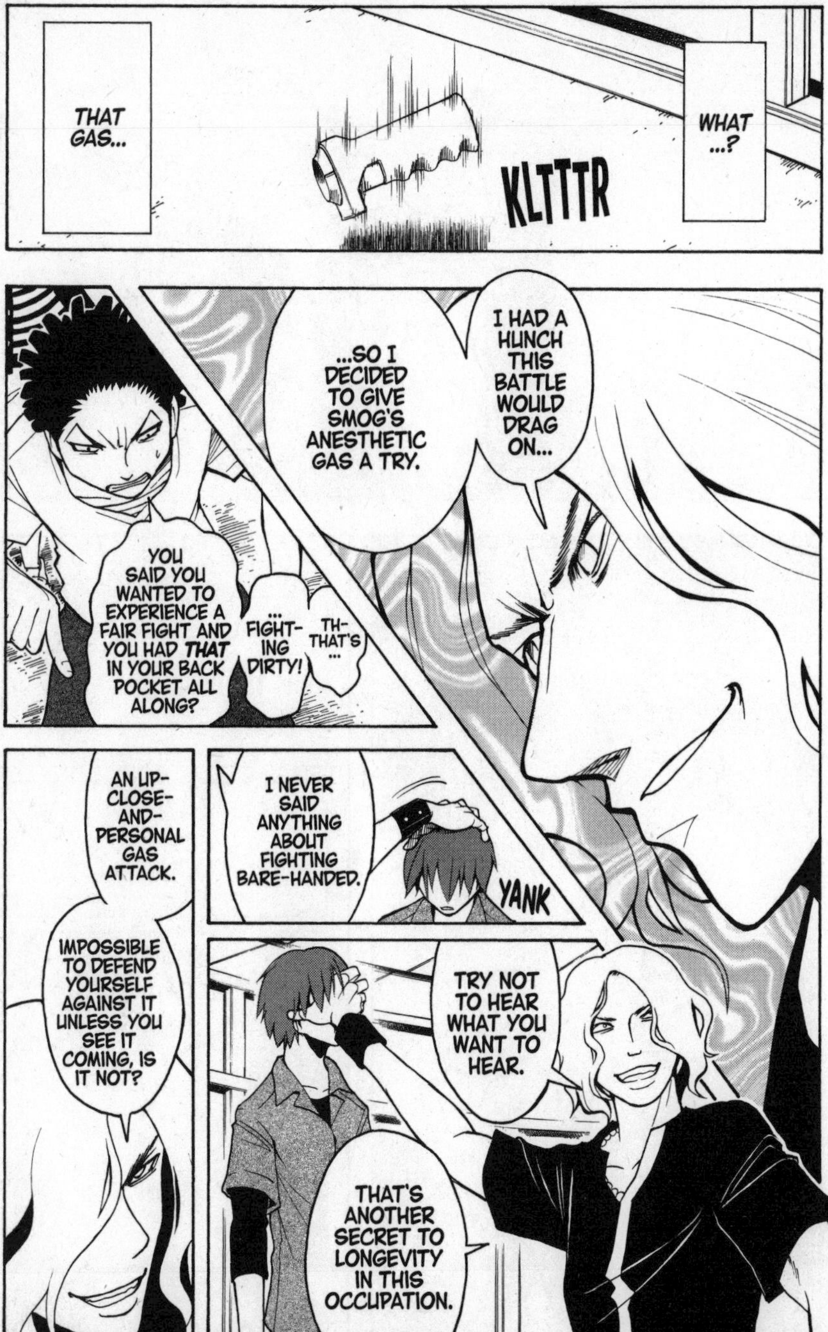
WHAT ...?
KLTTTR
THAT GAS...
I HAD A HUNCH THIS BATTLE WOULD DRAG ON...
...SO I DECIDED TO GIVE SMOG'S ANESTHETIC GAS A TRY.
TH-THAT'S...
...FIGHTING DIRTY!
YOU SAID YOU WANTED TO EXPERIENCE A FAIR FIGHT AND YOU HAD *THAT* IN YOUR BACK POCKET ALL ALONG?
I NEVER SAID ANYTHING ABOUT FIGHTING BARE-HANDED.
YANK
TRY NOT TO HEAR WHAT YOU WANT TO HEAR.
THAT'S ANOTHER SECRET TO LONGEVITY IN THIS OCCUPATION.
AN UP-CLOSE-AND-PERSONAL GAS ATTACK.
IMPOSSIBLE TO DEFEND YOURSELF AGAINST IT UNLESS YOU SEE IT COMING, IS IT NOT?

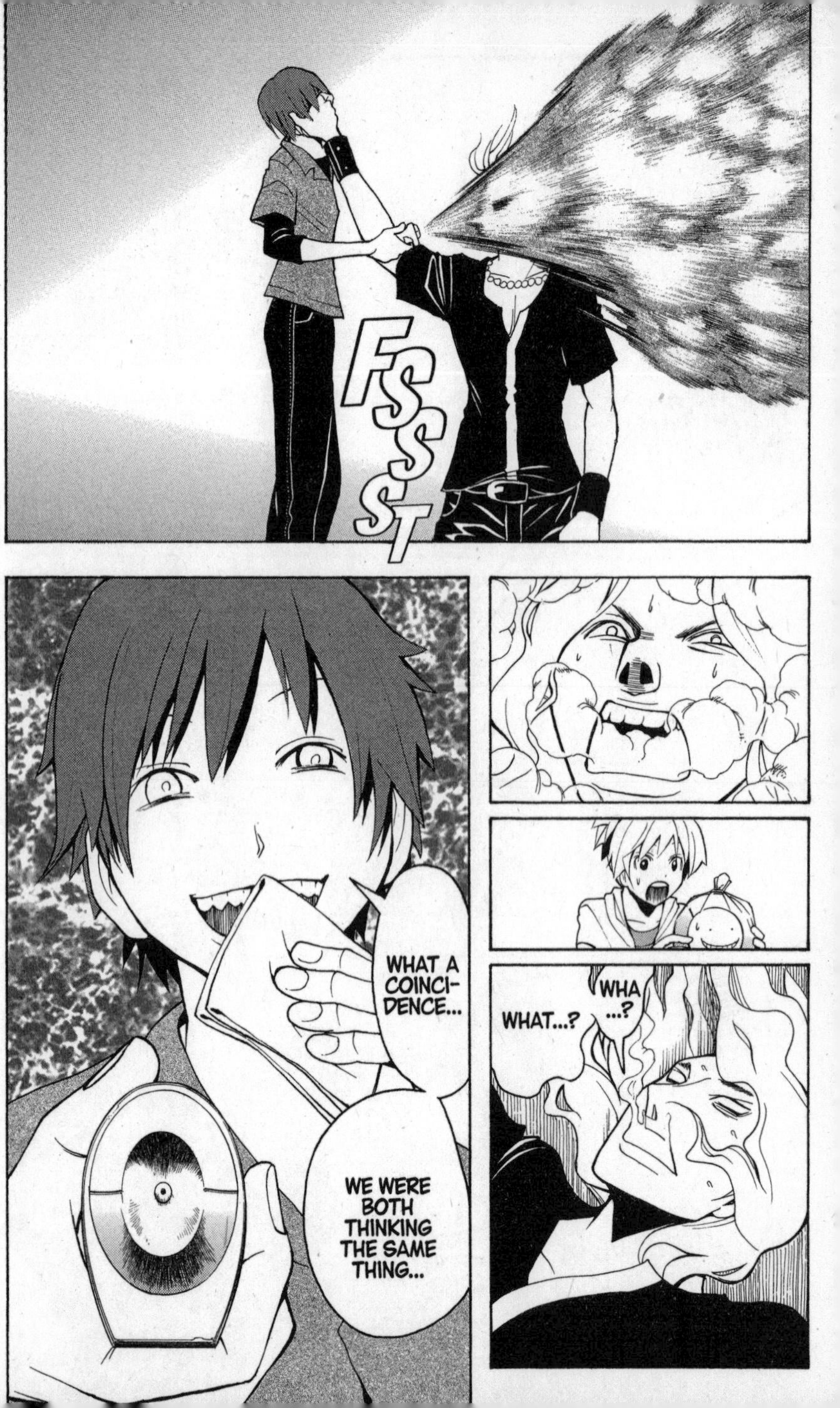
FSSST
WHA...?
WHAT...?
WHAT A COINCIDENCE...
WE WERE BOTH THINKING THE SAME THING...

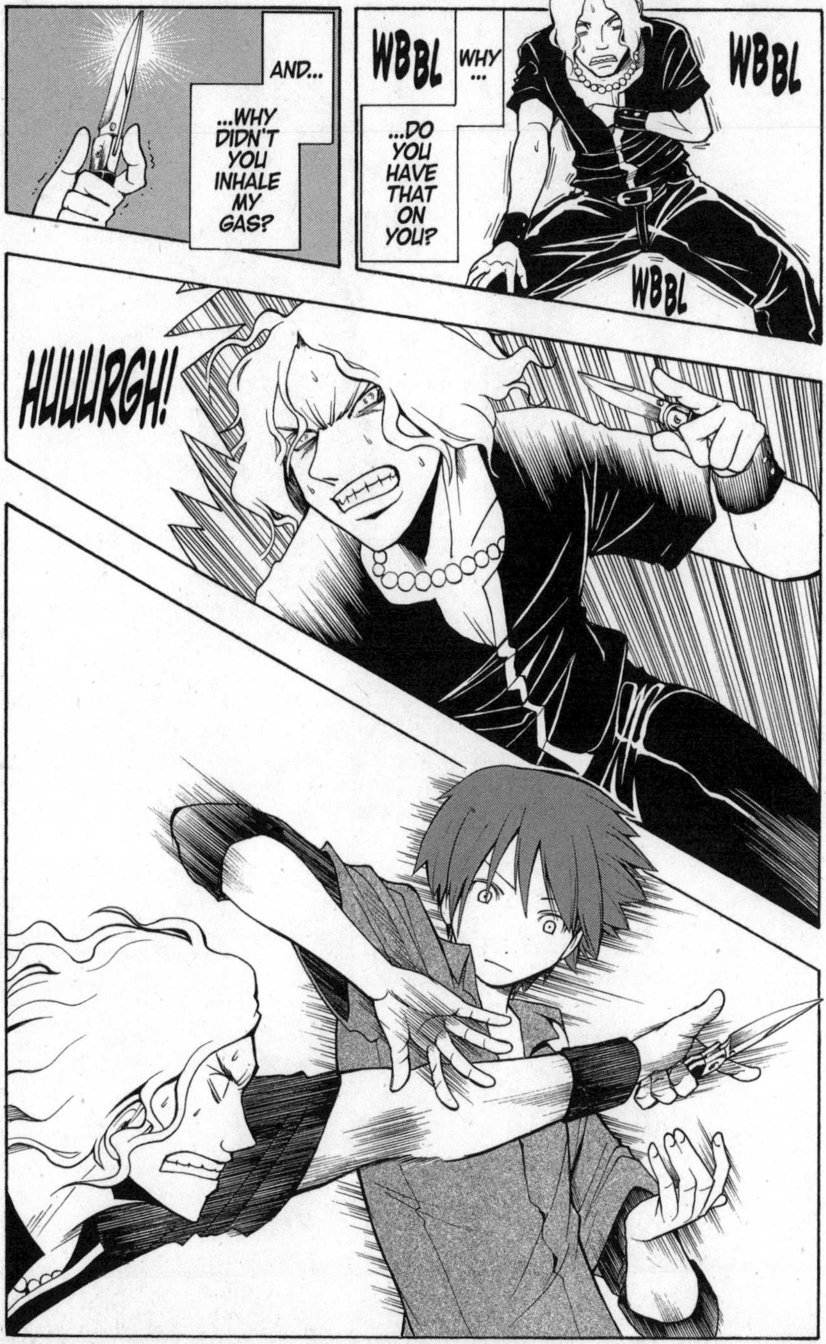
WBBL
WHY...
...DO YOU HAVE THAT ON YOU?
WBBL
WBBL
AND...
...WHY DIDN'T YOU INHALE MY GAS?
HUUURGH!

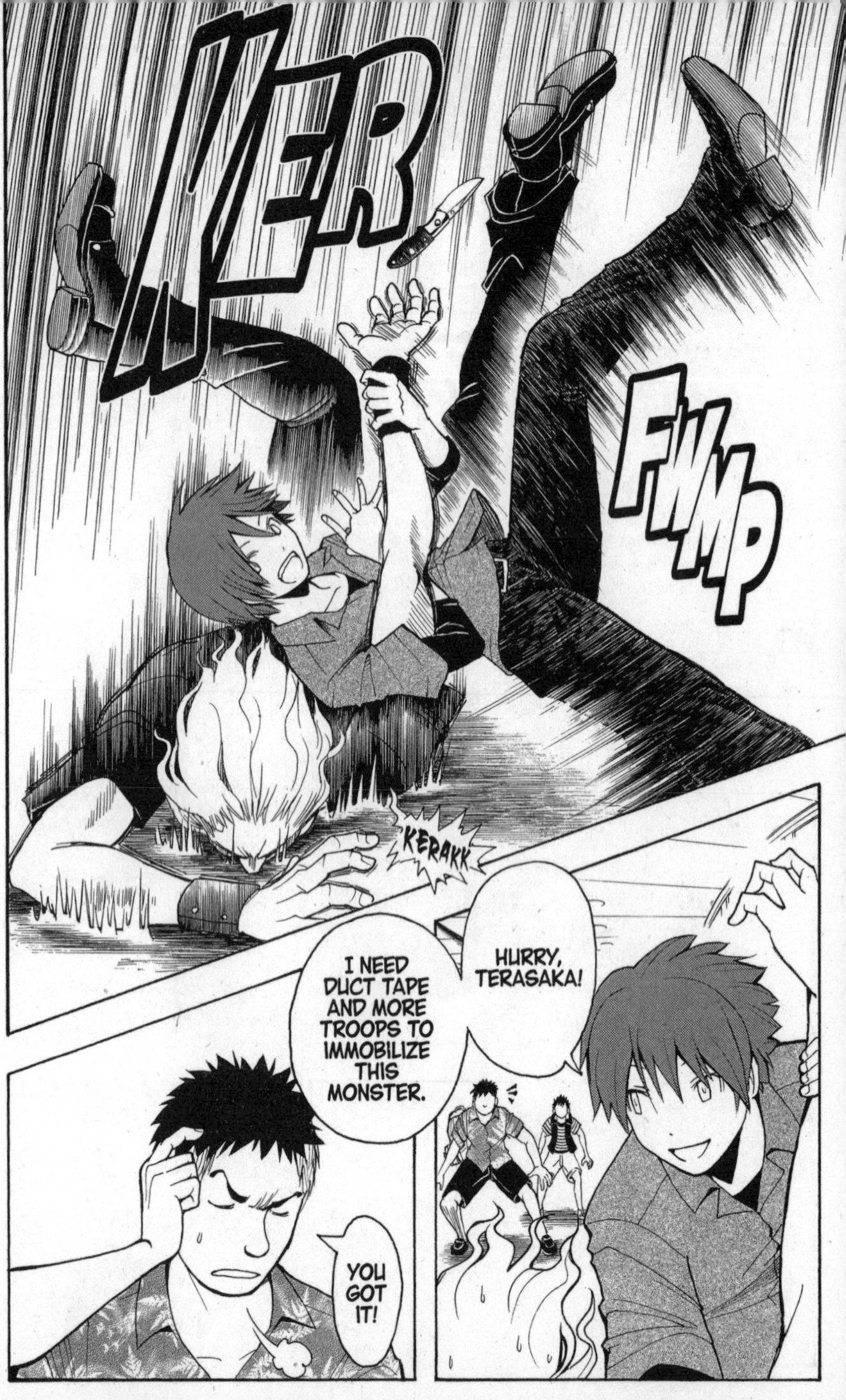
FWMP
KERAKK
HURRY, TERASAKA!
I NEED DUCT TAPE AND MORE TROOPS TO IMMOBILIZE THIS MONSTER.
YOU GOT IT!

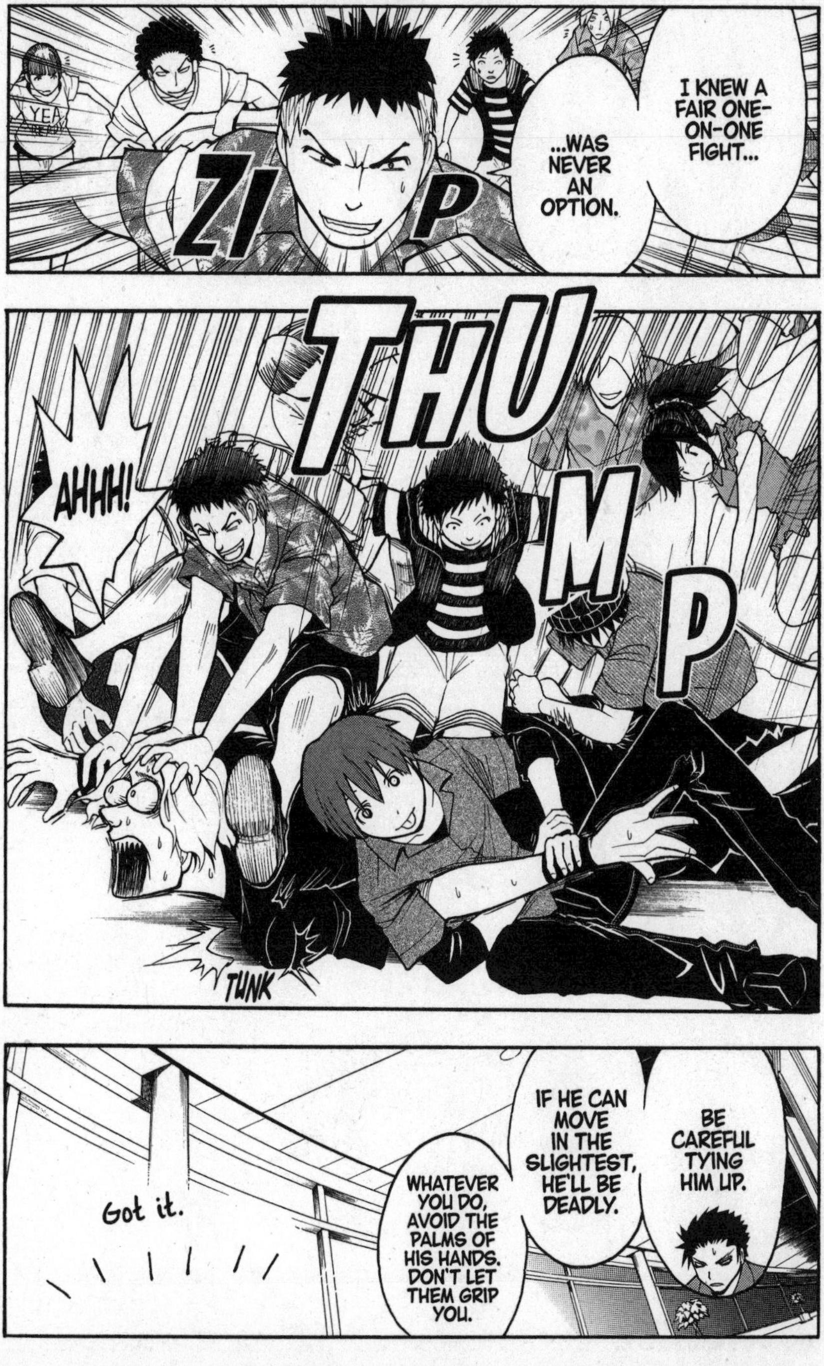
I KNEW A FAIR ONE-ON-ONE FIGHT...
...WAS NEVER AN OPTION.
ZIP
THUMP
AHHH!
TUNK
BE CAREFUL TYING HIM UP.
IF HE CAN MOVE IN THE SLIGHTEST, HE'LL BE DEADLY.
WHATEVER YOU DO, AVOID THE PALMS OF HIS HANDS. DON'T LET THEM GRIP YOU.
Got it.

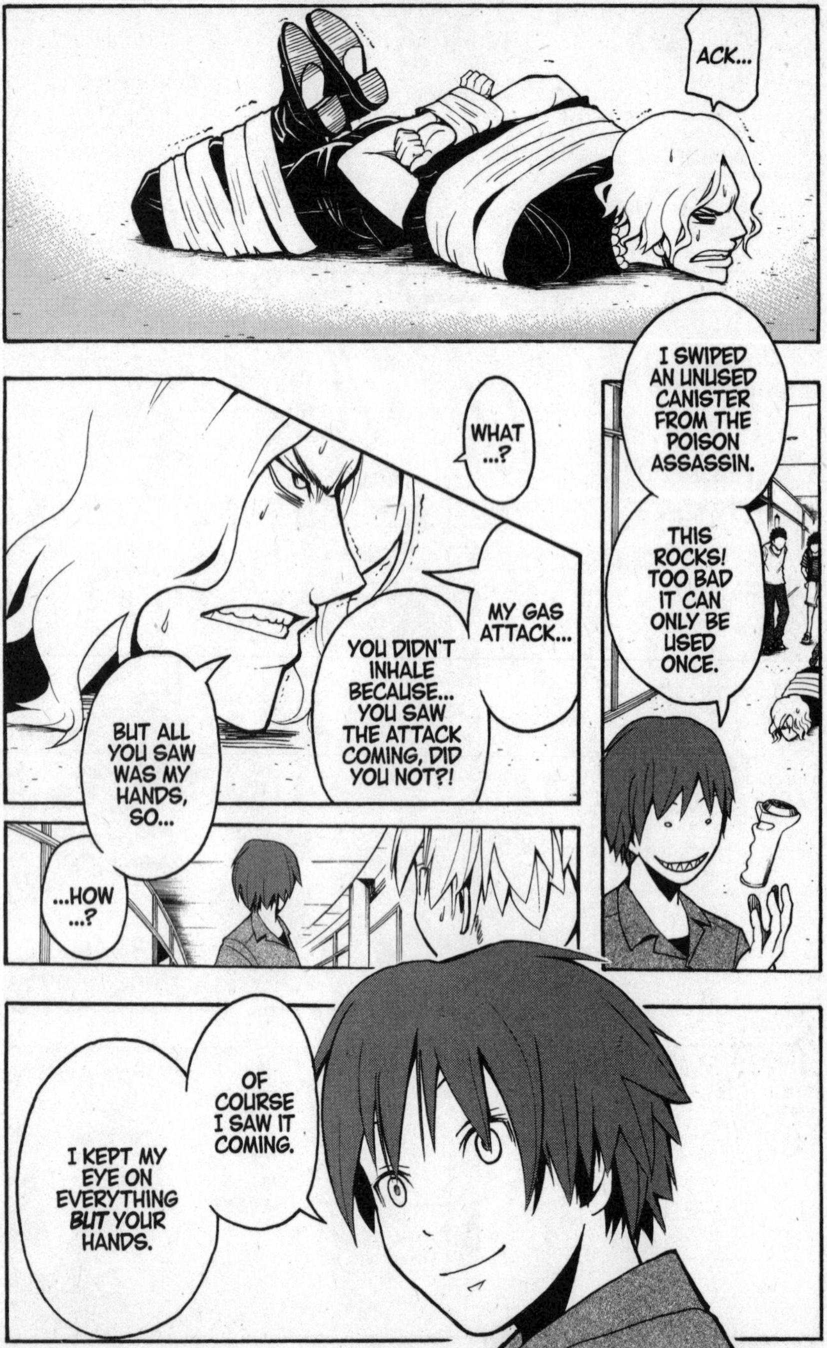
ACK...
I SWIPED AN UNUSED CANISTER FROM THE POISON ASSASSIN.
THIS ROCKS! TOO BAD IT CAN ONLY BE USED ONCE.
WHAT ...?
MY GAS ATTACK...
YOU DIDN'T INHALE BECAUSE... YOU SAW THE ATTACK COMING, DID YOU NOT?!
BUT ALL YOU SAW WAS MY HANDS, SO...
...HOW ...?
OF COURSE I SAW IT COMING.
I KEPT MY EYE ON EVERYTHING BUT YOUR HANDS.

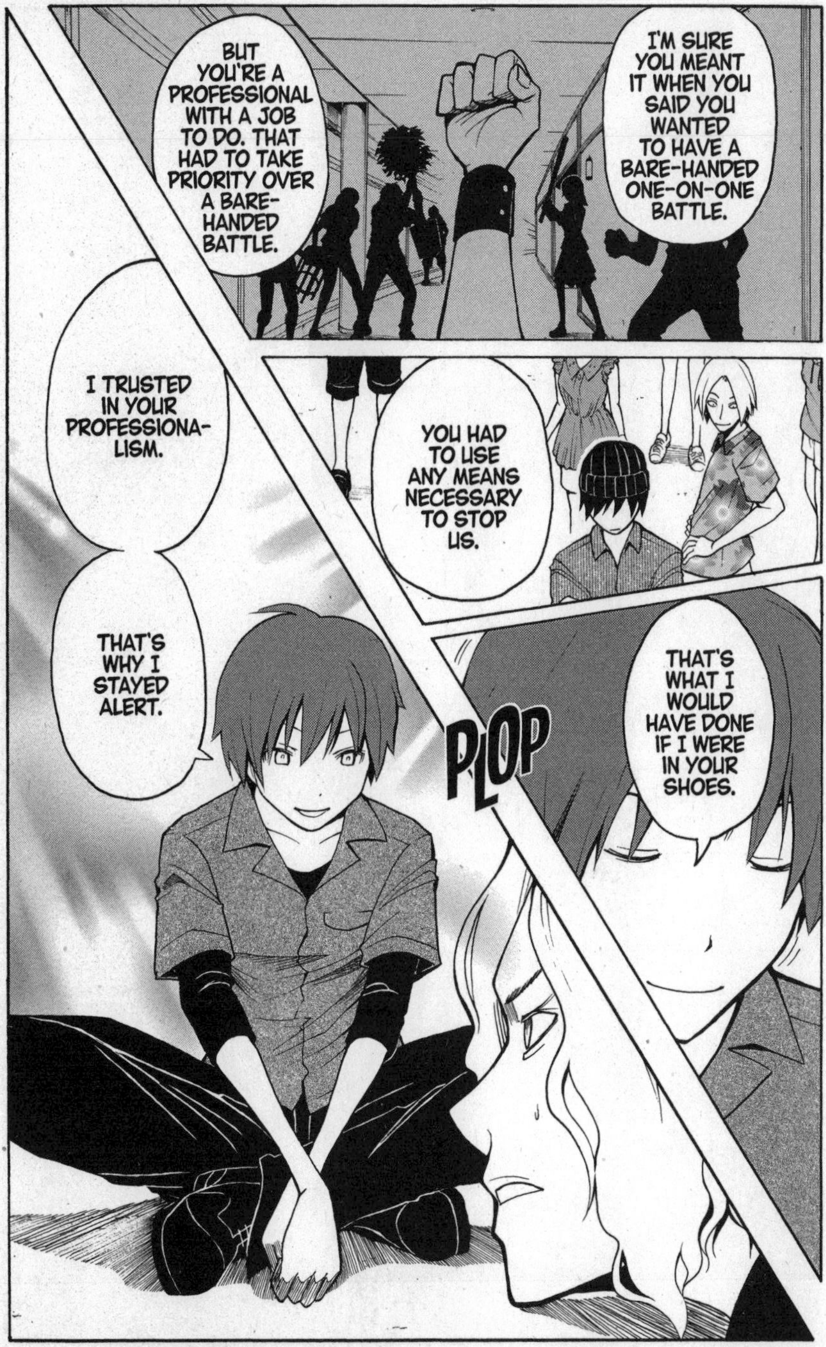
I'M SURE YOU MEANT IT WHEN YOU SAID YOU WANTED TO HAVE A BARE-HANDED ONE-ON-ONE BATTLE.
BUT YOU'RE A PROFESSIONAL WITH A JOB TO DO. THAT HAD TO TAKE PRIORITY OVER A BARE-HANDED BATTLE.
YOU HAD TO USE ANY MEANS NECESSARY TO STOP US.
PLOP
THAT'S WHAT I WOULD HAVE DONE IF I WERE IN YOUR SHOES.
I TRUSTED IN YOUR PROFESSIONA-LISM.
THAT'S WHY I STAYED ALERT.

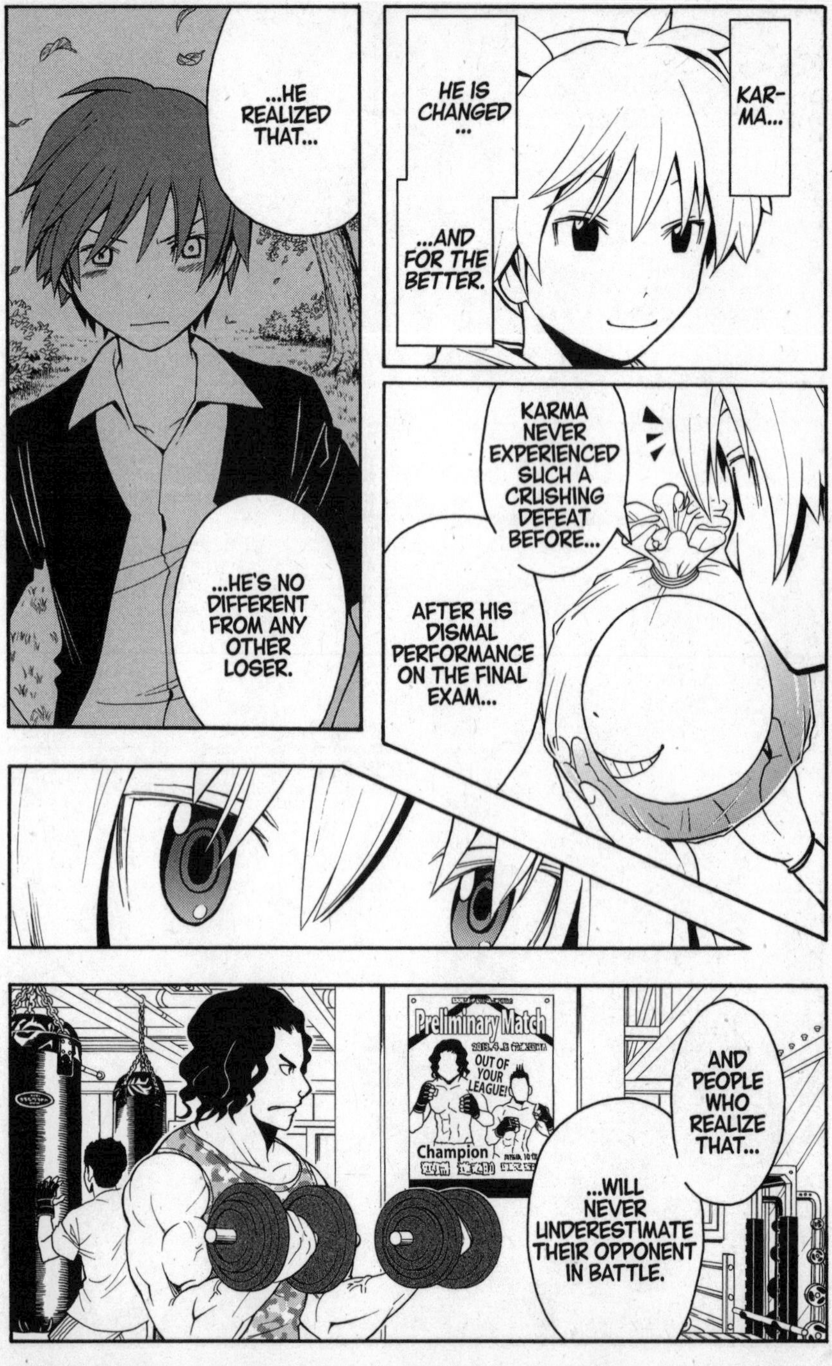
KAR-MA...
HE IS CHANGED...
...AND FOR THE BETTER.
KARMA NEVER EXPERIENCED SUCH A CRUSHING DEFEAT BEFORE...
AFTER HIS DISMAL PERFORMANCE ON THE FINAL EXAM...
...HE REALIZED THAT...
...HE'S NO DIFFERENT FROM ANY OTHER LOSER.
AND PEOPLE WHO REALIZE THAT...
...WILL NEVER UNDERESTIMATE THEIR OPPONENT IN BATTLE.
Preliminary Match
OUT OF YOUR LEAGUE!
Champion

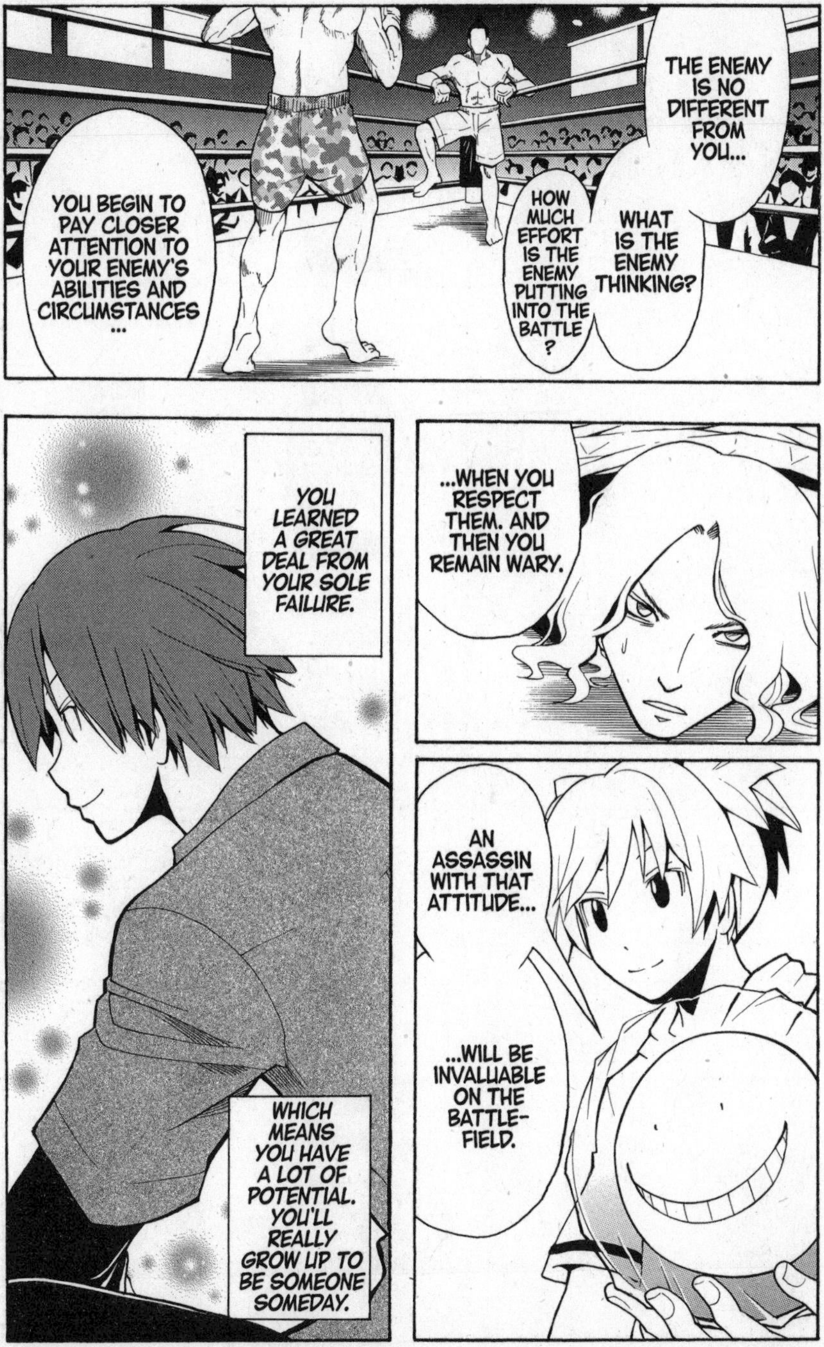
THE ENEMY IS NO DIFFERENT FROM YOU...
WHAT IS THE ENEMY THINKING?
HOW MUCH EFFORT IS THE ENEMY PUTTING INTO THE BATTLE?
YOU BEGIN TO PAY CLOSER ATTENTION TO YOUR ENEMY'S ABILITIES AND CIRCUMSTANCES...
...WHEN YOU RESPECT THEM. AND THEN YOU REMAIN WARY.
AN ASSASSIN WITH THAT ATTITUDE...
...WILL BE INVALUABLE ON THE BATTLE-FIELD.
YOU LEARNED A GREAT DEAL FROM YOUR SOLE FAILURE.
WHICH MEANS YOU HAVE A LOT OF POTENTIAL. YOU'LL REALLY GROW UP TO BE SOMEONE SOMEDAY.

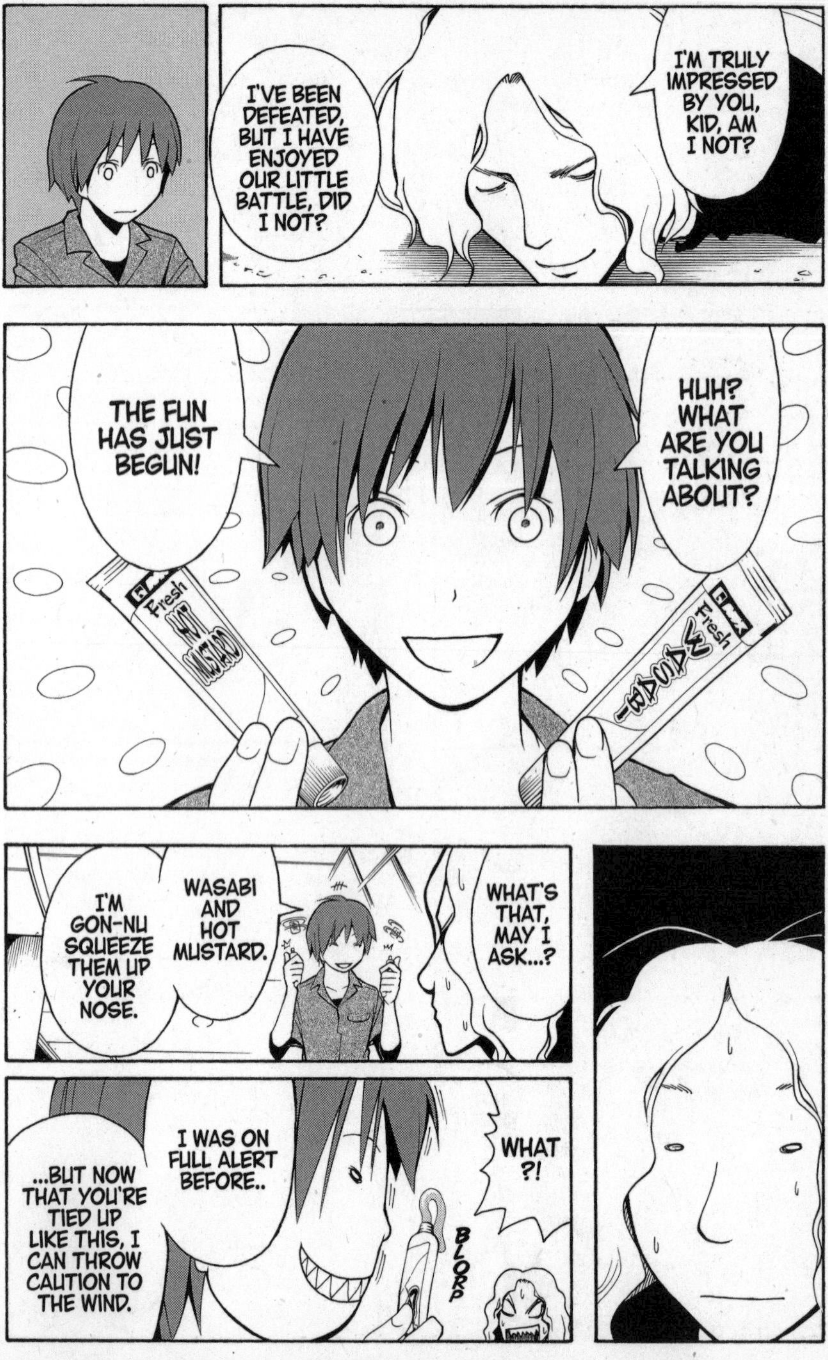
I'M TRULY IMPRESSED BY YOU, KID, AM I NOT?
I'VE BEEN DEFEATED, BUT I HAVE ENJOYED OUR LITTLE BATTLE, DID I NOT?
HUH? WHAT ARE YOU TALKING ABOUT?
THE FUN HAS JUST BEGUN!
Fresh
Fresh HOT MUSTARD
WHAT'S THAT, MAY I ASK...?
WASABI AND HOT MUSTARD.
I'M GON-NU SQUEEZE THEM UP YOUR NOSE.
WHAT?!
BLORP
I WAS ON FULL ALERT BEFORE..
...BUT NOW THAT YOU'RE TIED UP LIKE THIS, I CAN THROW CAUTION TO THE WIND.

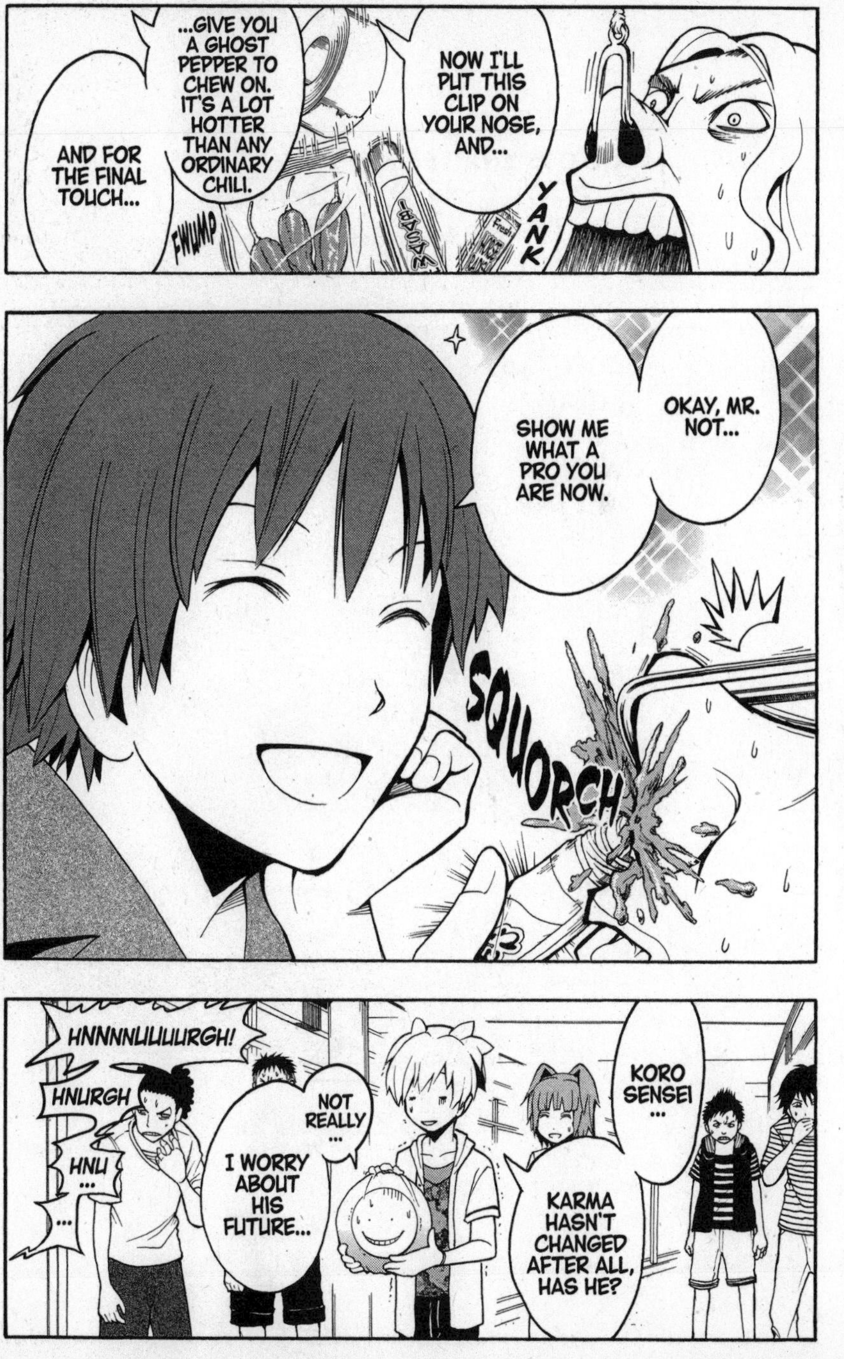
YANK
NOW I'LL PUT THIS CLIP ON YOUR NOSE, AND...
...GIVE YOU A GHOST PEPPER TO CHEW ON. IT'S A LOT HOTTER THAN ANY ORDINARY CHILI.
FWUMP
AND FOR THE FINAL TOUCH...
OKAY, MR. NOT...
SHOW ME WHAT A PRO YOU ARE NOW.
SQUORCH
KORO SENSEI ...
KARMA HASN'T CHANGED AFTER ALL, HAS HE?
NOT REALLY ...
I WORRY ABOUT HIS FUTURE...
HNNNNUUUURGH!
HNURGH
HNU ...
...

Karma's Emergency Tool Bag
(Currently stored inside Terasaka's backpack)

- Nosehook
- Clothespin
- Duct Tape
- Collar
- Safety Pin
- Wasabi
- Hot Mustard
- Garlic
- Ghost Pepper
- Green Gentian Tea
- Firecrackers
- Bad Luck Chain Letter
- Snap Chewing Gum
- "I Am an Idiot" Sticker
- Fake Cockroach
- Fake Poop
- Foul-Smelling Chemical Compound (Made by Okuda)

PRoviding is PReventing

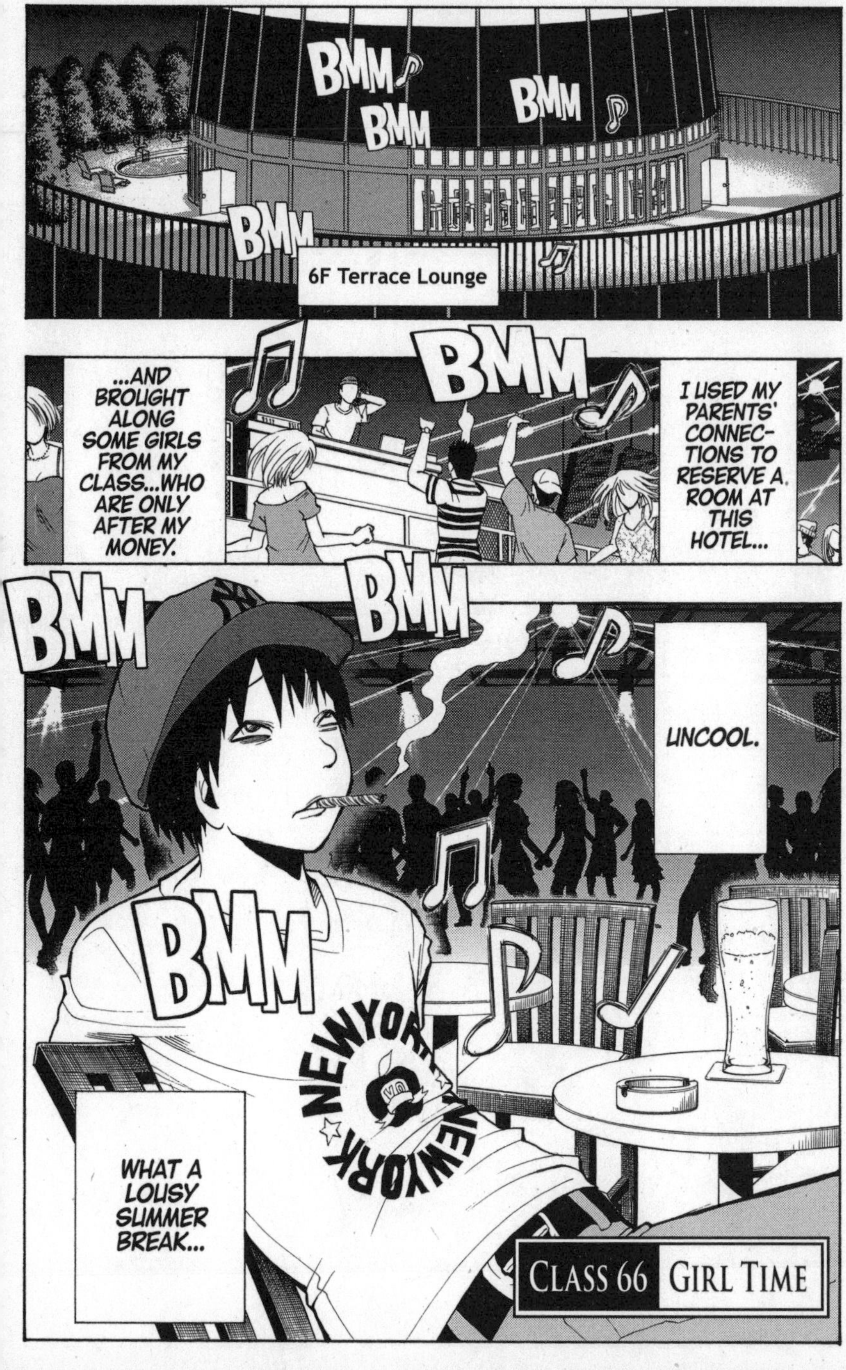
BMM
BMM
BMM
BMM
6F Terrace Lounge
BMM
I USED MY PARENTS' CONNECTIONS TO RESERVE A ROOM AT THIS HOTEL...
...AND BROUGHT ALONG SOME GIRLS FROM MY CLASS...WHO ARE ONLY AFTER MY MONEY.
BMM
BMM
UNCOOL.
BMM
NEWYORK NEWYORK
WHAT A LOUSY SUMMER BREAK...
CLASS 66 GIRL TIME

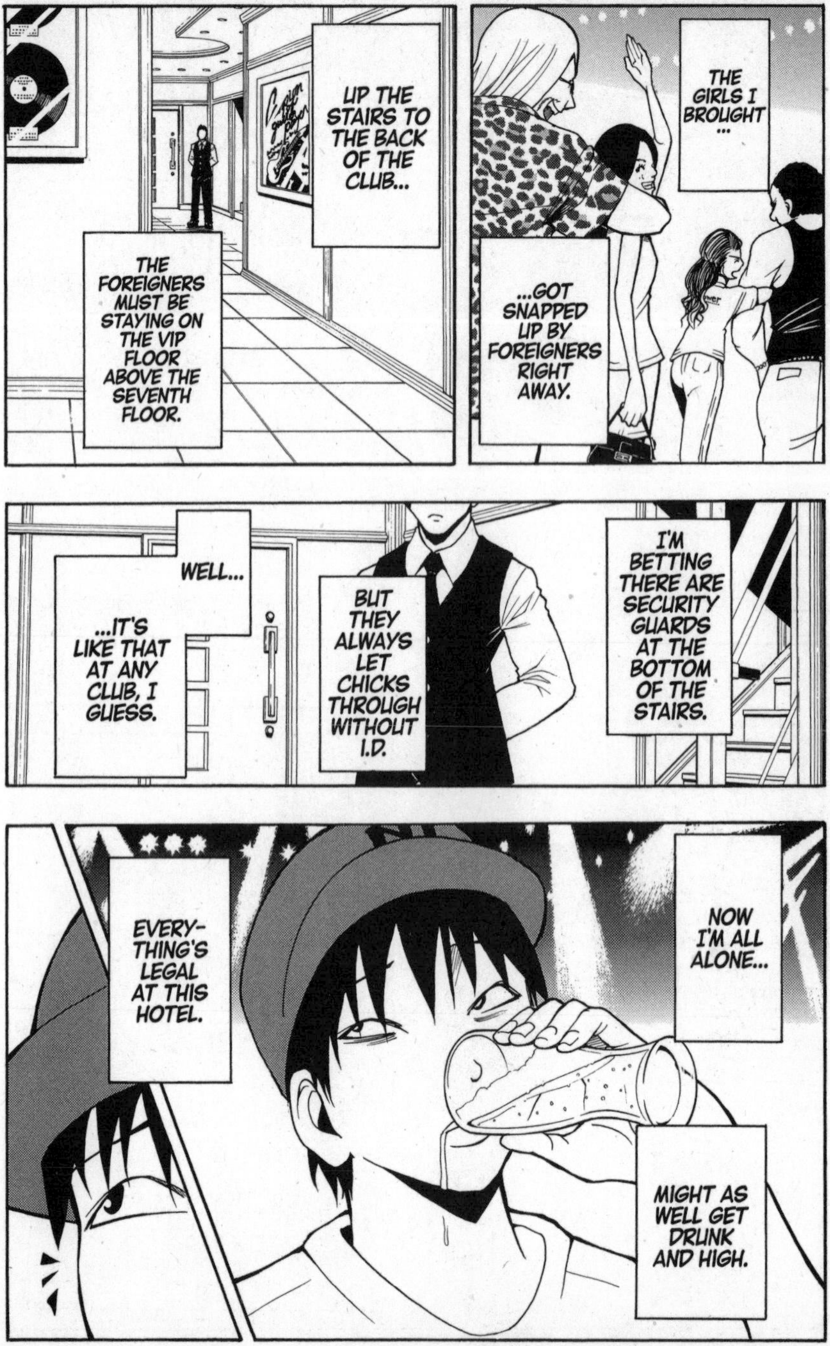
THE GIRLS I BROUGHT...
...GOT SNAPPED UP BY FOREIGNERS RIGHT AWAY.
UP THE STAIRS TO THE BACK OF THE CLUB...
THE FOREIGNERS MUST BE STAYING ON THE VIP FLOOR ABOVE THE SEVENTH FLOOR.
I'M BETTING THERE ARE SECURITY GUARDS AT THE BOTTOM OF THE STAIRS.
BUT THEY ALWAYS LET CHICKS THROUGH WITHOUT I.D.
WELL...
...IT'S LIKE THAT AT ANY CLUB, I GUESS.
NOW I'M ALL ALONE...
EVERYTHING'S LEGAL AT THIS HOTEL.
MIGHT AS WELL GET DRUNK AND HIGH.

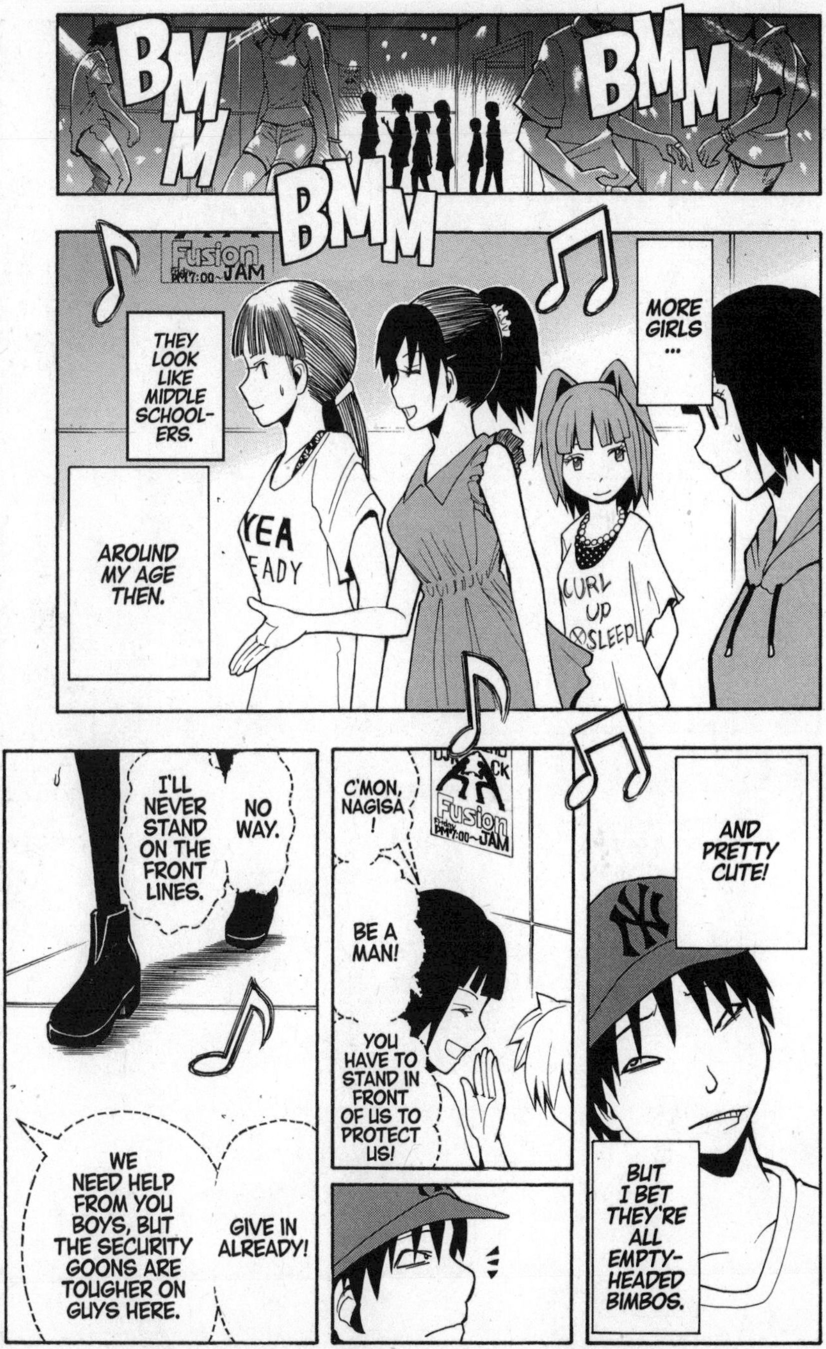
BMMM
BMMM
BMM
Fusion
Friday PM7:00~JAM
MORE GIRLS ...
THEY LOOK LIKE MIDDLE SCHOOLERS.
AROUND MY AGE THEN.
YEA
EADY
CURL UP SLEEP
AND PRETTY CUTE!
BUT I BET THEY'RE ALL EMPTY-HEADED BIMBOS.
Fusion
PM7:00~JAM
C'MON, NAGISA!
BE A MAN!
YOU HAVE TO STAND IN FRONT OF US TO PROTECT US!
NO WAY.
I'LL NEVER STAND ON THE FRONT LINES.
GIVE IN ALREADY!
WE NEED HELP FROM YOU BOYS, BUT THE SECURITY GOONS ARE TOUGHER ON GUYS HERE.

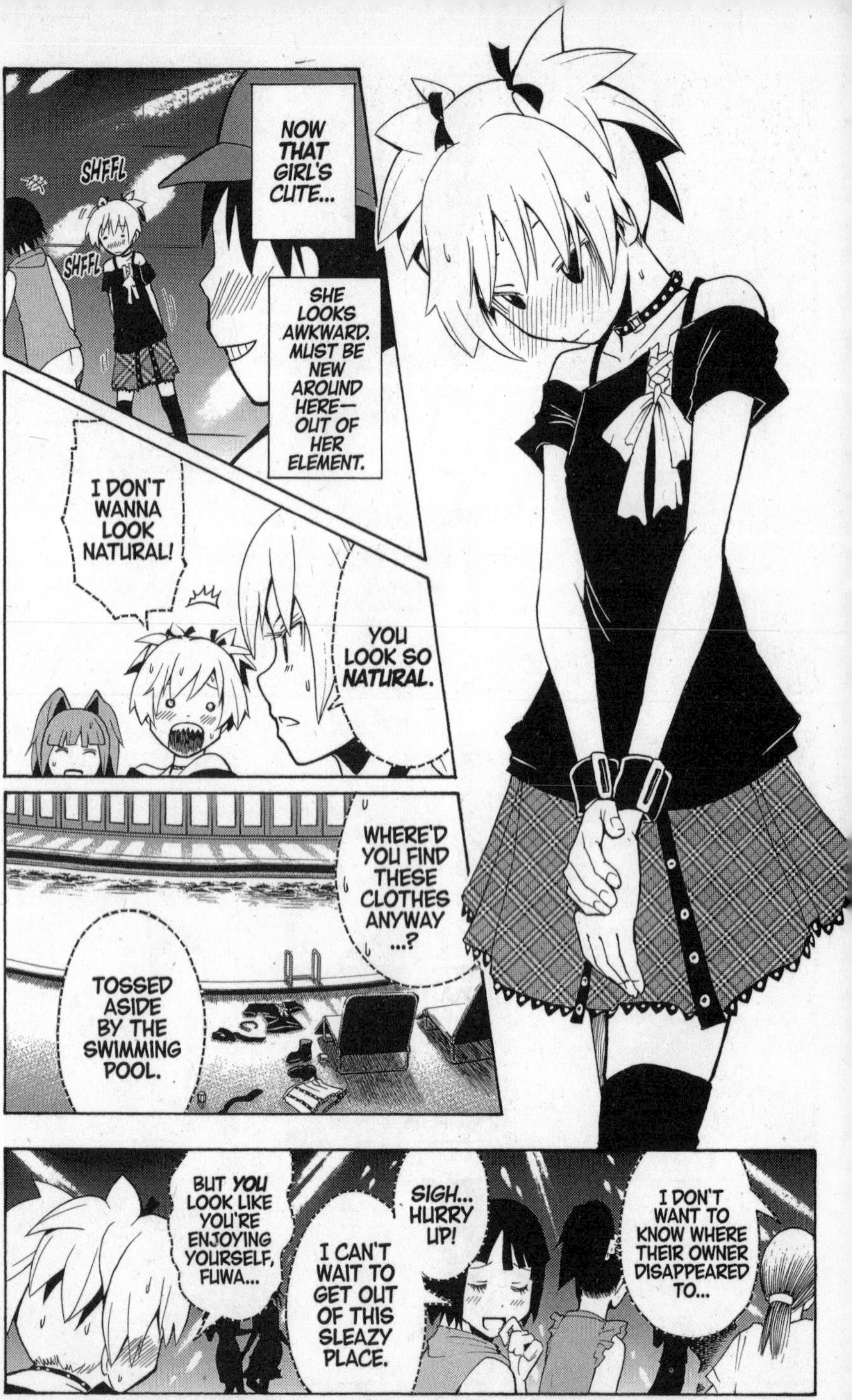
NOW THAT GIRL'S CUTE...
SHE LOOKS AWKWARD. MUST BE NEW AROUND HERE—OUT OF HER ELEMENT.
SHFFL
SHFFL
YOU LOOK SO *NATURAL*.
I DON'T WANNA LOOK NATURAL!
WHERE'D YOU FIND THESE CLOTHES ANYWAY...?
TOSSED ASIDE BY THE SWIMMING POOL.
I DON'T WANT TO KNOW WHERE THEIR OWNER DISAPPEARED TO...
SIGH... HURRY UP!
I CAN'T WAIT TO GET OUT OF THIS SLEAZY PLACE.
BUT *YOU* LOOK LIKE YOU'RE ENJOYING YOURSELF, FUWA...

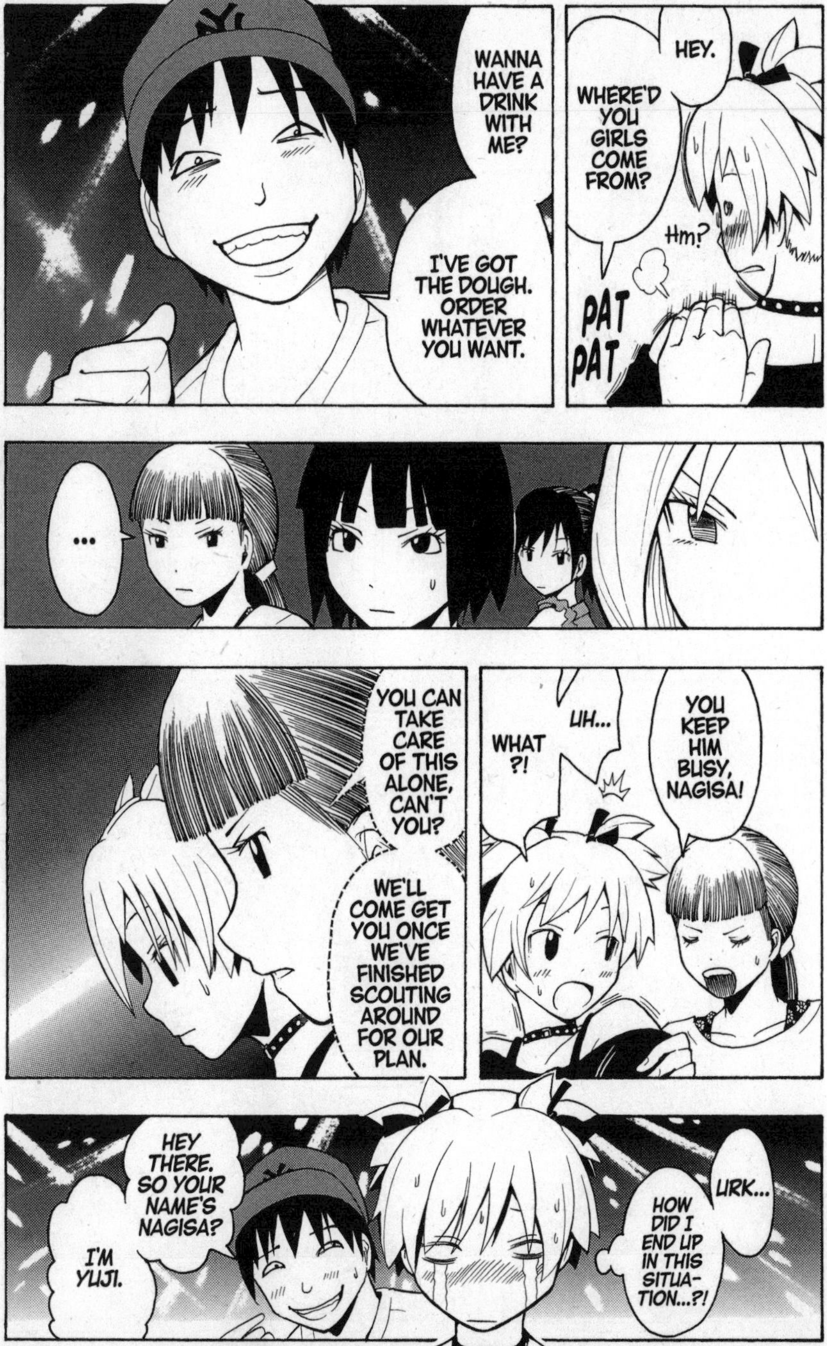
HEY.
WHERE'D YOU GIRLS COME FROM?
Hm?
PAT PAT
WANNA HAVE A DRINK WITH ME?
I'VE GOT THE DOUGH. ORDER WHATEVER YOU WANT.
...
YOU KEEP HIM BUSY, NAGISA!
UH...
WHAT?!
YOU CAN TAKE CARE OF THIS ALONE, CAN'T YOU?
WE'LL COME GET YOU ONCE WE'VE FINISHED SCOUTING AROUND FOR OUR PLAN.
URK...
HOW DID I END UP IN THIS SITUATION...?!
HEY THERE. SO YOUR NAME'S NAGISA?
I'M YUJI.

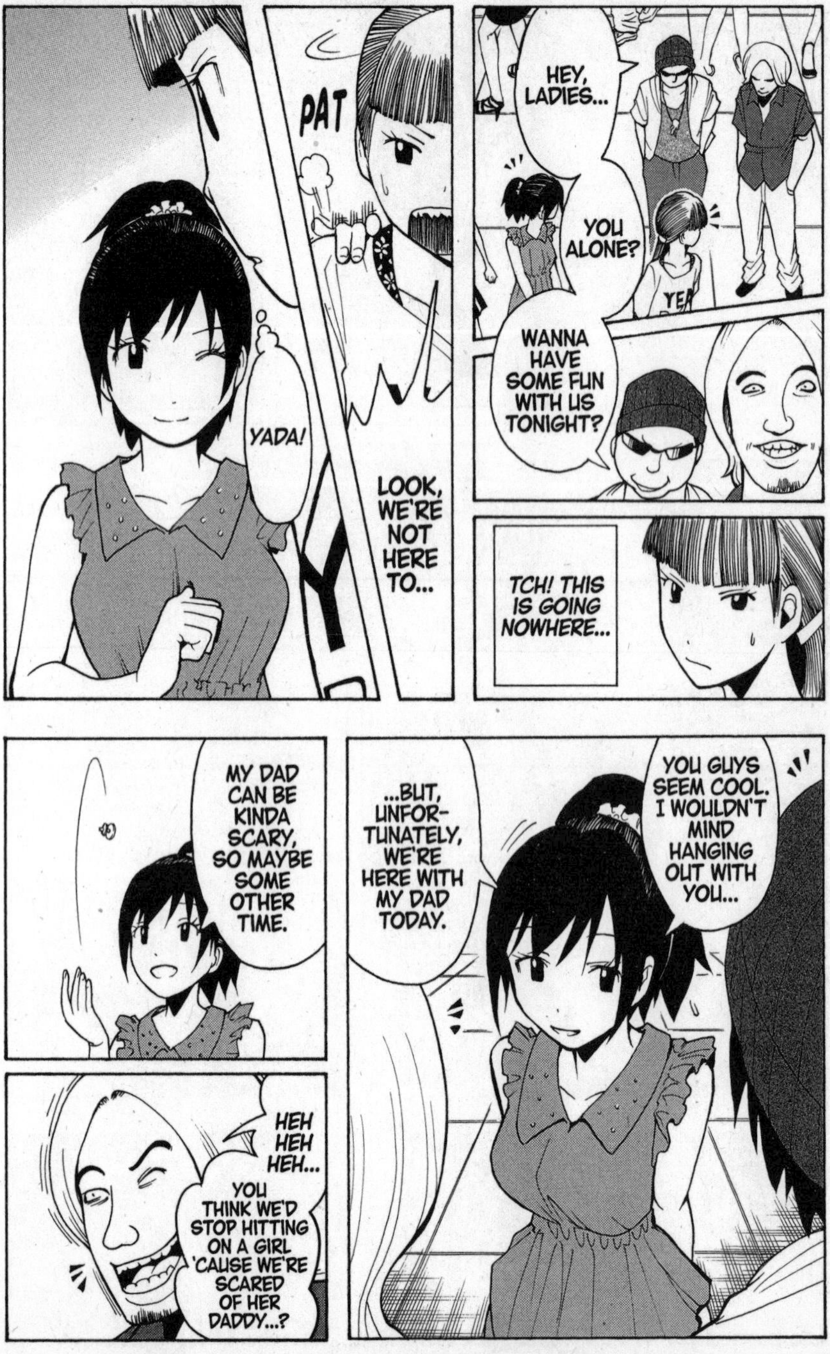
HEY, LADIES...
YOU ALONE?
WANNA HAVE SOME FUN WITH US TONIGHT?
TCH! THIS IS GOING NOWHERE...
PAT
LOOK, WE'RE NOT HERE TO...
YADA!
YOU GUYS SEEM COOL. I WOULDN'T MIND HANGING OUT WITH YOU...
...BUT, UNFORTUNATELY, WE'RE HERE WITH MY DAD TODAY.
MY DAD CAN BE KINDA SCARY, SO MAYBE SOME OTHER TIME.
HEH HEH HEH...
YOU THINK WE'D STOP HITTING ON A GIRL 'CAUSE WE'RE SCARED OF HER DADDY...?

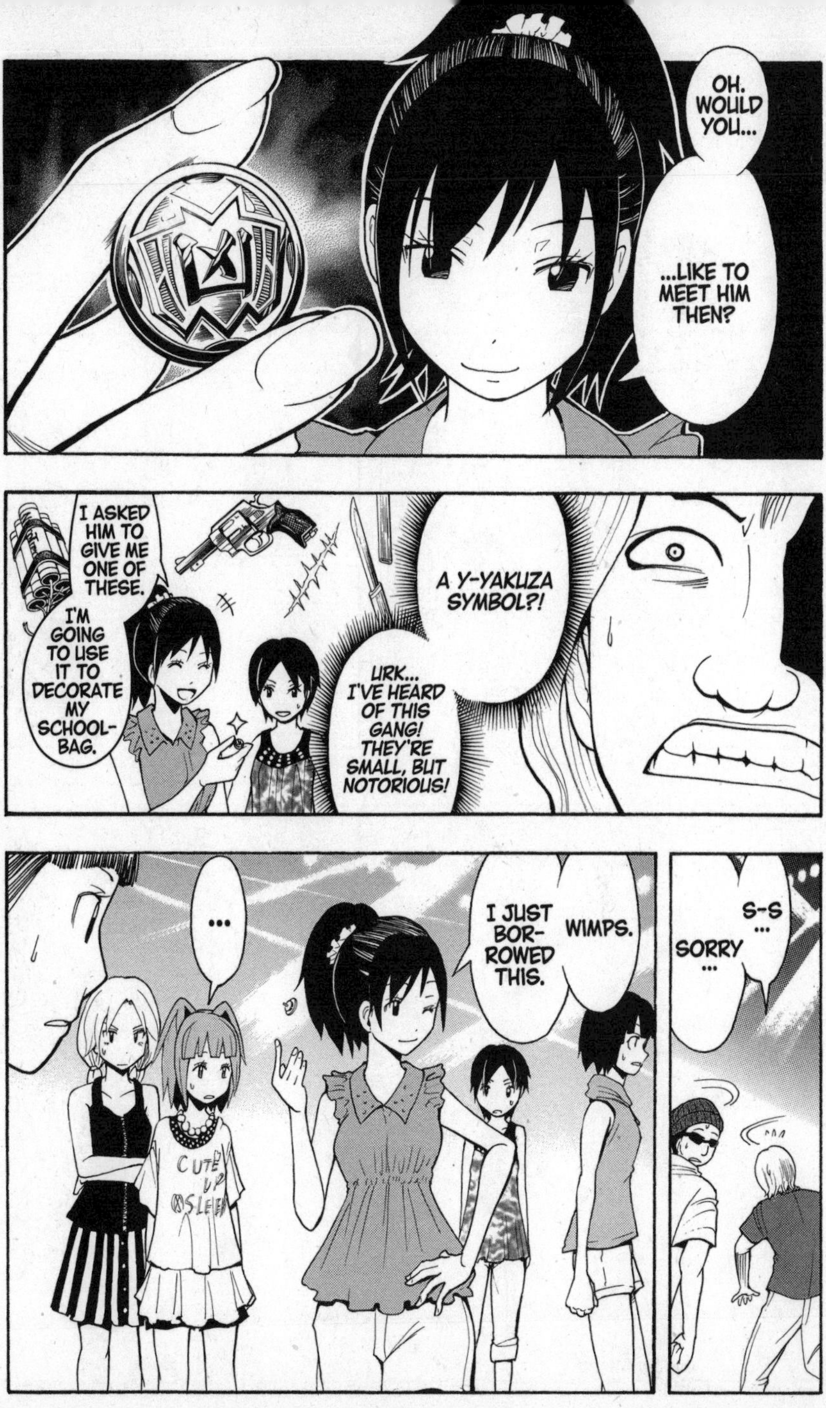
OH. WOULD YOU...
...LIKE TO MEET HIM THEN?
A Y-YAKUZA SYMBOL?!
URK... I'VE HEARD OF THIS GANG! THEY'RE SMALL, BUT NOTORIOUS!
I ASKED HIM TO GIVE ME ONE OF THESE.
I'M GOING TO USE IT TO DECORATE MY SCHOOL-BAG.
S-S...
SORRY...
WIMPS.
I JUST BOR-ROWED THIS.
...

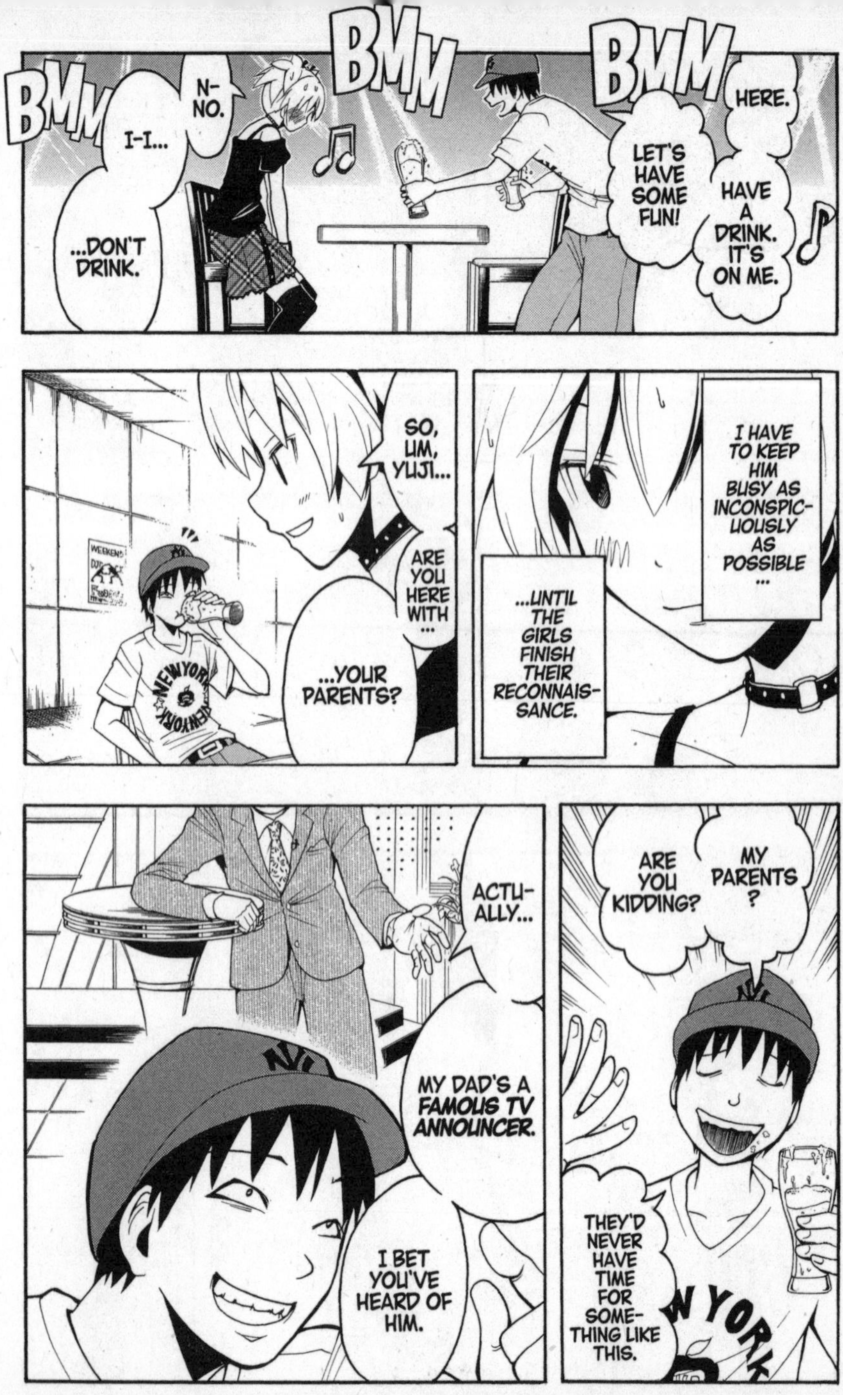
BMM
HERE.
HAVE A DRINK. IT'S ON ME.
LET'S HAVE SOME FUN!
BMM
N-NO.
I-I...
...DON'T DRINK.
BMM
I HAVE TO KEEP HIM BUSY AS INCONSPICUOUSLY AS POSSIBLE...
...UNTIL THE GIRLS FINISH THEIR RECONNAISSANCE.
SO, UM, YUJI...
ARE YOU HERE WITH...
...YOUR PARENTS?
MY PARENTS?
ARE YOU KIDDING?
THEY'D NEVER HAVE TIME FOR SOMETHING LIKE THIS.
ACTUALLY...
MY DAD'S A FAMOUS TV ANNOUNCER.
I BET YOU'VE HEARD OF HIM.

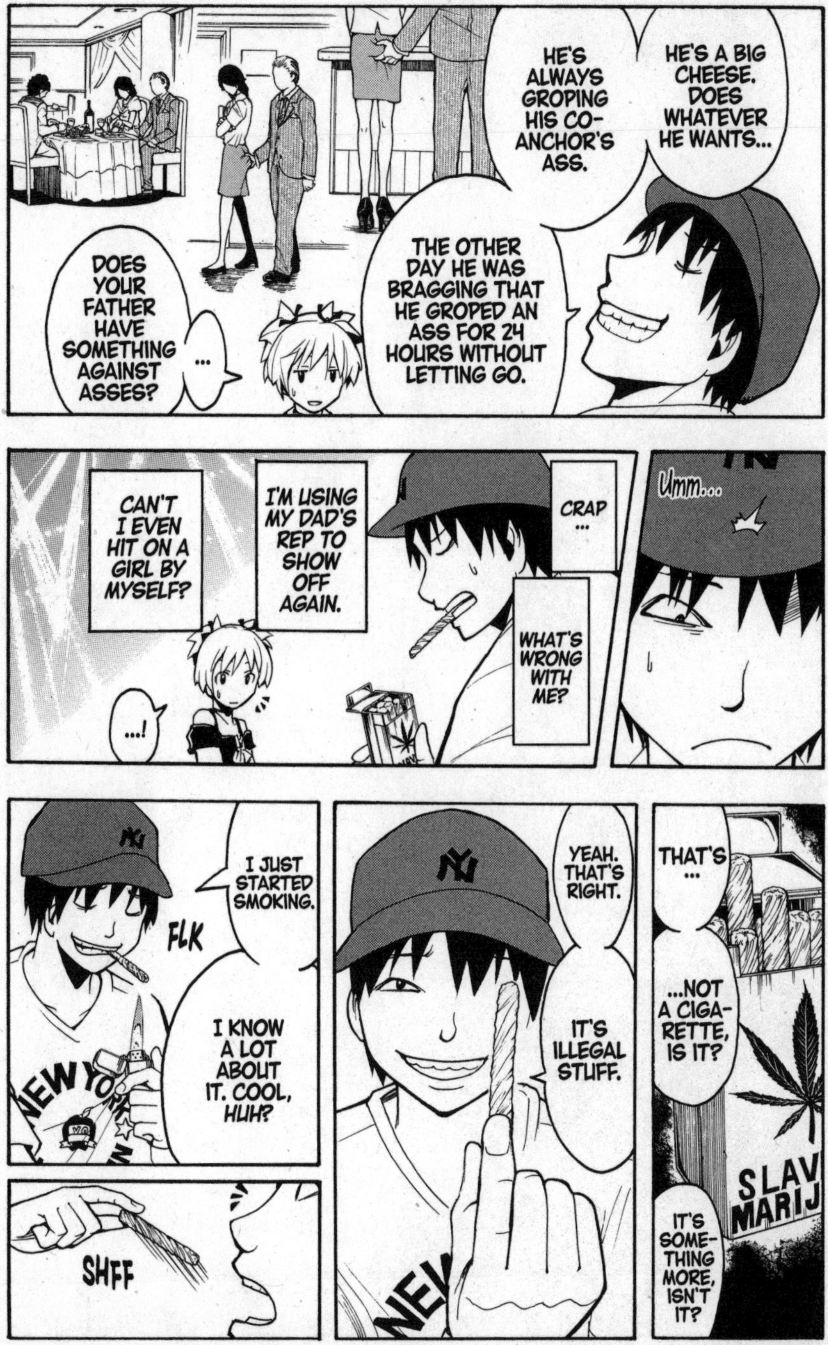
HE'S A BIG CHEESE. DOES WHATEVER HE WANTS...
HE'S ALWAYS GROPING HIS CO-ANCHOR'S ASS.
THE OTHER DAY HE WAS BRAGGING THAT HE GROPED AN ASS FOR 24 HOURS WITHOUT LETTING GO.
...
DOES YOUR FATHER HAVE SOMETHING AGAINST ASSES?
Umm...
CRAP...
WHAT'S WRONG WITH ME?
I'M USING MY DAD'S REP TO SHOW OFF AGAIN.
CAN'T I EVEN HIT ON A GIRL BY MYSELF?
...!
THAT'S...
...NOT A CIGARETTE, IS IT?
SLAV
MARIJ
IT'S SOMETHING MORE, ISN'T IT?
YEAH. THAT'S RIGHT.
IT'S ILLEGAL STUFF.
I JUST STARTED SMOKING.
FLK
NEW YORK
I KNOW A LOT ABOUT IT. COOL, HUH?
SHFF

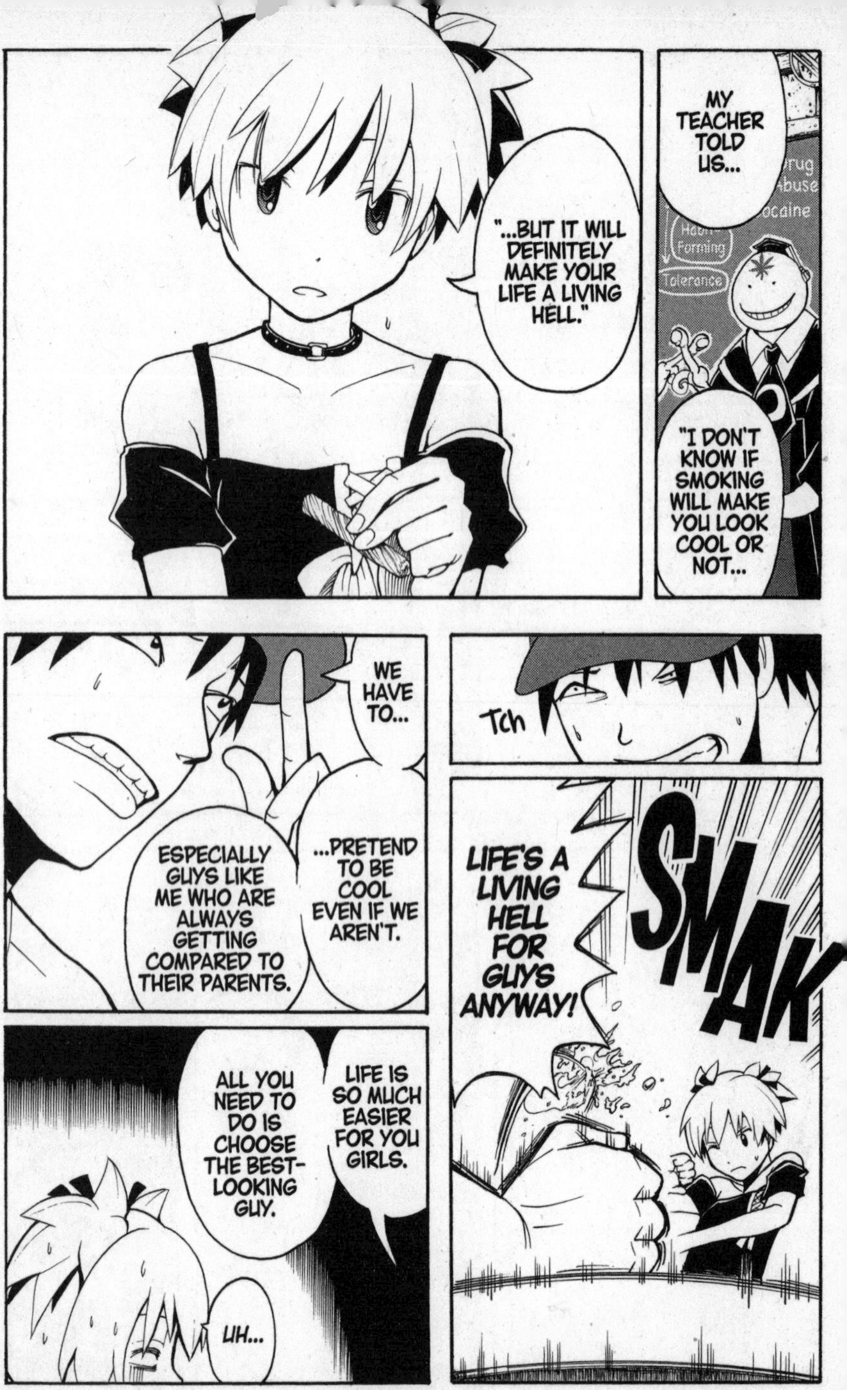
MY TEACHER TOLD US...
Tolerance
"I DON'T KNOW IF SMOKING WILL MAKE YOU LOOK COOL OR NOT...
"...BUT IT WILL DEFINITELY MAKE YOUR LIFE A LIVING HELL."
Tch
WE HAVE TO...
...PRETEND TO BE COOL EVEN IF WE AREN'T.
ESPECIALLY GUYS LIKE ME WHO ARE ALWAYS GETTING COMPARED TO THEIR PARENTS.
LIFE IS SO MUCH EASIER FOR YOU GIRLS.
ALL YOU NEED TO DO IS CHOOSE THE BEST-LOOKING GUY.
UH...
LIFE'S A LIVING HELL FOR GUYS ANYWAY!
SMAK

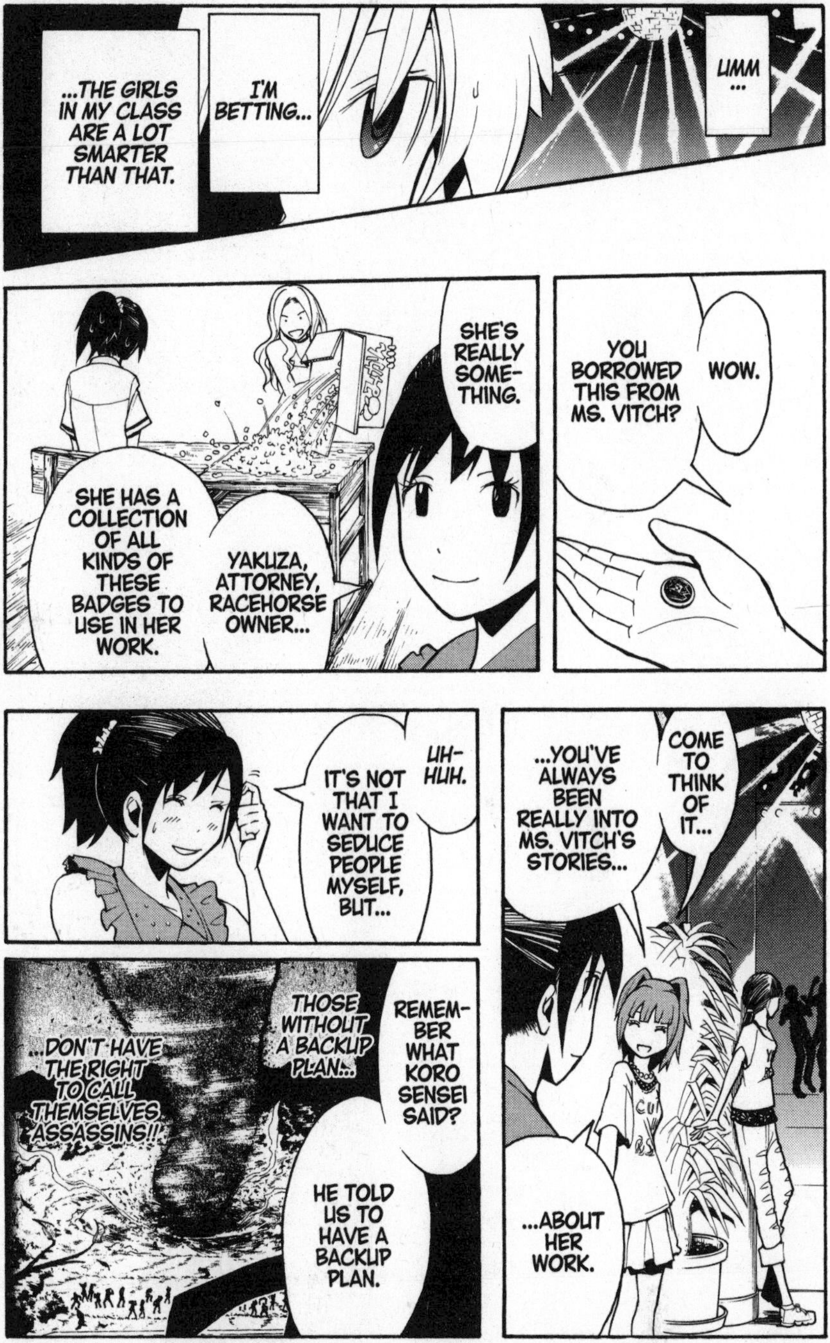
UMM...
I'M BETTING...
...THE GIRLS IN MY CLASS ARE A LOT SMARTER THAN THAT.
WOW.
YOU BORROWED THIS FROM MS. VITCH?
SHE'S REALLY SOME-THING.
YAKUZA, ATTORNEY, RACEHORSE OWNER...
SHE HAS A COLLECTION OF ALL KINDS OF THESE BADGES TO USE IN HER WORK.
COME TO THINK OF IT...
...YOU'VE ALWAYS BEEN REALLY INTO MS. VITCH'S STORIES...
...ABOUT HER WORK.
UH-HUH.
IT'S NOT THAT I WANT TO SEDUCE PEOPLE MYSELF, BUT...
REMEM-BER WHAT KORO SENSEI SAID?
HE TOLD US TO HAVE A BACKUP PLAN.
THOSE WITHOUT A BACKUP PLAN...
...DON'T HAVE THE RIGHT TO CALL THEMSELVES ASSASSINS!!

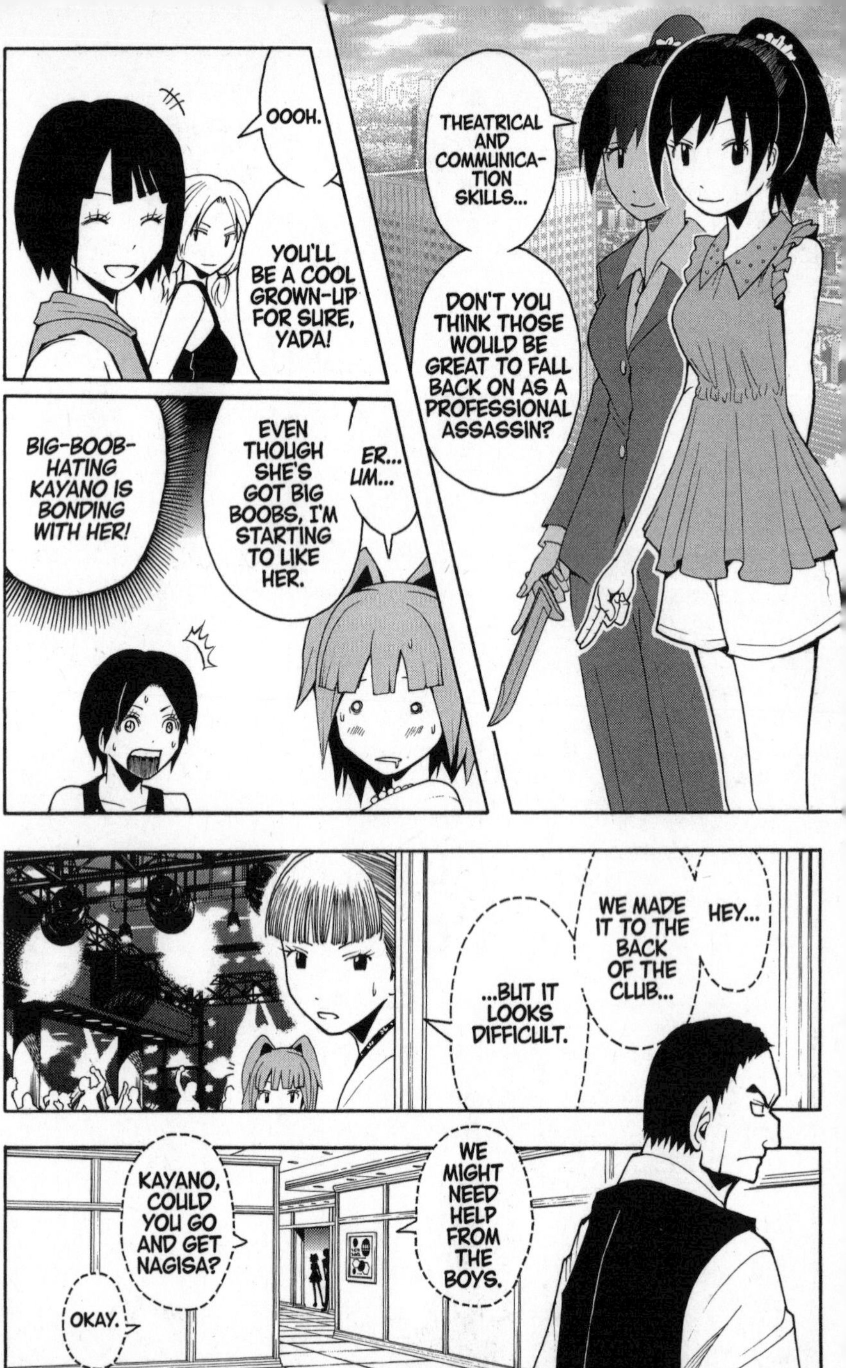
THEATRICAL AND COMMUNICATION SKILLS...
DON'T YOU THINK THOSE WOULD BE GREAT TO FALL BACK ON AS A PROFESSIONAL ASSASSIN?
OOOH.
YOU'LL BE A COOL GROWN-UP FOR SURE, YADA!
ER... UM...
EVEN THOUGH SHE'S GOT BIG BOOBS, I'M STARTING TO LIKE HER.
BIG-BOOB-HATING KAYANO IS BONDING WITH HER!
HEY...
WE MADE IT TO THE BACK OF THE CLUB...
...BUT IT LOOKS DIFFICULT.
WE MIGHT NEED HELP FROM THE BOYS.
KAYANO, COULD YOU GO AND GET NAGISA?
OKAY.

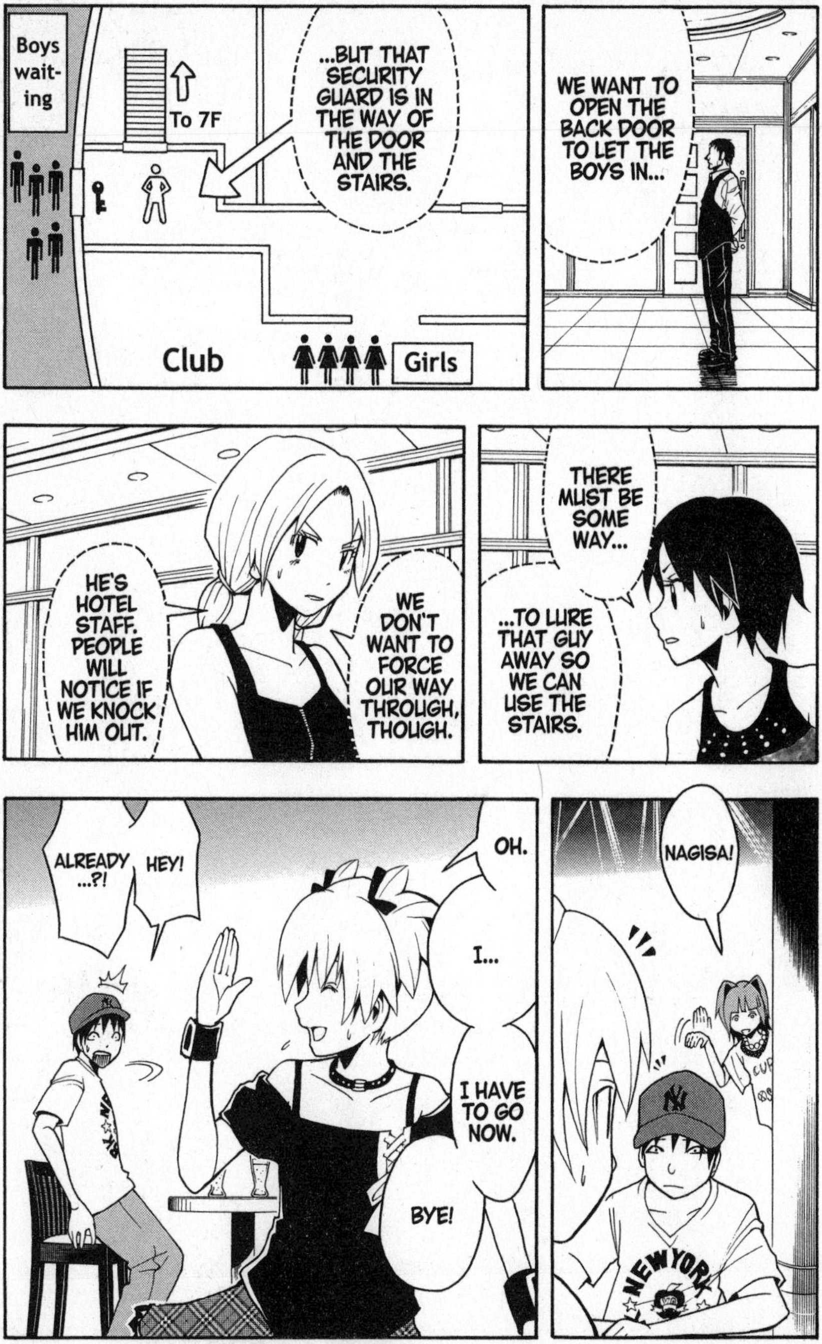
WE WANT TO OPEN THE BACK DOOR TO LET THE BOYS IN...
...BUT THAT SECURITY GUARD IS IN THE WAY OF THE DOOR AND THE STAIRS.
Boys waiting
To 7F
Club
Girls
THERE MUST BE SOME WAY...
...TO LURE THAT GUY AWAY SO WE CAN USE THE STAIRS.
WE DON'T WANT TO FORCE OUR WAY THROUGH, THOUGH.
HE'S HOTEL STAFF. PEOPLE WILL NOTICE IF WE KNOCK HIM OUT.
NAGISA!
OH.
I...
I HAVE TO GO NOW.
BYE!
HEY!
ALREADY ...?!

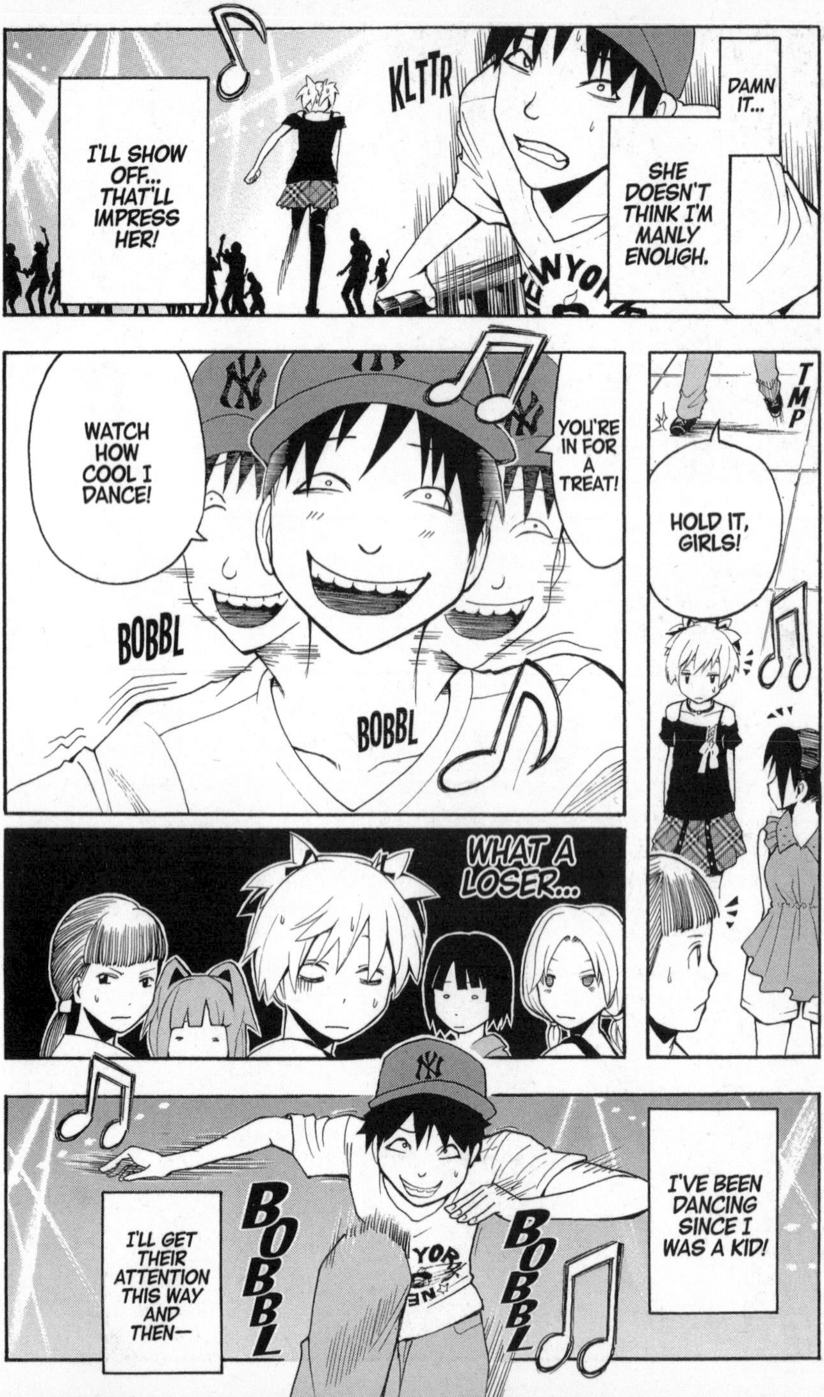
DAMN IT...
SHE DOESN'T THINK I'M MANLY ENOUGH.
KLTTR
I'LL SHOW OFF... THAT'LL IMPRESS HER!
TMP
HOLD IT, GIRLS!
YOU'RE IN FOR A TREAT!
WATCH HOW COOL I DANCE!
BOBBL
BOBBL
WHAT A LOSER...
I'VE BEEN DANCING SINCE I WAS A KID!
BOBBL
BOBBL
I'LL GET THEIR ATTENTION THIS WAY AND THEN—

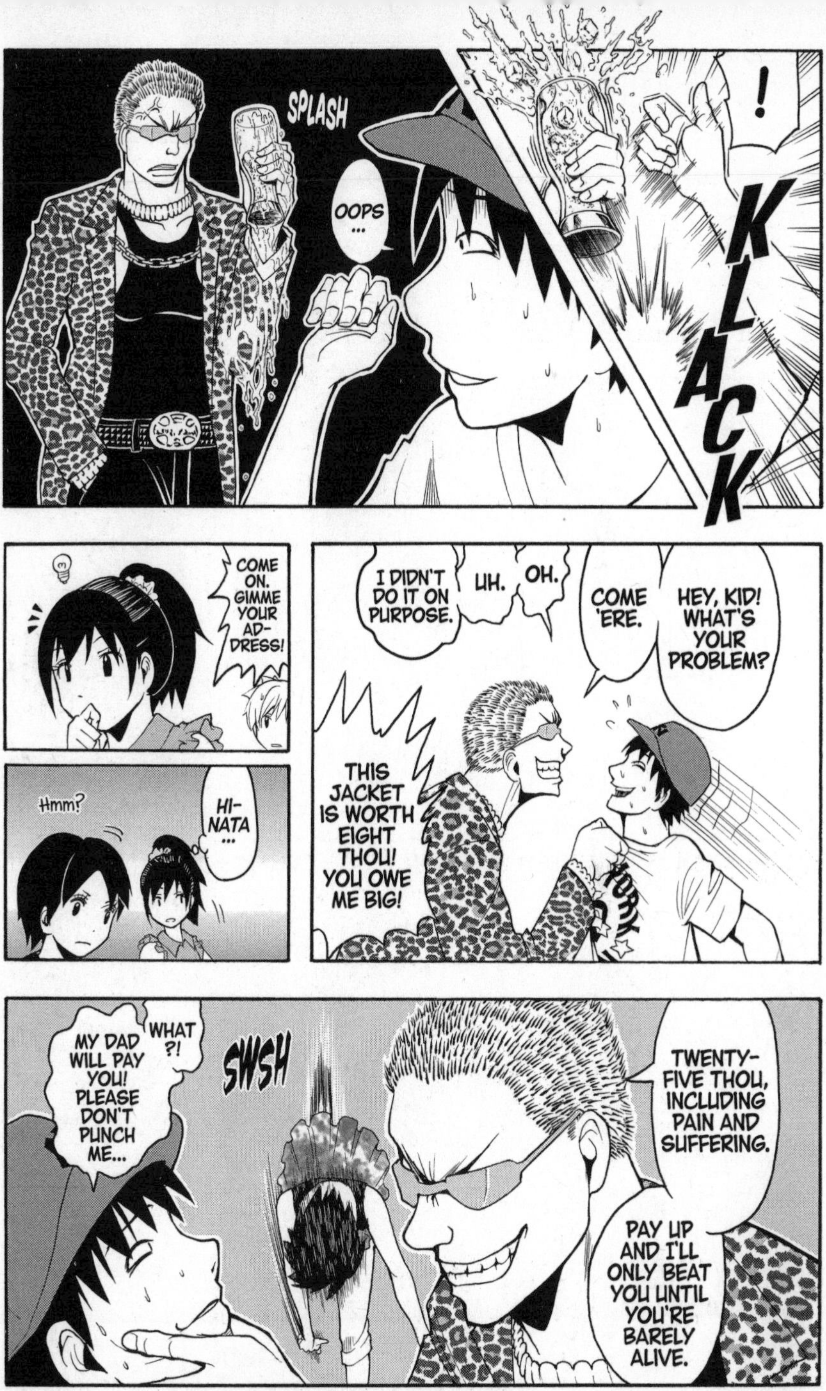
!
KLACK
SPLASH
OOPS ...
HEY, KID! WHAT'S YOUR PROBLEM?
COME 'ERE.
OH.
UH.
I DIDN'T DO IT ON PURPOSE.
THIS JACKET IS WORTH EIGHT THOU! YOU OWE ME BIG!
HURK
COME ON. GIMME YOUR AD-DRESS!
HI-NATA ...
Hmm?
TWENTY-FIVE THOU, INCLUDING PAIN AND SUFFERING.
PAY UP AND I'LL ONLY BEAT YOU UNTIL YOU'RE BARELY ALIVE.
SWSH
WHAT ?!
MY DAD WILL PAY YOU! PLEASE DON'T PUNCH ME...

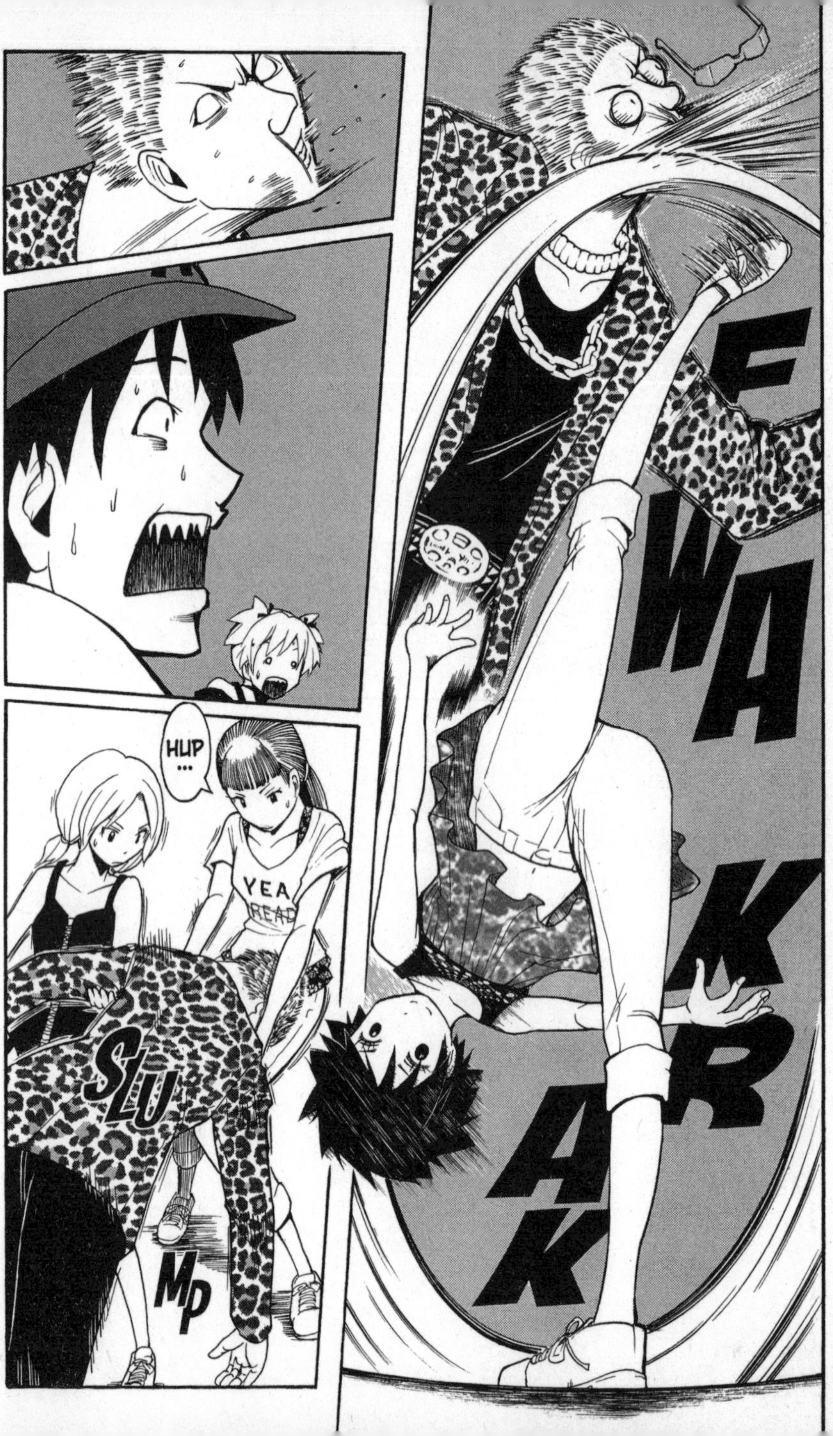
FWAAK KRAAK
HUP ...
SLUMP

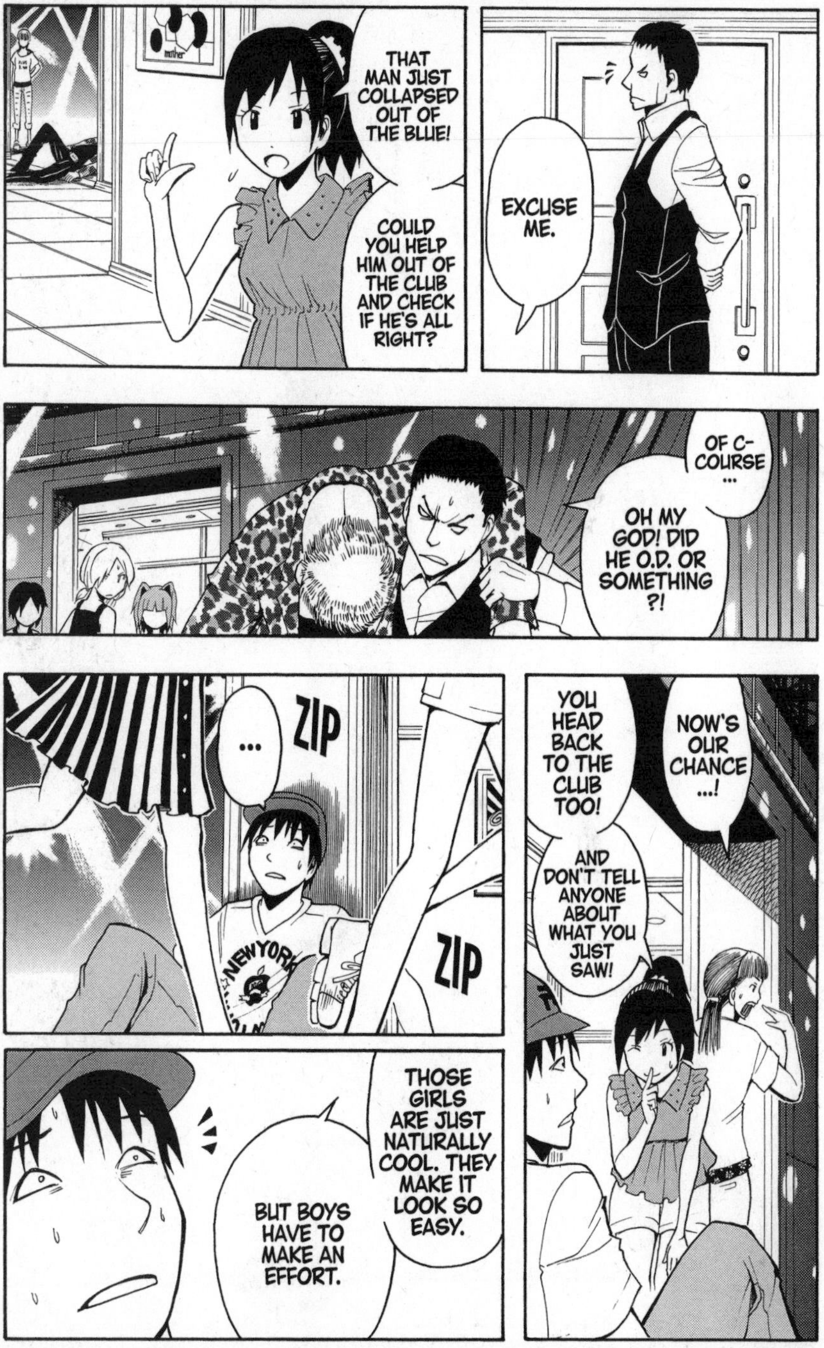
EXCUSE ME.
THAT MAN JUST COLLAPSED OUT OF THE BLUE!
COULD YOU HELP HIM OUT OF THE CLUB AND CHECK IF HE'S ALL RIGHT?
OF C-COURSE ...
OH MY GOD! DID HE O.D. OR SOMETHING?!
NOW'S OUR CHANCE ...!
YOU HEAD BACK TO THE CLUB TOO!
AND DON'T TELL ANYONE ABOUT WHAT YOU JUST SAW!
...
ZIP
ZIP
THOSE GIRLS ARE JUST NATURALLY COOL. THEY MAKE IT LOOK SO EASY.
BUT BOYS HAVE TO MAKE AN EFFORT.

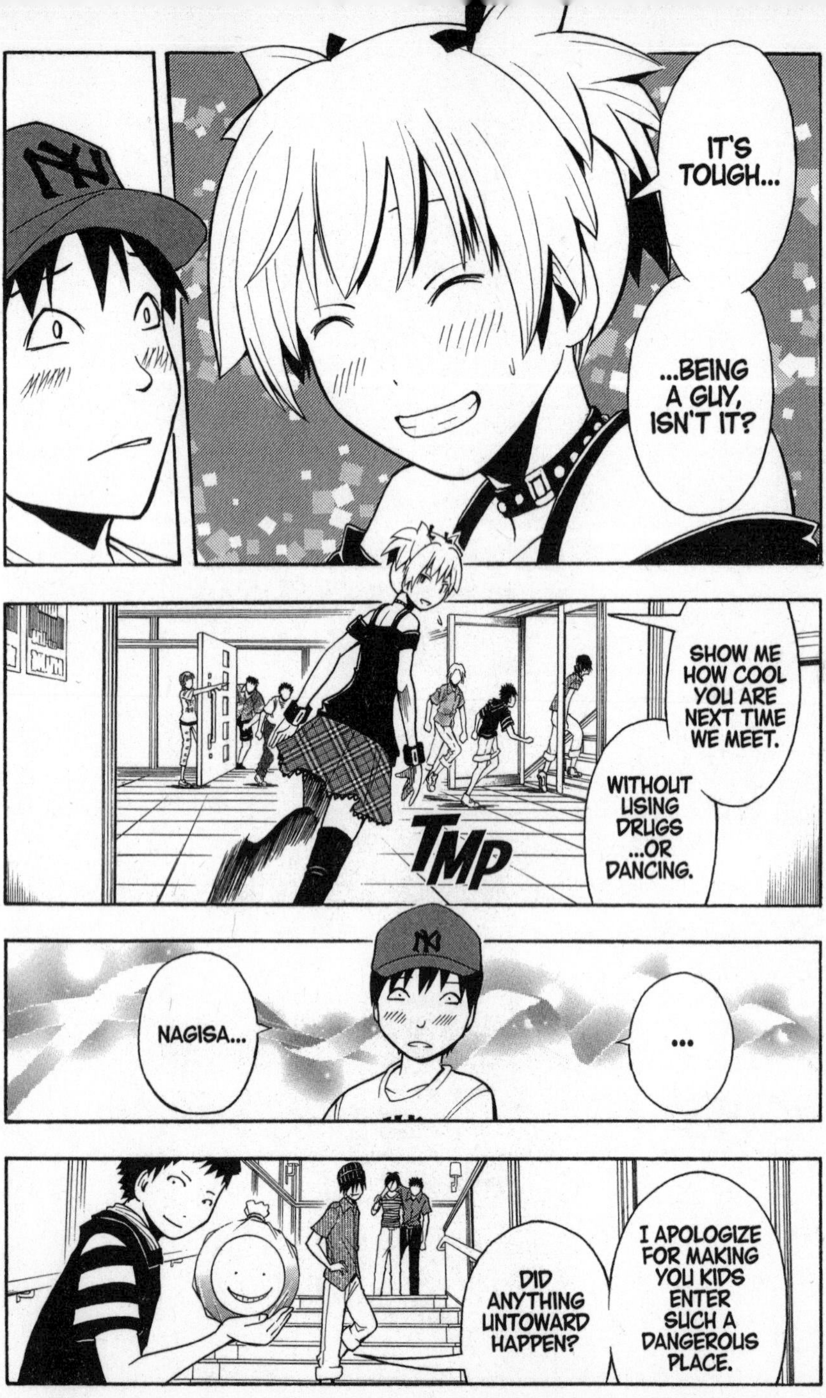
IT'S TOUGH...
...BEING A GUY, ISN'T IT?
SHOW ME HOW COOL YOU ARE NEXT TIME WE MEET.
WITHOUT USING DRUGS ...OR DANCING.
TMP
...
NAGISA...
I APOLOGIZE FOR MAKING YOU KIDS ENTER SUCH A DANGEROUS PLACE.
DID ANYTHING UNTOWARD HAPPEN?

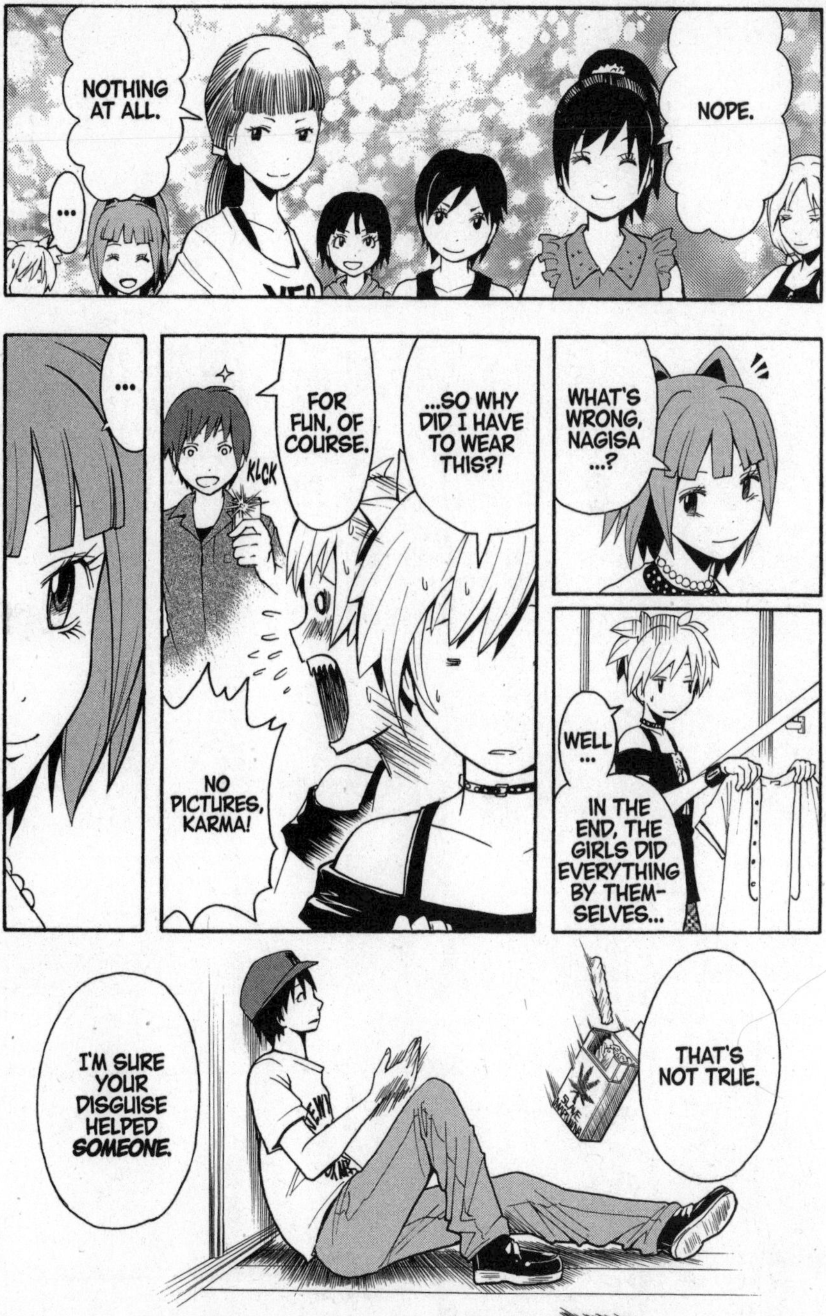
NOPE.
NOTHING AT ALL.
...
WHAT'S WRONG, NAGISA ...?
WELL ...
IN THE END, THE GIRLS DID EVERYTHING BY THEM-SELVES...
...SO WHY DID I HAVE TO WEAR THIS?!
FOR FUN, OF COURSE.
KLCK
NO PICTURES, KARMA!
...
THAT'S NOT TRUE.
I'M SURE YOUR DISGUISE HELPED SOMEONE.

Illegal Drugs

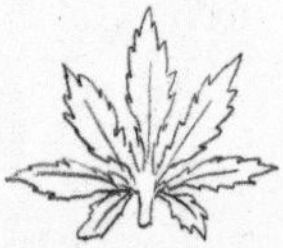

This is a manga, so the characters can easily quit. But you can't stop using that easily in real life. The risks of doing drugs aren't funny, so avoid them at all costs.

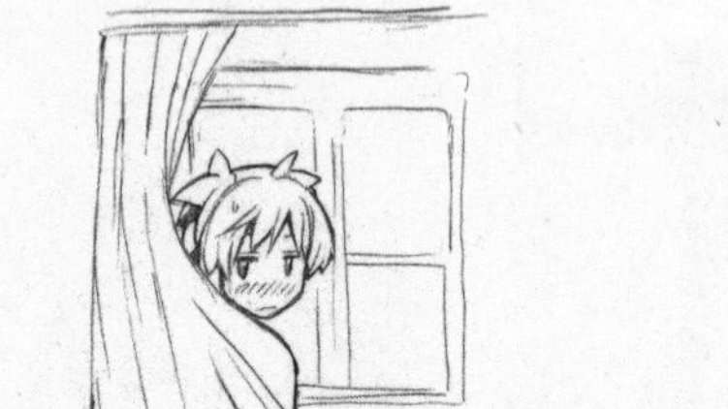
No. Never.

Class 67 Time for Weapons

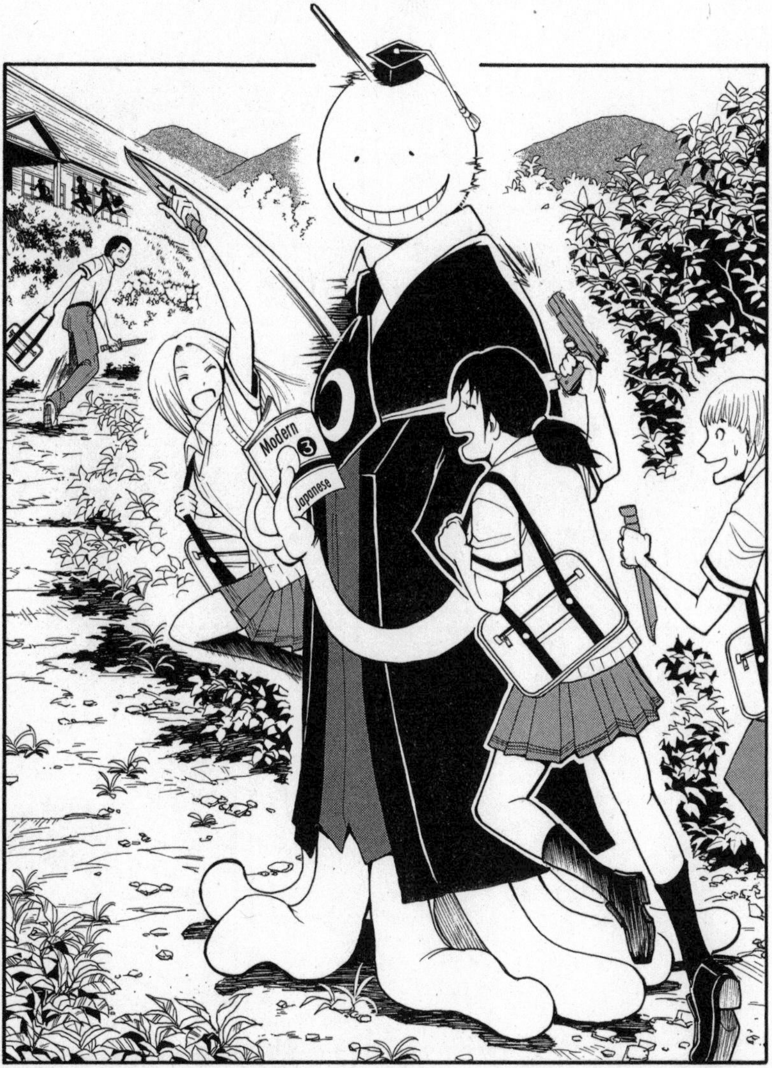
Modern
3
Japanese

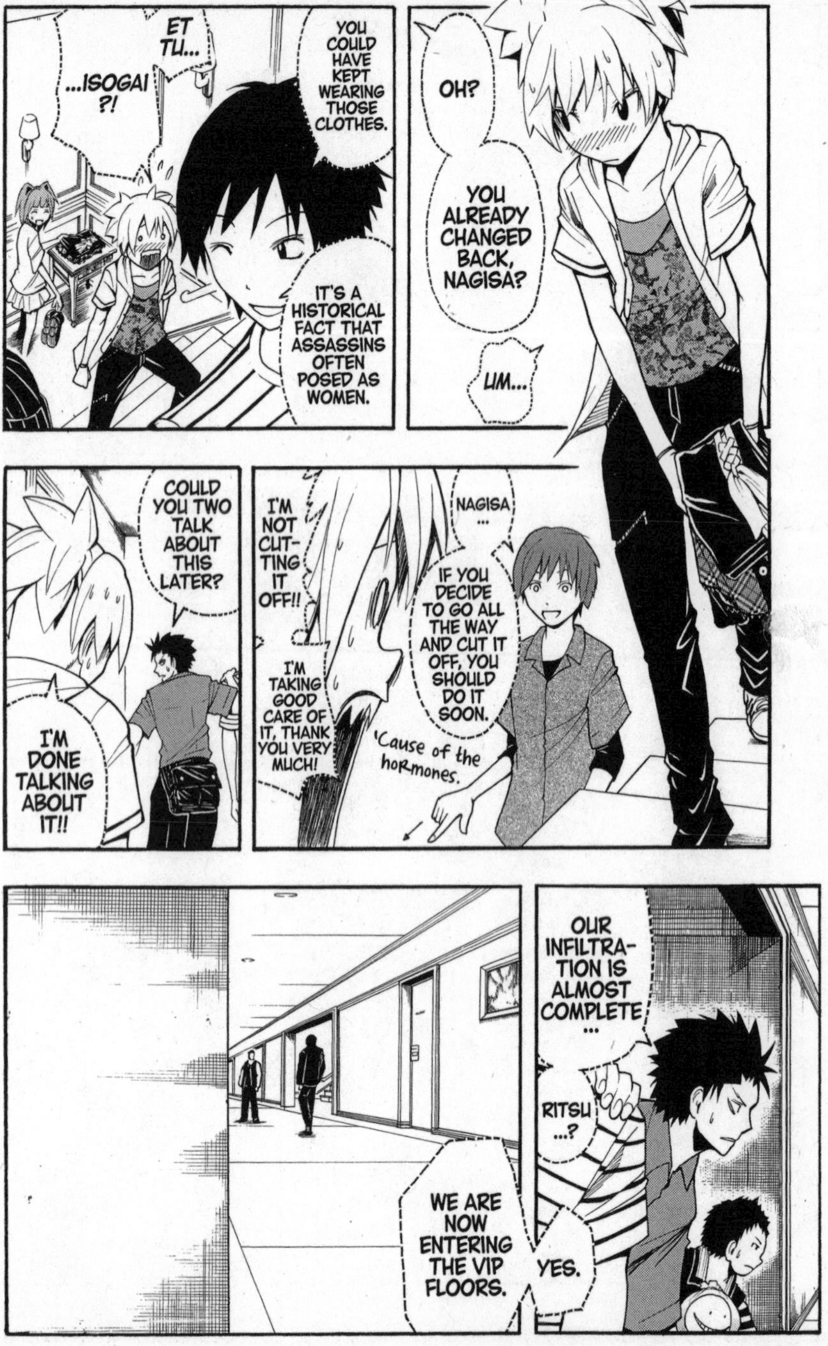
OH?
YOU ALREADY CHANGED BACK, NAGISA?
UM...
YOU COULD HAVE KEPT WEARING THOSE CLOTHES.
ET TU...
...ISOGAI ?!
IT'S A HISTORICAL FACT THAT ASSASSINS OFTEN POSED AS WOMEN.
NAGISA ...
IF YOU DECIDE TO GO ALL THE WAY AND CUT IT OFF, YOU SHOULD DO IT SOON.
'Cause of the hormones.
I'M NOT CUT-TING IT OFF!!
I'M TAKING GOOD CARE OF IT, THANK YOU VERY MUCH!
COULD YOU TWO TALK ABOUT THIS LATER?
I'M DONE TALKING ABOUT IT!!
OUR INFILTRA-TION IS ALMOST COMPLETE ...
RITSU ...?
YES.
WE ARE NOW ENTERING THE VIP FLOORS.

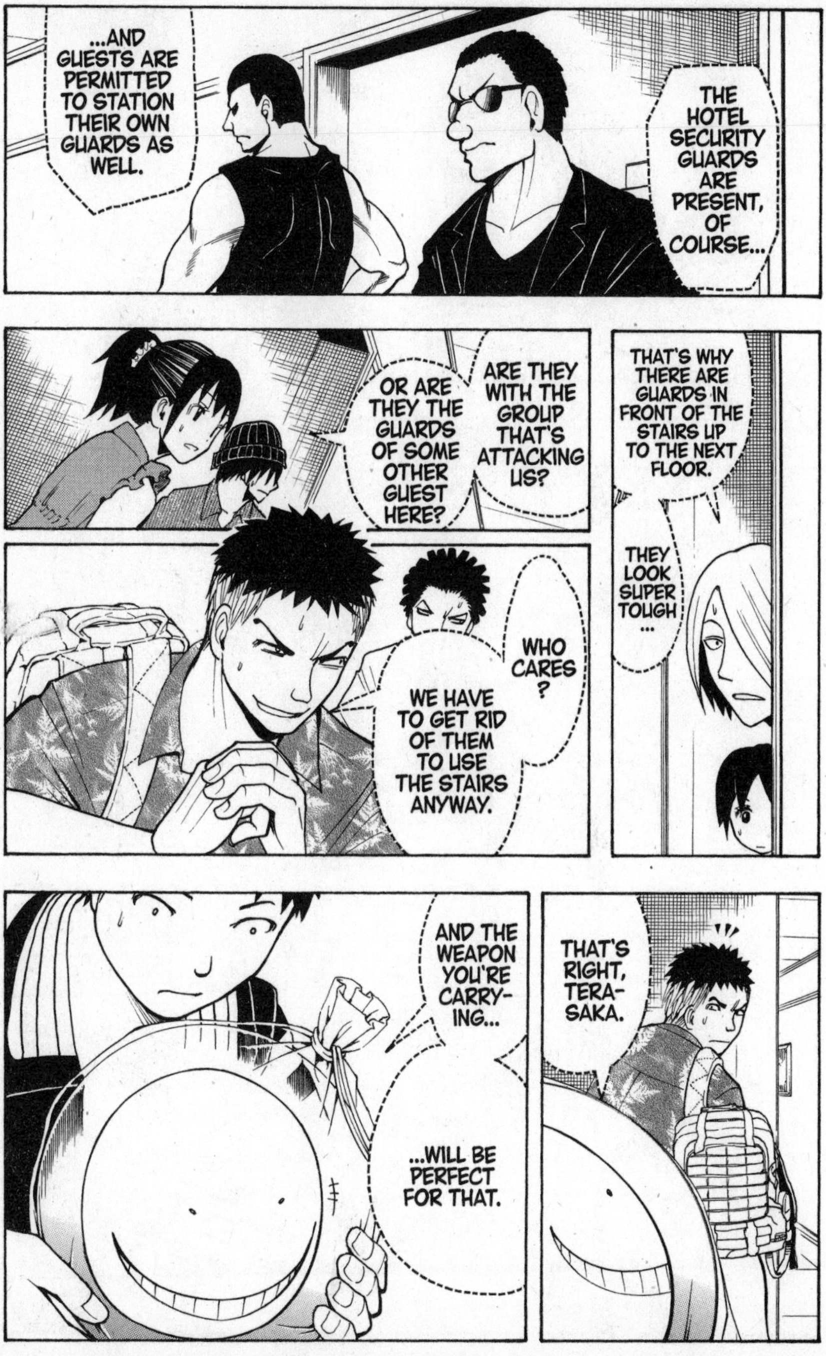
THE HOTEL SECURITY GUARDS ARE PRESENT, OF COURSE...
...AND GUESTS ARE PERMITTED TO STATION THEIR OWN GUARDS AS WELL.
THAT'S WHY THERE ARE GUARDS IN FRONT OF THE STAIRS UP TO THE NEXT FLOOR.
THEY LOOK SUPER TOUGH...
ARE THEY WITH THE GROUP THAT'S ATTACKING US?
OR ARE THEY THE GUARDS OF SOME OTHER GUEST HERE?
WHO CARES?
WE HAVE TO GET RID OF THEM TO USE THE STAIRS ANYWAY.
THAT'S RIGHT, TERA-SAKA.
AND THE WEAPON YOU'RE CARRY-ING...
...WILL BE PERFECT FOR THAT.

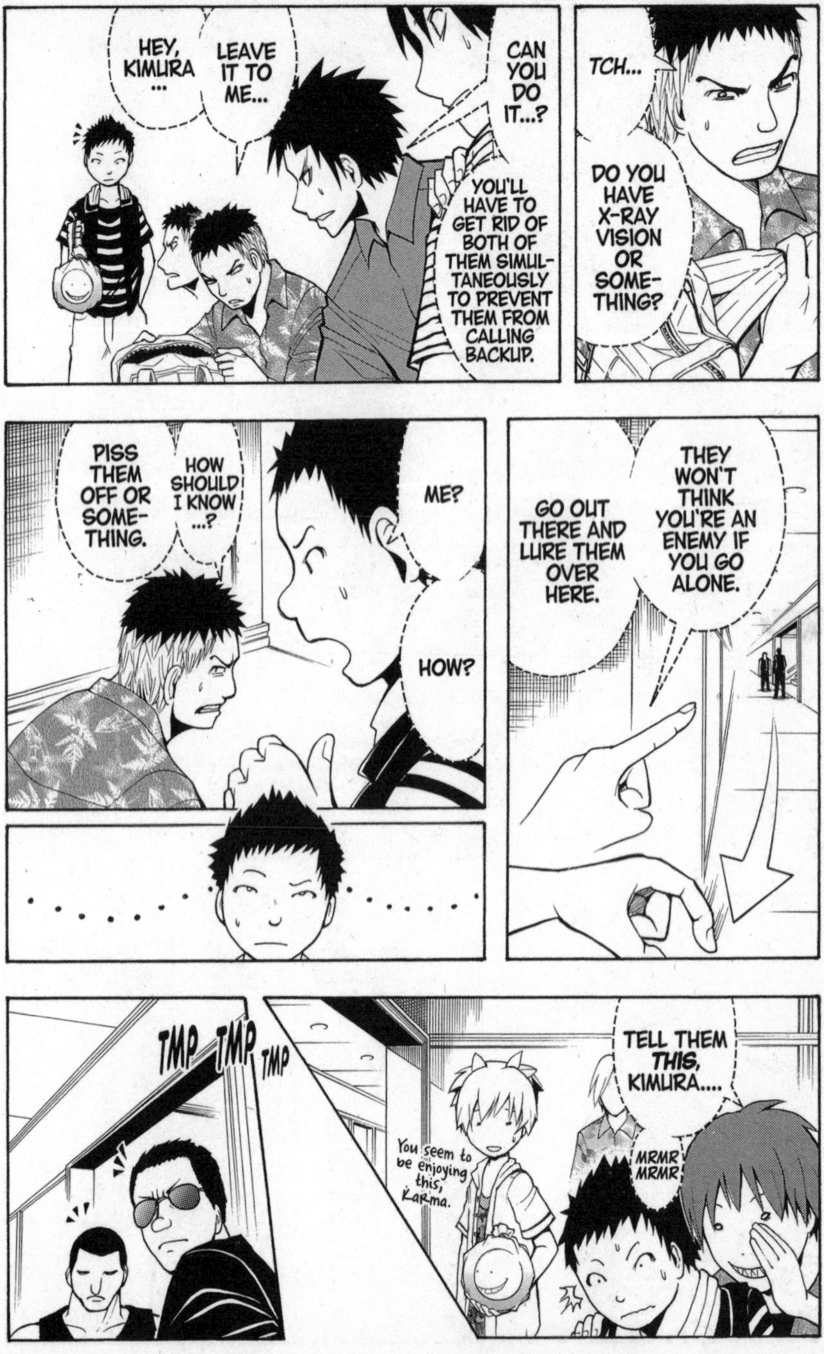
TCH...
DO YOU HAVE X-RAY VISION OR SOME-THING?
CAN YOU DO IT...?
YOU'LL HAVE TO GET RID OF BOTH OF THEM SIMUL-TANEOUSLY TO PREVENT THEM FROM CALLING BACKUP.
LEAVE IT TO ME...
HEY, KIMURA ...
THEY WON'T THINK YOU'RE AN ENEMY IF YOU GO ALONE.
GO OUT THERE AND LURE THEM OVER HERE.
ME?
HOW?
HOW SHOULD I KNOW ...?
PISS THEM OFF OR SOME-THING.
....
TELL THEM THIS, KIMURA....
MRMR MRMR
You seem to be enjoying this, Karma.
TMP TMP TMP

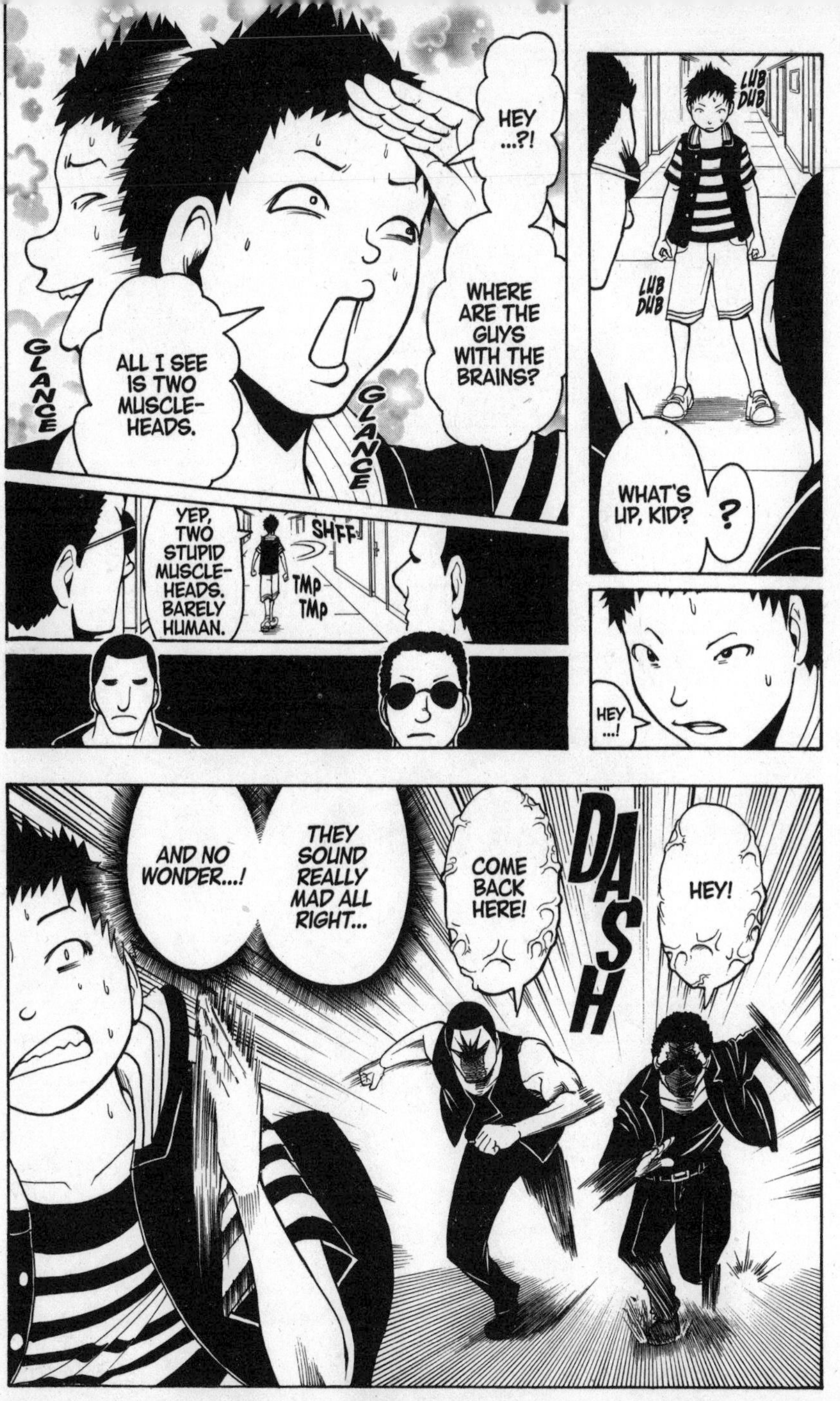
LUB DUB
LUB DUB
WHAT'S UP, KID?
?
HEY ...!
HEY ...?!
WHERE ARE THE GUYS WITH THE BRAINS?
GLANCE
ALL I SEE IS TWO MUSCLE-HEADS.
GLANCE
SHFF
TMP TMP
YEP, TWO STUPID MUSCLE-HEADS. BARELY HUMAN.
HEY!
DASH
COME BACK HERE!
THEY SOUND REALLY MAD ALL RIGHT...
AND NO WONDER...!

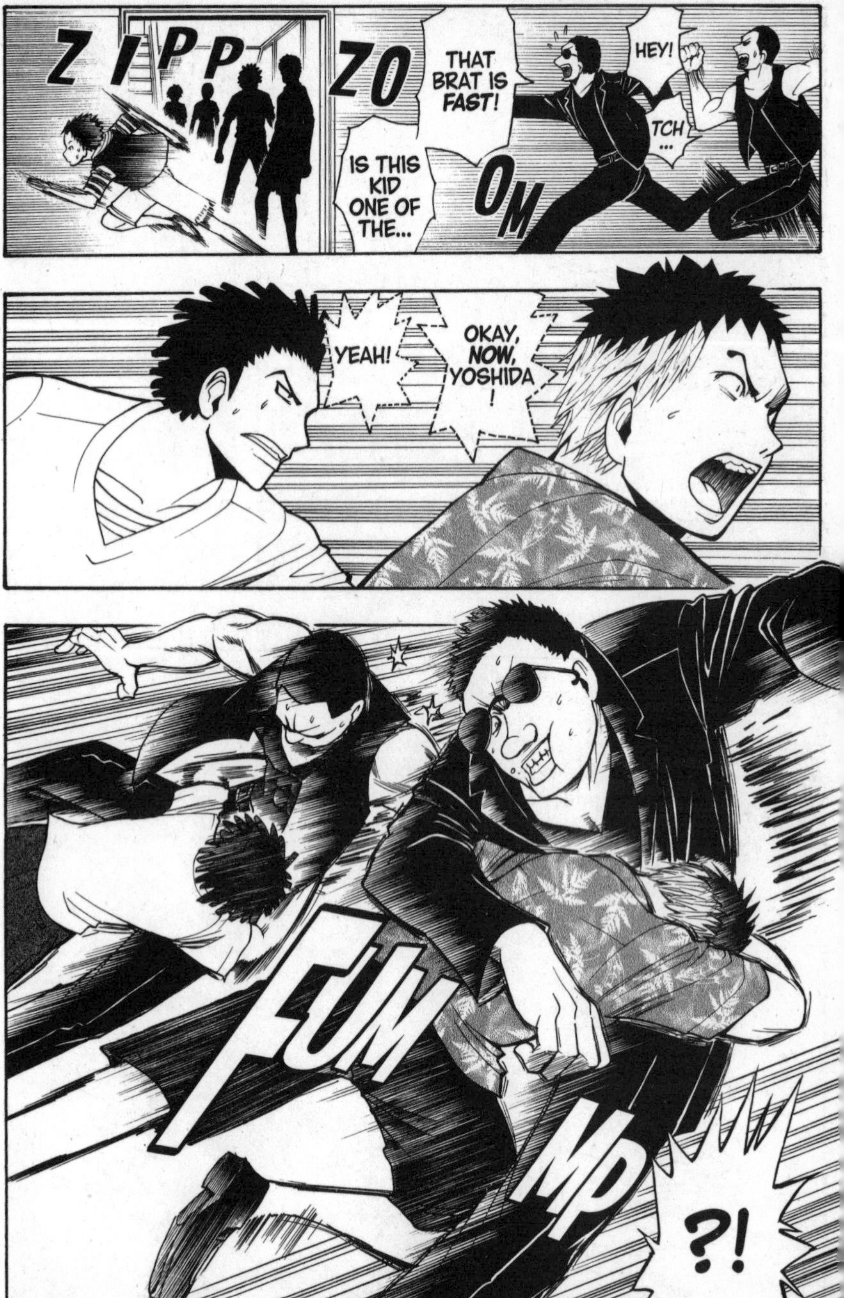
HEY!
TCH...
THAT BRAT IS FAST!
ZO
OM
IS THIS KID ONE OF THE...
ZIPP
OKAY, NOW, YOSHIDA!
YEAH!
?!
FUM
MP

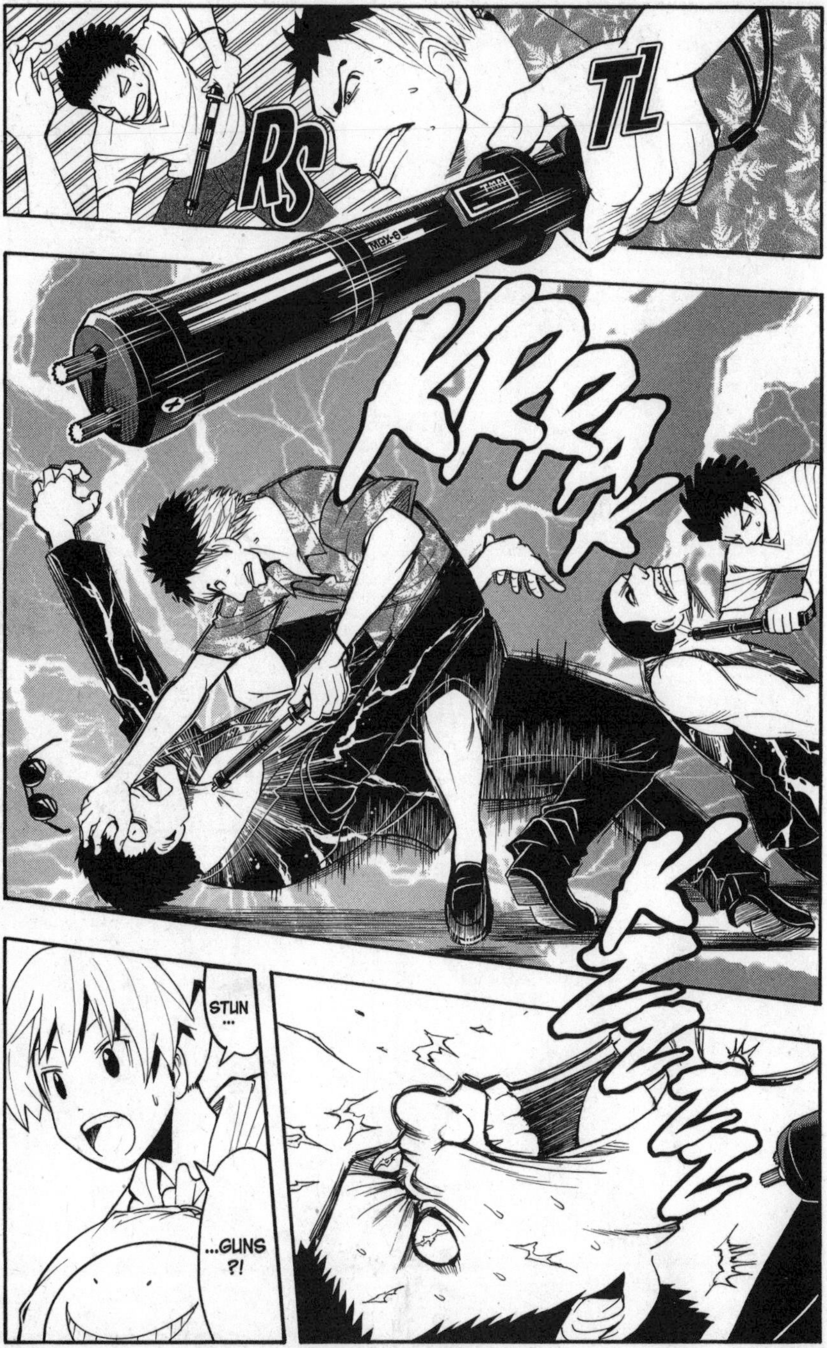
TL
RS
STUN ...
...GUNS ?!

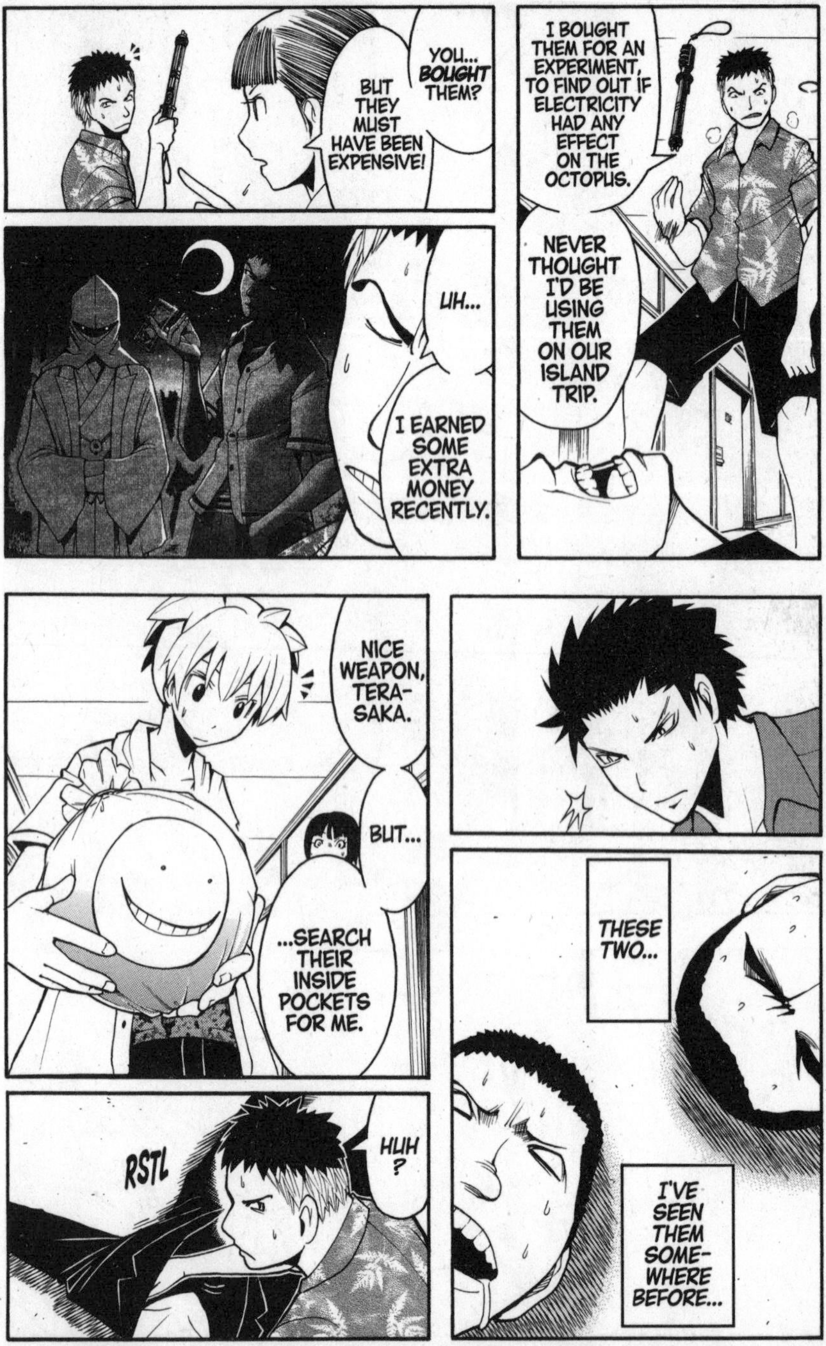
I BOUGHT THEM FOR AN EXPERIMENT, TO FIND OUT IF ELECTRICITY HAD ANY EFFECT ON THE OCTOPUS.
NEVER THOUGHT I'D BE USING THEM ON OUR ISLAND TRIP.
YOU... BOUGHT THEM?
BUT THEY MUST HAVE BEEN EXPENSIVE!
UH...
I EARNED SOME EXTRA MONEY RECENTLY.
NICE WEAPON, TERA-SAKA.
BUT...
...SEARCH THEIR INSIDE POCKETS FOR ME.
HUH?
RSTL
THESE TWO...
I'VE SEEN THEM SOME-WHERE BEFORE...

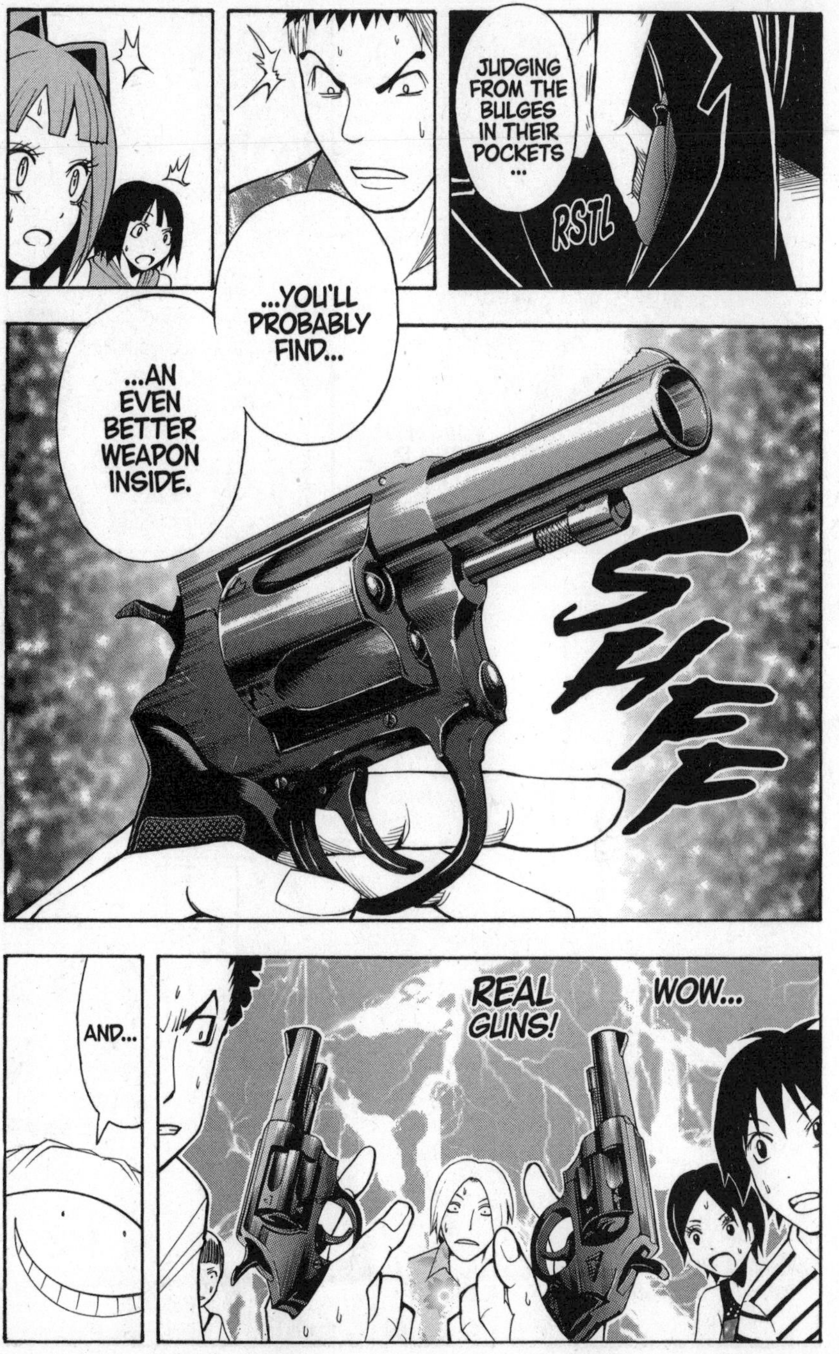
JUDGING FROM THE BULGES IN THEIR POCKETS ...
RSTL
...YOU'LL PROBABLY FIND...
...AN EVEN BETTER WEAPON INSIDE.
SHFF
WOW...
REAL GUNS!
AND...

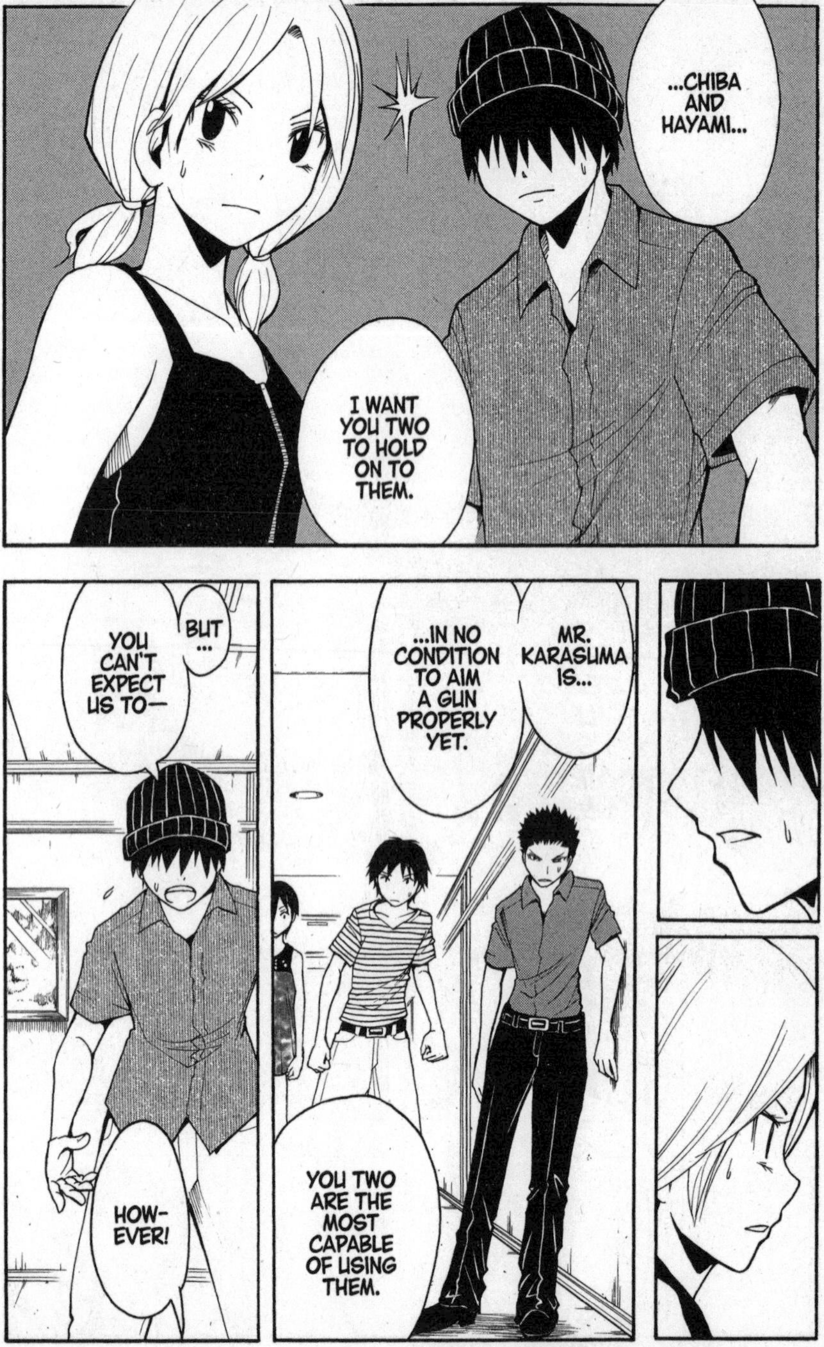
...CHIBA AND HAYAMI...
I WANT YOU TWO TO HOLD ON TO THEM.
MR. KARASUMA IS...
...IN NO CONDITION TO AIM A GUN PROPERLY YET.
YOU TWO ARE THE MOST CAPABLE OF USING THEM.
BUT ...
YOU CAN'T EXPECT US TO—
HOW-EVER!

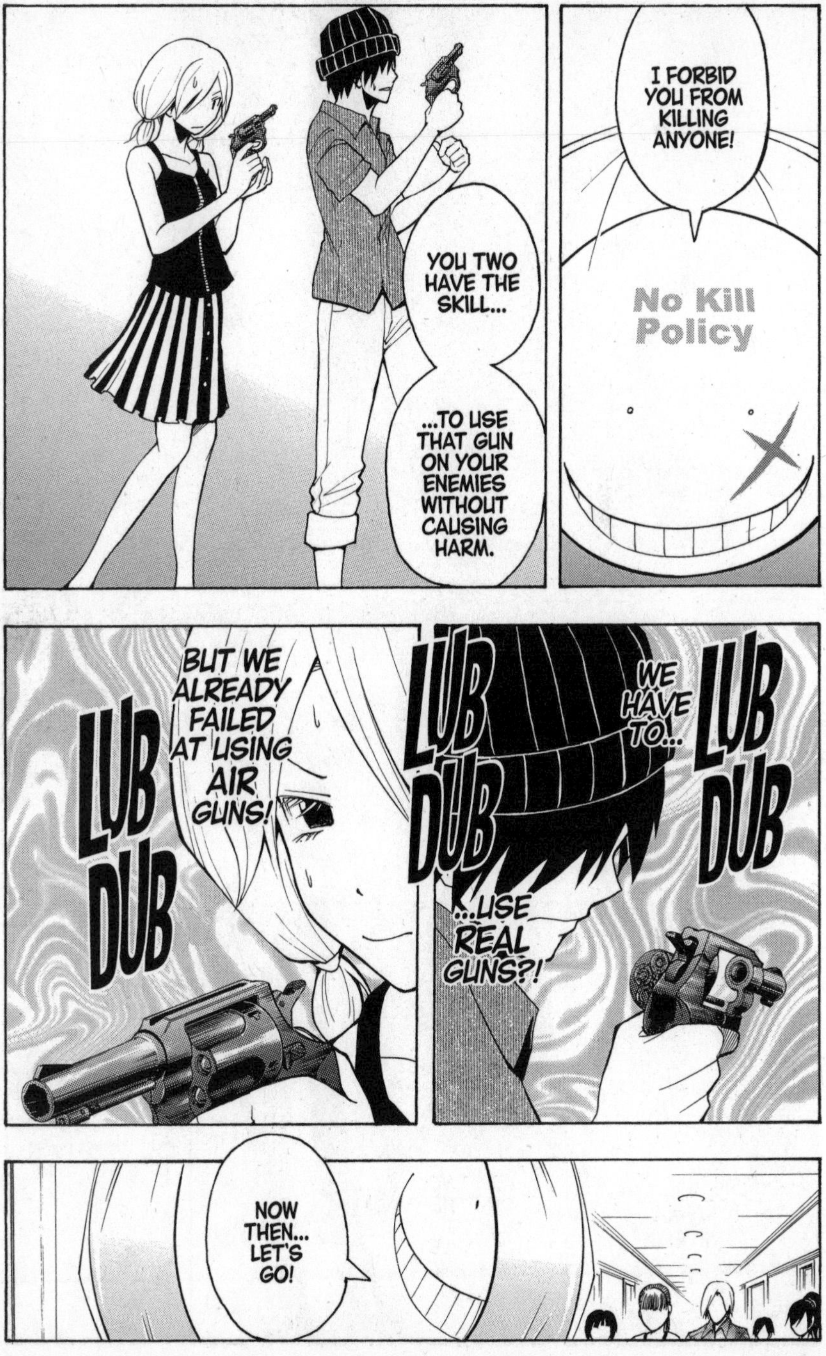
I FORBID YOU FROM KILLING ANYONE!
No Kill Policy
YOU TWO HAVE THE SKILL...
...TO USE THAT GUN ON YOUR ENEMIES WITHOUT CAUSING HARM.
LUB DUB
WE HAVE TO...
LUB DUB
...USE REAL GUNS?!
LUB DUB
BUT WE ALREADY FAILED AT USING AIR GUNS!
NOW THEN... LET'S GO!

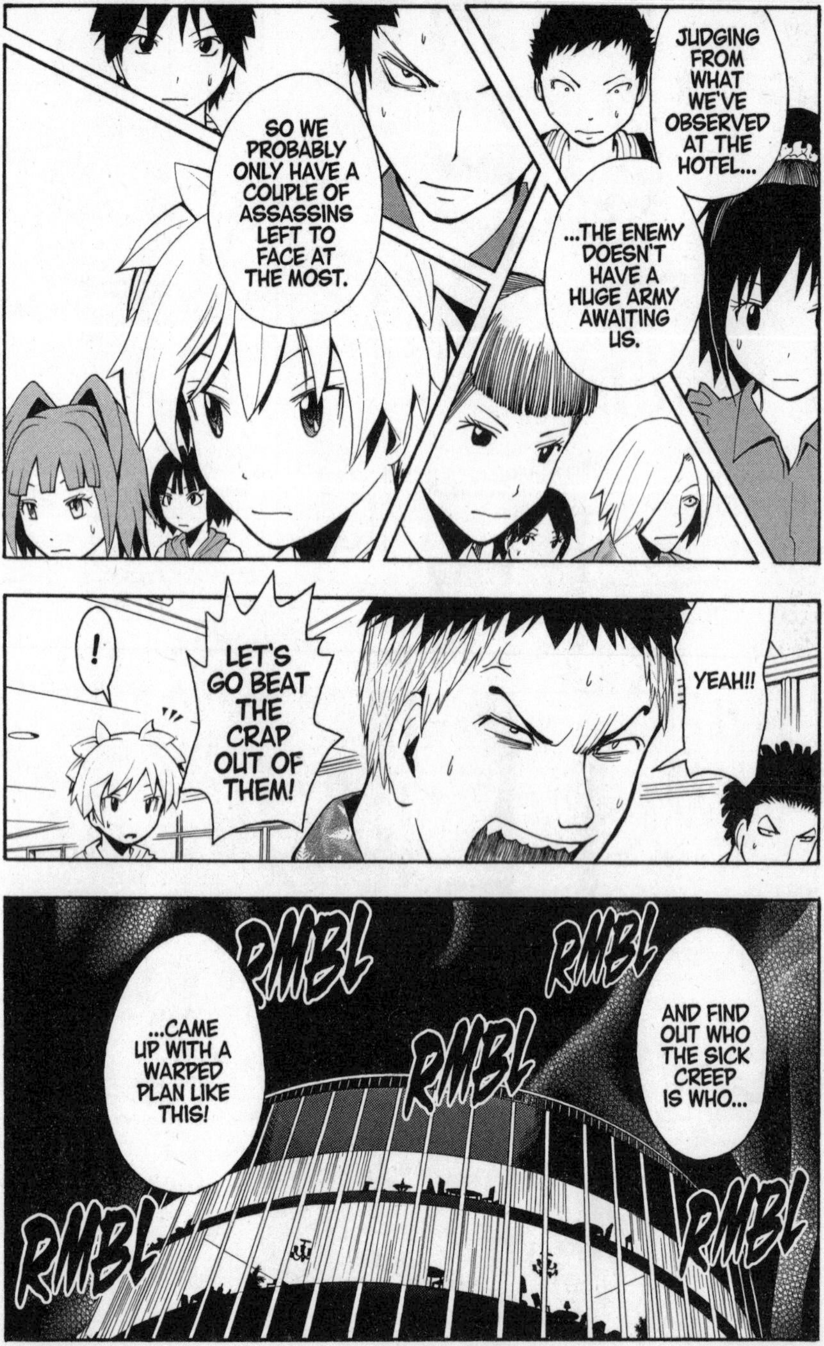
JUDGING FROM WHAT WE'VE OBSERVED AT THE HOTEL...
...THE ENEMY DOESN'T HAVE A HUGE ARMY AWAITING US.
SO WE PROBABLY ONLY HAVE A COUPLE OF ASSASSINS LEFT TO FACE AT THE MOST.
LET'S GO BEAT THE CRAP OUT OF THEM!
YEAH!!
!
RMBL
RMBL
AND FIND OUT WHO THE SICK CREEP IS WHO...
RMBL
...CAME UP WITH A WARPED PLAN LIKE THIS!
RMBL
RMBL

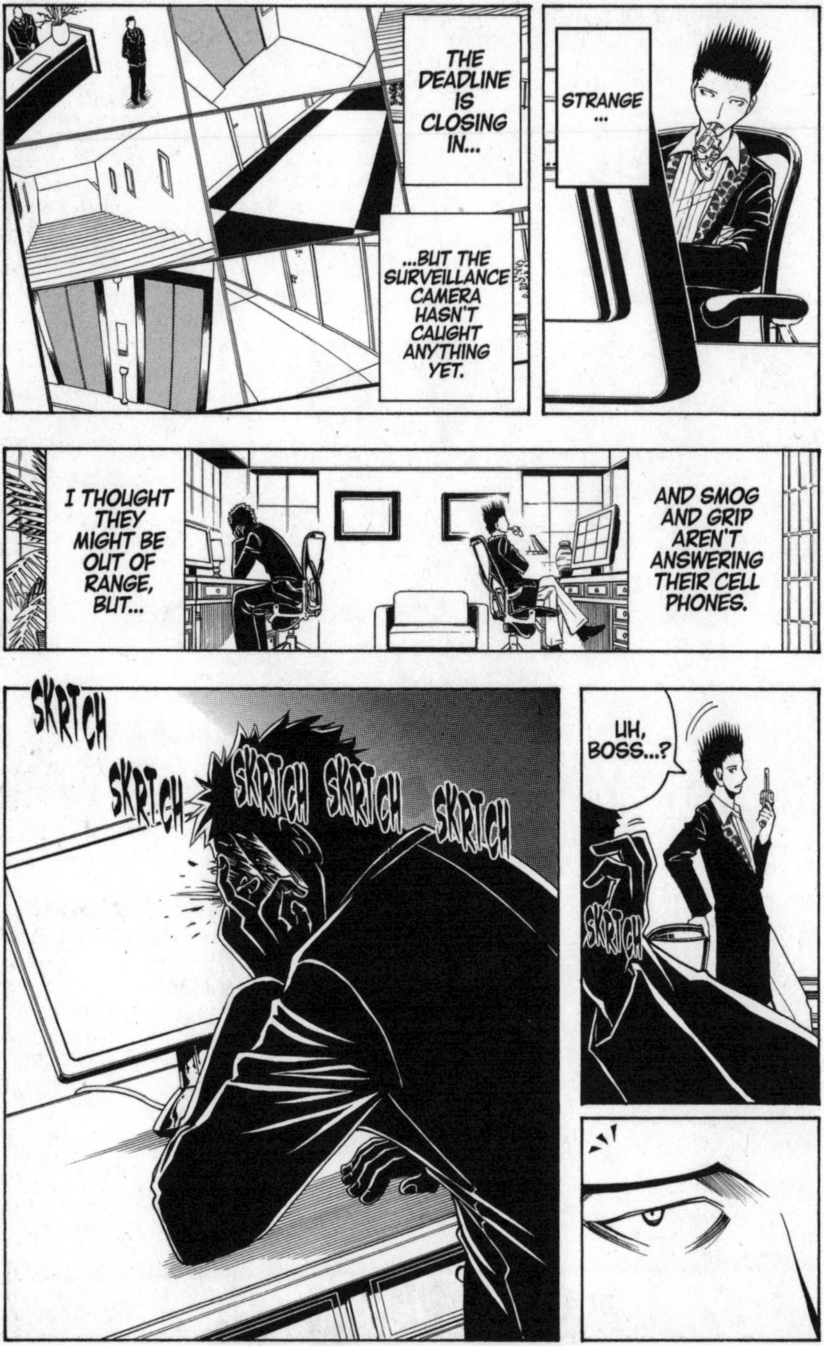
STRANGE...
THE DEADLINE IS CLOSING IN...
...BUT THE SURVEILLANCE CAMERA HASN'T CAUGHT ANYTHING YET.
AND SMOG AND GRIP AREN'T ANSWERING THEIR CELL PHONES.
I THOUGHT THEY MIGHT BE OUT OF RANGE, BUT...
UH, BOSS...?
SKRTCH
SKRTCH
SKRTCH
SKRTCH
SKRTCH
SKRTCH
SKRTCH

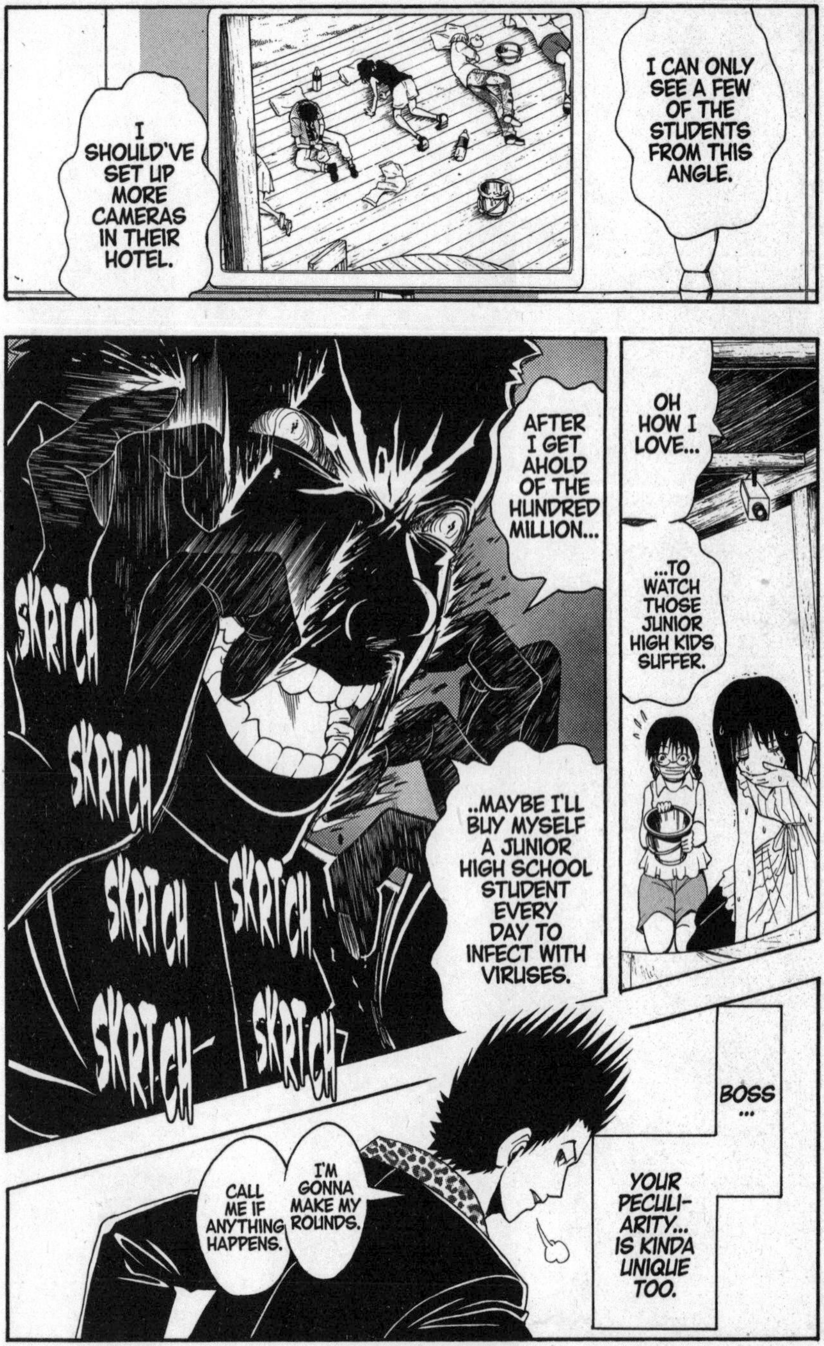
I CAN ONLY SEE A FEW OF THE STUDENTS FROM THIS ANGLE.
I SHOULD'VE SET UP MORE CAMERAS IN THEIR HOTEL.
OH HOW I LOVE...
...TO WATCH THOSE JUNIOR HIGH KIDS SUFFER.
AFTER I GET AHOLD OF THE HUNDRED MILLION...
...MAYBE I'LL BUY MYSELF A JUNIOR HIGH SCHOOL STUDENT EVERY DAY TO INFECT WITH VIRUSES.
SKRTCH
SKRTCH
SKRTCH
SKRTCH
SKRTCH
SKRTCH
BOSS...
YOUR PECULIARITY... IS KINDA UNIQUE TOO.
I'M GONNA MAKE MY ROUNDS.
CALL ME IF ANYTHING HAPPENS.

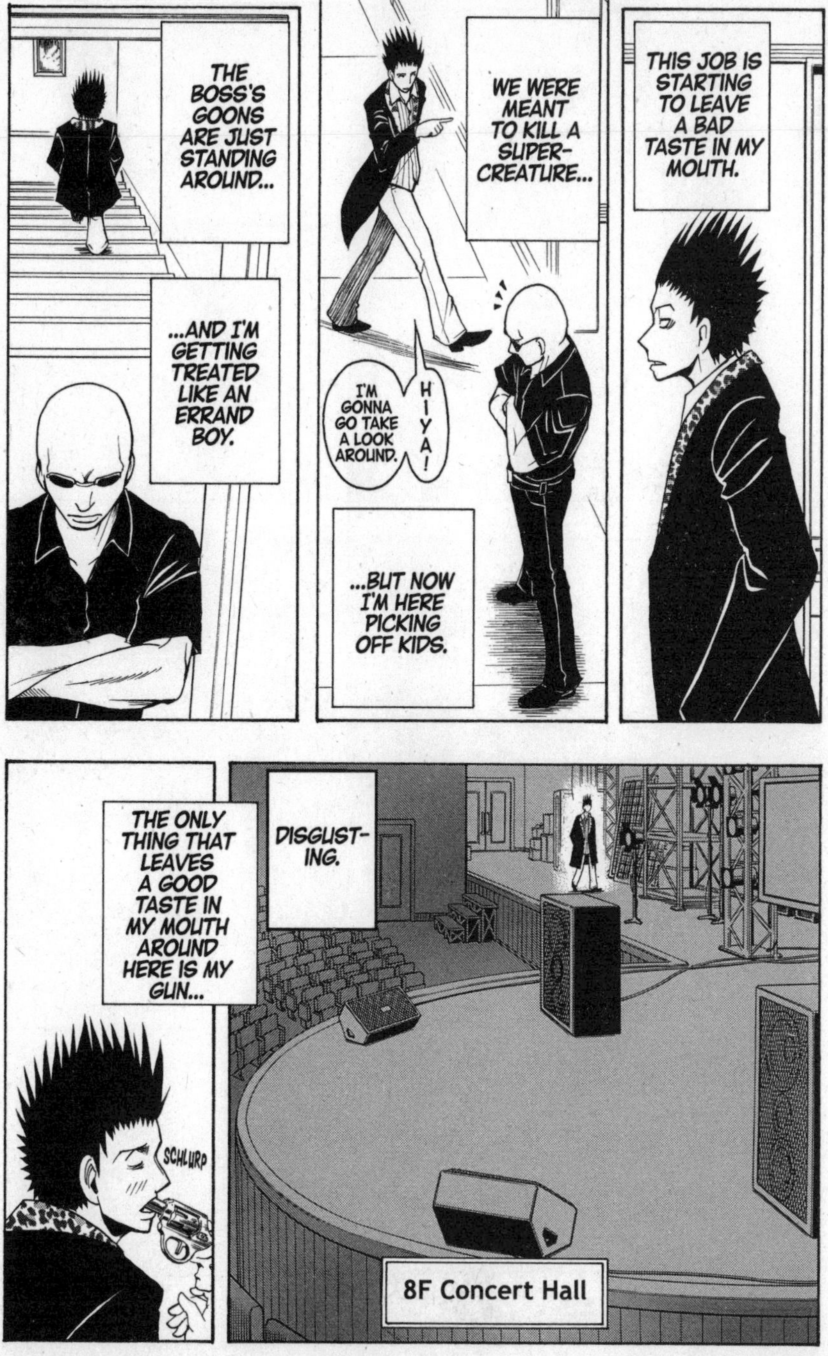
THIS JOB IS STARTING TO LEAVE A BAD TASTE IN MY MOUTH.
WE WERE MEANT TO KILL A SUPER-CREATURE...
HIYA!
I'M GONNA GO TAKE A LOOK AROUND.
...BUT NOW I'M HERE PICKING OFF KIDS.
THE BOSS'S GOONS ARE JUST STANDING AROUND...
...AND I'M GETTING TREATED LIKE AN ERRAND BOY.
DISGUST-ING.
8F Concert Hall
THE ONLY THING THAT LEAVES A GOOD TASTE IN MY MOUTH AROUND HERE IS MY GUN...
SCHLURP

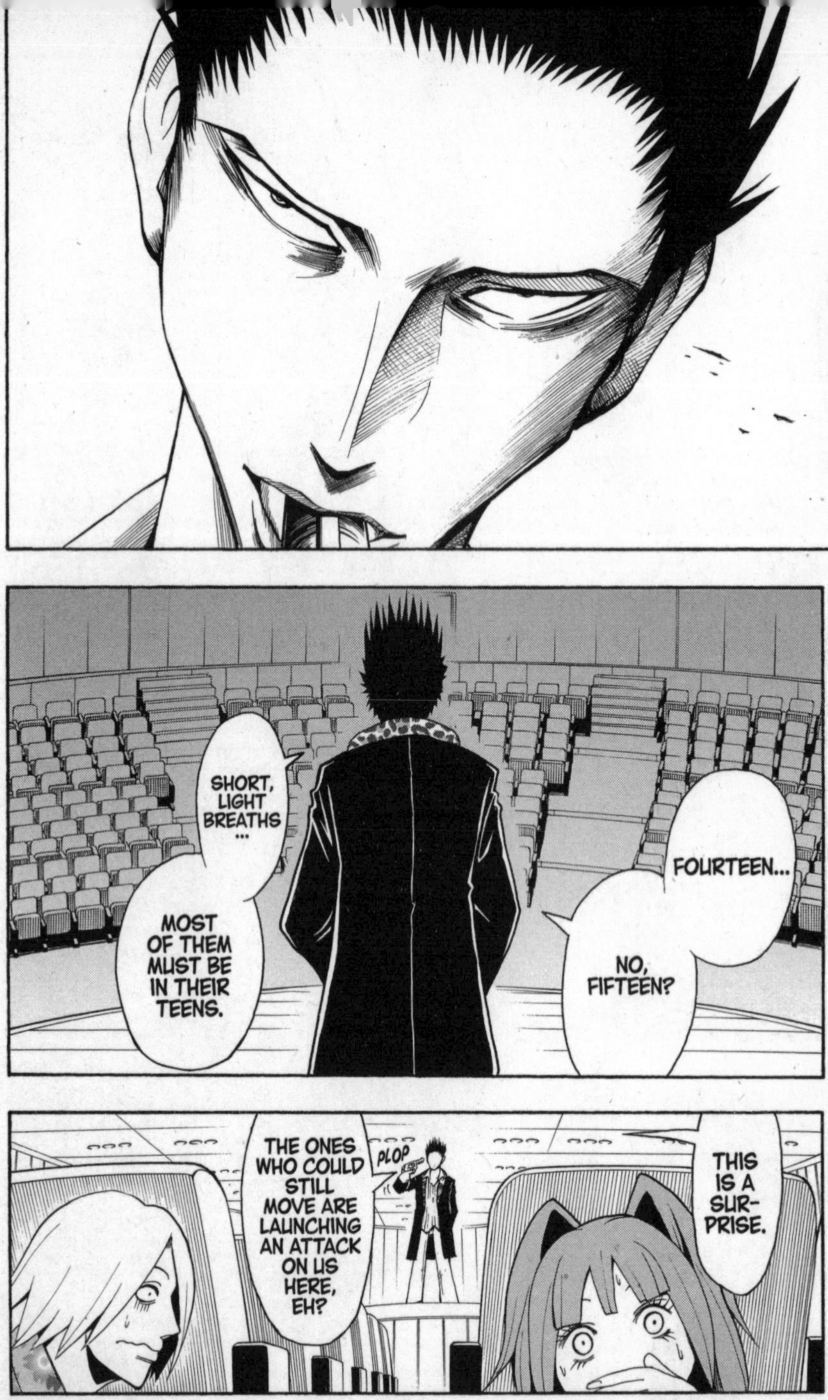
FOURTEEN...
NO, FIFTEEN?
SHORT, LIGHT BREATHS...
MOST OF THEM MUST BE IN THEIR TEENS.
THIS IS A SUR-PRISE.
PLOP
THE ONES WHO COULD STILL MOVE ARE LAUNCHING AN ATTACK ON US HERE, EH?

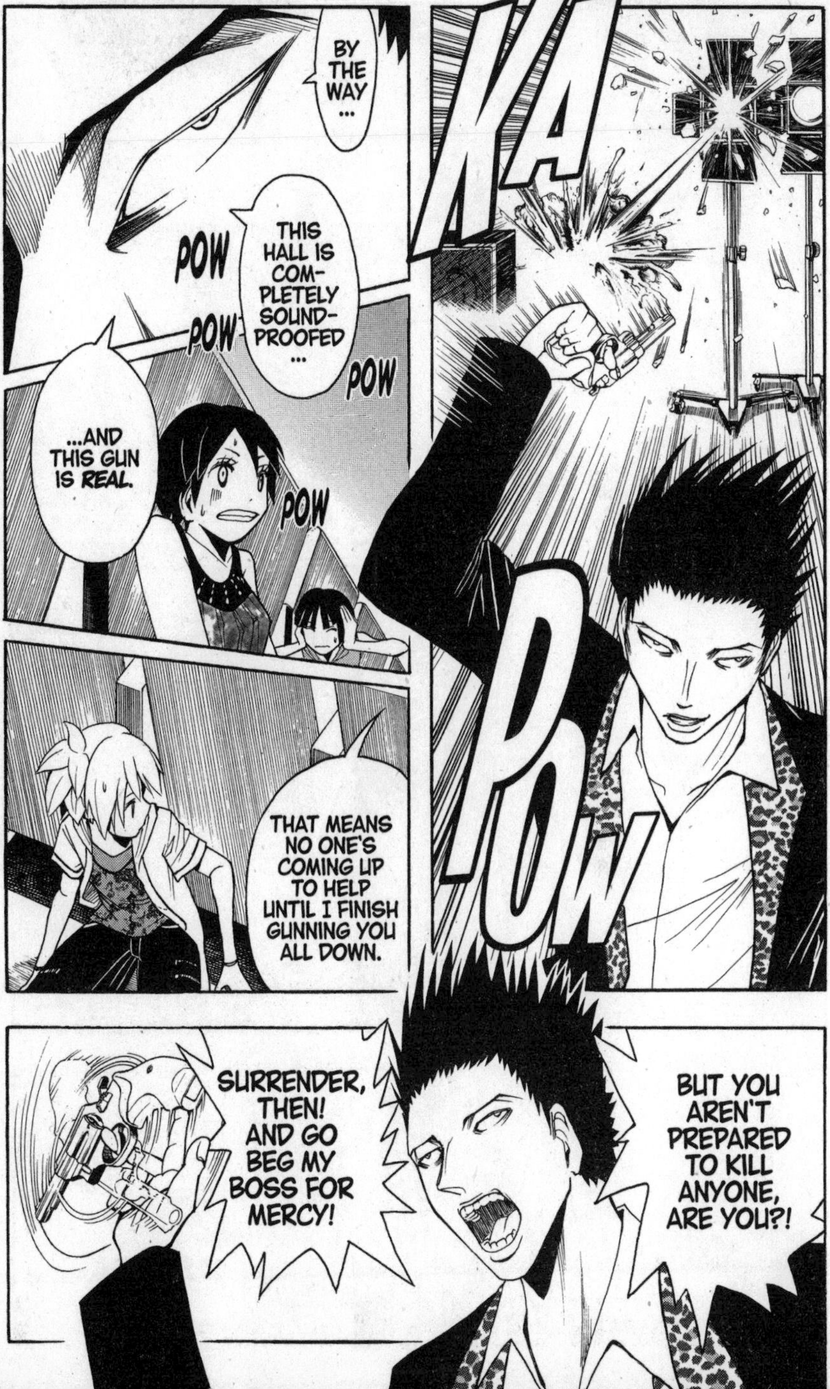
KA
POW
BY THE WAY...
POW
THIS HALL IS COMPLETELY SOUNDPROOFED...
POW
POW
...AND THIS GUN IS *REAL*.
POW
THAT MEANS NO ONE'S COMING UP TO HELP UNTIL I FINISH GUNNING YOU ALL DOWN.
BUT YOU AREN'T PREPARED TO KILL ANYONE, ARE YOU?!
SURRENDER, THEN! AND GO BEG MY BOSS FOR MERCY!

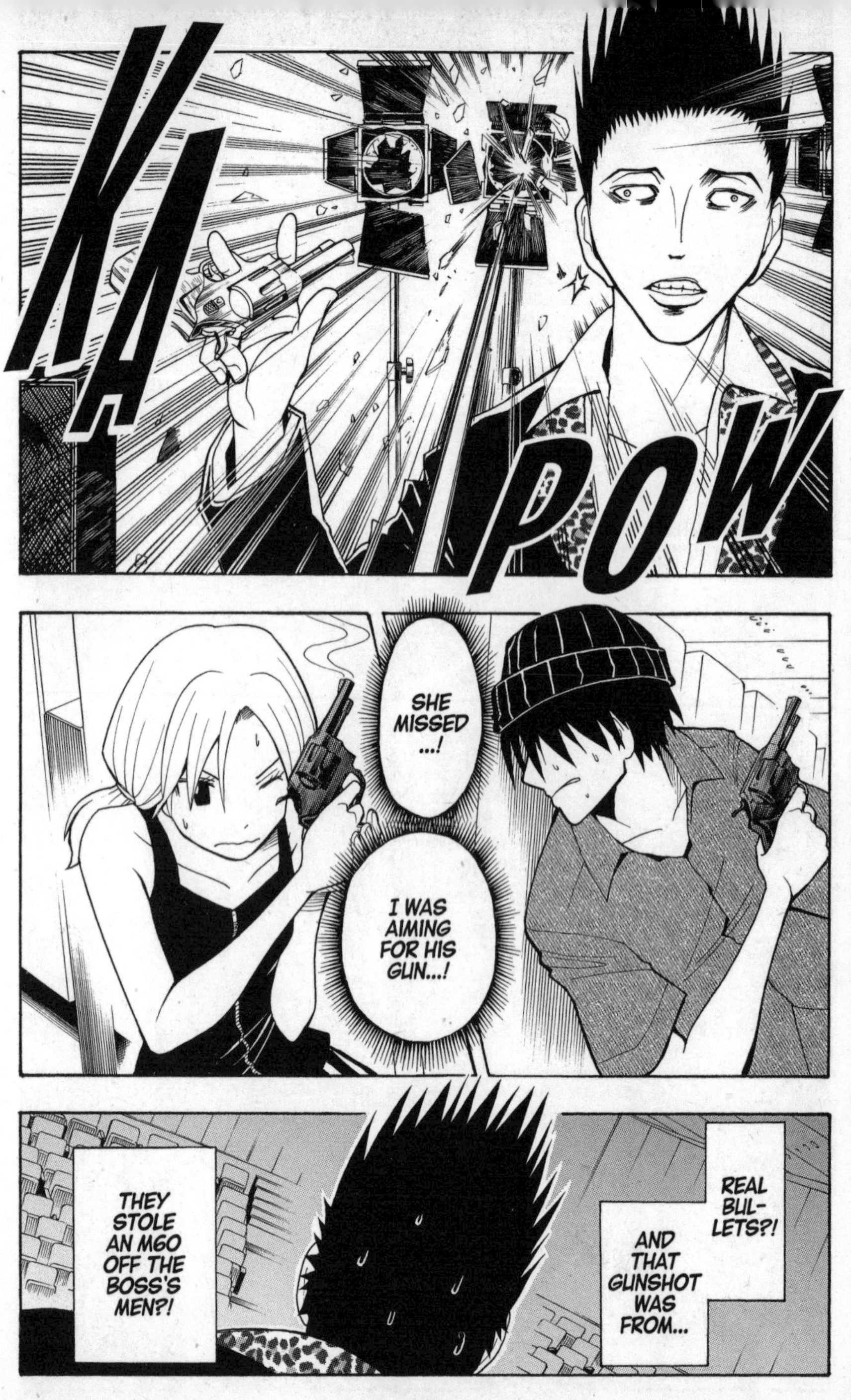
KA
POW
SHE MISSED ...!
I WAS AIMING FOR HIS GUN...!
REAL BUL-LETS?!
AND THAT GUNSHOT WAS FROM...
THEY STOLE AN M60 OFF THE BOSS'S MEN?!

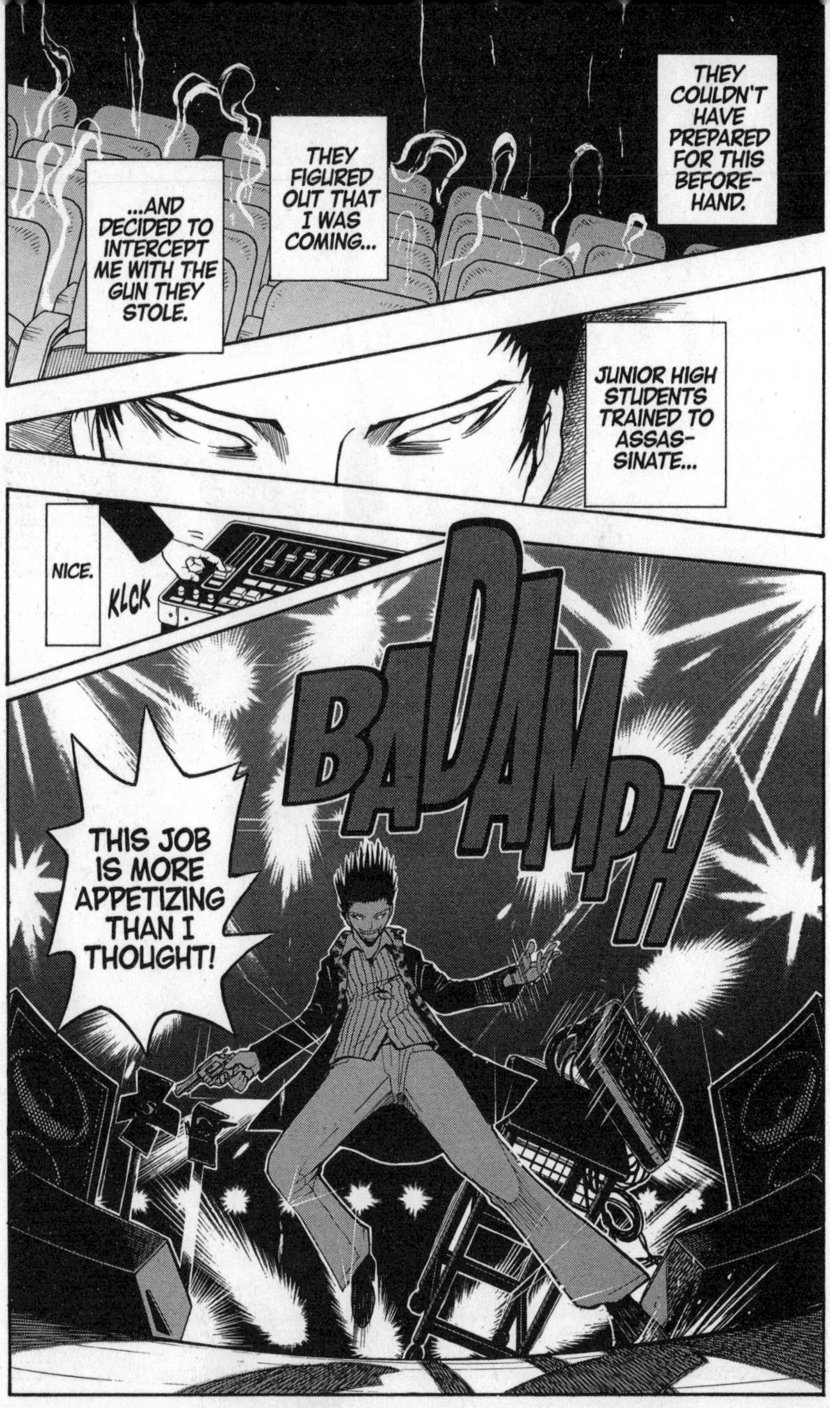
THEY COULDN'T HAVE PREPARED FOR THIS BEFORE-HAND.
THEY FIGURED OUT THAT I WAS COMING...
...AND DECIDED TO INTERCEPT ME WITH THE GUN THEY STOLE.
JUNIOR HIGH STUDENTS TRAINED TO ASSAS-SINATE...
KLCK
NICE.
BADAMPH
THIS JOB IS MORE APPETIZING THAN I THOUGHT!

Gastro's Gun Cuisine Recipe

Meat and
Gun Stew

Unagi Gun

Ooh-Yum-Style Gun
with Strawberry
Gun Sauce, served
with a side of
seasonal gun

CLASS 68 TIME FOR AN OPPORTUNITY

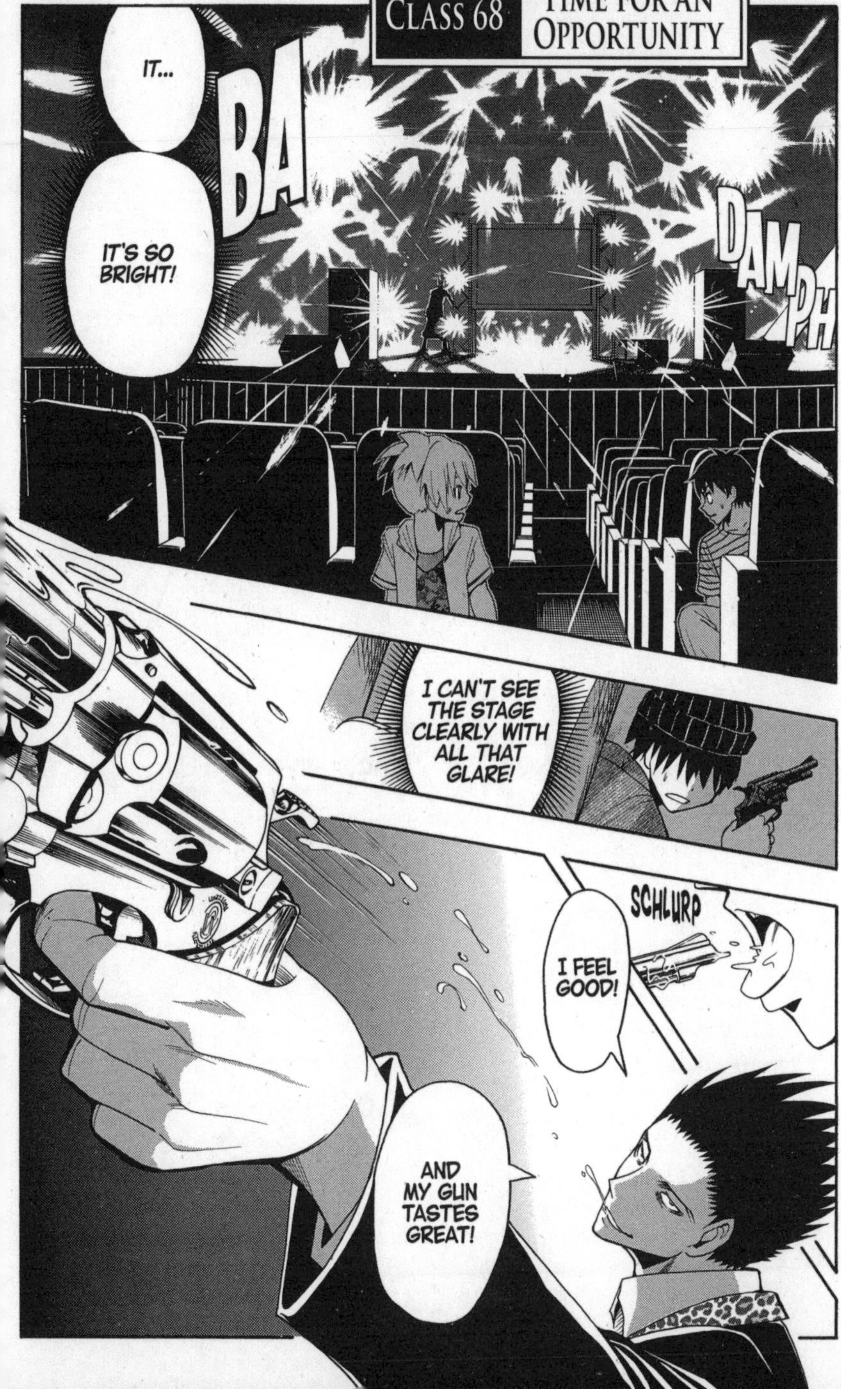

DAMPH
BA
IT...
IT'S SO BRIGHT!
I CAN'T SEE THE STAGE CLEARLY WITH ALL THAT GLARE!
SCHLURP
I FEEL GOOD!
AND MY GUN TASTES GREAT!

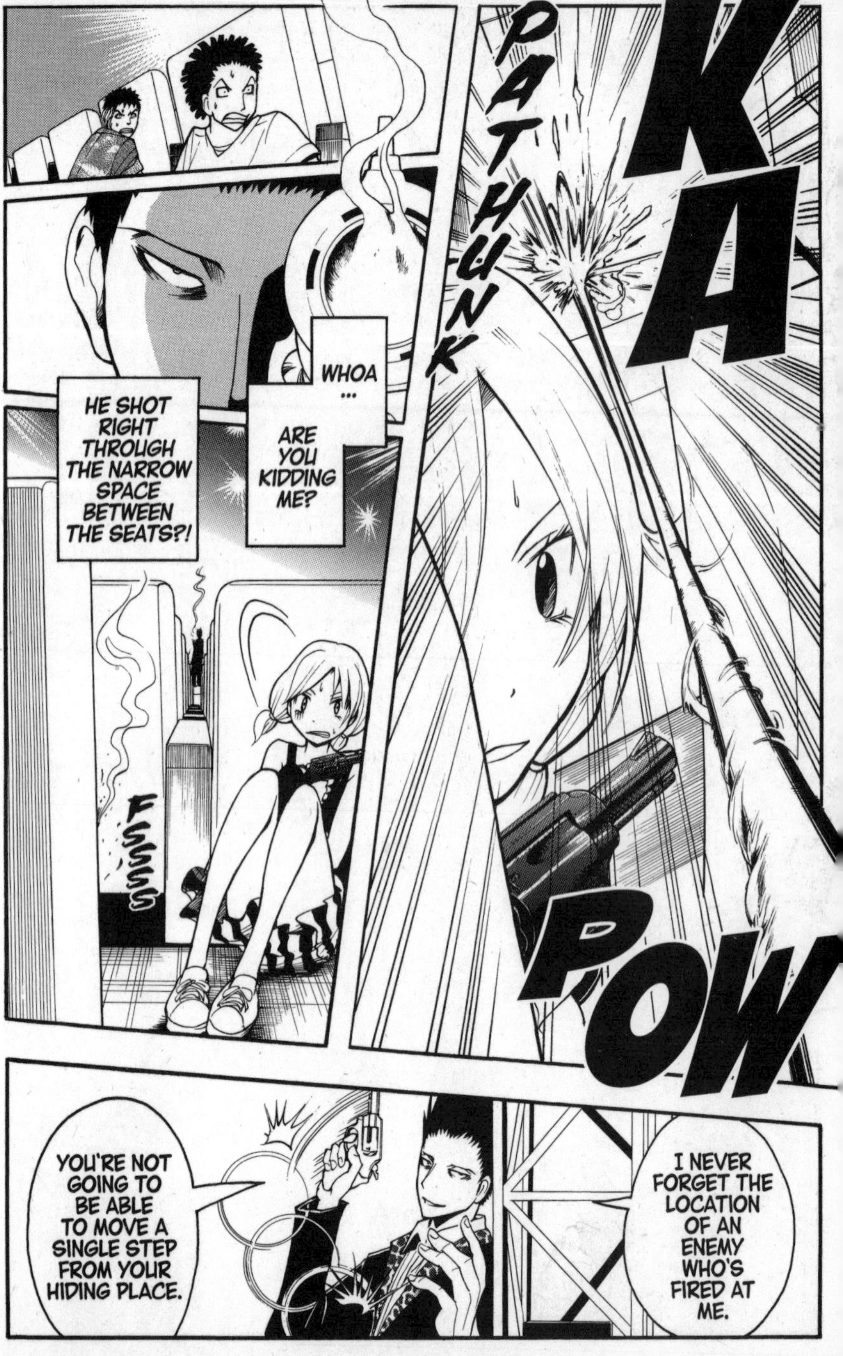
KA
PATHUNK
POW
WHOA ...
ARE YOU KIDDING ME?
HE SHOT RIGHT THROUGH THE NARROW SPACE BETWEEN THE SEATS?!
FSSSS
I NEVER FORGET THE LOCATION OF AN ENEMY WHO'S FIRED AT ME.
YOU'RE NOT GOING TO BE ABLE TO MOVE A SINGLE STEP FROM YOUR HIDING PLACE.

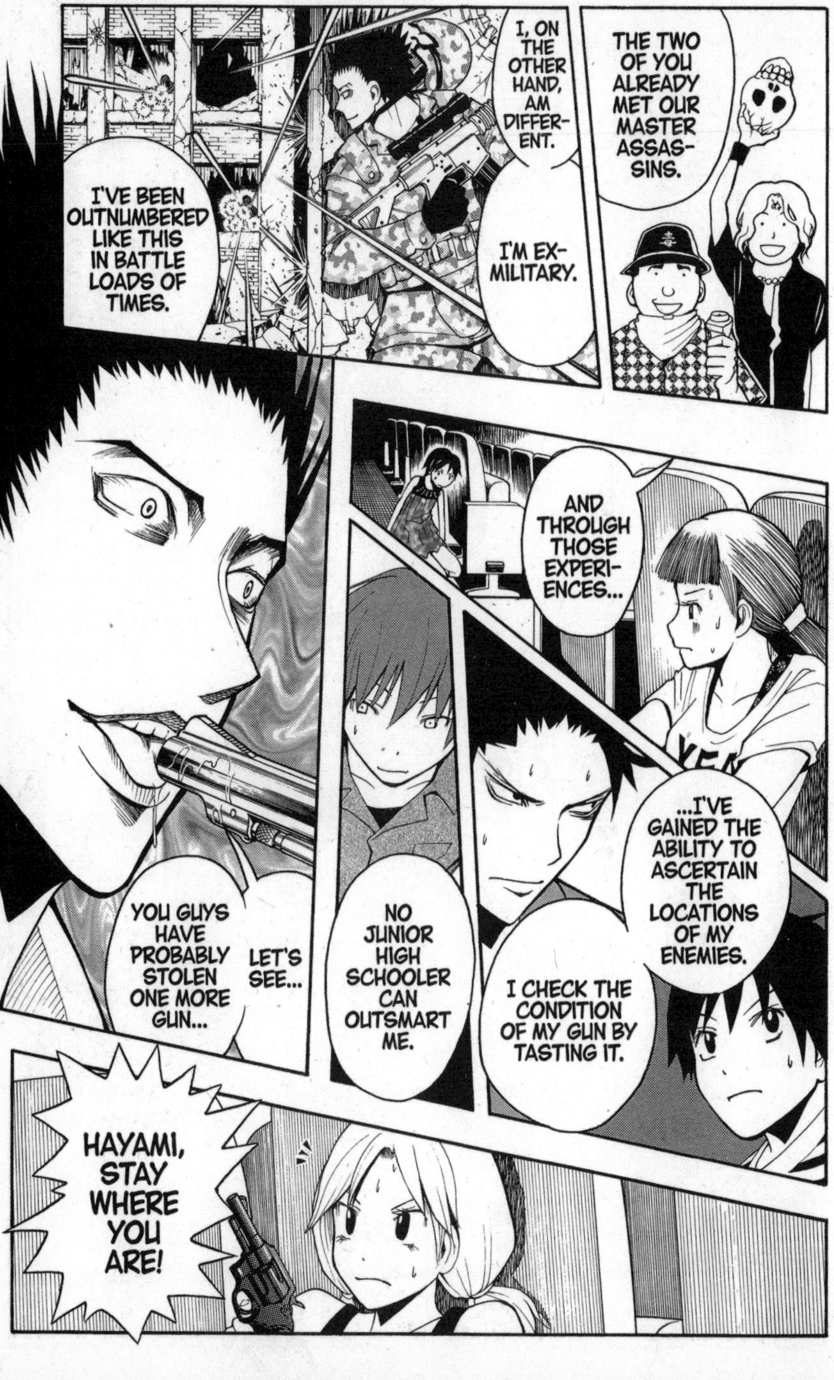
THE TWO OF YOU ALREADY MET OUR MASTER ASSAS-SINS.
I, ON THE OTHER HAND, AM DIFFER-ENT.
I'M EX-MILITARY.
I'VE BEEN OUTNUMBERED LIKE THIS IN BATTLE LOADS OF TIMES.
AND THROUGH THOSE EXPERI-ENCES...
...I'VE GAINED THE ABILITY TO ASCERTAIN THE LOCATIONS OF MY ENEMIES.
I CHECK THE CONDITION OF MY GUN BY TASTING IT.
NO JUNIOR HIGH SCHOOLER CAN OUTSMART ME.
LET'S SEE...
YOU GUYS HAVE PROBABLY STOLEN ONE MORE GUN...
HAYAMI, STAY WHERE YOU ARE!

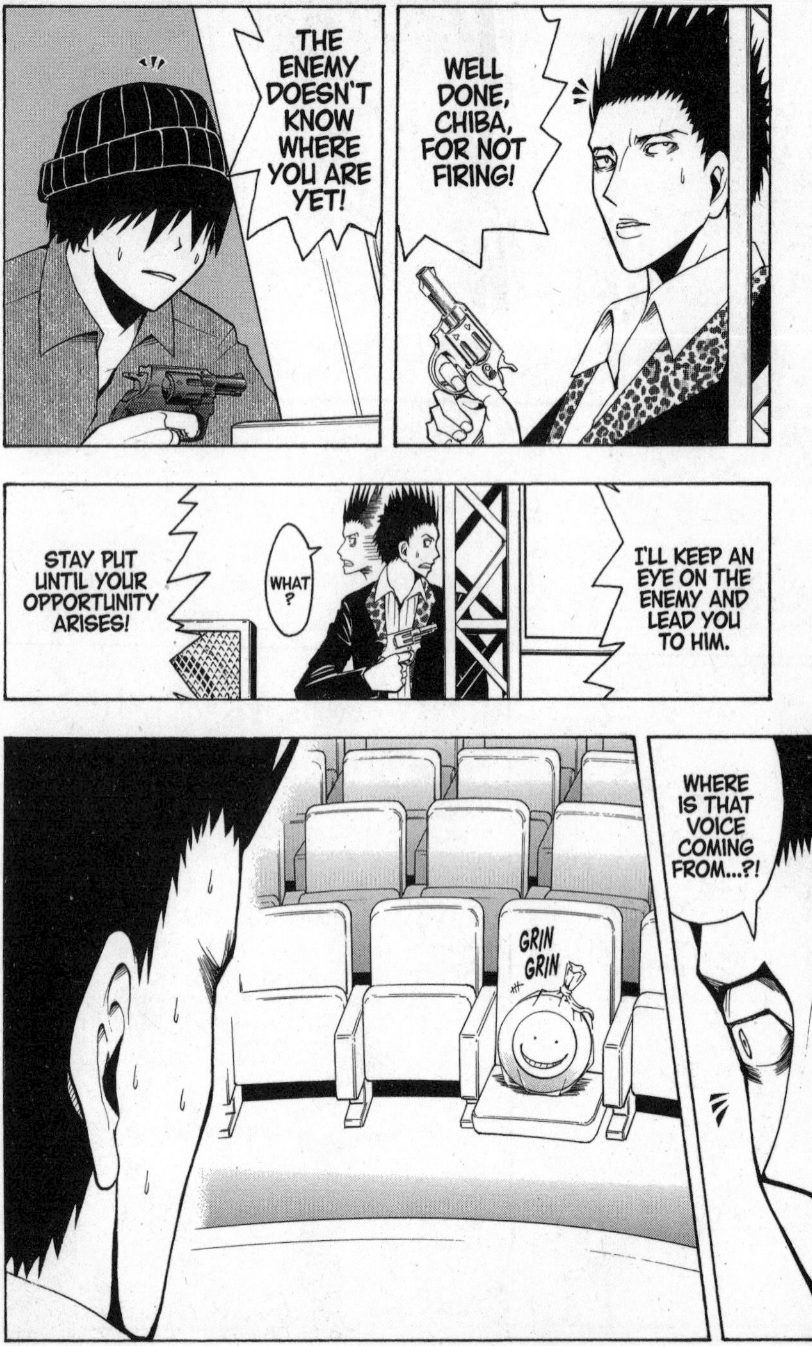
WELL DONE, CHIBA, FOR NOT FIRING!
THE ENEMY DOESN'T KNOW WHERE YOU ARE YET!
I'LL KEEP AN EYE ON THE ENEMY AND LEAD YOU TO HIM.
WHAT?
STAY PUT UNTIL YOUR OPPORTUNITY ARISES!
WHERE IS THAT VOICE COMING FROM...?!
GRIN GRIN

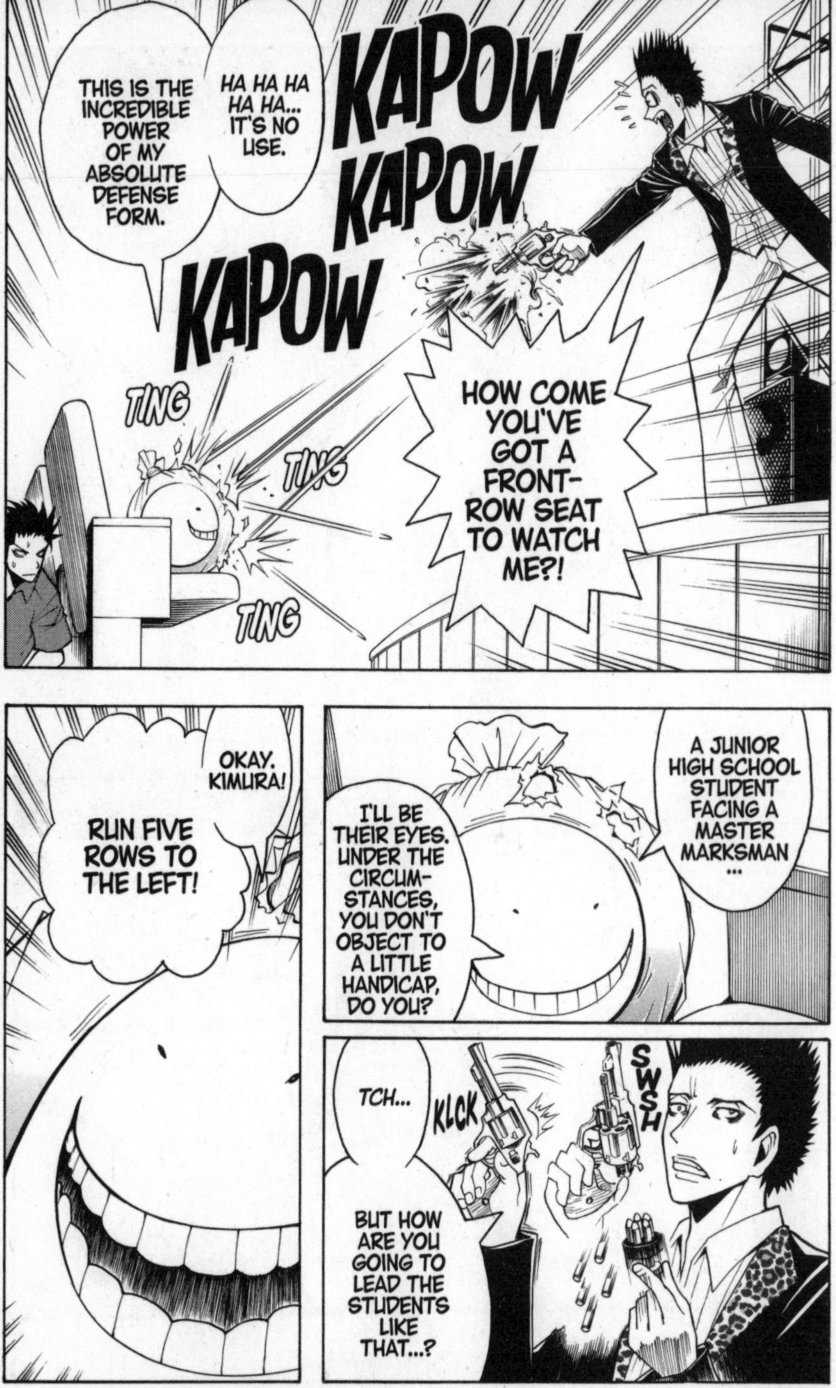
KAPOW
KAPOW
KAPOW
HOW COME YOU'VE GOT A FRONT-ROW SEAT TO WATCH ME?!
TING
TING
TING
HA HA HA HA HA... IT'S NO USE.
THIS IS THE INCREDIBLE POWER OF MY ABSOLUTE DEFENSE FORM.
A JUNIOR HIGH SCHOOL STUDENT FACING A MASTER MARKSMAN...
I'LL BE THEIR EYES. UNDER THE CIRCUM-STANCES, YOU DON'T OBJECT TO A LITTLE HANDICAP, DO YOU?
SWSH
KLCK
TCH...
BUT HOW ARE YOU GOING TO LEAD THE STUDENTS LIKE THAT...?
OKAY. KIMURA!
RUN FIVE ROWS TO THE LEFT!

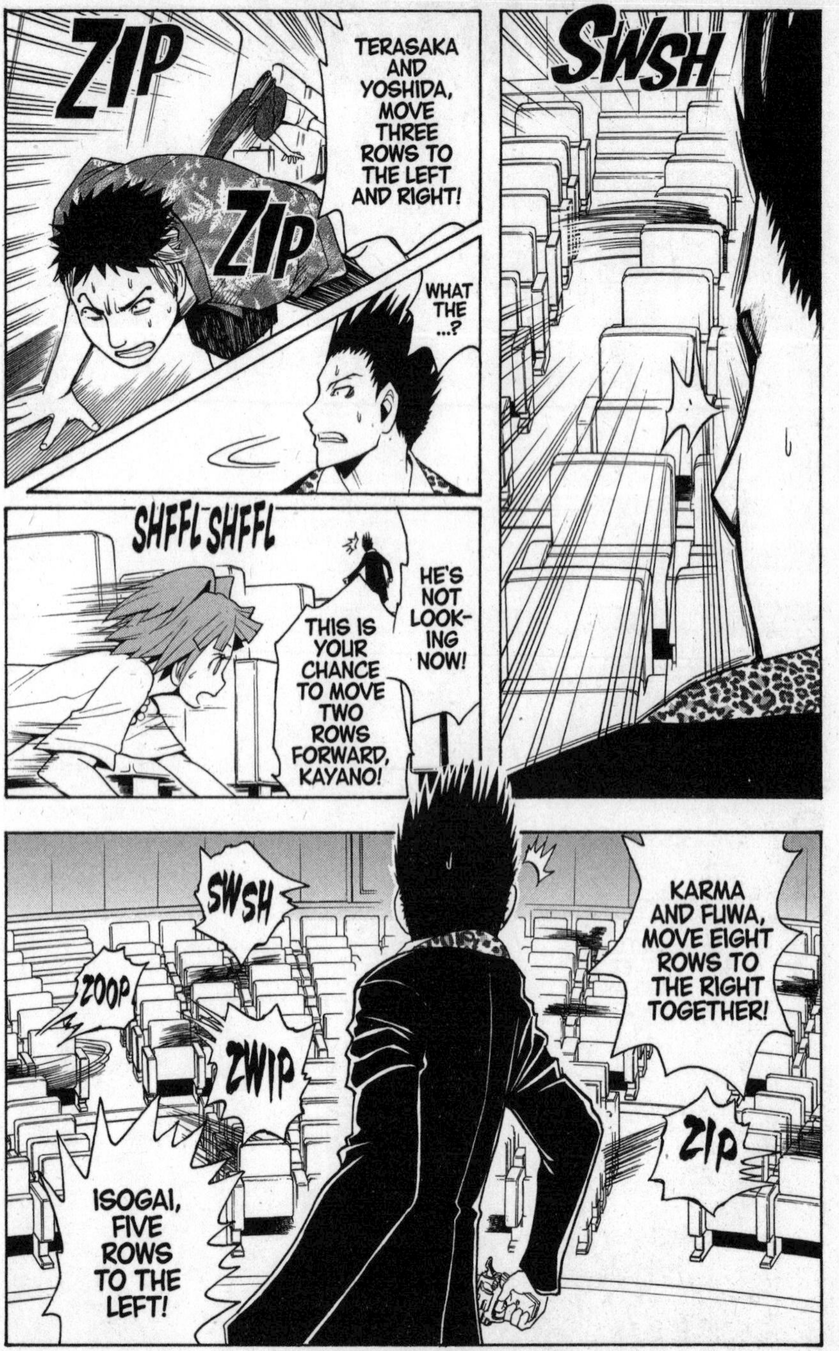
SWSH
ZIP
TERASAKA AND YOSHIDA, MOVE THREE ROWS TO THE LEFT AND RIGHT!
ZIP
WHAT THE ...?
SHFFL SHFFL
HE'S NOT LOOKING NOW!
THIS IS YOUR CHANCE TO MOVE TWO ROWS FORWARD, KAYANO!
KARMA AND FUWA, MOVE EIGHT ROWS TO THE RIGHT TOGETHER!
ZIP
SWSH
ZOOP
ZWIP
ISOGAI, FIVE ROWS TO THE LEFT!

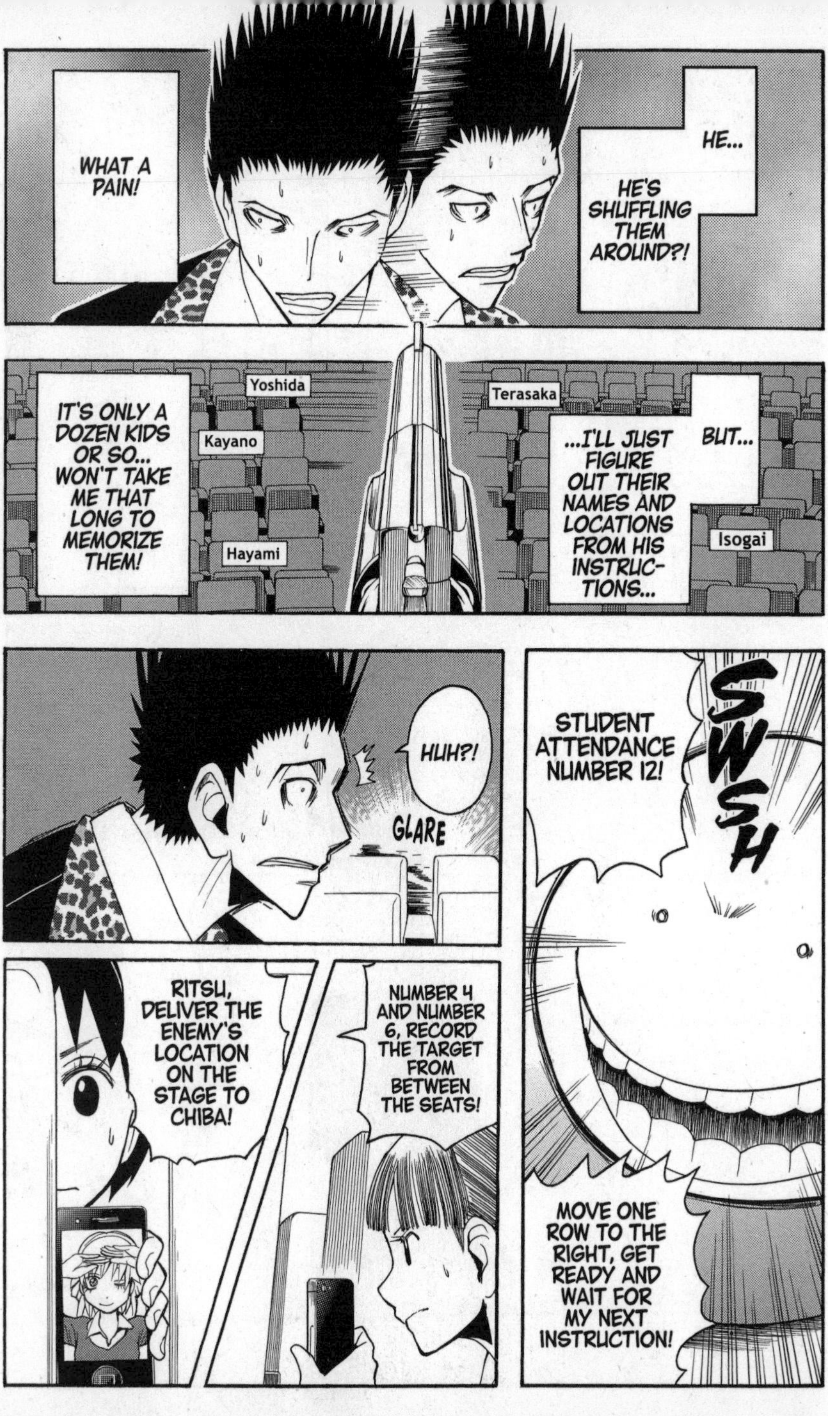
HE...
HE'S SHUFFLING THEM AROUND?!
WHAT A PAIN!
BUT...
...I'LL JUST FIGURE OUT THEIR NAMES AND LOCATIONS FROM HIS INSTRUCTIONS...
Terasaka
Isogai
Yoshida
Kayano
Hayami
IT'S ONLY A DOZEN KIDS OR SO... WON'T TAKE ME THAT LONG TO MEMORIZE THEM!
SWSH
STUDENT ATTENDANCE NUMBER 12!
MOVE ONE ROW TO THE RIGHT, GET READY AND WAIT FOR MY NEXT INSTRUCTION!
HUH?!
GLARE
NUMBER 4 AND NUMBER 6, RECORD THE TARGET FROM BETWEEN THE SEATS!
RITSU, DELIVER THE ENEMY'S LOCATION ON THE STAGE TO CHIBA!

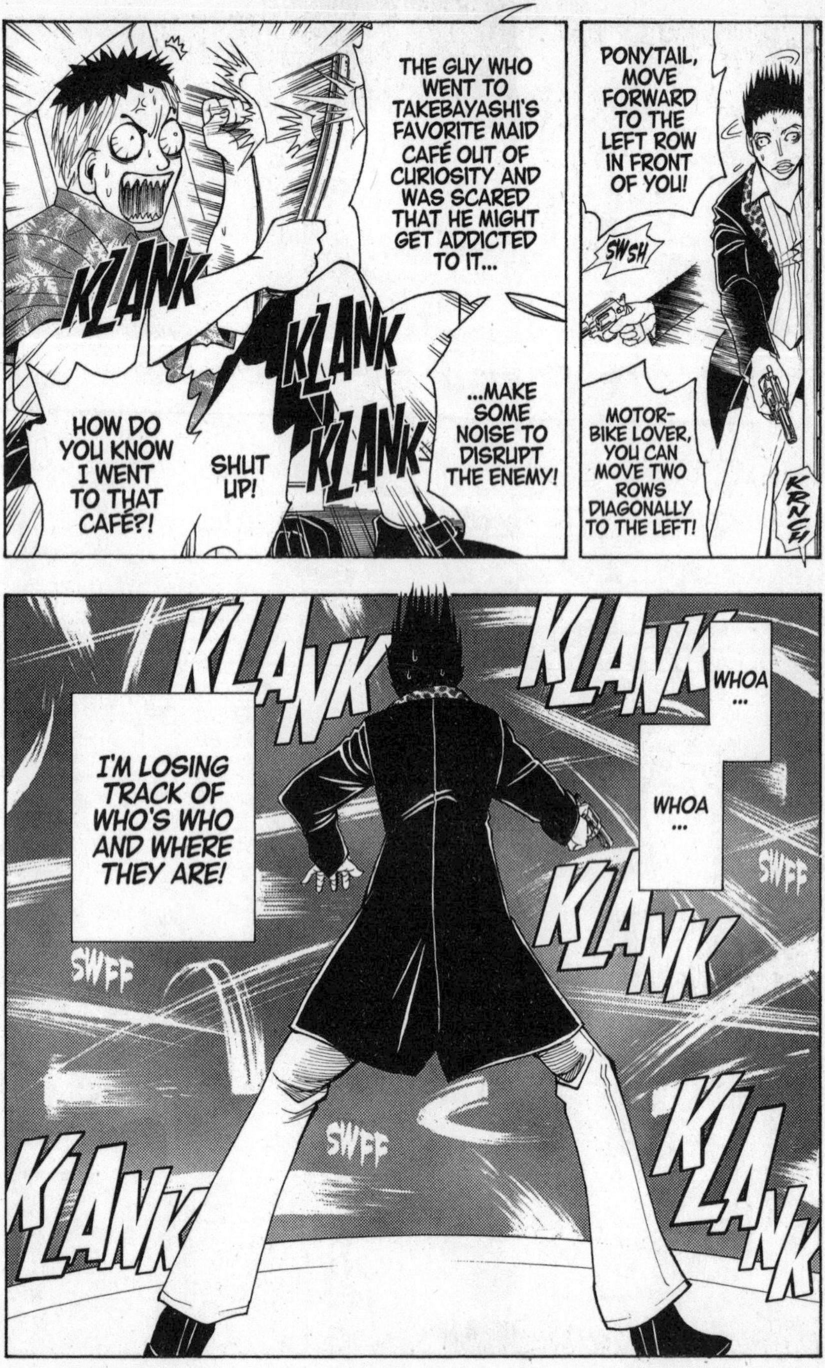
PONYTAIL, MOVE FORWARD TO THE LEFT ROW IN FRONT OF YOU!
SWSH
MOTOR-BIKE LOVER, YOU CAN MOVE TWO ROWS DIAGONALLY TO THE LEFT!
KRNCH
THE GUY WHO WENT TO TAKEBAYASHI'S FAVORITE MAID CAFÉ OUT OF CURIOSITY AND WAS SCARED THAT HE MIGHT GET ADDICTED TO IT...
KLANK
KLANK
KLANK
...MAKE SOME NOISE TO DISRUPT THE ENEMY!
SHUT UP!
HOW DO YOU KNOW I WENT TO THAT CAFÉ?!
KLANK
WHOA ...
WHOA ...
KLANK
I'M LOSING TRACK OF WHO'S WHO AND WHERE THEY ARE!
SWFF
KLANK
SWFF
KLANK
SWFF
KLANK

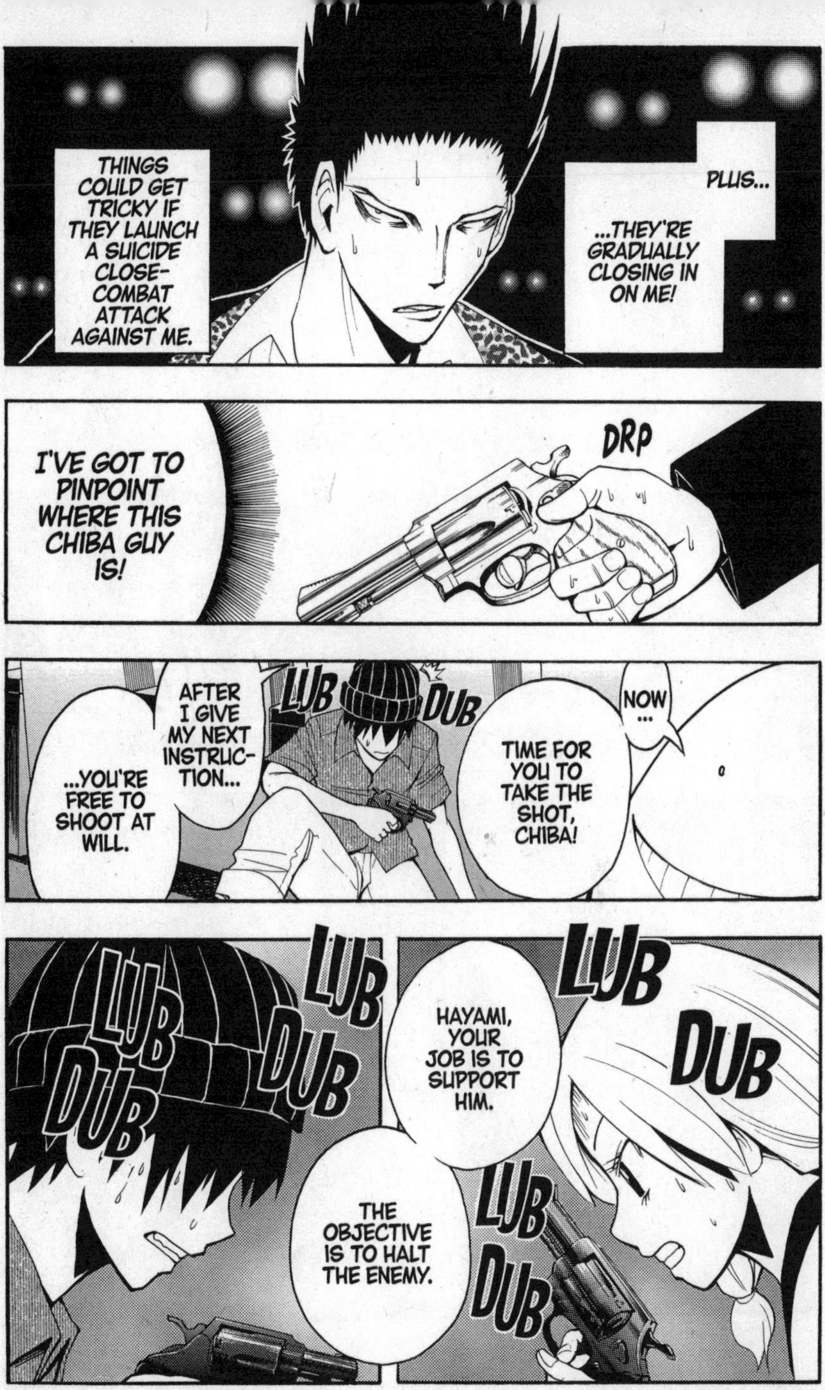
THINGS COULD GET TRICKY IF THEY LAUNCH A SUICIDE CLOSE-COMBAT ATTACK AGAINST ME.
PLUS...
...THEY'RE GRADUALLY CLOSING IN ON ME!
DRP
I'VE GOT TO PINPOINT WHERE THIS CHIBA GUY IS!
NOW...
TIME FOR YOU TO TAKE THE SHOT, CHIBA!
LUB DUB
AFTER I GIVE MY NEXT INSTRUCTION...
...YOU'RE FREE TO SHOOT AT WILL.
LUB DUB
HAYAMI, YOUR JOB IS TO SUPPORT HIM.
THE OBJECTIVE IS TO HALT THE ENEMY.
LUB DUB
LUB DUB
LUB DUB

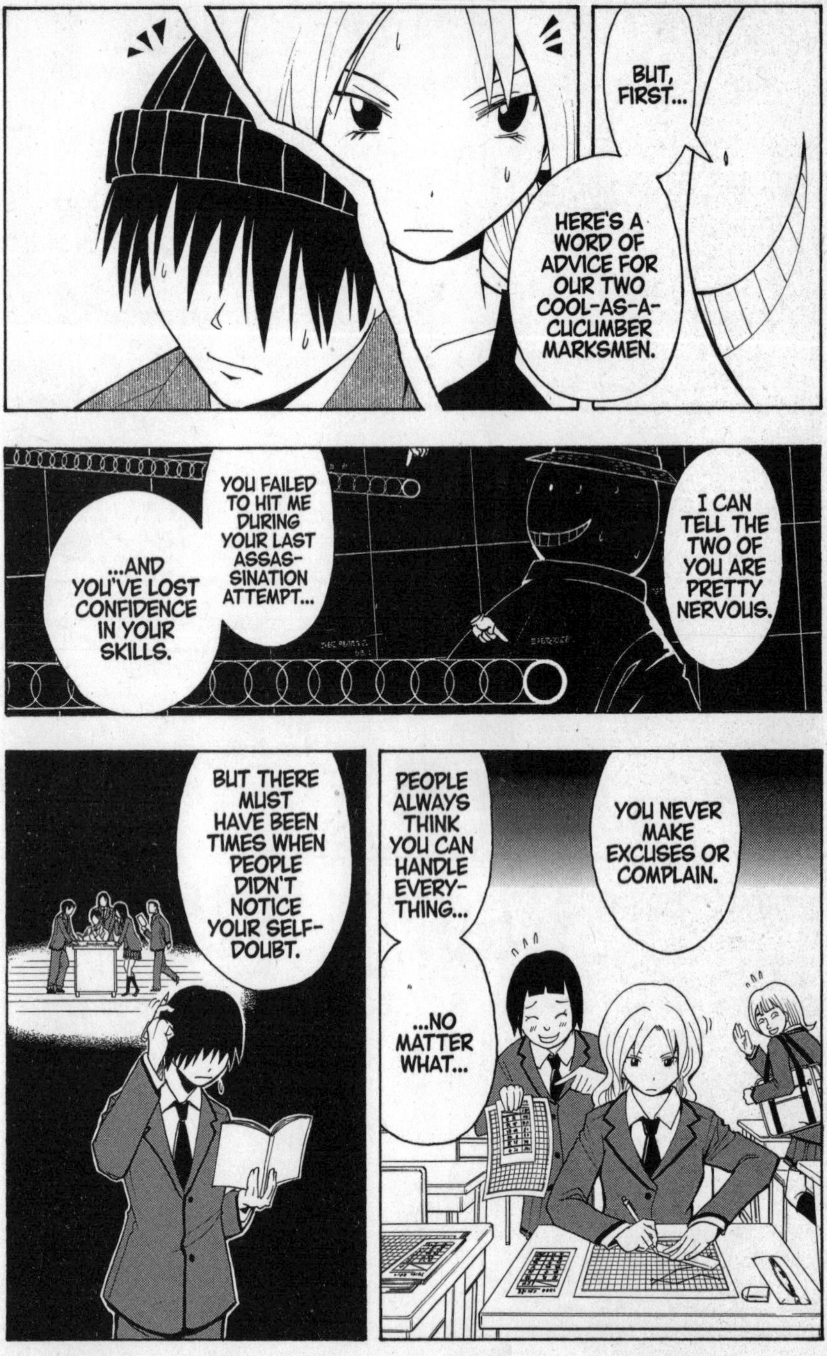
BUT, FIRST...
HERE'S A WORD OF ADVICE FOR OUR TWO COOL-AS-A-CUCUMBER MARKSMEN.
I CAN TELL THE TWO OF YOU ARE PRETTY NERVOUS.
YOU FAILED TO HIT ME DURING YOUR LAST ASSAS-SINATION ATTEMPT...
...AND YOU'VE LOST CONFIDENCE IN YOUR SKILLS.
YOU NEVER MAKE EXCUSES OR COMPLAIN.
PEOPLE ALWAYS THINK YOU CAN HANDLE EVERY-THING...
...NO MATTER WHAT...
BUT THERE MUST HAVE BEEN TIMES WHEN PEOPLE DIDN'T NOTICE YOUR SELF-DOUBT.

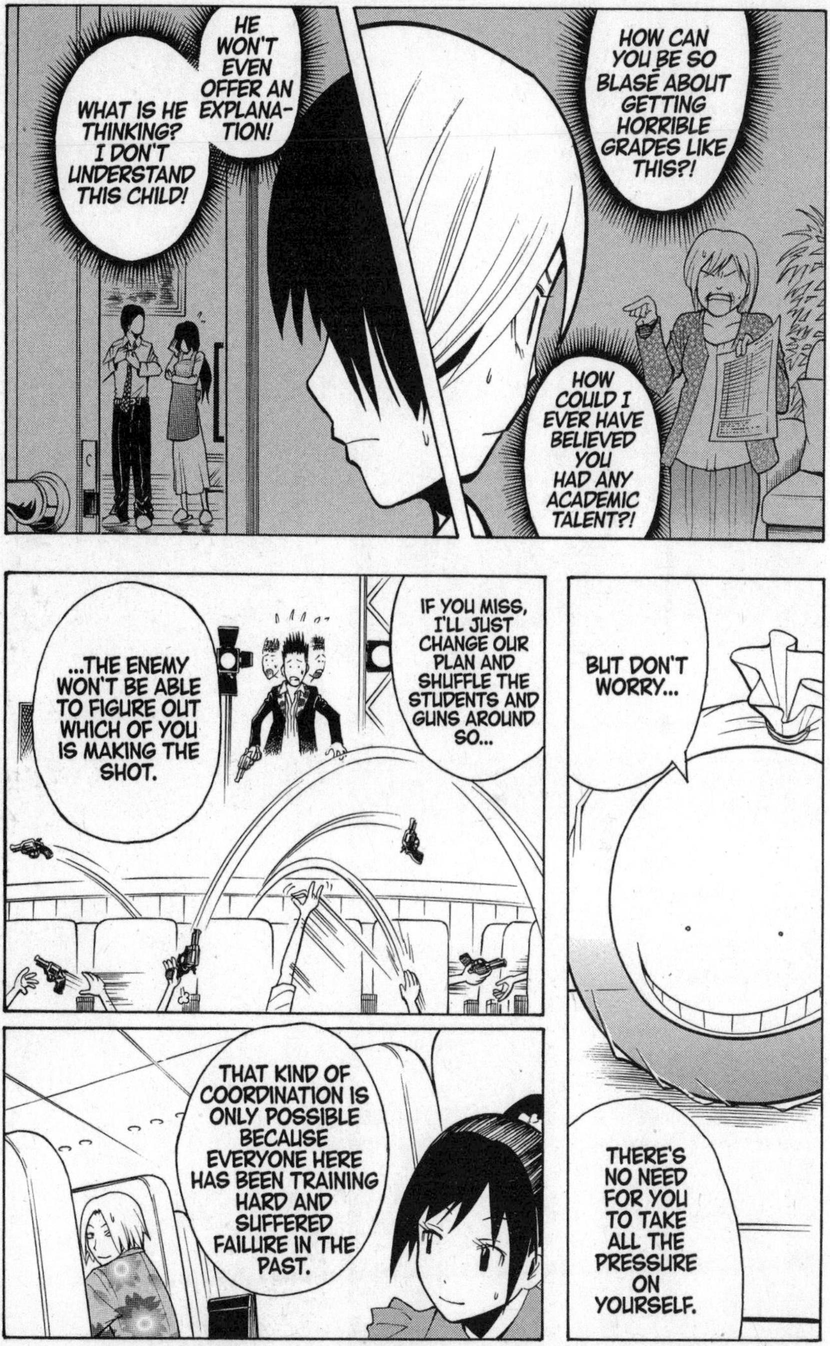
HOW CAN YOU BE SO BLASÉ ABOUT GETTING HORRIBLE GRADES LIKE THIS?!
HOW COULD I EVER HAVE BELIEVED YOU HAD ANY ACADEMIC TALENT?!
HE WON'T EVEN OFFER AN EXPLANATION!
WHAT IS HE THINKING? I DON'T UNDERSTAND THIS CHILD!
BUT DON'T WORRY...
THERE'S NO NEED FOR YOU TO TAKE ALL THE PRESSURE ON YOURSELF.
IF YOU MISS, I'LL JUST CHANGE OUR PLAN AND SHUFFLE THE STUDENTS AND GUNS AROUND SO...
...THE ENEMY WON'T BE ABLE TO FIGURE OUT WHICH OF YOU IS MAKING THE SHOT.
THAT KIND OF COORDINATION IS ONLY POSSIBLE BECAUSE EVERYONE HERE HAS BEEN TRAINING HARD AND SUFFERED FAILURE IN THE PAST.

YOU'RE SURROUNDED BY FRIENDS WHO'VE GONE THROUGH THE SAME EXPERIENCE AS YOU.

DON'T WORRY ABOUT A THING. JUST PULL THE TRIGGER.

KLCK

...!!

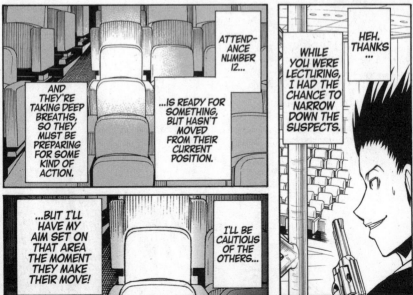

HEH. THANKS...

WHILE YOU WERE LECTURING, I HAD THE CHANCE TO NARROW DOWN THE SUSPECTS.

ATTENDANCE NUMBER 12...

...IS READY FOR SOMETHING, BUT HASN'T MOVED FROM THEIR CURRENT POSITION.

AND THEY'RE TAKING DEEP BREATHS, SO THEY MUST BE PREPARING FOR SOME KIND OF ACTION.

I'LL BE CAUTIOUS OF THE OTHERS...

...BUT I'LL HAVE MY AIM SET ON THAT AREA THE MOMENT THEY MAKE THEIR MOVE!

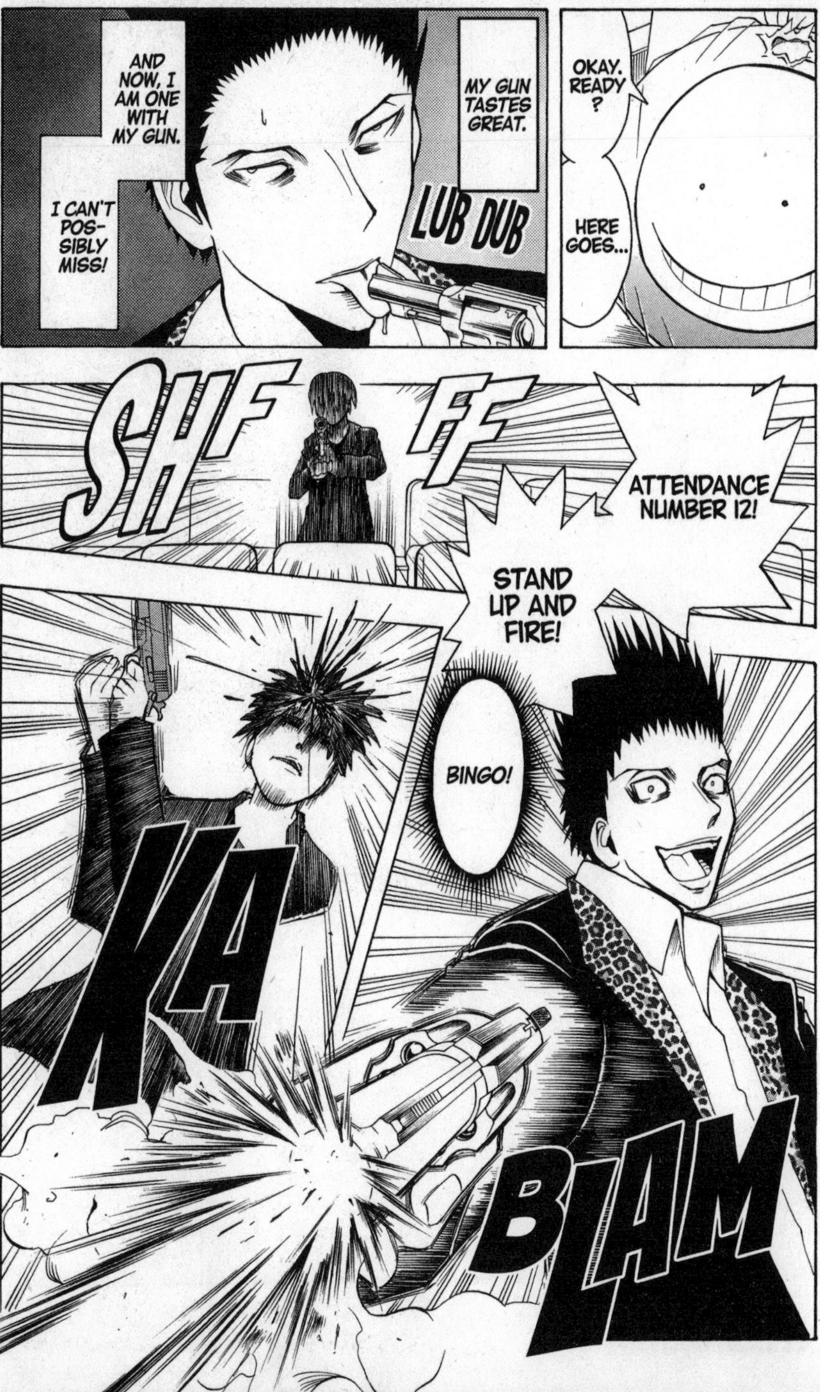
OKAY. READY?
HERE GOES...
MY GUN TASTES GREAT.
LUB DUB
AND NOW, I AM ONE WITH MY GUN.
I CAN'T POSSIBLY MISS!
ATTENDANCE NUMBER 12!
SHFF
STAND UP AND FIRE!
BINGO!
BLAM
KA

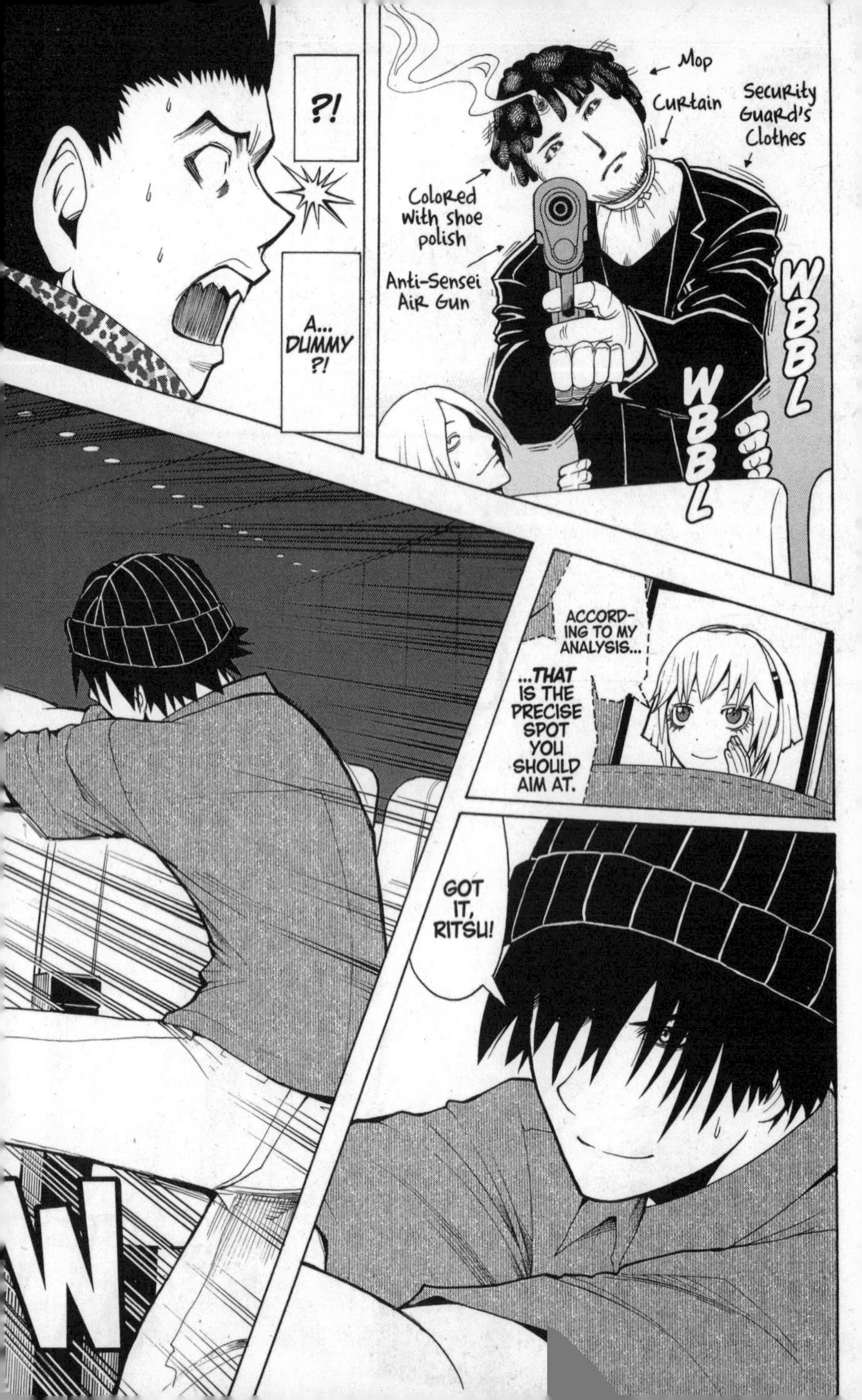
Mop
Curtain
Security Guard's Clothes
Colored with shoe polish
Anti-Sensei Air Gun
WBBL
WBBL
?!
A... DUMMY?!
ACCORDING TO MY ANALYSIS...
...THAT IS THE PRECISE SPOT YOU SHOULD AIM AT.
GOT IT, RITSU!
W

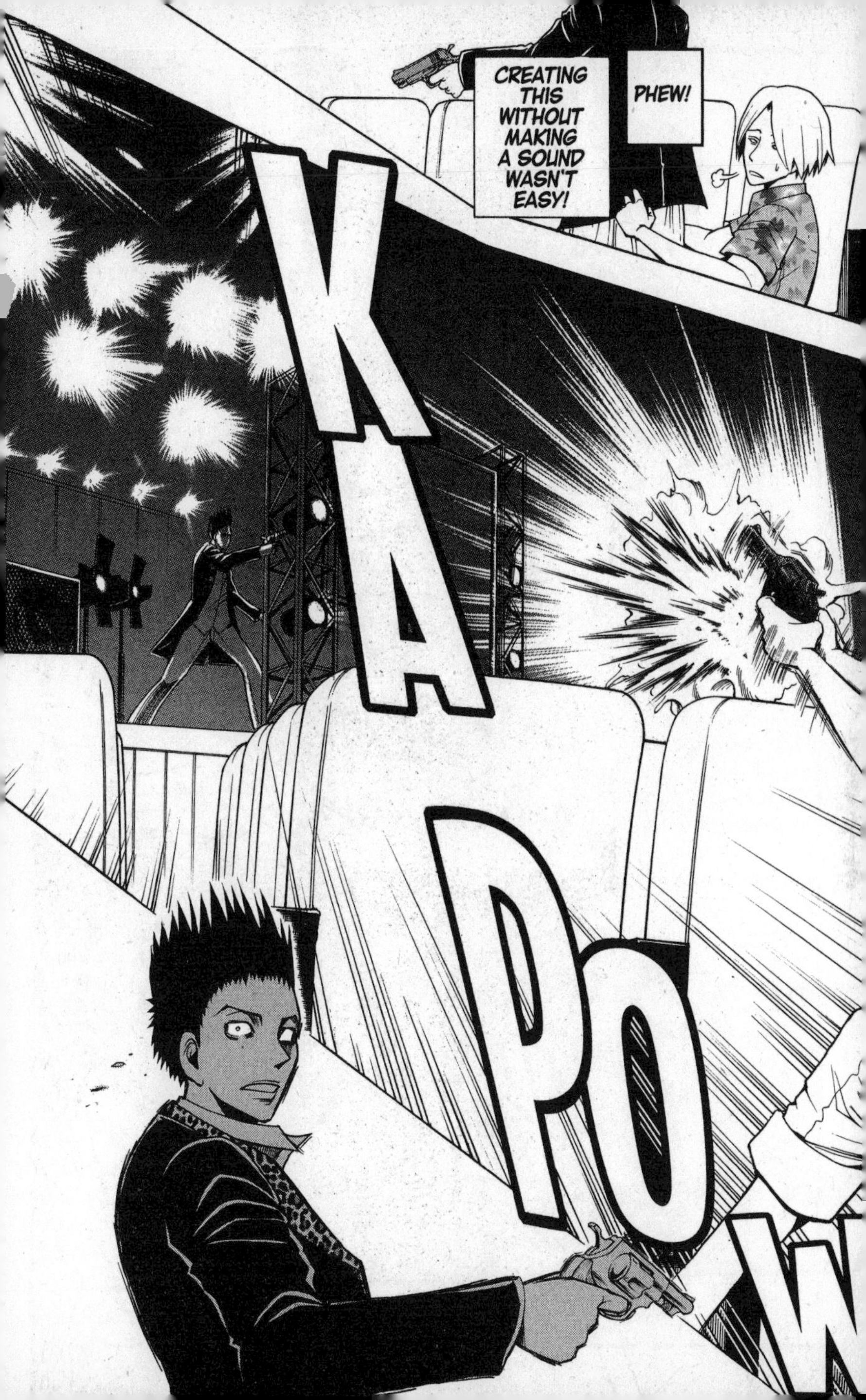

PHEW!
CREATING THIS WITHOUT MAKING A SOUND WASN'T EASY!
KAPOW

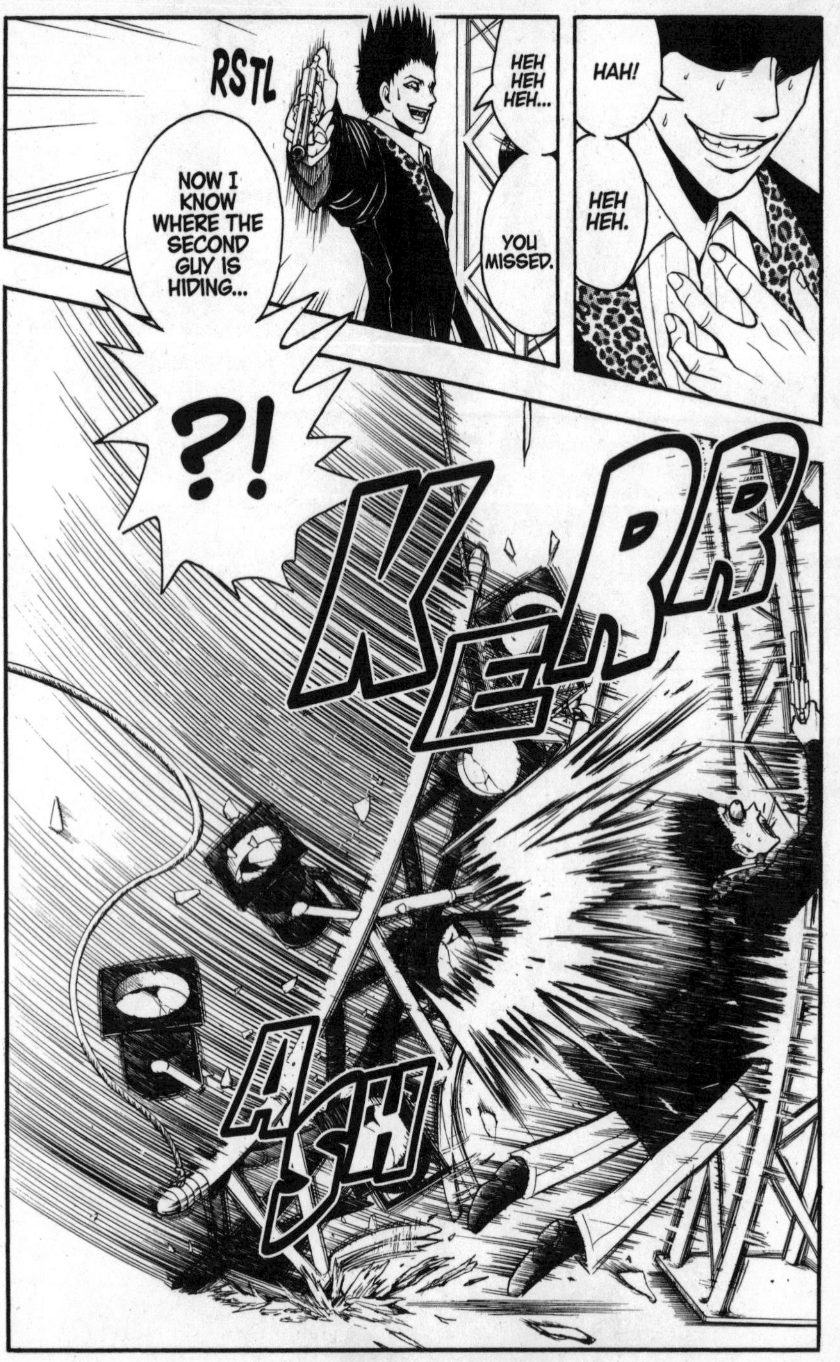
HAH!
HEH HEH.
HEH HEH HEH...
YOU MISSED.
RSTL
NOW I KNOW WHERE THE SECOND GUY IS HIDING...
?!
KERR
ASH

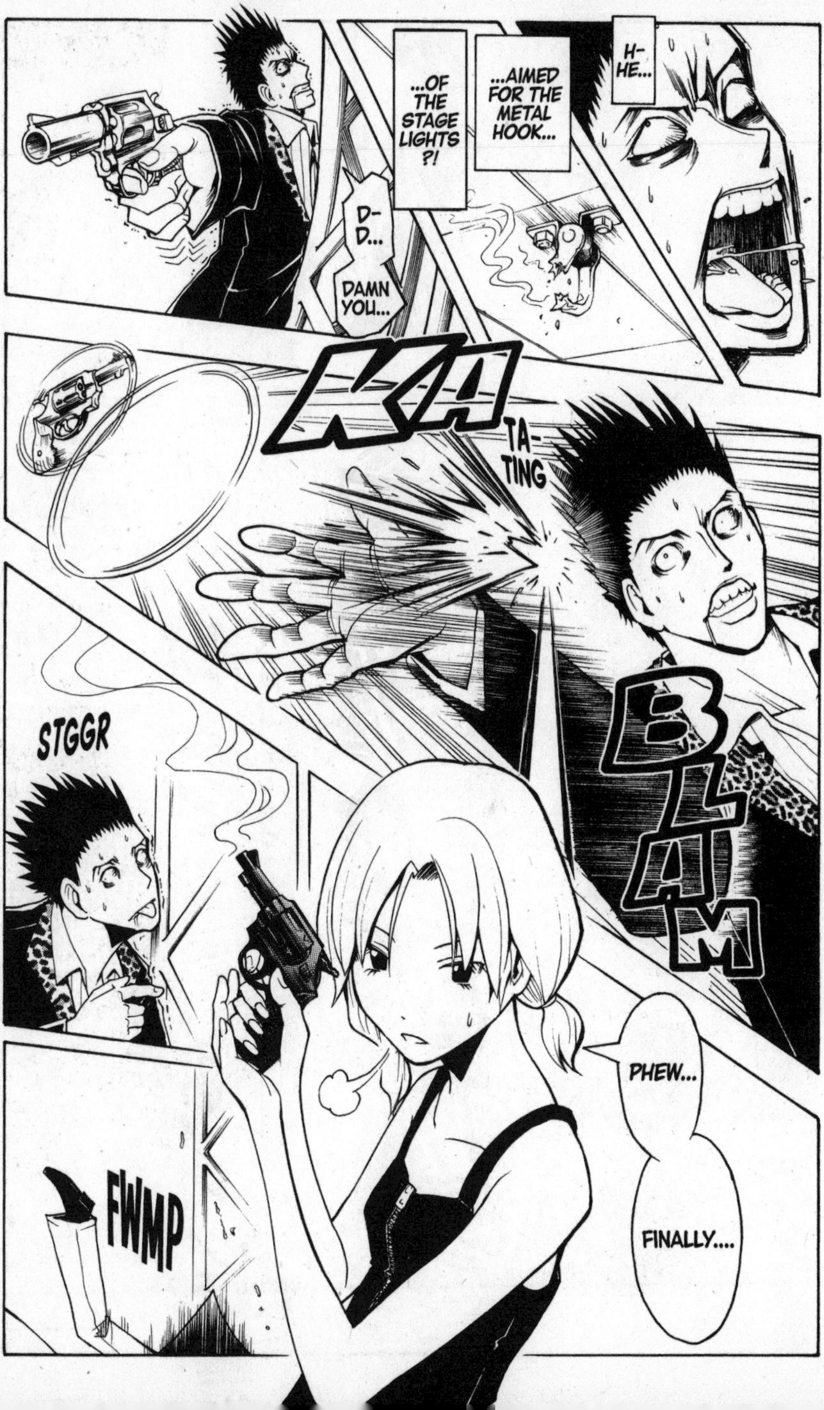
H-HE...
...AIMED FOR THE METAL HOOK...
...OF THE STAGE LIGHTS?!
D-D...
DAMN YOU...
KA
TA-TING
BLAM
STGGR
PHEW...
FINALLY....
FWMP

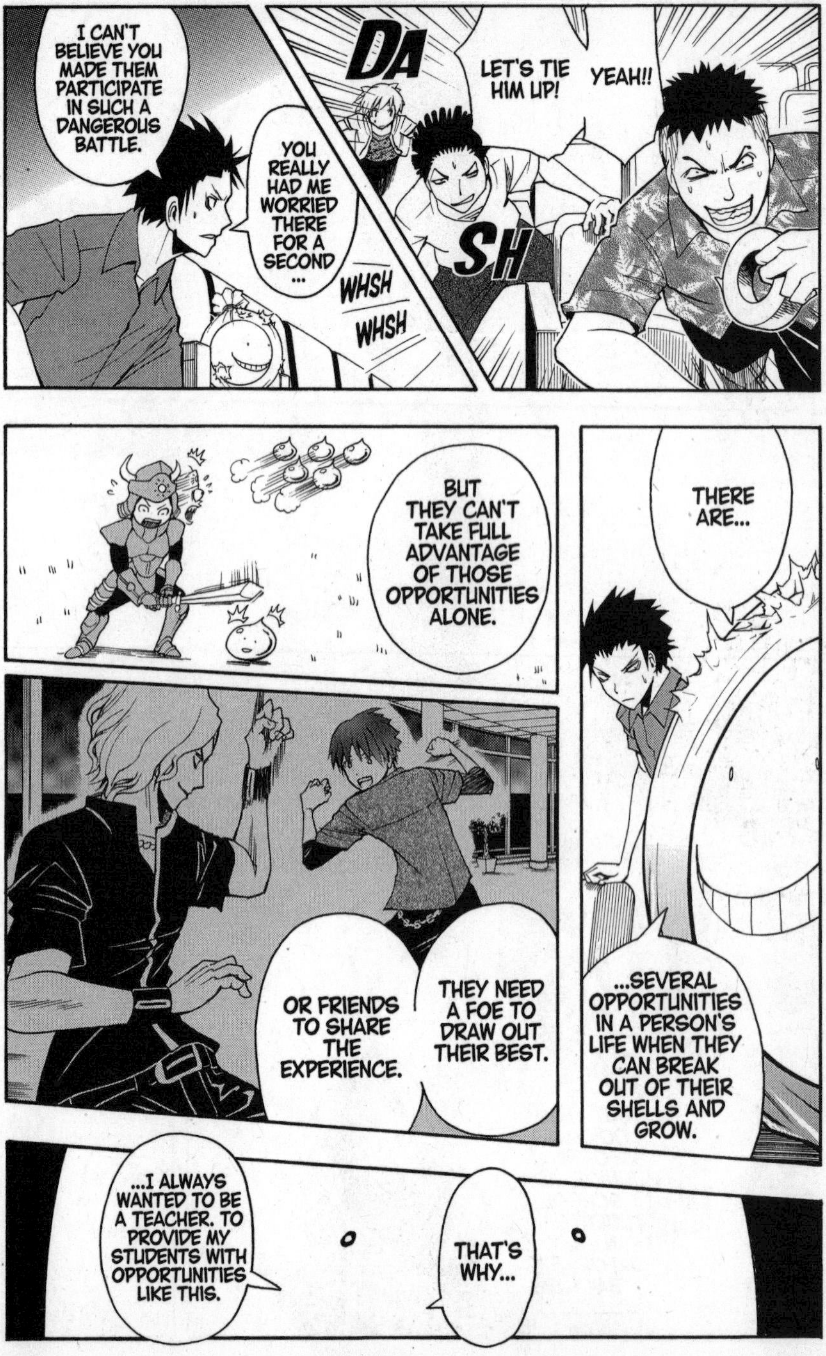
YEAH!!
LET'S TIE HIM UP!
DA
SH
I CAN'T BELIEVE YOU MADE THEM PARTICIPATE IN SUCH A DANGEROUS BATTLE.
YOU REALLY HAD ME WORRIED THERE FOR A SECOND...
WHSH
WHSH
THERE ARE...
...SEVERAL OPPORTUNITIES IN A PERSON'S LIFE WHEN THEY CAN BREAK OUT OF THEIR SHELLS AND GROW.
BUT THEY CAN'T TAKE FULL ADVANTAGE OF THOSE OPPORTUNITIES ALONE.
THEY NEED A FOE TO DRAW OUT THEIR BEST.
OR FRIENDS TO SHARE THE EXPERIENCE.
THAT'S WHY...
...I ALWAYS WANTED TO BE A TEACHER. TO PROVIDE MY STUDENTS WITH OPPORTUNITIES LIKE THIS.

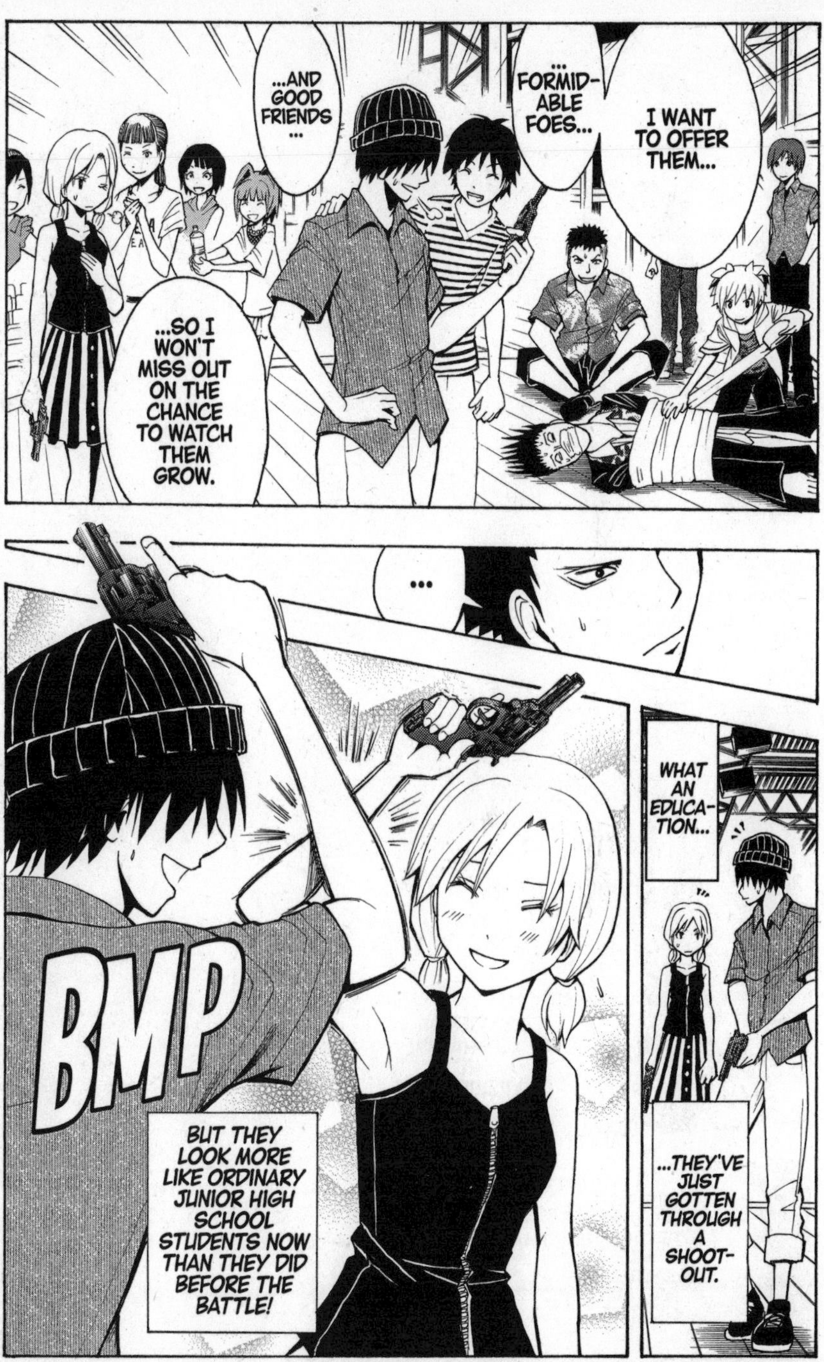
I WANT TO OFFER THEM...
...FORMID-ABLE FOES...
...AND GOOD FRIENDS...
...SO I WON'T MISS OUT ON THE CHANCE TO WATCH THEM GROW.
...
WHAT AN EDUCA-TION...
...THEY'VE JUST GOTTEN THROUGH A SHOOT-OUT.
BMP
BUT THEY LOOK MORE LIKE ORDINARY JUNIOR HIGH SCHOOL STUDENTS NOW THAN THEY DID BEFORE THE BATTLE!

E-15 RYUNOSUKE CHIBA

- ☺ BIRTHDAY: MAY 20
- ☺ HEIGHT: 5' 8"
- ☺ WEIGHT: 128 LBS.
- ☺ FAVORITE SUBJECT: MATHEMATICS
- ☺ LEAST FAVORITE SUBJECT: BIOLOGY
- ☺ HOBBY/SKILL: TRIANGULAR SURVEYING
- ☺ FUTURE GOAL: ARCHITECT
- ☺ FAVORITE FOOD: HARDBOILED EGG
- ☺ THE REASON HE'S GOOD AT SNIPING EVEN WHEN HIS EYES ARE HIDDEN IS THAT HE USES THE STRANDS OF HAIR THAT COVER THEM AS A GUN SIGHT.

Class 69 The Puppet Master's Time

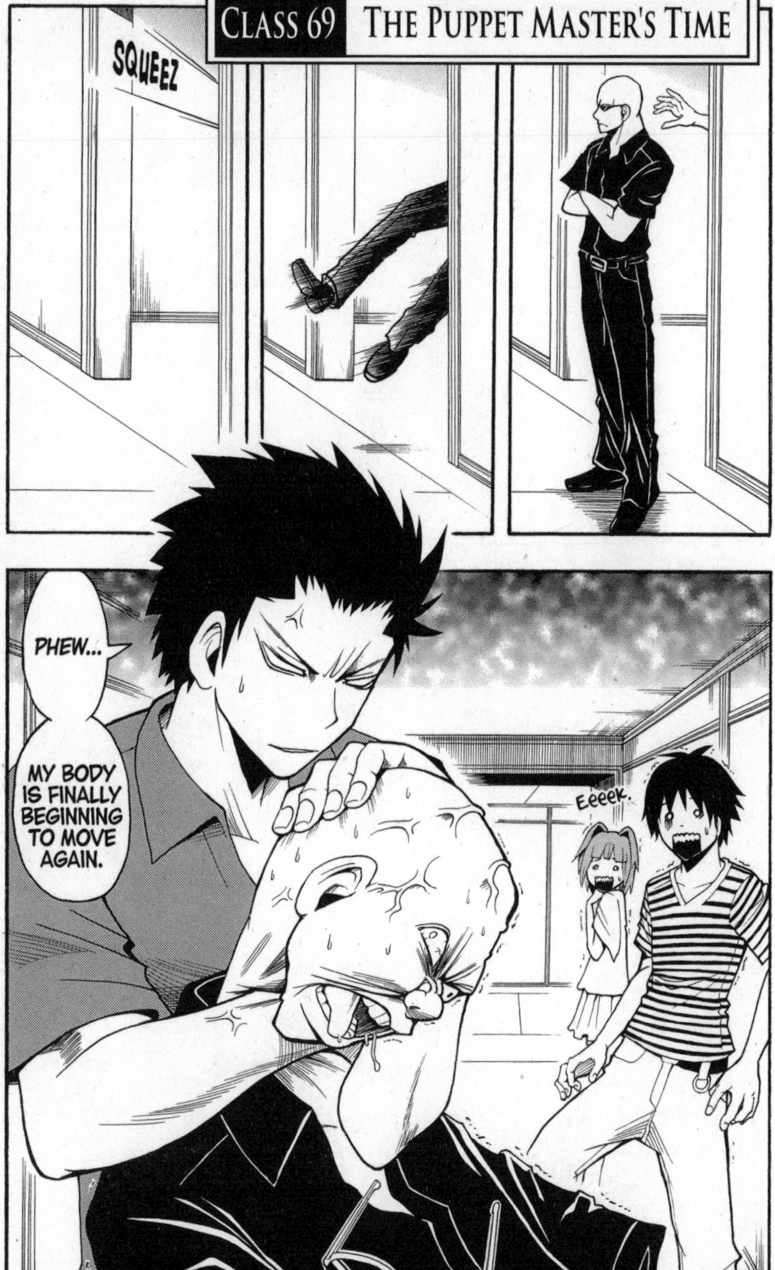
SQUEEZ
PHEW...
MY BODY IS FINALLY BEGINNING TO MOVE AGAIN.
Eeeek.

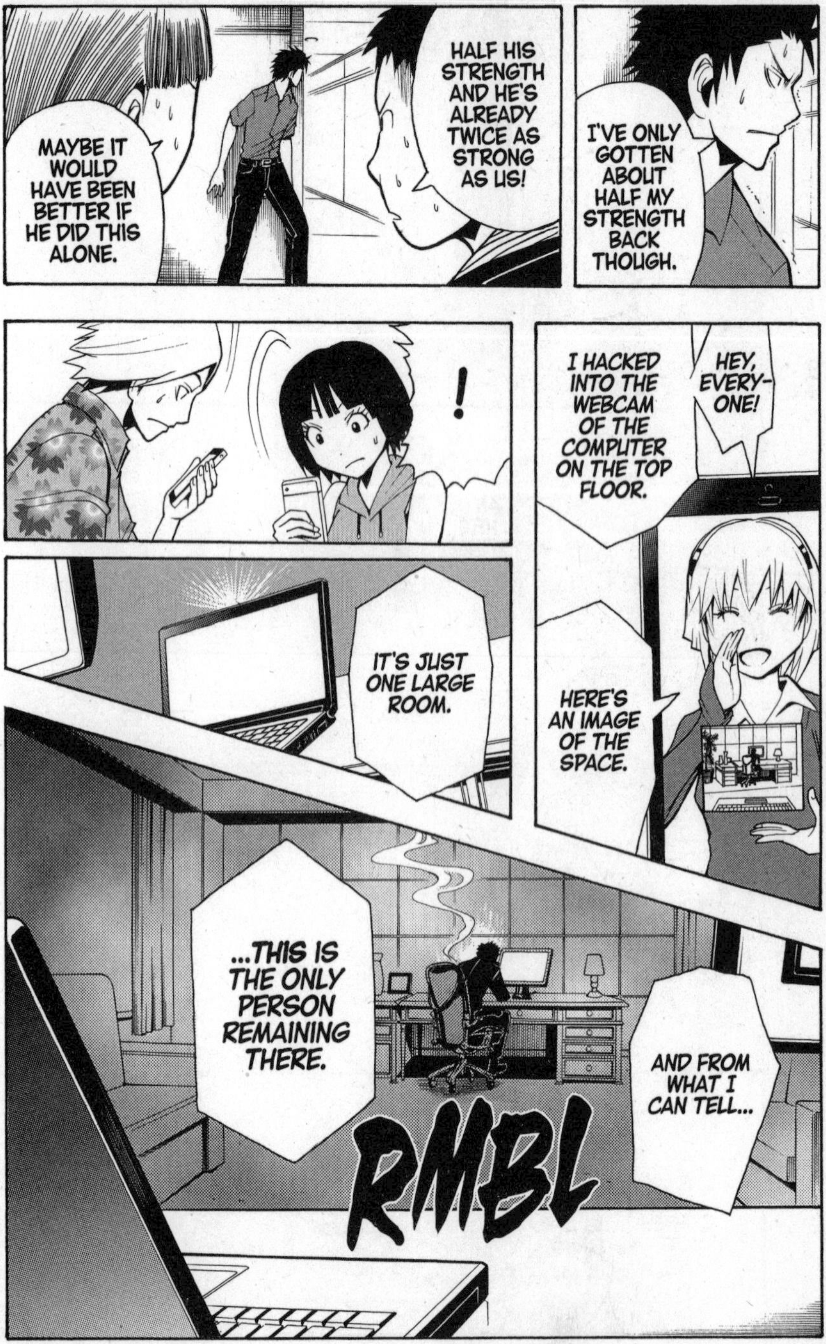
I'VE ONLY GOTTEN ABOUT HALF MY STRENGTH BACK THOUGH.
HALF HIS STRENGTH AND HE'S ALREADY TWICE AS STRONG AS US!
MAYBE IT WOULD HAVE BEEN BETTER IF HE DID THIS ALONE.
HEY, EVERYONE!
I HACKED INTO THE WEBCAM OF THE COMPUTER ON THE TOP FLOOR.
HERE'S AN IMAGE OF THE SPACE.
!
IT'S JUST ONE LARGE ROOM.
AND FROM WHAT I CAN TELL...
...THIS IS THE ONLY PERSON REMAINING THERE.
RMBL

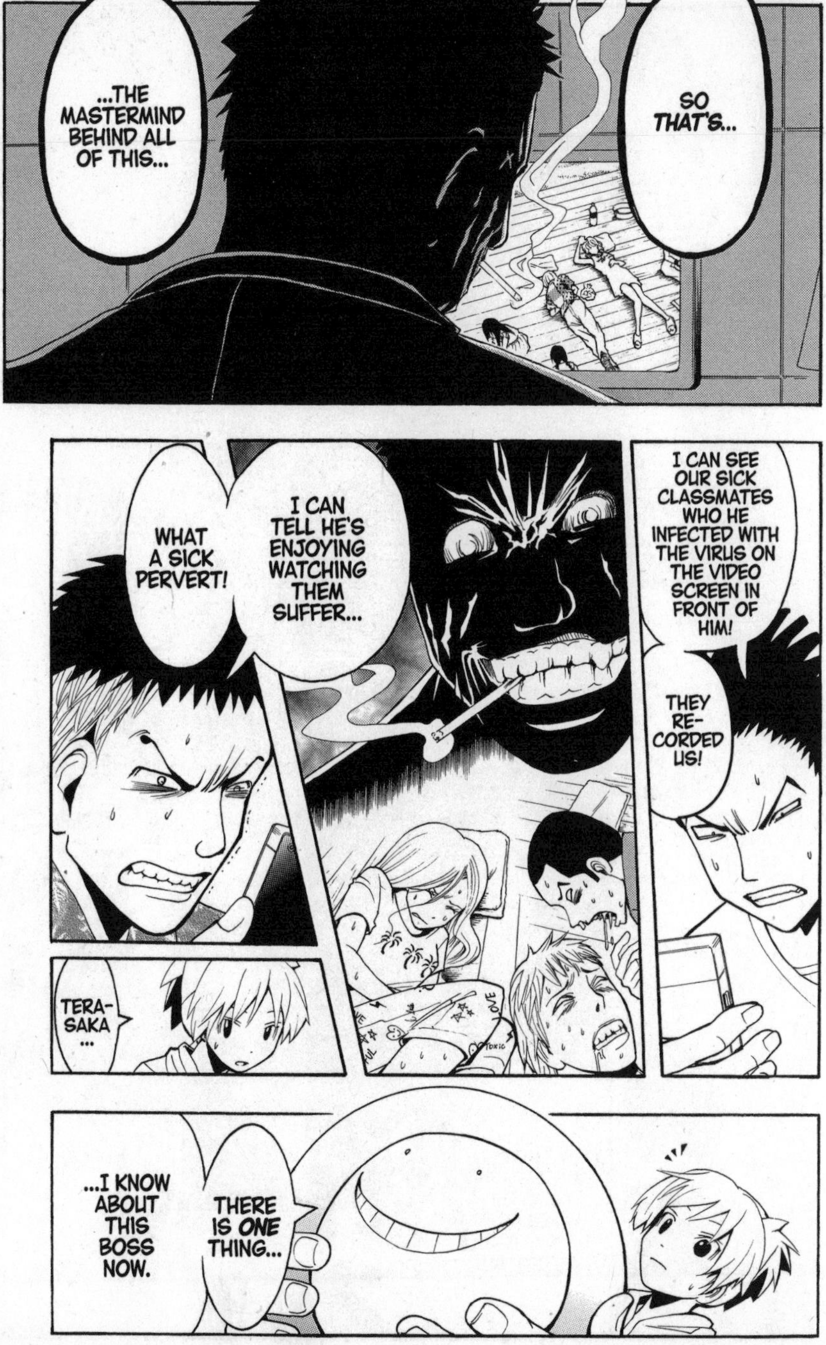
SO THAT'S...
...THE MASTERMIND BEHIND ALL OF THIS...
I CAN SEE OUR SICK CLASSMATES WHO HE INFECTED WITH THE VIRUS ON THE VIDEO SCREEN IN FRONT OF HIM!
THEY RE-CORDED US!
I CAN TELL HE'S ENJOYING WATCHING THEM SUFFER...
WHAT A SICK PERVERT!
TERA-SAKA...
THERE IS ONE THING...
...I KNOW ABOUT THIS BOSS NOW.

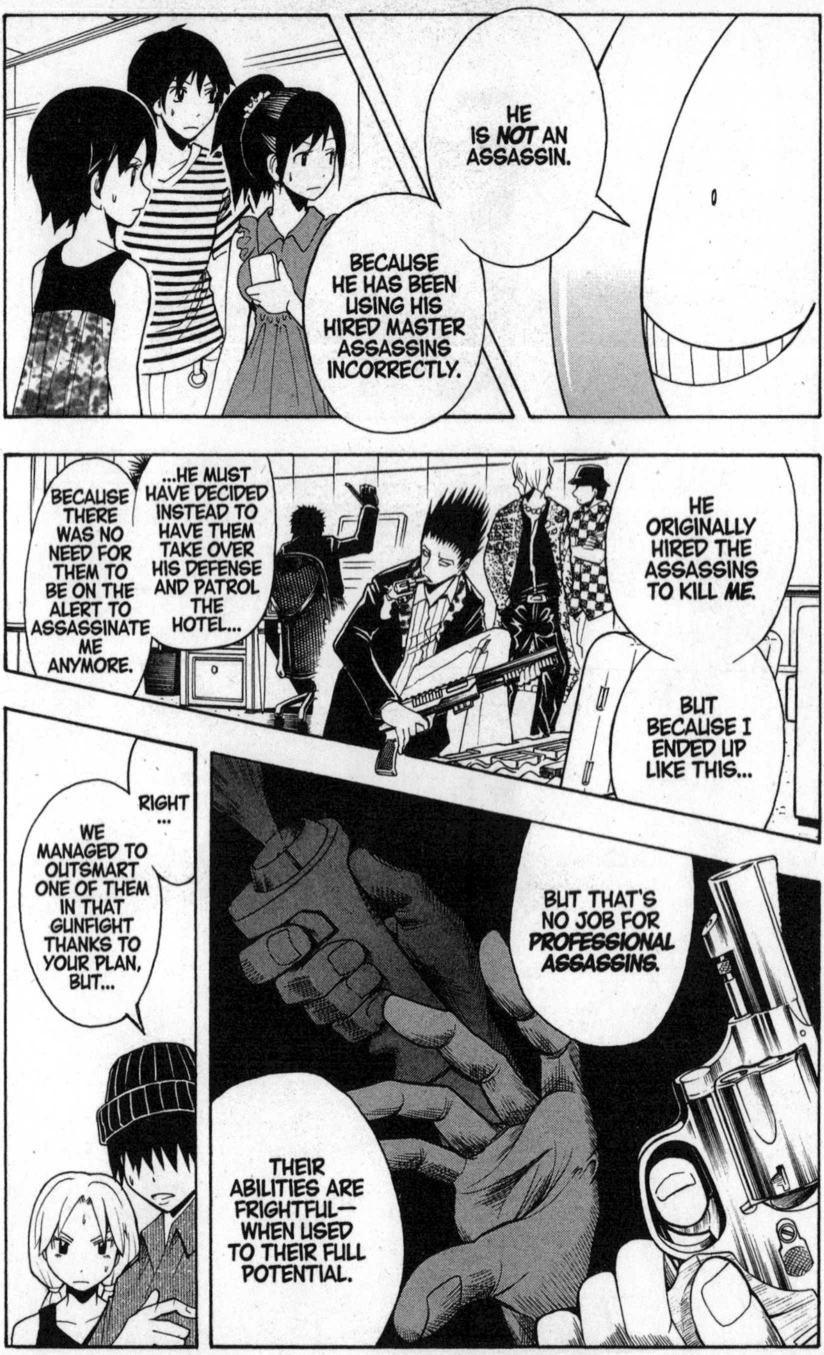
HE IS *NOT* AN ASSASSIN.
BECAUSE HE HAS BEEN USING HIS HIRED MASTER ASSASSINS INCORRECTLY.
HE ORIGINALLY HIRED THE ASSASSINS TO KILL *ME*.
BUT BECAUSE I ENDED UP LIKE THIS...
...HE MUST HAVE DECIDED INSTEAD TO HAVE THEM TAKE OVER HIS DEFENSE AND PATROL THE HOTEL...
BECAUSE THERE WAS NO NEED FOR THEM TO BE ON THE ALERT TO ASSASSINATE ME ANYMORE.
BUT THAT'S NO JOB FOR *PROFESSIONAL ASSASSINS*.
THEIR ABILITIES ARE FRIGHTFUL— WHEN USED TO THEIR FULL POTENTIAL.
RIGHT...
WE MANAGED TO OUTSMART ONE OF THEM IN THAT GUNFIGHT THANKS TO YOUR PLAN, BUT...

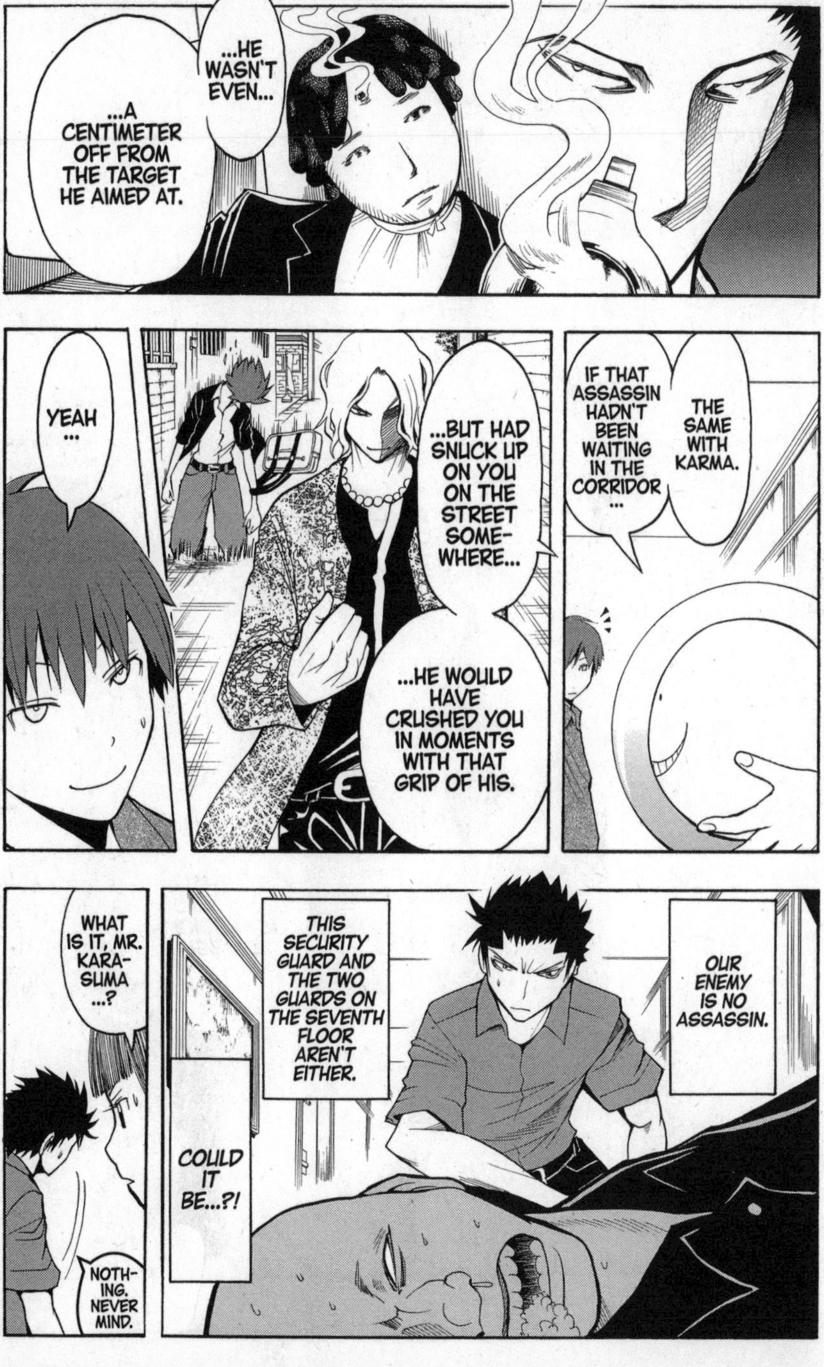
...HE WASN'T EVEN...
...A CENTIMETER OFF FROM THE TARGET HE AIMED AT.
THE SAME WITH KARMA.
IF THAT ASSASSIN HADN'T BEEN WAITING IN THE CORRIDOR...
...BUT HAD SNUCK UP ON YOU ON THE STREET SOME-WHERE...
...HE WOULD HAVE CRUSHED YOU IN MOMENTS WITH THAT GRIP OF HIS.
YEAH...
OUR ENEMY IS NO ASSASSIN.
THIS SECURITY GUARD AND THE TWO GUARDS ON THE SEVENTH FLOOR AREN'T EITHER.
COULD IT BE...?!
WHAT IS IT, MR. KARA-SUMA...?
NOTH-ING. NEVER MIND.

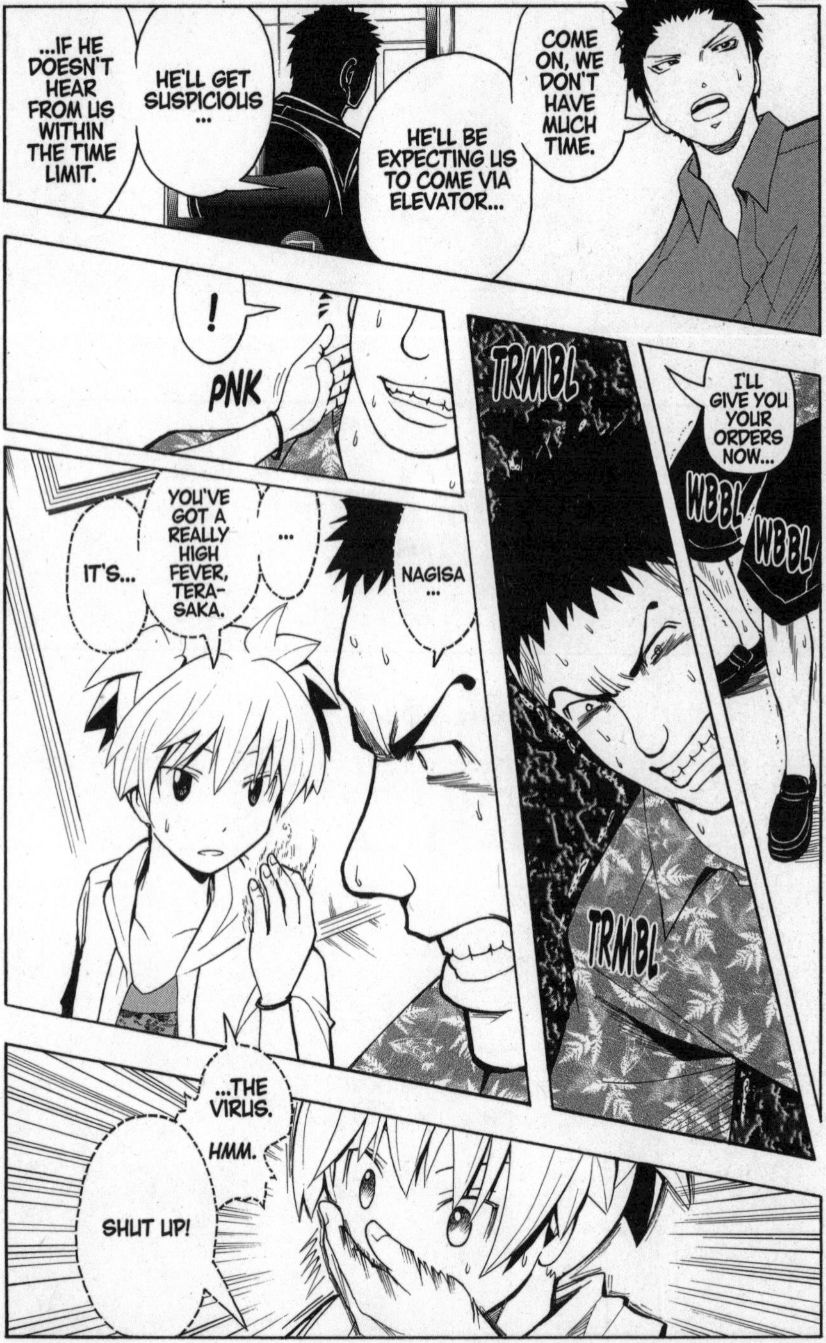
COME ON, WE DON'T HAVE MUCH TIME.
HE'LL BE EXPECTING US TO COME VIA ELEVATOR...
HE'LL GET SUSPICIOUS...
...IF HE DOESN'T HEAR FROM US WITHIN THE TIME LIMIT.
I'LL GIVE YOU YOUR ORDERS NOW...
WBBL
WBBL
TRMBL
TRMBL
!
PNK
NAGISA...
...
YOU'VE GOT A REALLY HIGH FEVER, TERA-SAKA.
IT'S...
...THE VIRUS.
HMM.
SHUT UP!

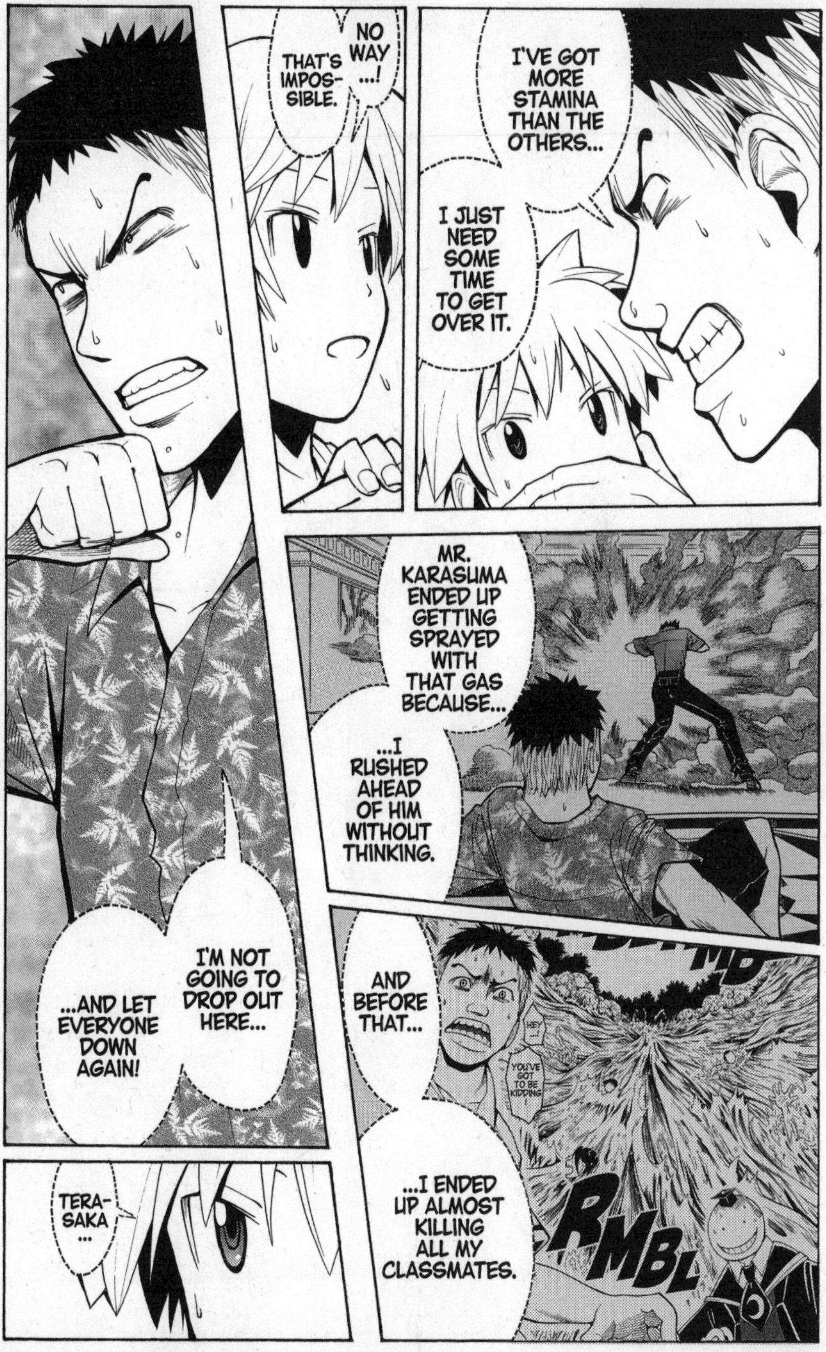
I'VE GOT MORE STAMINA THAN THE OTHERS...
I JUST NEED SOME TIME TO GET OVER IT.
NO WAY ...!
THAT'S IMPOSSIBLE.
MR. KARASUMA ENDED UP GETTING SPRAYED WITH THAT GAS BECAUSE...
...I RUSHED AHEAD OF HIM WITHOUT THINKING.
AND BEFORE THAT...
HEY
YOU'VE GOT TO BE KIDDING!
...I ENDED UP ALMOST KILLING ALL MY CLASSMATES.
RMBL
I'M NOT GOING TO DROP OUT HERE...
...AND LET EVERYONE DOWN AGAIN!
TERA-SAKA...

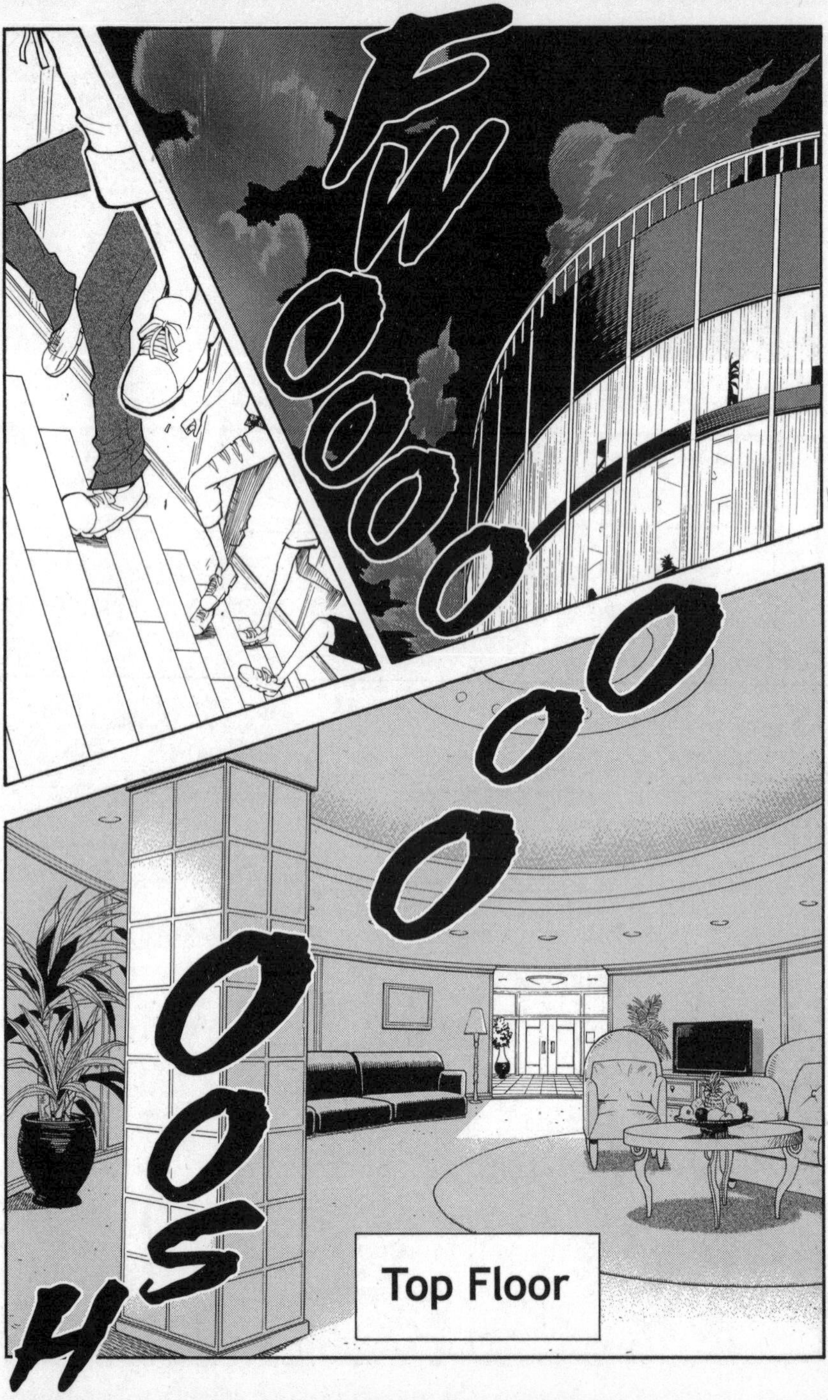
SWOOOOOOOOOOSH
Top Floor

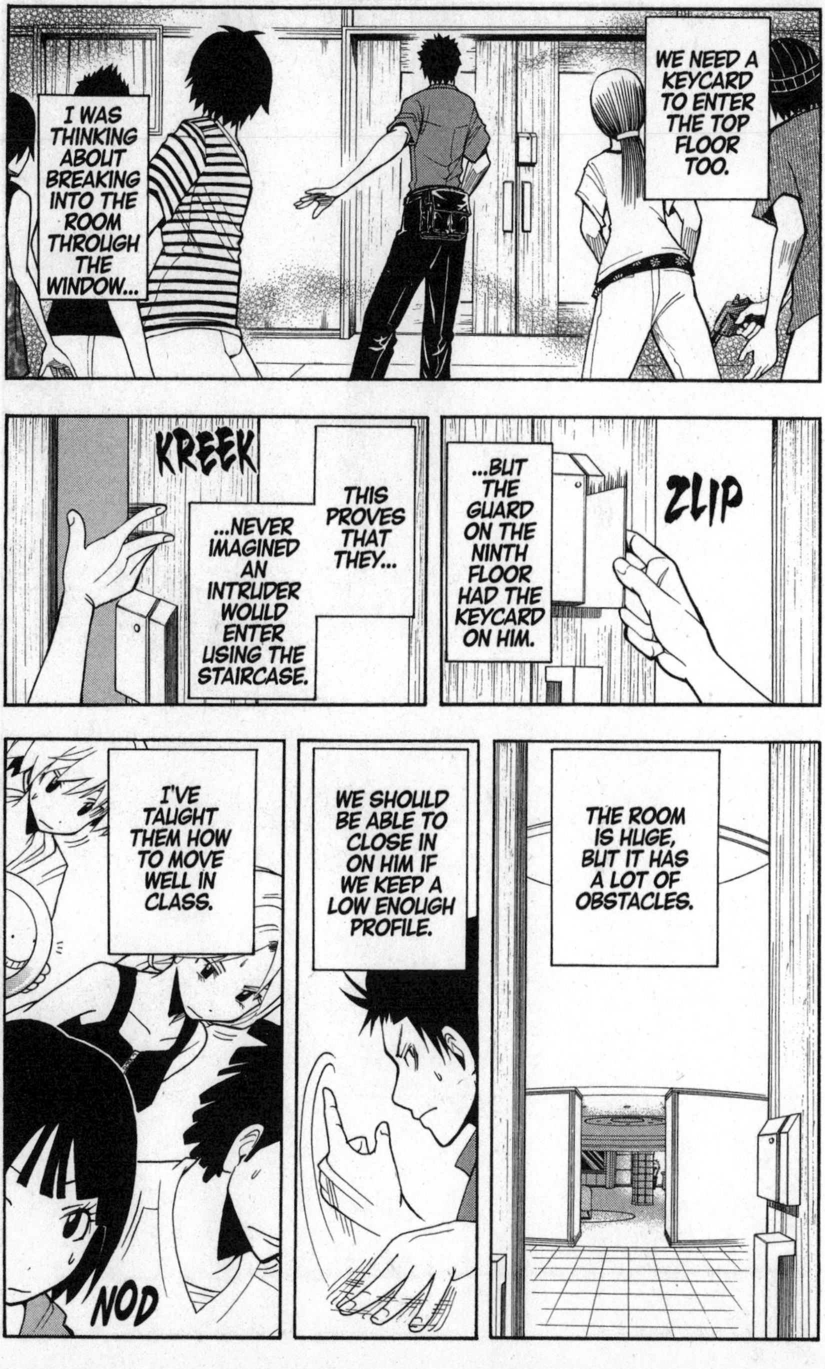
WE NEED A KEYCARD TO ENTER THE TOP FLOOR TOO.
I WAS THINKING ABOUT BREAKING INTO THE ROOM THROUGH THE WINDOW...
ZLIP
...BUT THE GUARD ON THE NINTH FLOOR HAD THE KEYCARD ON HIM.
THIS PROVES THAT THEY...
...NEVER IMAGINED AN INTRUDER WOULD ENTER USING THE STAIRCASE.
KREEK
THE ROOM IS HUGE, BUT IT HAS A LOT OF OBSTACLES.
WE SHOULD BE ABLE TO CLOSE IN ON HIM IF WE KEEP A LOW ENOUGH PROFILE.
I'VE TAUGHT THEM HOW TO MOVE WELL IN CLASS.
NOD

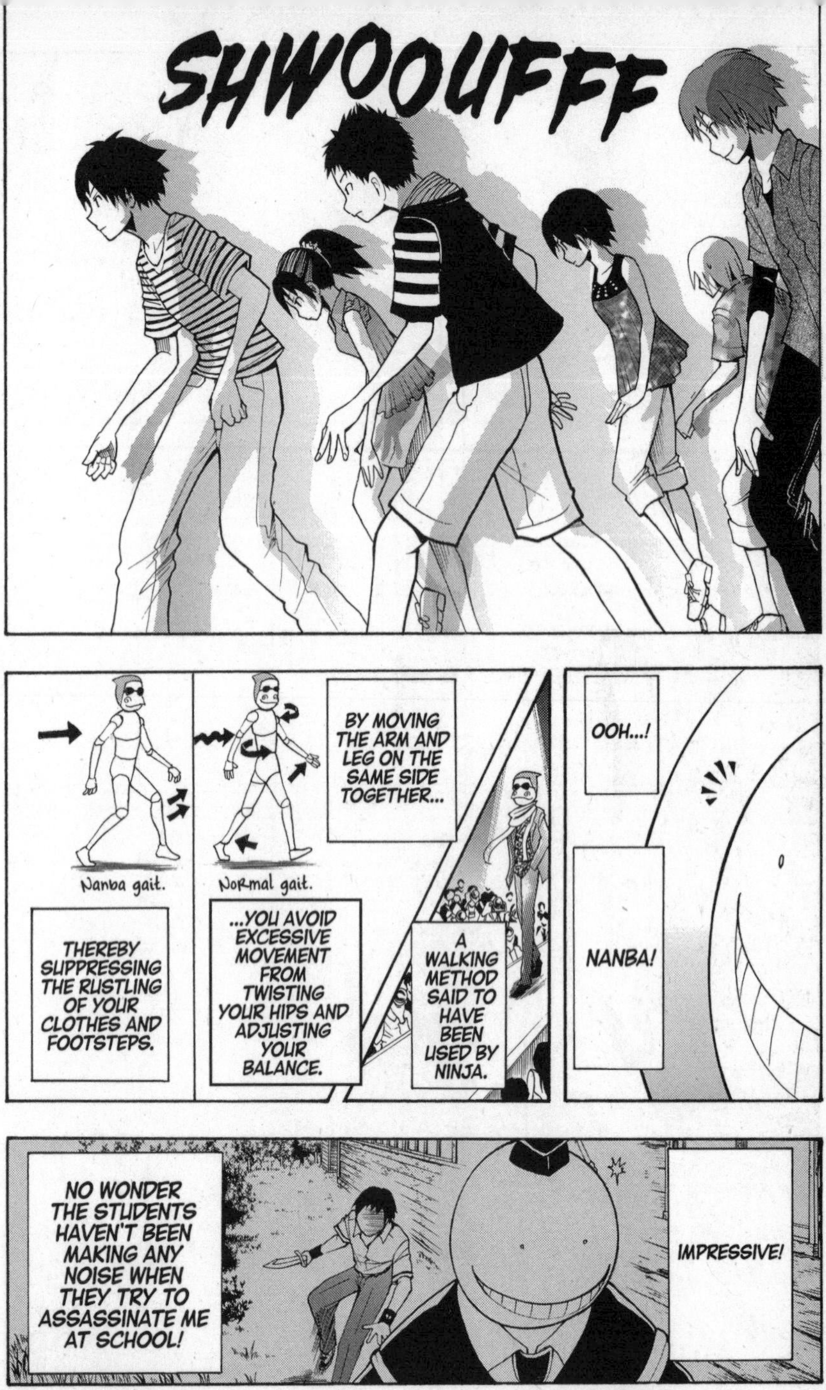
SHWOOUFFF
OOH...!
NANBA!
A WALKING METHOD SAID TO HAVE BEEN USED BY NINJA.
BY MOVING THE ARM AND LEG ON THE SAME SIDE TOGETHER...
Normal gait.
...YOU AVOID EXCESSIVE MOVEMENT FROM TWISTING YOUR HIPS AND ADJUSTING YOUR BALANCE.
Nanba gait.
THEREBY SUPPRESSING THE RUSTLING OF YOUR CLOTHES AND FOOTSTEPS.
IMPRESSIVE!
NO WONDER THE STUDENTS HAVEN'T BEEN MAKING ANY NOISE WHEN THEY TRY TO ASSASSINATE ME AT SCHOOL!

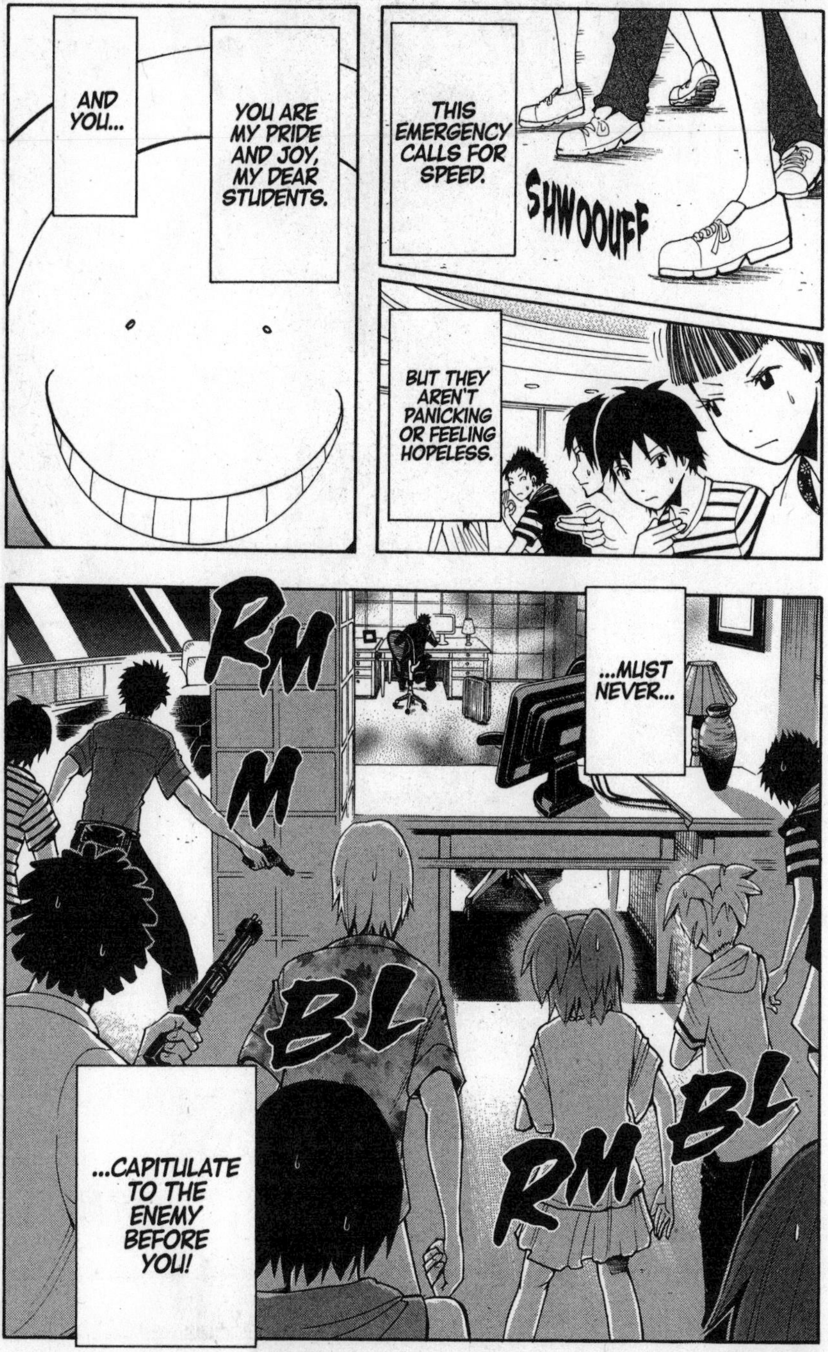
THIS EMERGENCY CALLS FOR SPEED.
SHWOOUFF
BUT THEY AREN'T PANICKING OR FEELING HOPELESS.
YOU ARE MY PRIDE AND JOY, MY DEAR STUDENTS.
AND YOU...
...MUST NEVER...
RMMBL
...CAPITULATE TO THE ENEMY BEFORE YOU!
RMBL

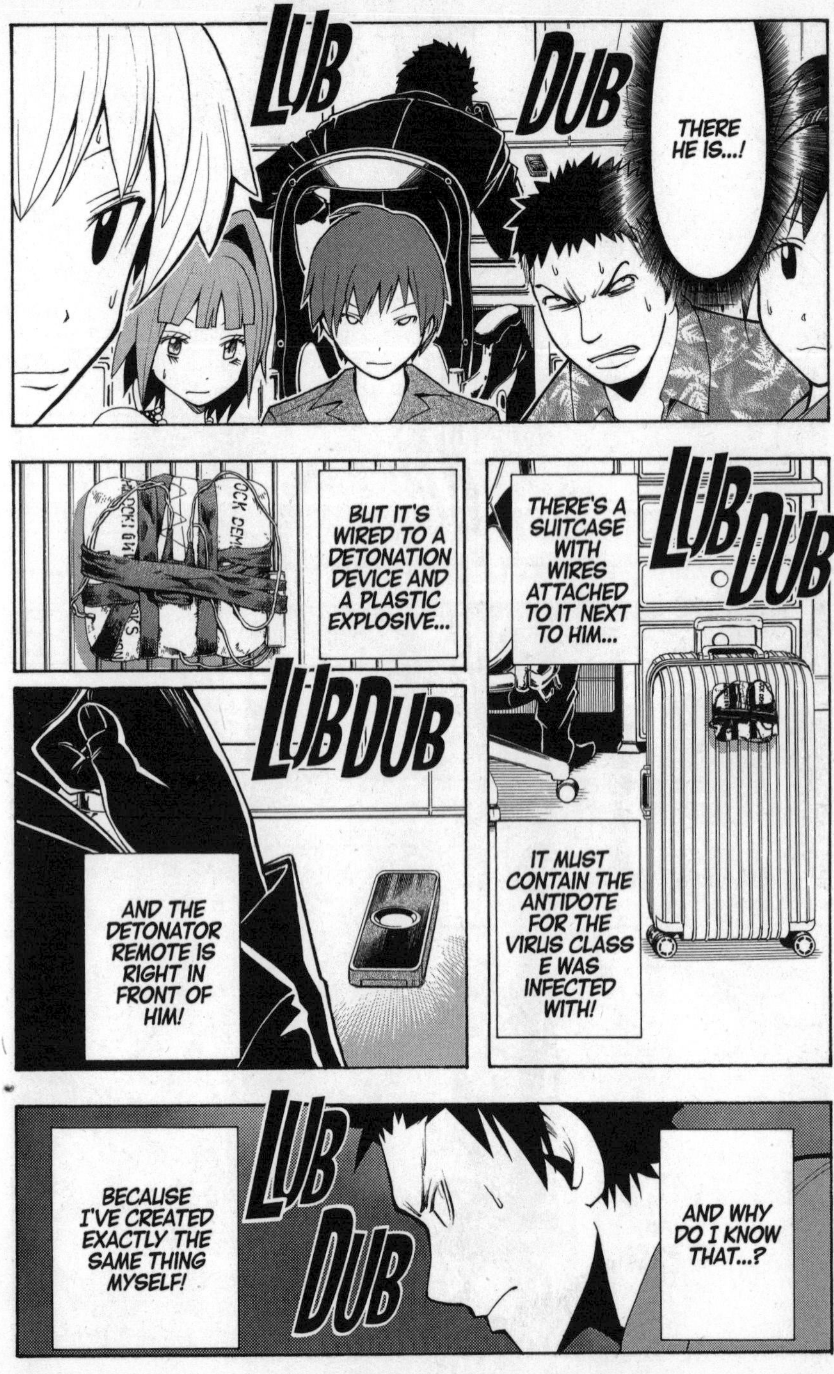
THERE HE IS...!
LUB
DUB
THERE'S A SUITCASE WITH WIRES ATTACHED TO IT NEXT TO HIM...
LUB DUB
IT MUST CONTAIN THE ANTIDOTE FOR THE VIRUS CLASS E WAS INFECTED WITH!
BUT IT'S WIRED TO A DETONATION DEVICE AND A PLASTIC EXPLOSIVE...
LUB DUB
AND THE DETONATOR REMOTE IS RIGHT IN FRONT OF HIM!
AND WHY DO I KNOW THAT...?
LUB
DUB
BECAUSE I'VE CREATED EXACTLY THE SAME THING MYSELF!

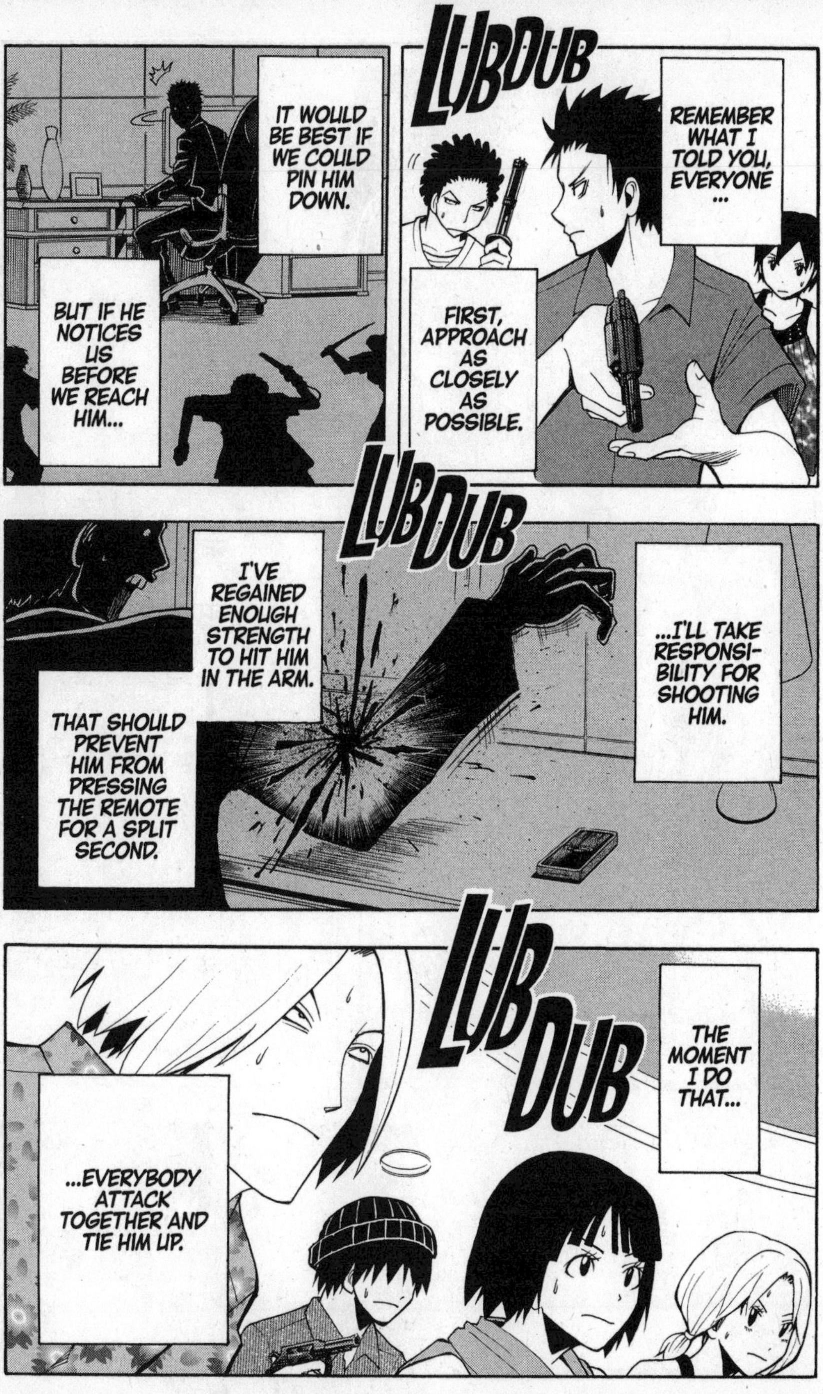
LUBDUB
REMEMBER WHAT I TOLD YOU, EVERYONE ...
FIRST, APPROACH AS CLOSELY AS POSSIBLE.
IT WOULD BE BEST IF WE COULD PIN HIM DOWN.
BUT IF HE NOTICES US BEFORE WE REACH HIM...
LUBDUB
...I'LL TAKE RESPONSI-BILITY FOR SHOOTING HIM.
I'VE REGAINED ENOUGH STRENGTH TO HIT HIM IN THE ARM.
THAT SHOULD PREVENT HIM FROM PRESSING THE REMOTE FOR A SPLIT SECOND.
LUB DUB
THE MOMENT I DO THAT...
...EVERYBODY ATTACK TOGETHER AND TIE HIM UP.

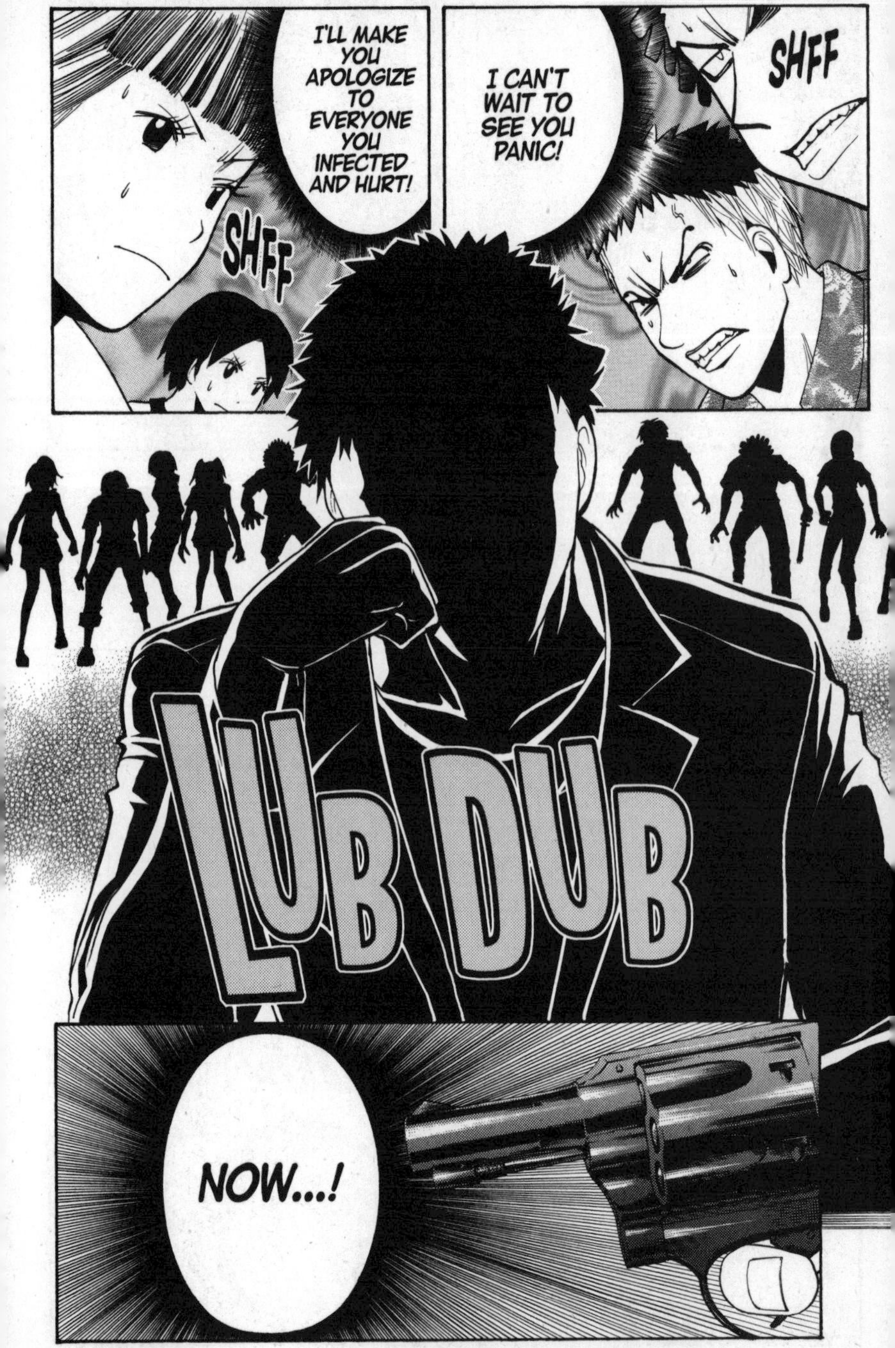
I CAN'T WAIT TO SEE YOU PANIC!
SHFF
I'LL MAKE YOU APOLOGIZE TO EVERYONE YOU INFECTED AND HURT!
SHFF
LUB DUB
NOW...!

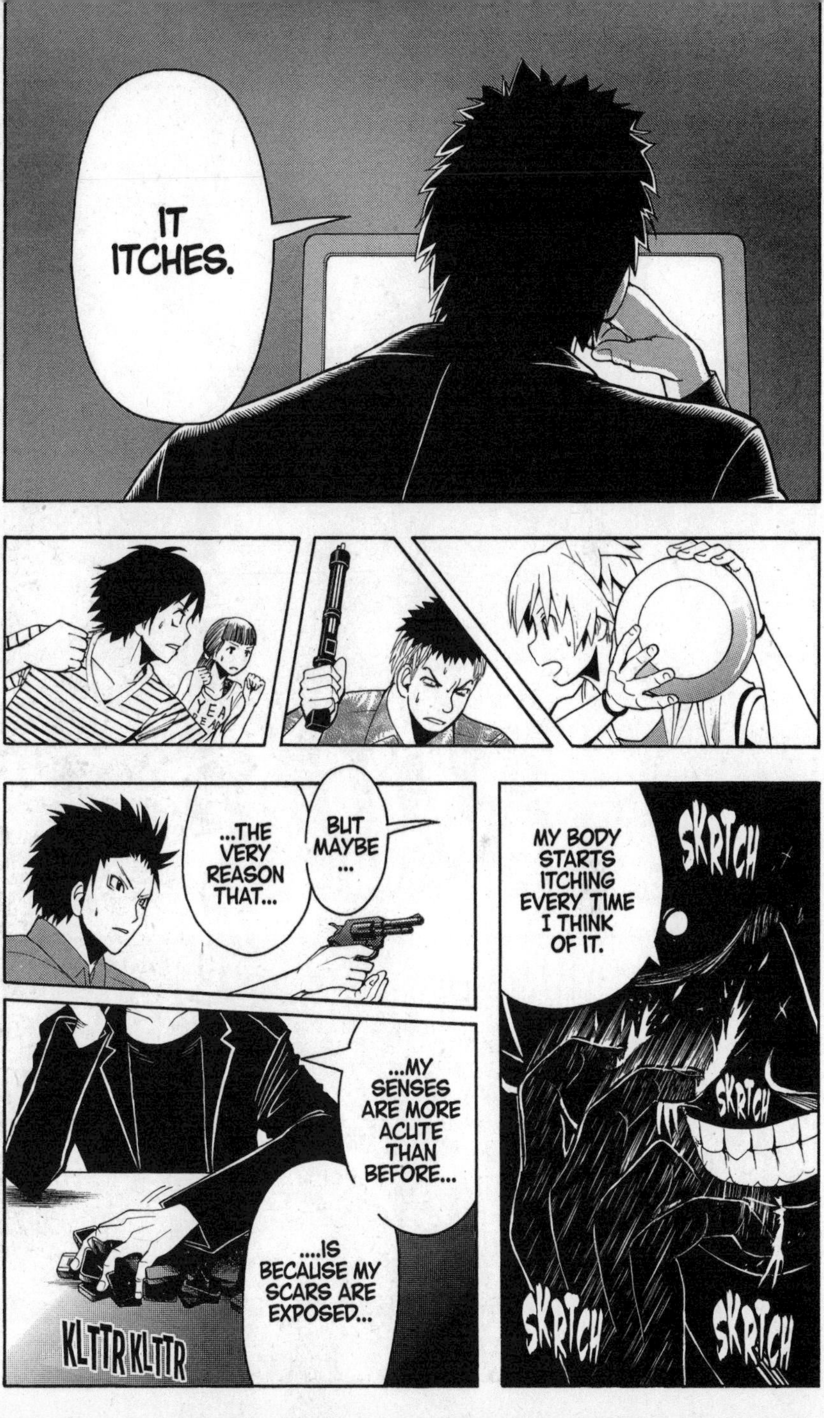
IT ITCHES.
MY BODY STARTS ITCHING EVERY TIME I THINK OF IT.
SKRTCH
SKRTCH
SKRTCH
SKRTCH
BUT MAYBE ...
...THE VERY REASON THAT...
...MY SENSES ARE MORE ACUTE THAN BEFORE...
....IS BECAUSE MY SCARS ARE EXPOSED...
KLTTR KLTTR

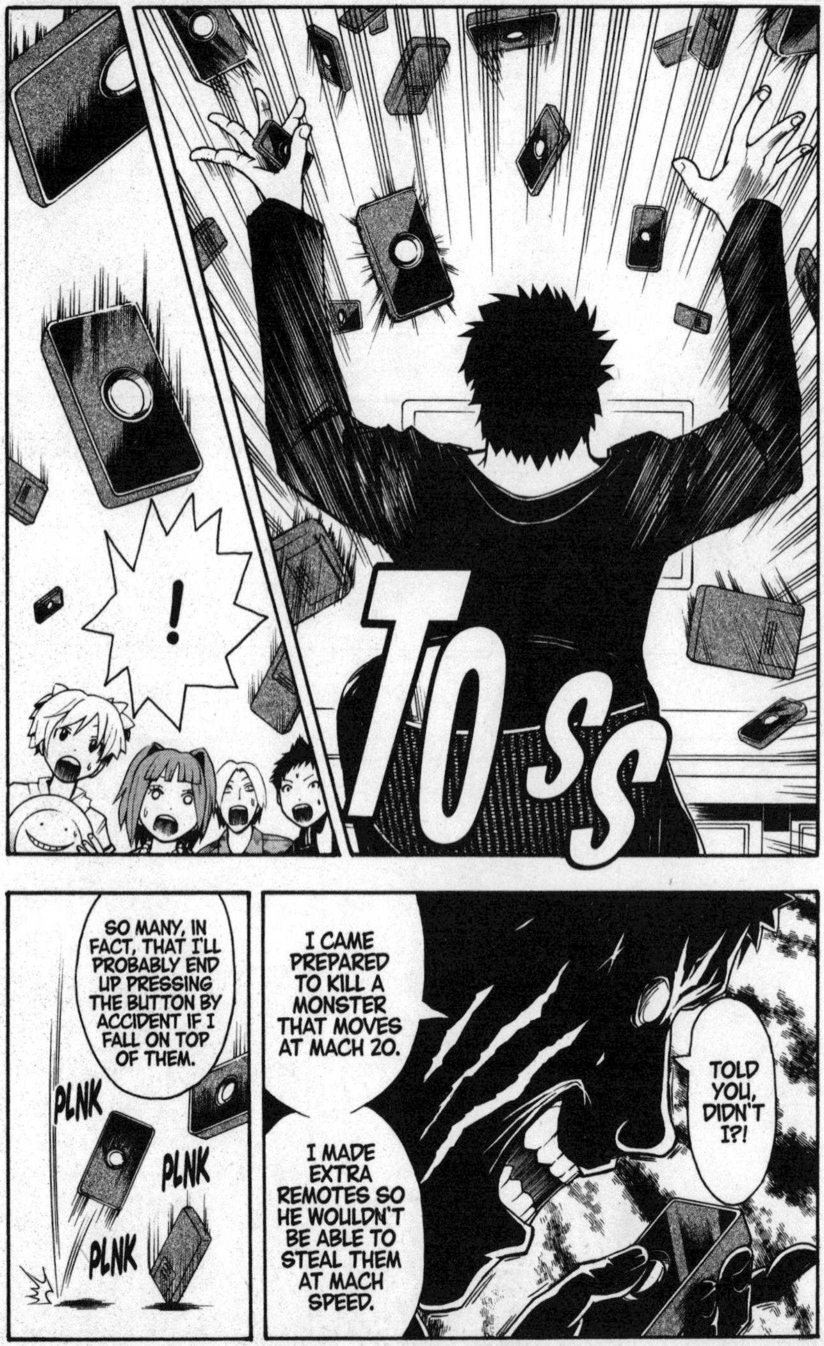
TOSS
!
I CAME PREPARED TO KILL A MONSTER THAT MOVES AT MACH 20.
TOLD YOU, DIDN'T I?!
I MADE EXTRA REMOTES SO HE WOULDN'T BE ABLE TO STEAL THEM AT MACH SPEED.
SO MANY, IN FACT, THAT I'LL PROBABLY END UP PRESSING THE BUTTON BY ACCIDENT IF I FALL ON TOP OF THEM.
PLNK
PLNK
PLNK

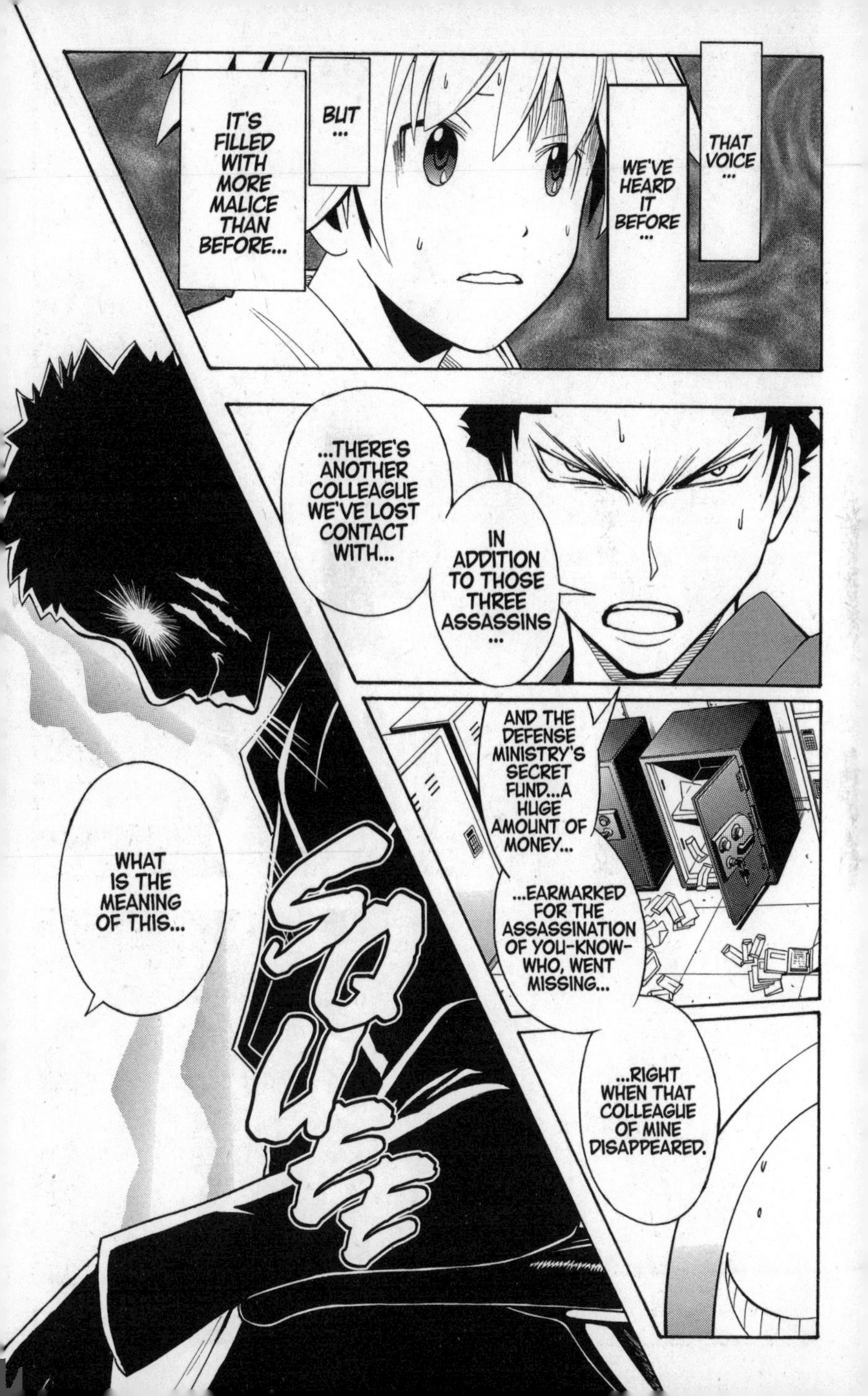
THAT VOICE...
WE'VE HEARD IT BEFORE...
BUT...
IT'S FILLED WITH MORE MALICE THAN BEFORE...
IN ADDITION TO THOSE THREE ASSASSINS...
...THERE'S ANOTHER COLLEAGUE WE'VE LOST CONTACT WITH...
AND THE DEFENSE MINISTRY'S SECRET FUND...A HUGE AMOUNT OF MONEY...
...EARMARKED FOR THE ASSASSINATION OF YOU-KNOW-WHO, WENT MISSING...
...RIGHT WHEN THAT COLLEAGUE OF MINE DISAPPEARED.
WHAT IS THE MEANING OF THIS...
SQUEE

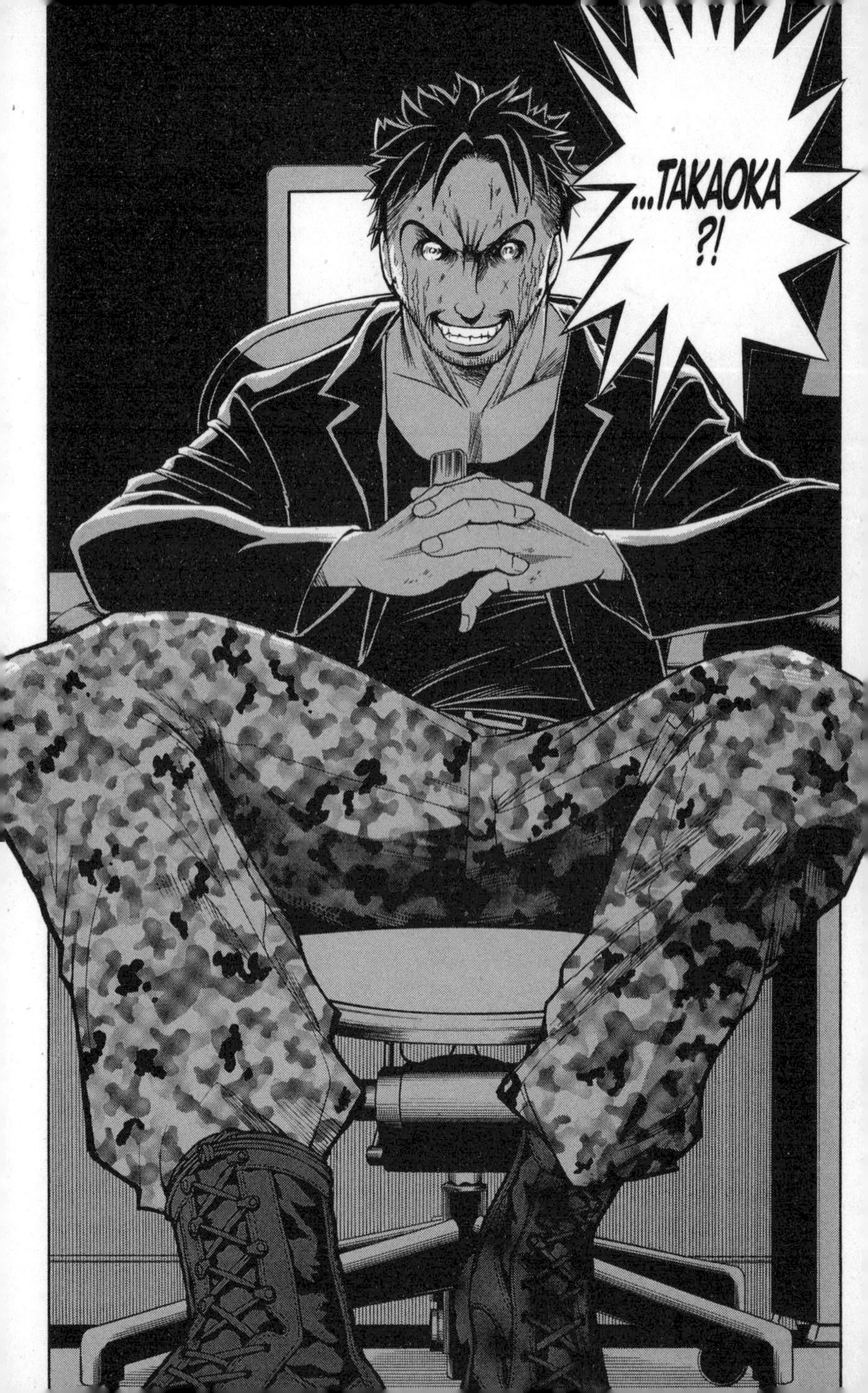
...TAKAOKA
?!

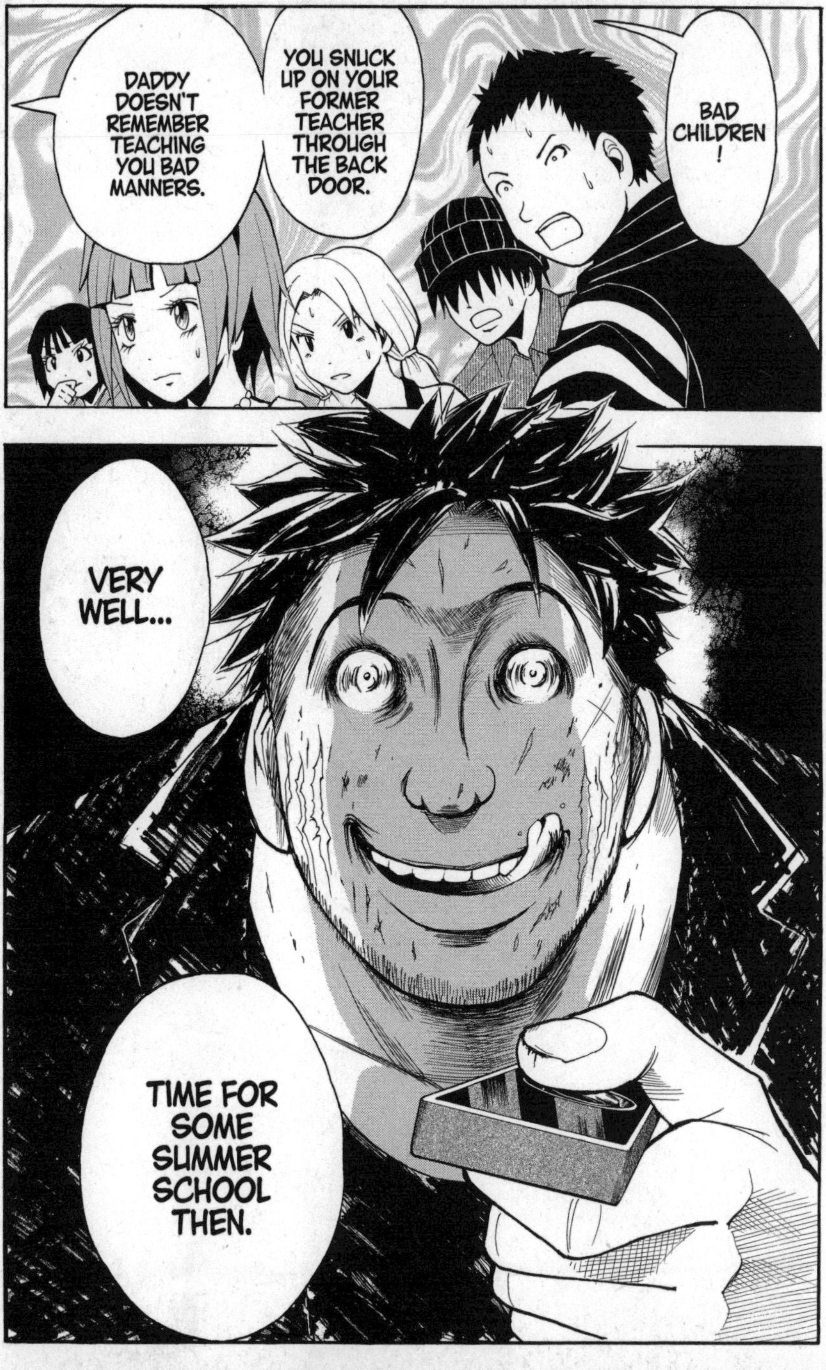
BAD CHILDREN!
YOU SNUCK UP ON YOUR FORMER TEACHER THROUGH THE BACK DOOR.
DADDY DOESN'T REMEMBER TEACHING YOU BAD MANNERS.
VERY WELL...
TIME FOR SOME SUMMER SCHOOL THEN.

E-19 RINKA HAYAMI

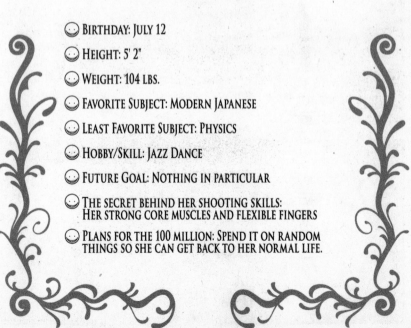

- BIRTHDAY: JULY 12
- HEIGHT: 5' 2"
- WEIGHT: 104 LBS.
- FAVORITE SUBJECT: MODERN JAPANESE
- LEAST FAVORITE SUBJECT: PHYSICS
- HOBBY/SKILL: JAZZ DANCE
- FUTURE GOAL: NOTHING IN PARTICULAR
- THE SECRET BEHIND HER SHOOTING SKILLS: HER STRONG CORE MUSCLES AND FLEXIBLE FINGERS
- PLANS FOR THE 100 MILLION: SPEND IT ON RANDOM THINGS SO SHE CAN GET BACK TO HER NORMAL LIFE.

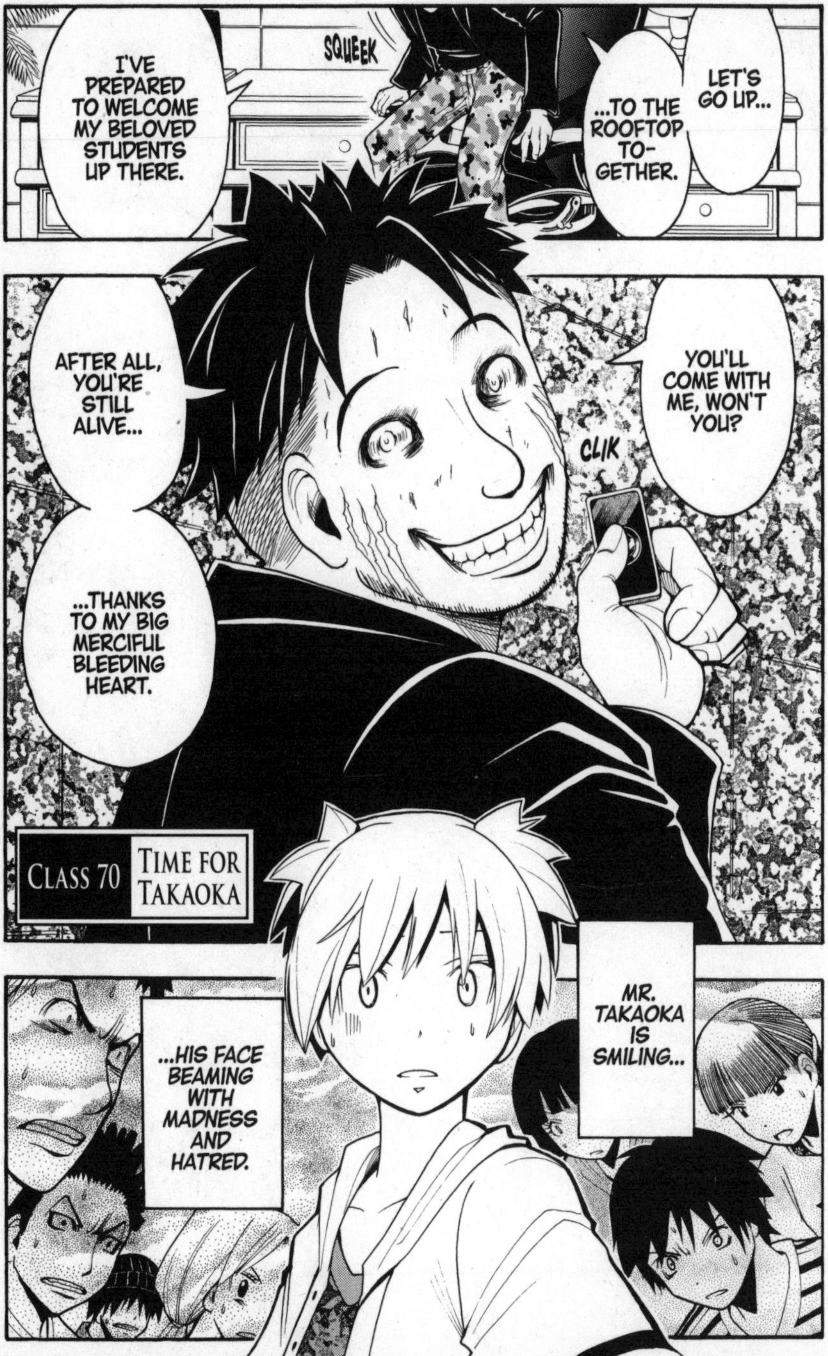
LET'S GO UP...
...TO THE ROOFTOP TOGETHER.
SQUEEK
I'VE PREPARED TO WELCOME MY BELOVED STUDENTS UP THERE.
YOU'LL COME WITH ME, WON'T YOU?
CLIK
AFTER ALL, YOU'RE STILL ALIVE...
...THANKS TO MY BIG MERCIFUL BLEEDING HEART.
CLASS 70 TIME FOR TAKAOKA
MR. TAKAOKA IS SMILING...
...HIS FACE BEAMING WITH MADNESS AND HATRED.

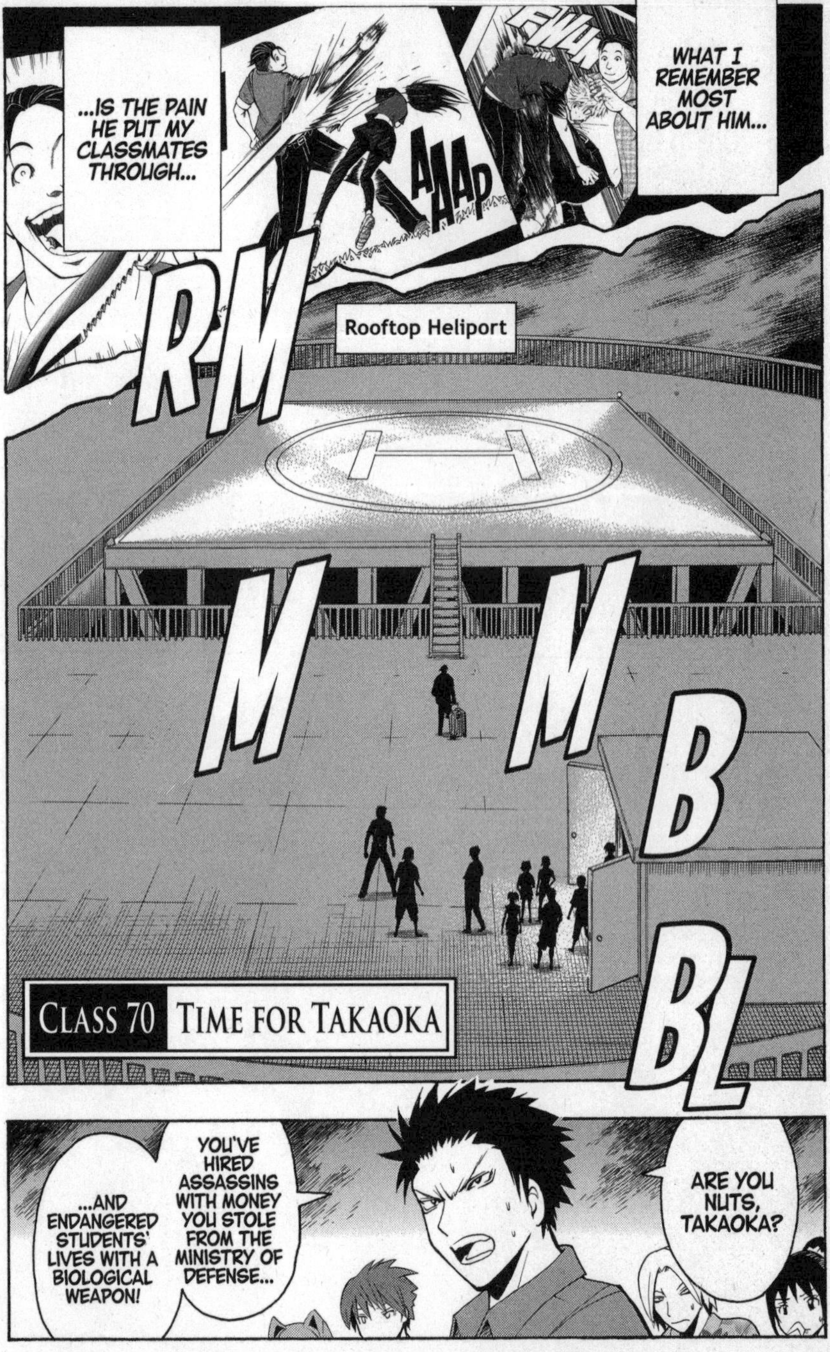
WHAT I REMEMBER MOST ABOUT HIM...
FWUM
...IS THE PAIN HE PUT MY CLASSMATES THROUGH...
AAAP
RMMMBBL
Rooftop Heliport
CLASS 70 TIME FOR TAKAOKA
ARE YOU NUTS, TAKAOKA?
YOU'VE HIRED ASSASSINS WITH MONEY YOU STOLE FROM THE MINISTRY OF DEFENSE...
...AND ENDANGERED STUDENTS' LIVES WITH A BIOLOGICAL WEAPON!

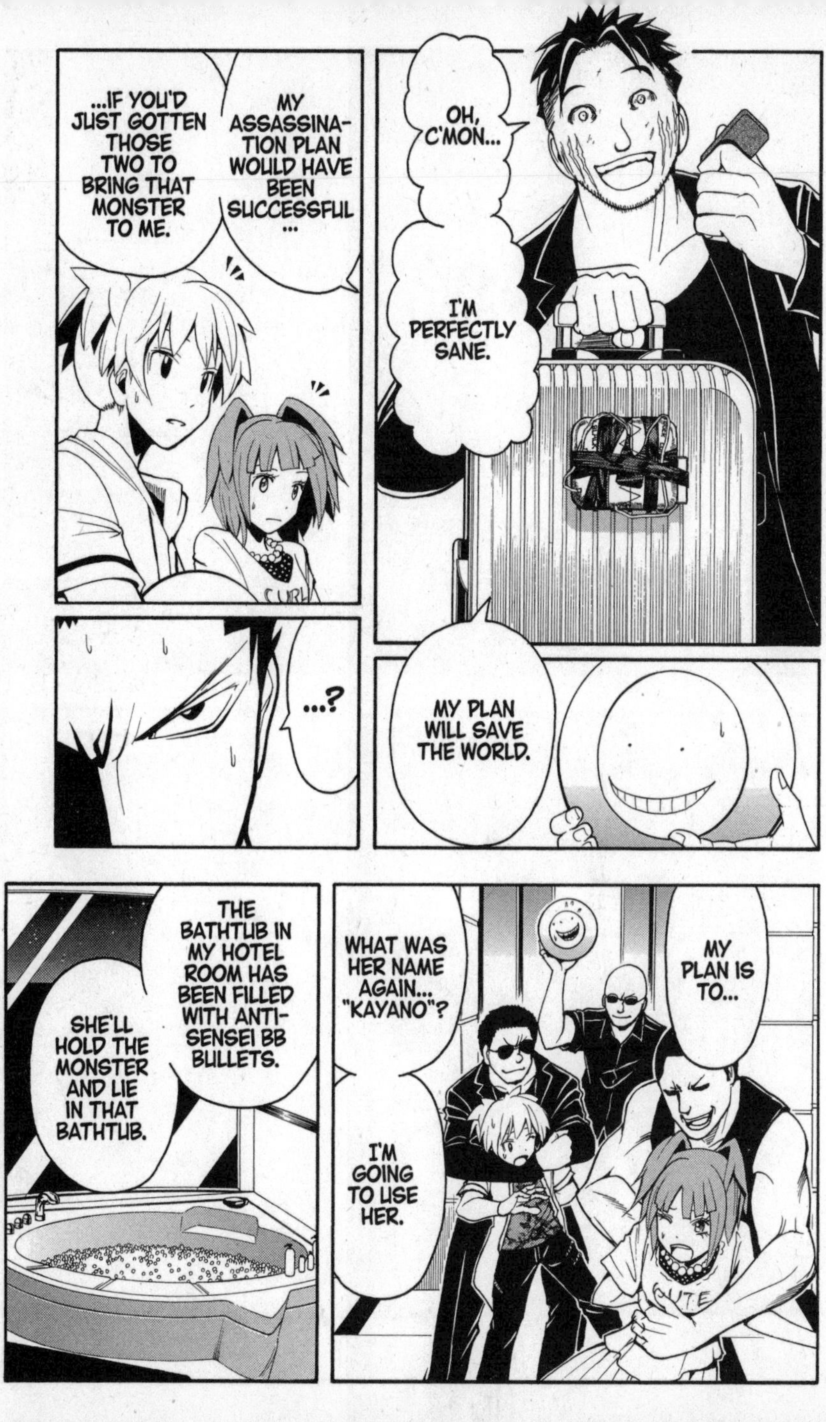
OH, C'MON...
I'M PERFECTLY SANE.
MY ASSASSINATION PLAN WOULD HAVE BEEN SUCCESSFUL...
...IF YOU'D JUST GOTTEN THOSE TWO TO BRING THAT MONSTER TO ME.
MY PLAN WILL SAVE THE WORLD.
...?
MY PLAN IS TO...
WHAT WAS HER NAME AGAIN... "KAYANO"?
I'M GOING TO USE HER.
THE BATHTUB IN MY HOTEL ROOM HAS BEEN FILLED WITH ANTI-SENSEI BB BULLETS.
SHE'LL HOLD THE MONSTER AND LIE IN THAT BATHTUB.

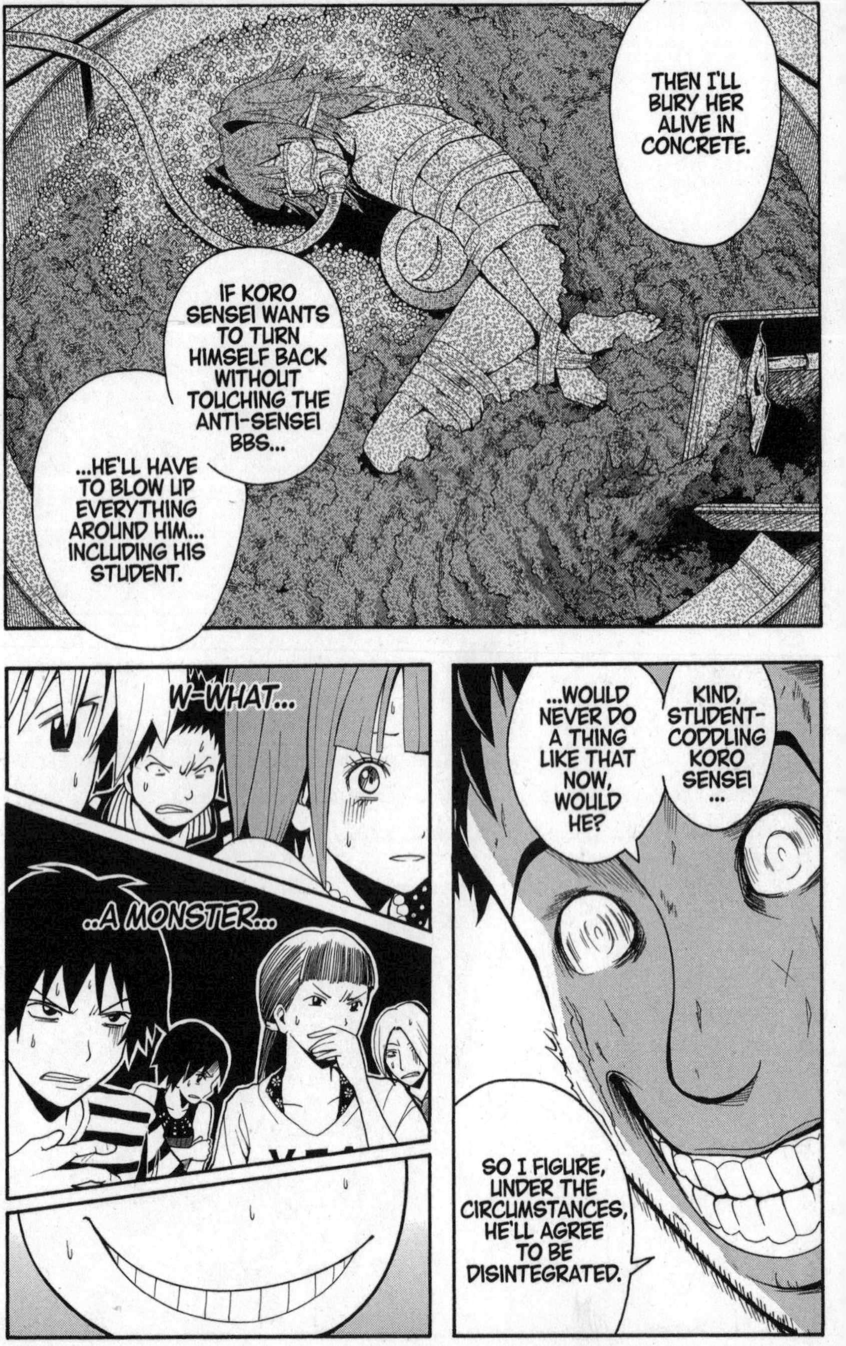
THEN I'LL BURY HER ALIVE IN CONCRETE.
IF KORO SENSEI WANTS TO TURN HIMSELF BACK WITHOUT TOUCHING THE ANTI-SENSEI BBS...
...HE'LL HAVE TO BLOW UP EVERYTHING AROUND HIM... INCLUDING HIS STUDENT.
KIND, STUDENT-CODDLING KORO SENSEI ...
...WOULD NEVER DO A THING LIKE THAT NOW, WOULD HE?
SO I FIGURE, UNDER THE CIRCUMSTANCES, HE'LL AGREE TO BE DISINTEGRATED.
W-WHAT...
..A MONSTER...

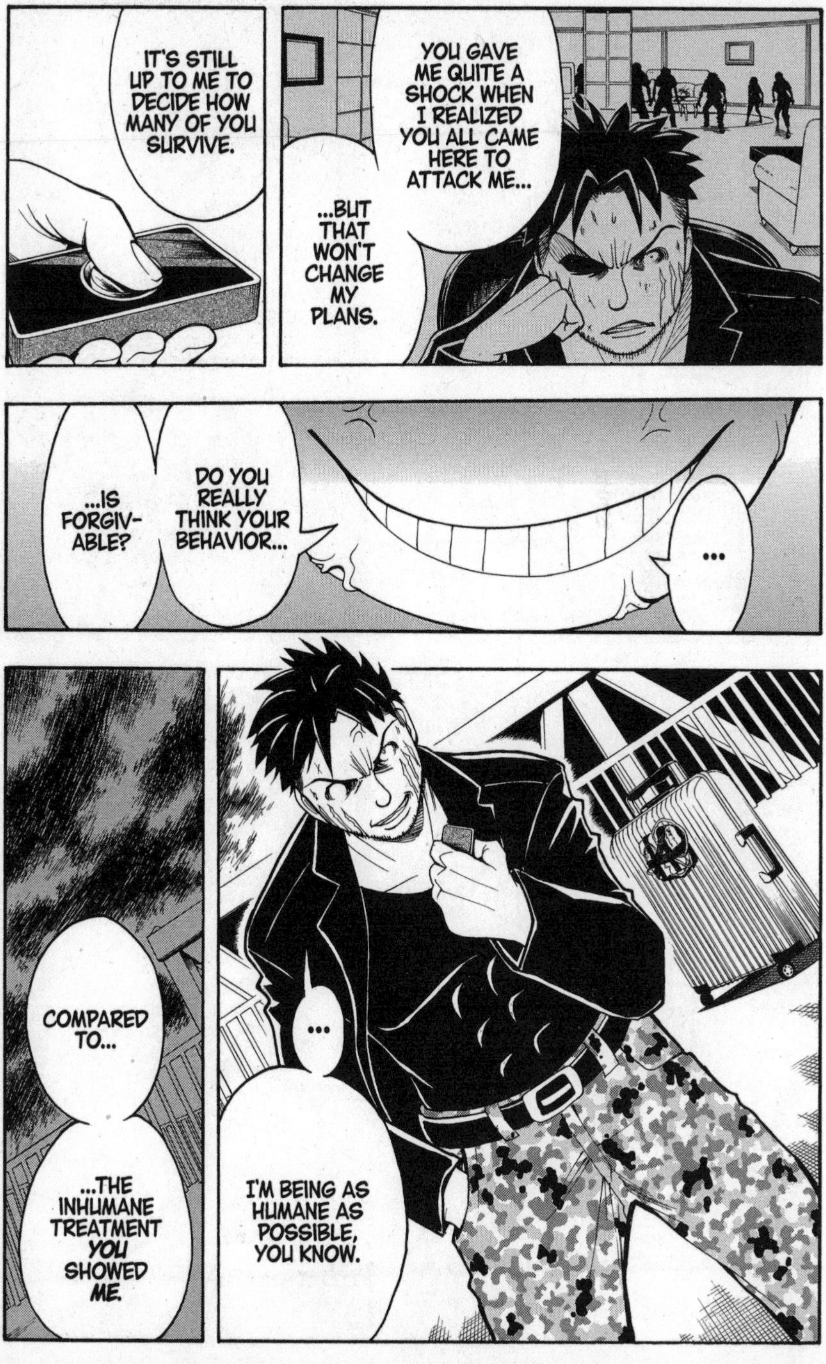
YOU GAVE ME QUITE A SHOCK WHEN I REALIZED YOU ALL CAME HERE TO ATTACK ME...
...BUT THAT WON'T CHANGE MY PLANS.
IT'S STILL UP TO ME TO DECIDE HOW MANY OF YOU SURVIVE.
...
DO YOU REALLY THINK YOUR BEHAVIOR...
...IS FORGIV-ABLE?
...
I'M BEING AS HUMANE AS POSSIBLE, YOU KNOW.
COMPARED TO...
...THE INHUMANE TREATMENT *YOU* SHOWED *ME*.

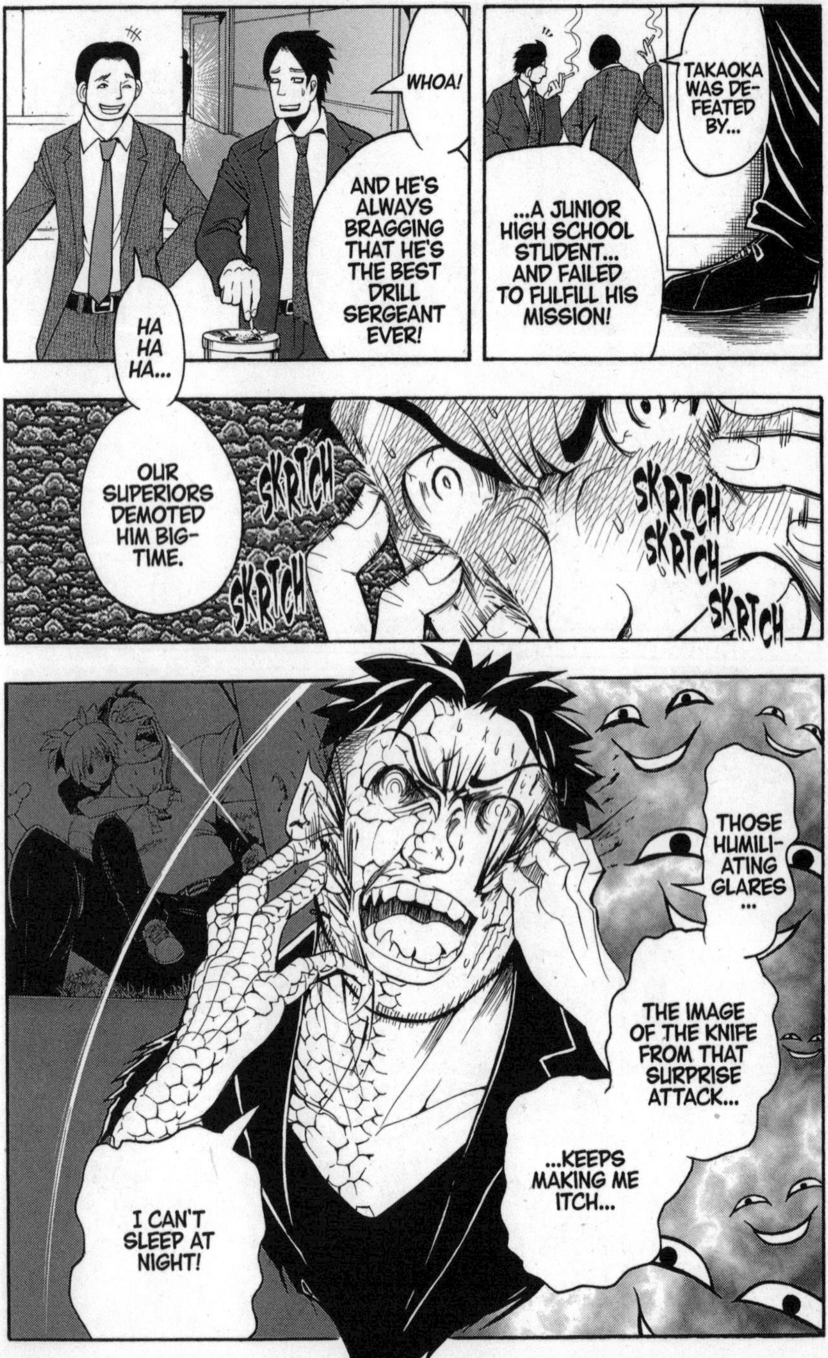
TAKAOKA WAS DEFEATED BY...
...A JUNIOR HIGH SCHOOL STUDENT... AND FAILED TO FULFILL HIS MISSION!
WHOA!
AND HE'S ALWAYS BRAGGING THAT HE'S THE BEST DRILL SERGEANT EVER!
HA HA HA...
SKRTCH
SKRTCH
SKRTCH
OUR SUPERIORS DEMOTED HIM BIG-TIME.
SKRTCH
SKRTCH
THOSE HUMILIATING GLARES...
THE IMAGE OF THE KNIFE FROM THAT SURPRISE ATTACK...
...KEEPS MAKING ME ITCH...
I CAN'T SLEEP AT NIGHT!

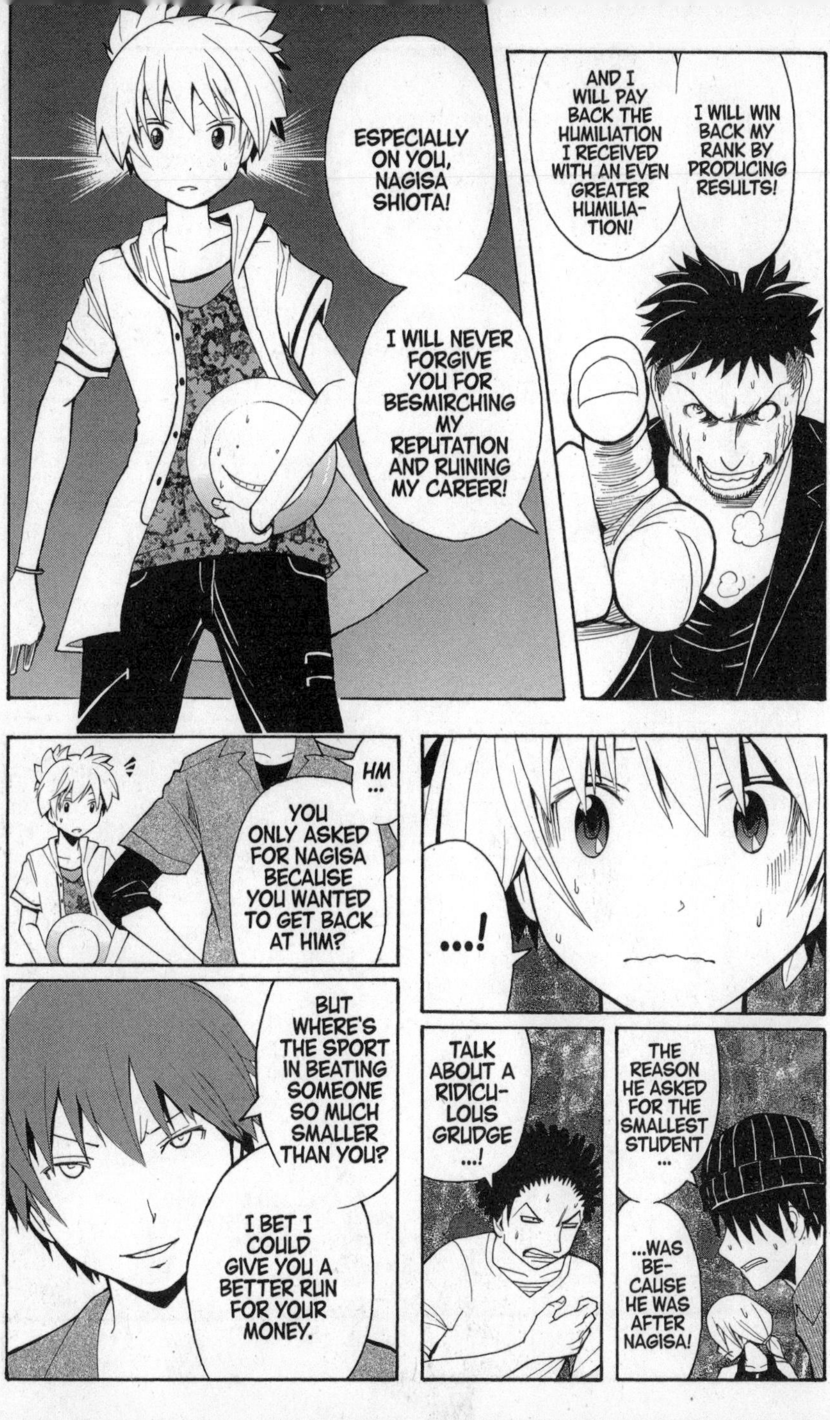
I WILL WIN BACK MY RANK BY PRODUCING RESULTS!
AND I WILL PAY BACK THE HUMILIATION I RECEIVED WITH AN EVEN GREATER HUMILIA-TION!
ESPECIALLY ON YOU, NAGISA SHIOTA!
I WILL NEVER FORGIVE YOU FOR BESMIRCHING MY REPUTATION AND RUINING MY CAREER!
...!
HM ...
YOU ONLY ASKED FOR NAGISA BECAUSE YOU WANTED TO GET BACK AT HIM?
THE REASON HE ASKED FOR THE SMALLEST STUDENT ...
...WAS BE-CAUSE HE WAS AFTER NAGISA!
TALK ABOUT A RIDICU-LOUS GRUDGE ...!
BUT WHERE'S THE SPORT IN BEATING SOMEONE SO MUCH SMALLER THAN YOU?
I BET I COULD GIVE YOU A BETTER RUN FOR YOUR MONEY.

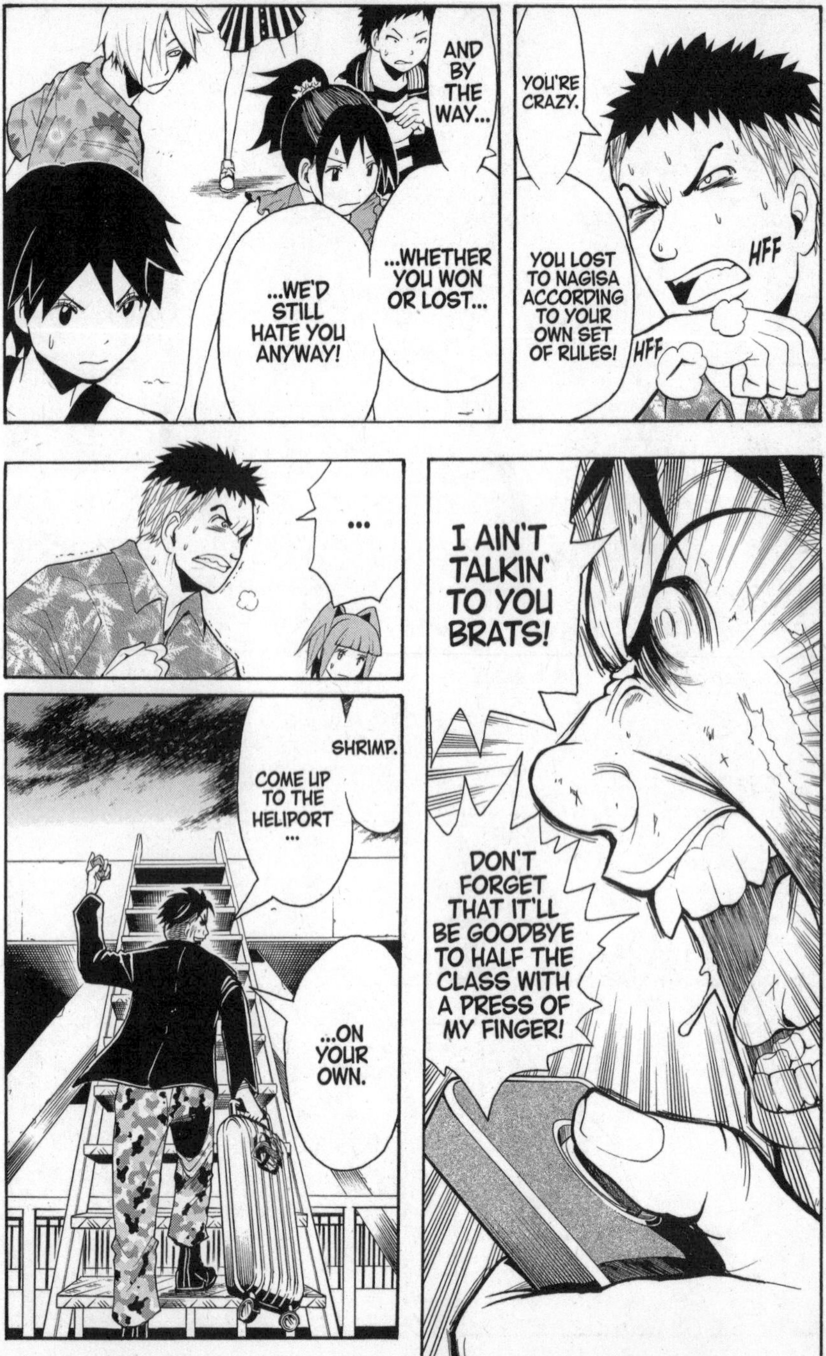
YOU'RE CRAZY.
YOU LOST TO NAGISA ACCORDING TO YOUR OWN SET OF RULES!
HFF
HFF
AND BY THE WAY...
...WHETHER YOU WON OR LOST...
...WE'D STILL HATE YOU ANYWAY!
I AIN'T TALKIN' TO YOU BRATS!
DON'T FORGET THAT IT'LL BE GOODBYE TO HALF THE CLASS WITH A PRESS OF MY FINGER!
...
SHRIMP.
COME UP TO THE HELIPORT ...
...ON YOUR OWN.

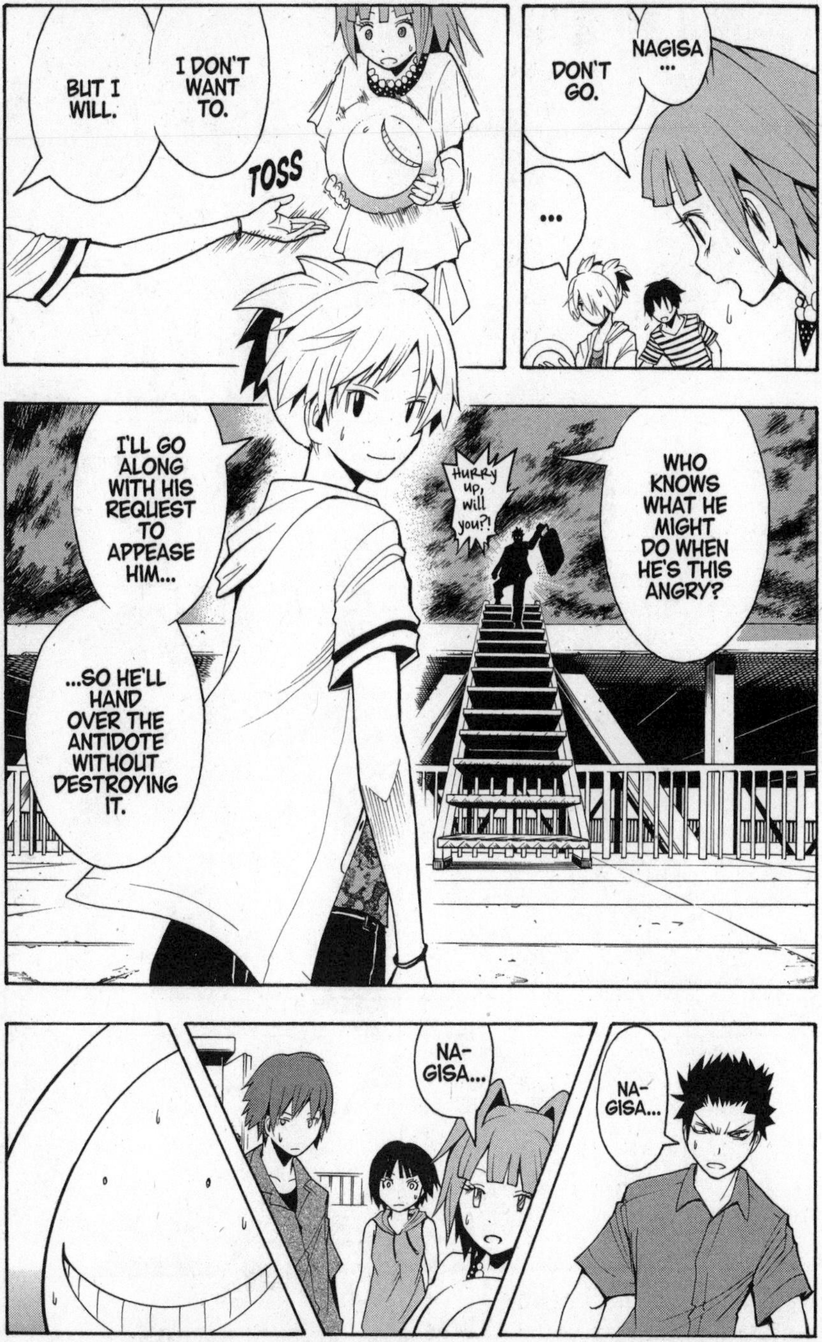
NAGISA...
DON'T GO.
...
I DON'T WANT TO.
BUT I WILL.
TOSS
WHO KNOWS WHAT HE MIGHT DO WHEN HE'S THIS ANGRY?
Hurry up, will you?!
I'LL GO ALONG WITH HIS REQUEST TO APPEASE HIM...
...SO HE'LL HAND OVER THE ANTIDOTE WITHOUT DESTROYING IT.
NA-GISA...
NA-GISA...

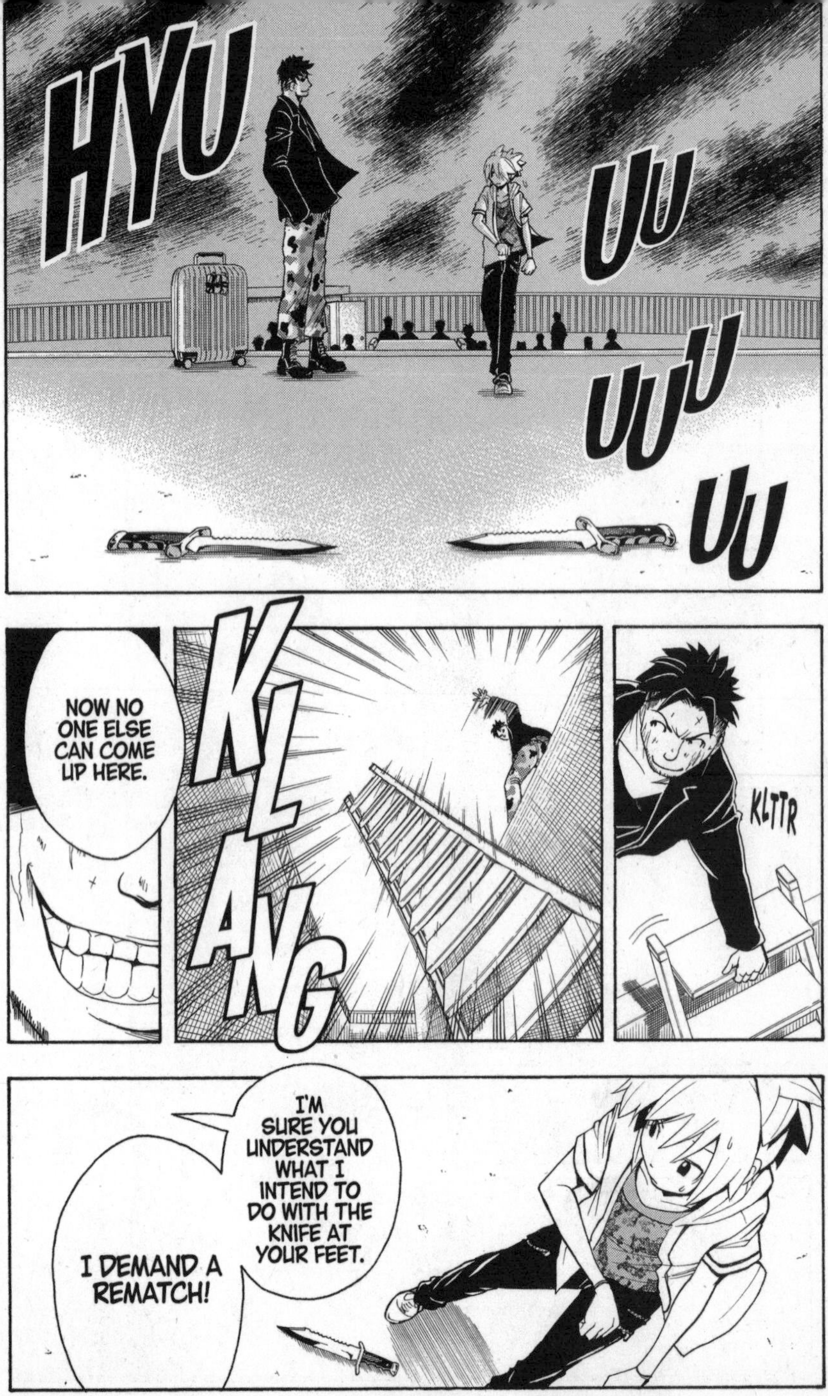
HYU
UU
UUU
UU
KLTTR
KLANG
NOW NO ONE ELSE CAN COME UP HERE.
I'M SURE YOU UNDERSTAND WHAT I INTEND TO DO WITH THE KNIFE AT YOUR FEET.
I DEMAND A REMATCH!

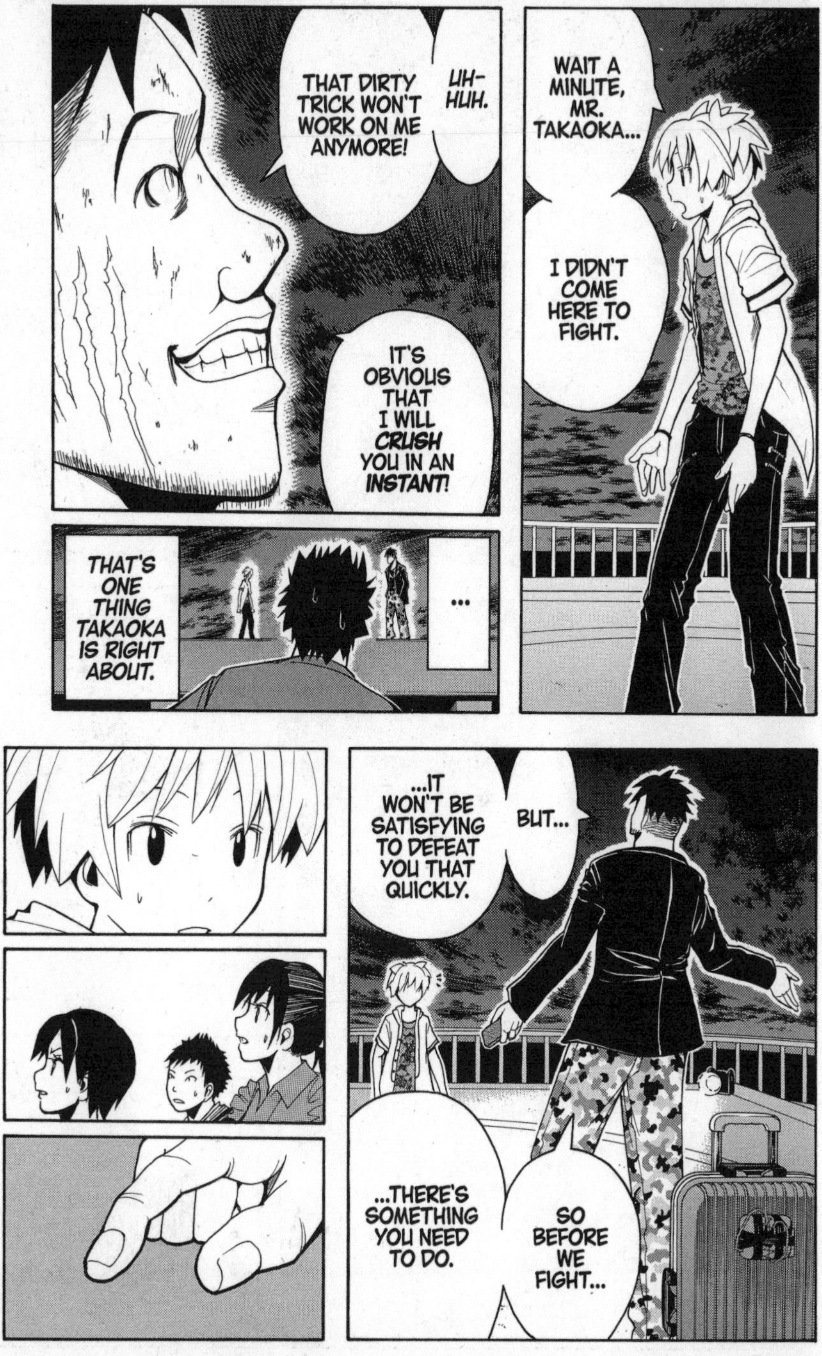
WAIT A MINUTE, MR. TAKAOKA...
I DIDN'T COME HERE TO FIGHT.
UH-HUH.
THAT DIRTY TRICK WON'T WORK ON ME ANYMORE!
IT'S OBVIOUS THAT I WILL CRUSH YOU IN AN INSTANT!
...
THAT'S ONE THING TAKAOKA IS RIGHT ABOUT.
BUT...
...IT WON'T BE SATISFYING TO DEFEAT YOU THAT QUICKLY.
SO BEFORE WE FIGHT...
...THERE'S SOMETHING YOU NEED TO DO.

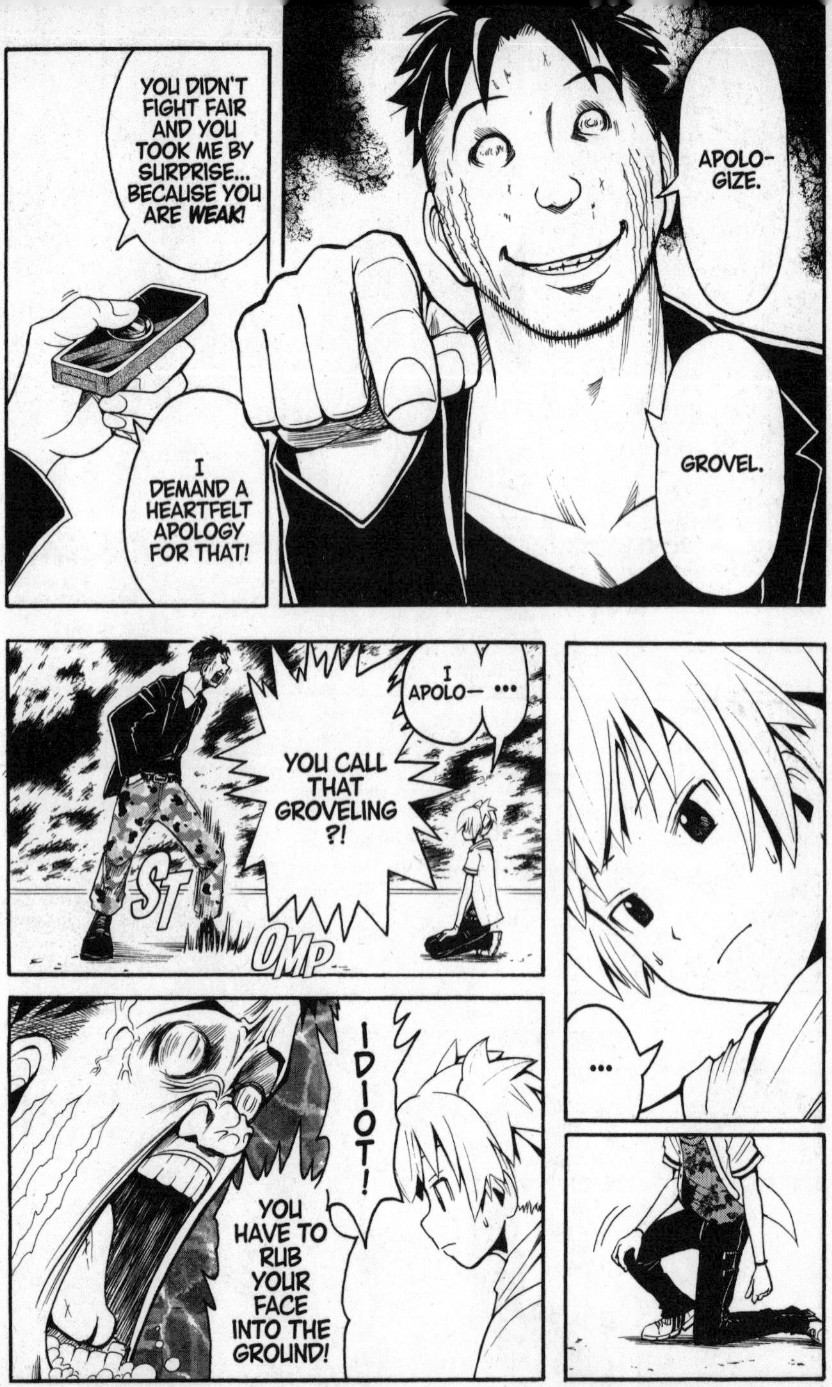
APOLO-GIZE.
GROVEL.
YOU DIDN'T FIGHT FAIR AND YOU TOOK ME BY SURPRISE... BECAUSE YOU ARE WEAK!
I DEMAND A HEARTFELT APOLOGY FOR THAT!
...
I APOLO— ...
YOU CALL THAT GROVELING?!
STOMP
IDIOT!
YOU HAVE TO RUB YOUR FACE INTO THE GROUND!

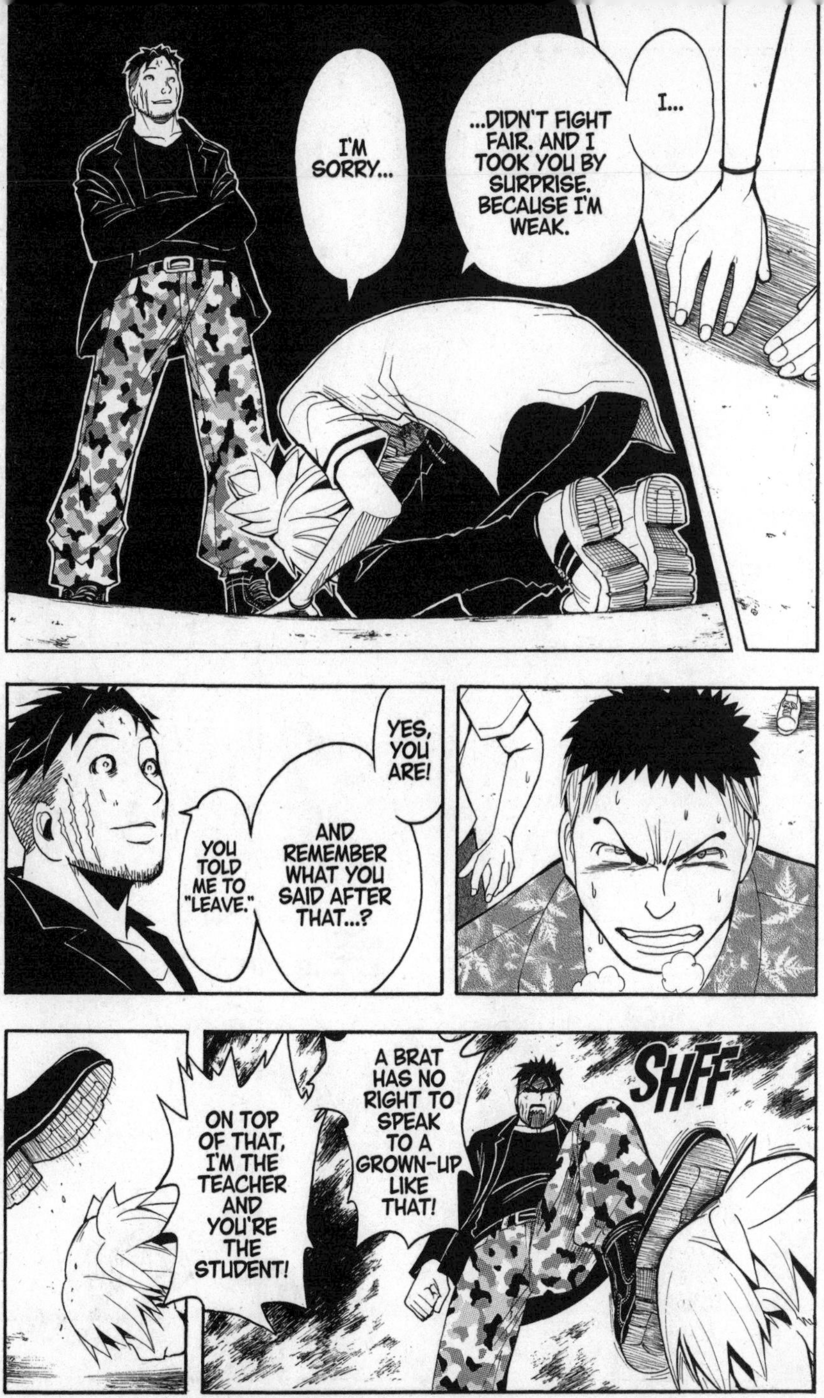
I...
...DIDN'T FIGHT FAIR. AND I TOOK YOU BY SURPRISE. BECAUSE I'M WEAK.
I'M SORRY...
YES, YOU ARE!
AND REMEMBER WHAT YOU SAID AFTER THAT...?
YOU TOLD ME TO "LEAVE."
SHFF
A BRAT HAS NO RIGHT TO SPEAK TO A GROWN-UP LIKE THAT!
ON TOP OF THAT, I'M THE TEACHER AND YOU'RE THE STUDENT!

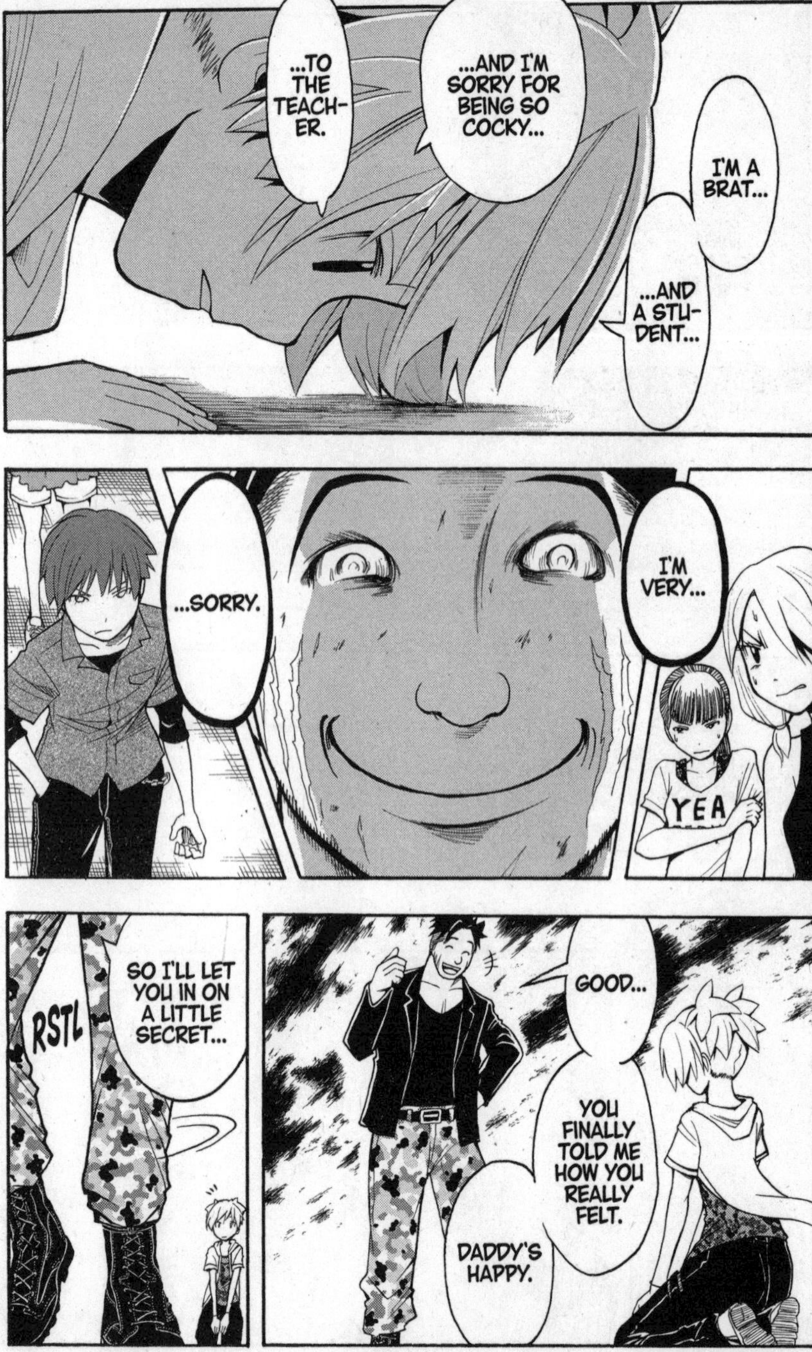
I'M A BRAT...
...AND A STUDENT...
...AND I'M SORRY FOR BEING SO COCKY...
...TO THE TEACHER.
I'M VERY...
...SORRY.
YEA
GOOD...
YOU FINALLY TOLD ME HOW YOU REALLY FELT.
DADDY'S HAPPY.
SO I'LL LET YOU IN ON A LITTLE SECRET...
RSTL

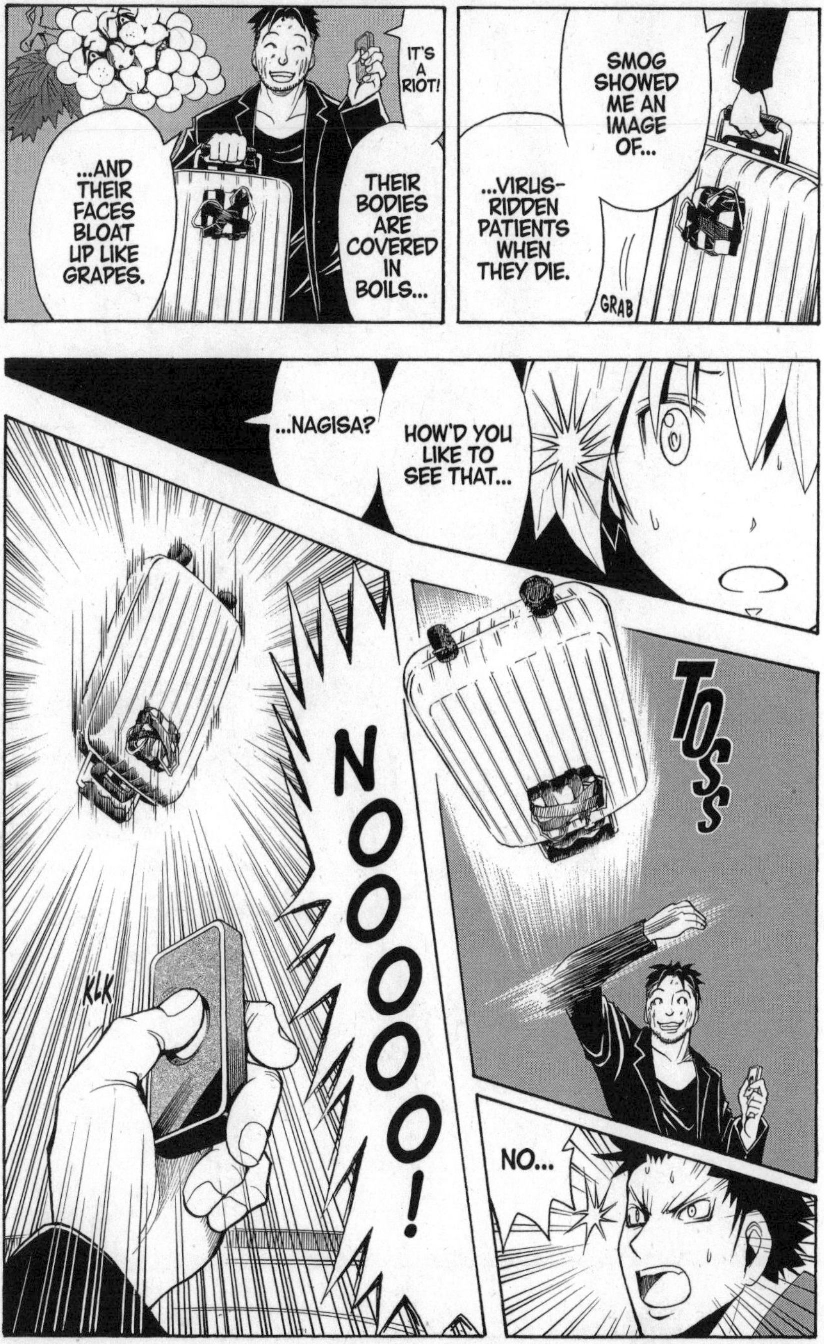
SMOG SHOWED ME AN IMAGE OF...
...VIRUS-RIDDEN PATIENTS WHEN THEY DIE.
GRAB
IT'S A RIOT!
THEIR BODIES ARE COVERED IN BOILS...
...AND THEIR FACES BLOAT UP LIKE GRAPES.
HOW'D YOU LIKE TO SEE THAT...
...NAGISA?
TOSS
NO...
KLK
NOOOOO!

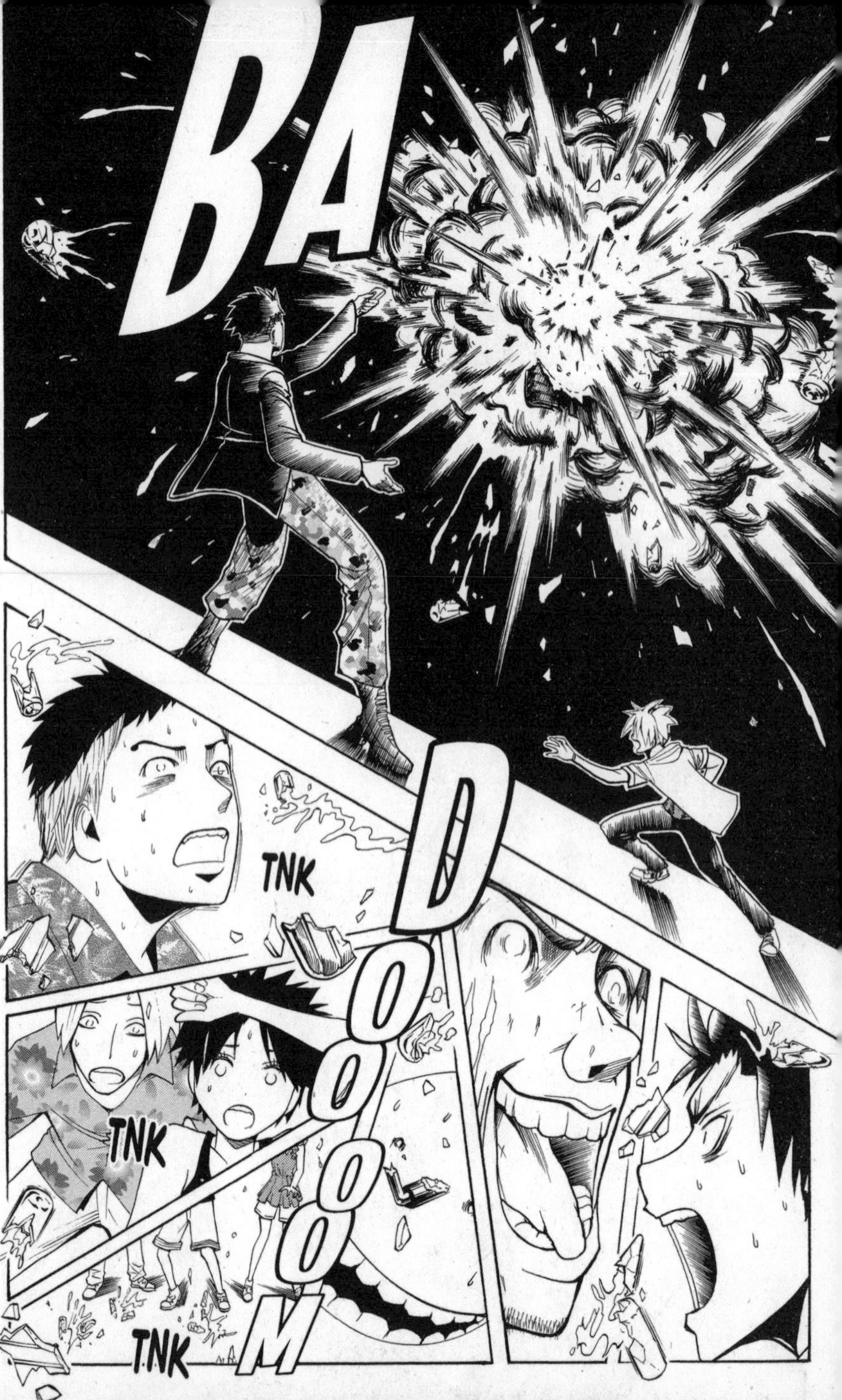
BA-
DOOOOM
TNK
TNK
TNK

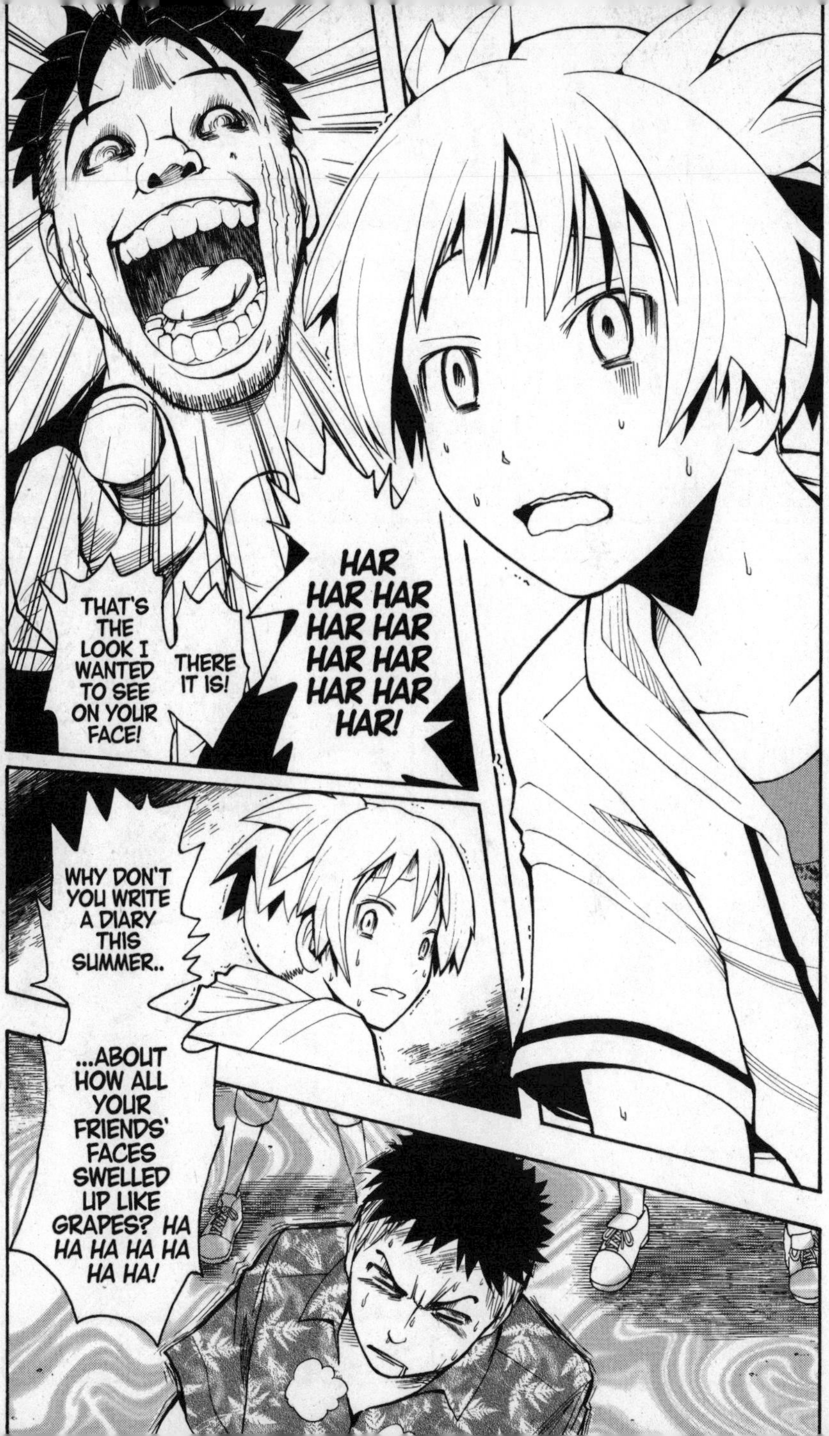
HAR HAR HAR HAR HAR HAR HAR HAR HAR HAR HAR!
THERE IT IS!
THAT'S THE LOOK I WANTED TO SEE ON YOUR FACE!
WHY DON'T YOU WRITE A DIARY THIS SUMMER..
...ABOUT HOW ALL YOUR FRIENDS' FACES SWELLED UP LIKE GRAPES? HA HA HA HA HA HA HA!

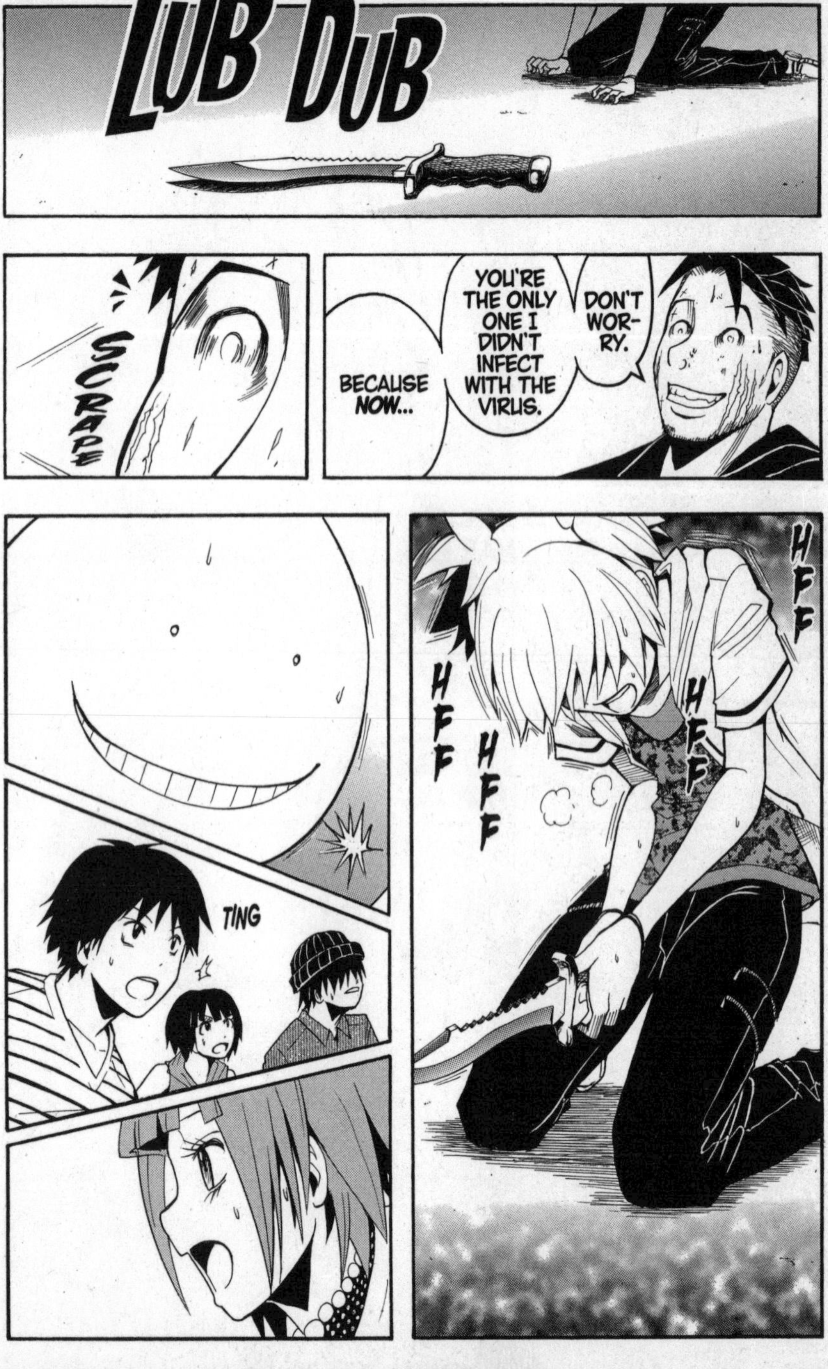
LUB DUB
DON'T WORRY.
YOU'RE THE ONLY ONE I DIDN'T INFECT WITH THE VIRUS.
BECAUSE NOW...
SCRAPE
HFF
HFF HFF
HFF HFF
HFF
TING

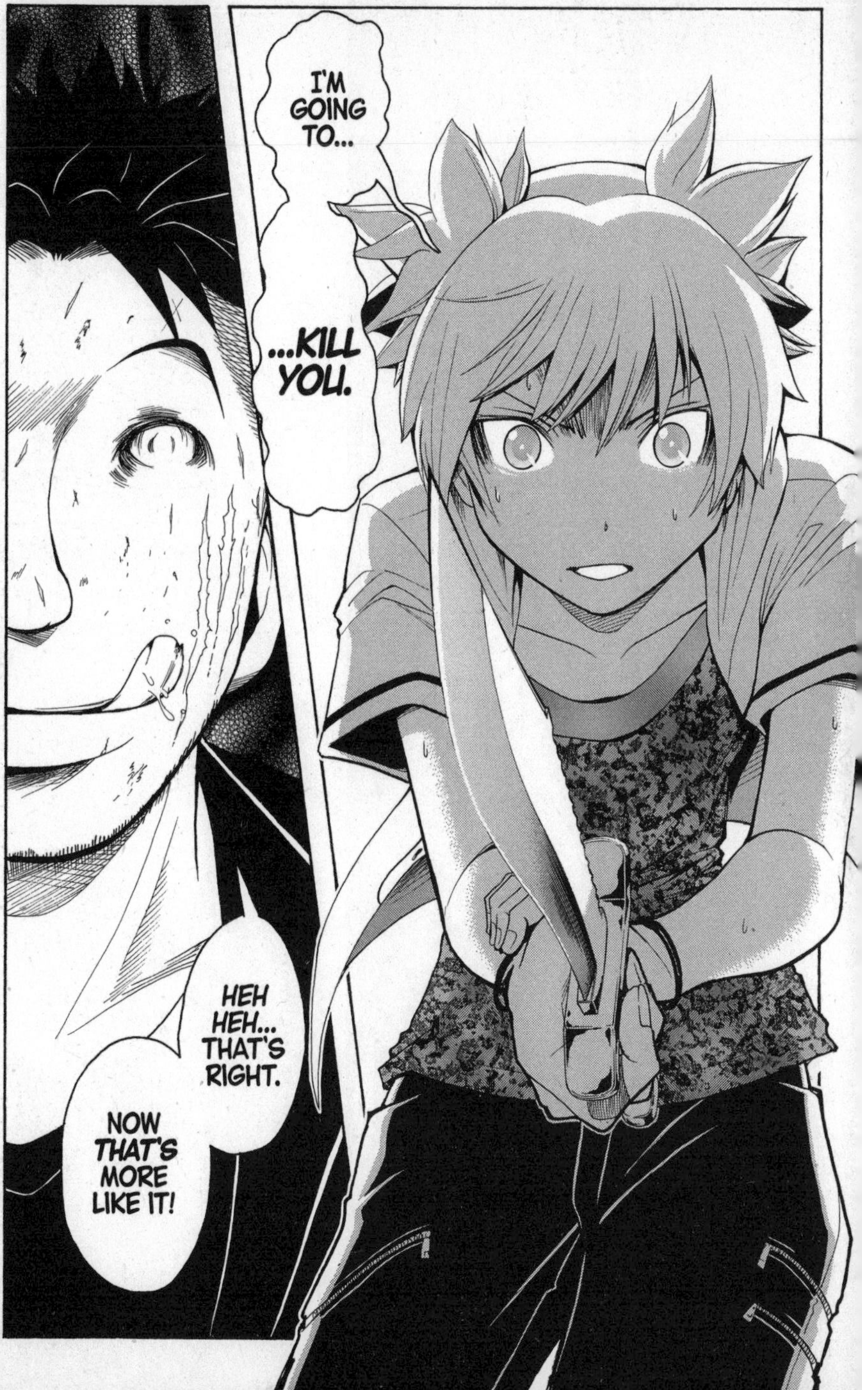
I'M GOING TO...
...KILL YOU.
HEH HEH... THAT'S RIGHT.
NOW THAT'S MORE LIKE IT!

to   be   continued   ...

Sleeping
sleeping
sleeping
sleeping...

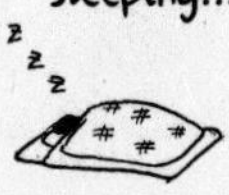
z z z

SamuRai
Insomnia

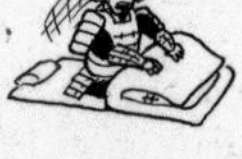

I created a business card for the first time in my life because I've had opportunities to meet more people recently.

I enjoy handing the cards out to my old friends saying, "Sorry for the super-belated introduction..."

It's a very ordinary business card, so I can give it to anyone in any situation.

Manga artists don't often get the chance to take part in social customs like this, so I really enjoy this exchange of business cards.

My dream is to eat lunch in a park in the Marunouchi area with a handcrafted employee ID card hanging from my neck.

—Yusei Matsui

Yusei Matsui was born on the last day of January in Saitama Prefecture, Japan. He has been drawing manga since elementary school. Some of his favorite manga series are *Bobobo-bo Bo-bobo*, *JoJo's Bizarre Adventure* and *Ultimate Muscle*. Matsui learned his trade working as an assistant to manga artist Yoshio Sawai, creator of *Bobobo-bo Bo-bobo*. In 2005, Matsui debuted his original manga *Neuro: Supernatural Detective* in *Weekly Shonen Jump*. In 2007, *Neuro* was adapted into an anime. In 2012, *Assassination Classroom* began serialization in *Weekly Shonen Jump*.

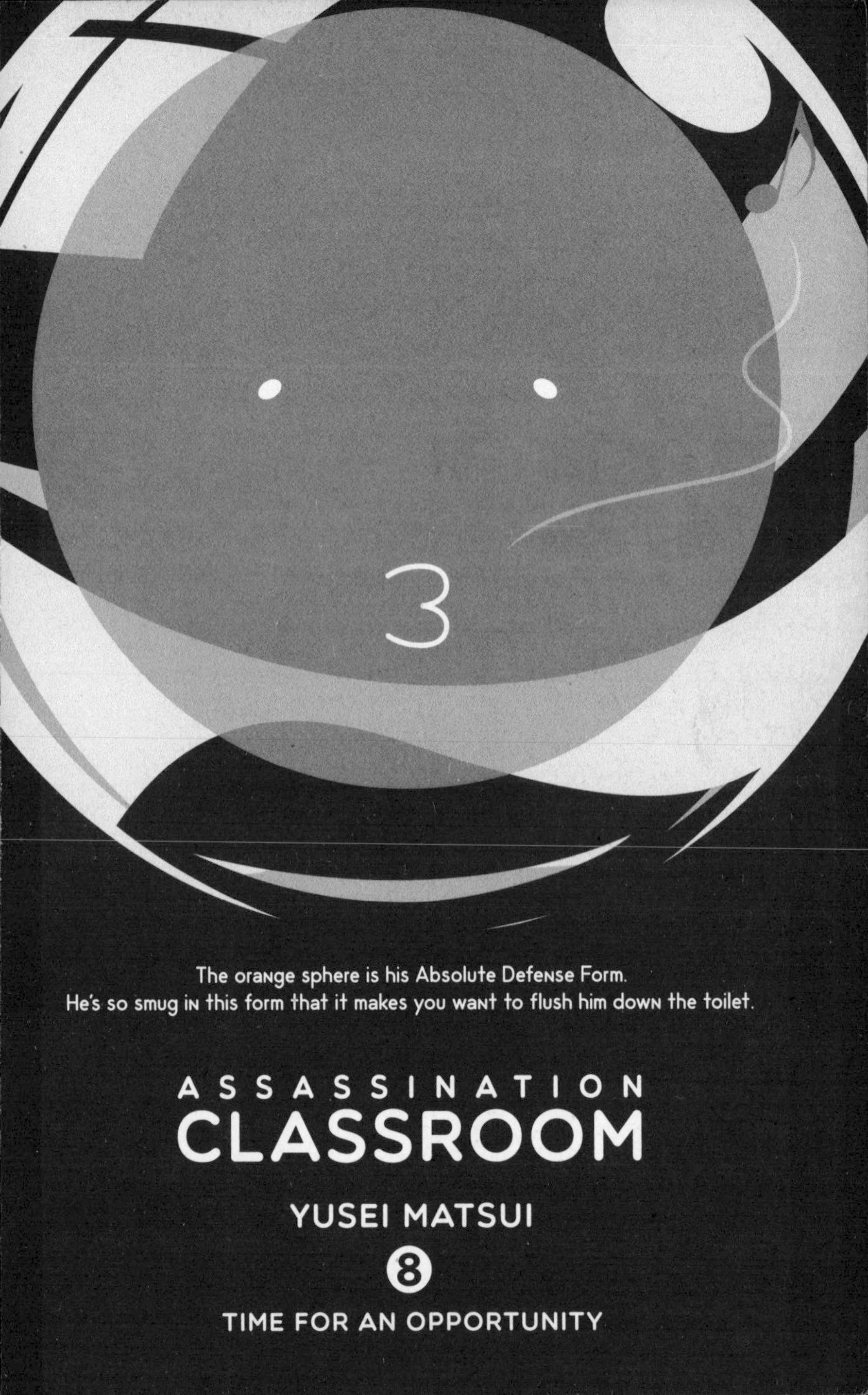

The orange sphere is his Absolute Defense Form.
He's so smug in this form that it makes you want to flush him down the toilet.

ASSASSINATION CLASSROOM

YUSEI MATSUI

8

TIME FOR AN OPPORTUNITY

A MOMENT OF TENTACLE ZEN

Veni. Vidi. Slimum.

– Korius Saensar
(100 B.C. to 44 B.C.)

ASSASSINATION
CLASSROOM

Volume 8
SHONEN JUMP ADVANCED Manga Edition

Story and Art by YUSEI MATSUI

Translation/Tetsuichiro Miyaki
English Adaptation/Bryant Turnage
Touch-up Art & Lettering/Stephen Dutro
Cover & Interior Design/Sam Elzway
Editor/Annette Roman

ANSATSU KYOSHITSU © 2012 by Yusei Matsui
All rights reserved.
First published in Japan in 2012 by SHUEISHA Inc., Tokyo.
English translation rights arranged by SHUEISHA Inc.

Printed in the U.S.A.

Published by VIZ Media, LLC
P.O. Box 77010
San Francisco, CA 94107

10 9 8 7 6 5 4 3
First printing, February 2016
Third printing, January 2018

www.viz.com

www.shonenjump.com

Syllabus for
Assassination Classroom, Vol. 9

Nagisa risks it all in an attempt to take down the mastermind behind the biological attack on his classmates. After the dust settles, Koro Sensei gives *his* all to ignite summer romances between his students. Turns out their English teacher Ms. Jelavitch has her sights on someone...and everyone wants to help her get her target—er, the man of her dreams. Then, back at school, one of the students defects from the 3–E ranks for all the wrong reasons. How will they win him back before he inflicts irrevocable damage on them all...?!

Available Now!

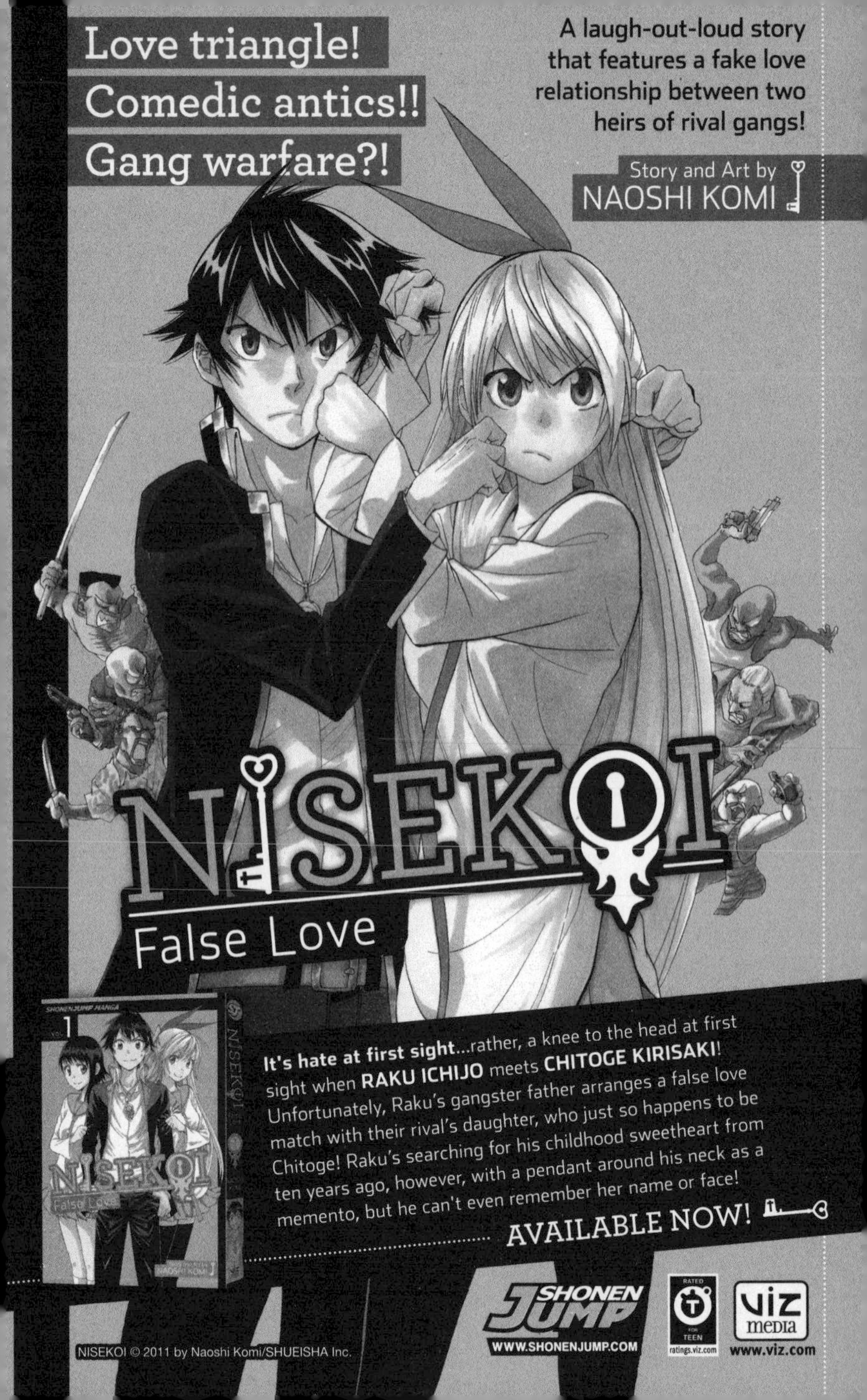
Love triangle!
Comedic antics!!
Gang warfare?!
A laugh-out-loud story that features a fake love relationship between two heirs of rival gangs!
Story and Art by
NAOSHI KOMI
NISEKOI
False Love
SHONEN JUMP MANGA
VOL. 1
NISEKOI
False Love
NAOSHI KOMI
It's hate at first sight...rather, a knee to the head at first sight when RAKU ICHIJO meets CHITOGE KIRISAKI! Unfortunately, Raku's gangster father arranges a false love match with their rival's daughter, who just so happens to be Chitoge! Raku's searching for his childhood sweetheart from ten years ago, however, with a pendant around his neck as a memento, but he can't even remember her name or face!
AVAILABLE NOW!
SHONEN JUMP
WWW.SHONENJUMP.COM
RATED
T
FOR
TEEN
ratings.viz.com
viz media
www.viz.com
NISEKOI © 2011 by Naoshi Komi/SHUEISHA Inc.

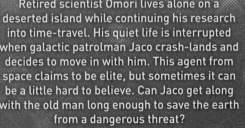

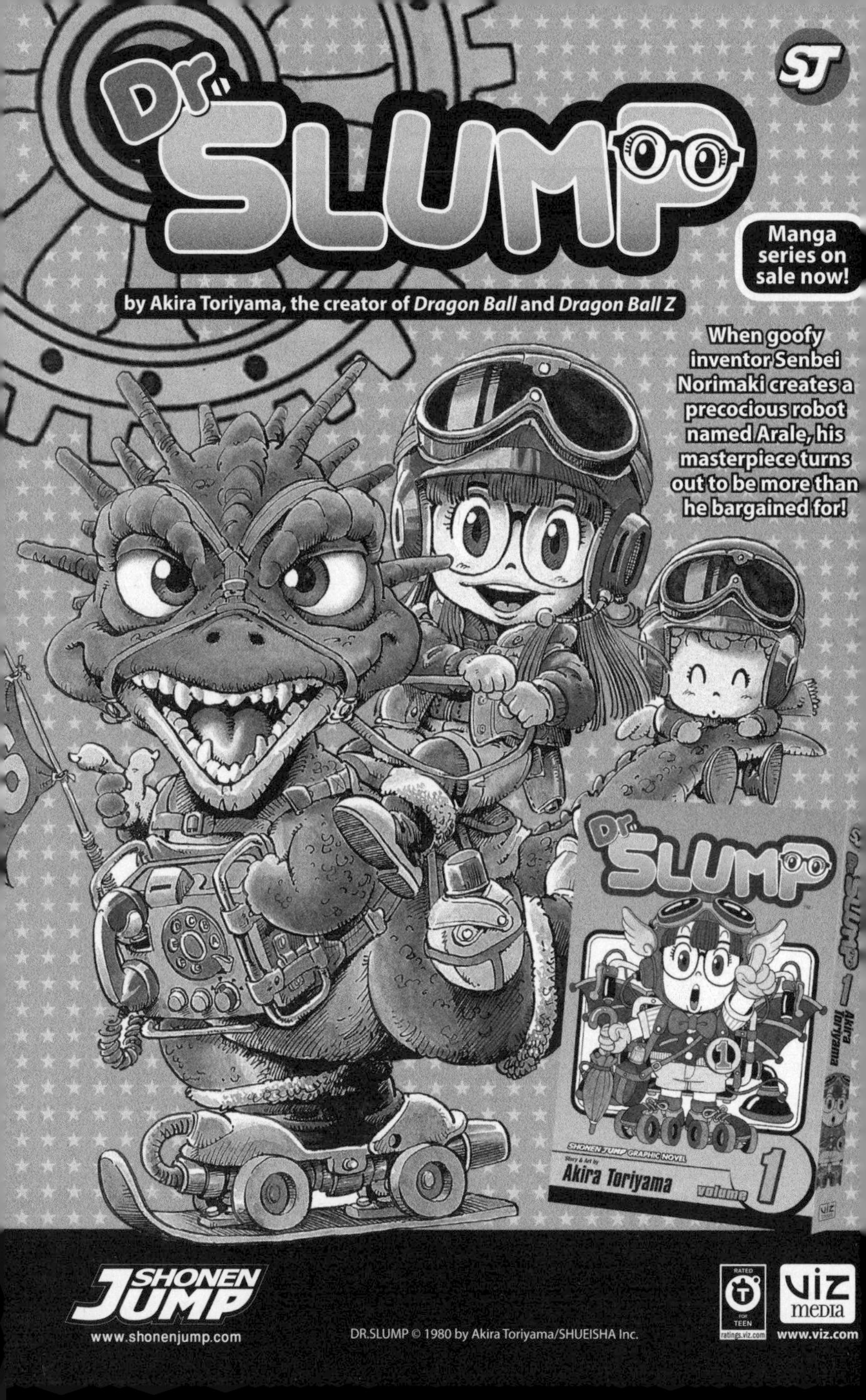
SJ
Dr. SLUMP
Manga series on sale now!
by Akira Toriyama, the creator of *Dragon Ball* and *Dragon Ball Z*
When goofy inventor Senbei Norimaki creates a precocious robot named Arale, his masterpiece turns out to be more than he bargained for!
Dr. SLUMP
SHONEN JUMP GRAPHIC NOVEL
Story & Art by
Akira Toriyama
volume 1
Dr. SLUMP 1 Akira Toriyama
SHONEN JUMP
www.shonenjump.com
DR.SLUMP © 1980 by Akira Toriyama/SHUEISHA Inc.
RATED T FOR TEEN
ratings.viz.com
VIZ media
www.viz.com

THE BEST SELLING MANGA SERIES IN THE WORLD!

ONE PIECE

Story & Art by EIICHIRO ODA

As a child, **Monkey D. Luffy** was inspired to become a pirate by listening to the tales of the buccaneer "Red-Haired" Shanks. But Luffy's life changed when he accidentally ate the Gum-Gum Devil Fruit and gained the power to stretch like rubber...at the cost of never being able to swim again! Years later, still vowing to become the king of the pirates, Luffy sets out on his adventure in search of the legendary "One Piece," said to be the greatest treasure in the world...

A PREMIUM BOX SET OF THE FIRST TWO STORY ARCS OF ONE PIECE!

A PIRATE'S TREASURE FOR ANY MANGA FAN!

STORY AND ART BY EIICHIRO ODA

Comes with
EXCLUSIVE
POSTER
and the
ROMANCE
DAWN
mini-comic!

As a child, Monkey D. Luffy dreamed of becoming King of the Pirates.
But his life changed when he accidentally gained the power to stretch like
rubber...at the cost of never being able to swim again! Years later, Luffy sets off
in search of the "One Piece," said to be the greatest treasure in the world...

**This box set includes VOLUMES 1-23, which comprise
the EAST BLUE and BAROQUE WORKS story arcs.**

EXCLUSIVE PREMIUMS and GREAT SAVINGS
over buying the individual volumes!

You're Reading in the Wrong Direction!!

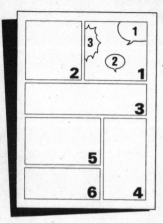

Whoops! Guess what? You're starting at the wrong end of the comic!

...It's true! In keeping with the original Japanese format, **Assassination Classroom** is meant to be read from right to left, starting in the upper-right corner.

Unlike English, which is read from left to right, Japanese is read from right to left, meaning that action, sound effects and word-balloon order are completely reversed... something which can make readers unfamiliar with Japanese feel pretty backwards themselves. For this reason, manga or Japanese comics published in the U.S. in English have sometimes been published "flopped"—that is, printed in exact reverse order, as though seen from the other side of a mirror.

By flopping pages, U.S. publishers can avoid confusing readers, but the compromise is not without its downside. For one thing, a character in a flopped manga series who once wore in the original Japanese version a T-shirt emblazoned with "M A Y" (as in "the merry month of") now wears one which reads "Y A M"! Additionally, many manga creators in Japan are themselves unhappy with the process, as some feel the mirror-imaging of their art skews their original intentions.

We are proud to bring you Yusei Matsui's **Assassination Classroom** in the original unflopped format.
For now, though, turn to the other side of the book and let the adventure begin...!

—Editor